THE PURSUIT OF UNHAPPINESS

The Pursuit of Unhappiness

The Elusive Psychology of Well-Being

DANIEL M. HAYBRON

OXFORD
UNIVERSITY PRESS

OXFORD
UNIVERSITY PRESS

Great Clarendon Street, Oxford OX2 6DP

Oxford University Press is a department of the University of Oxford.
It furthers the University's objective of excellence in research, scholarship,
and education by publishing worldwide in

Oxford New York

Auckland Cape Town Dar es Salaam Hong Kong Karachi
Kuala Lumpur Madrid Melbourne Mexico City Nairobi
New Delhi Shanghai Taipei Toronto

With offices in

Argentina Austria Brazil Chile Czech Republic France Greece
Guatemala Hungary Italy Japan Poland Portugal Singapore
South Korea Switzerland Thailand Turkey Ukraine Vietnam

Oxford is a registered trade mark of Oxford University Press
in the UK and in certain other countries

Published in the United States
by Oxford University Press Inc., New York

© Daniel M. Haybron 2008

The moral rights of the author have been asserted
Database right Oxford University Press (maker)

First published 2008

British Library Cataloguing in Publication Data

Data available

Library of Congress Cataloging in Publication Data

Data available

Typeset by Laserwords Private Limited, Chennai, India
Printed in Great Britain
on acid-free paper by
CPI Antony Rowe, Chippenham, Wiltshire

ISBN 978-0-19-954598-8

1 3 5 7 9 10 8 6 4 2

In memory of Alice and Ron

Preface

We cannot think clearly about a plant or animal until we have a name for it.

E. O. Wilson[1]

White people think they can learn everything right away, by reading it out of a book and asking questions at everyone. But it doesn't work that way, you got to *experience* it and *live* it to learn it . . . Stop asking questions. You ask too many fucking questions. Because when you're ready to know, it'll be shown to you. Maybe by the end of this trip, you'll know just a little, tiny bit . . . Yeah, but then maybe you won't want to write a book anymore, because it's impossible to write down those kinds of things . . . And people won't understand anyway, because they didn't *experience* it.

Lewis Atcitty, a Navajo[2]

There are many good reasons not to write a book on happiness. Not least of these is the inherently paradoxical nature of the enterprise. On the one hand, serious inquiry, particularly philosophical argument, demands clarity of expression; we need to know exactly what is being said so that we can assess the merits of our claims and the arguments for them. Philosophers like to wade in clear streams, not murky swamps. On the other hand, happiness is a *paradigm* of unclarity, the Mother of All Swamps. Even if you can get past the endless verbal squabbling that has tended to cripple discussion of the subject—or is it subjects?—you will still find yourself dealing with some of the most rich, complex, nebulous, diaphanous, fluid, and evanescent phenomena known to humankind. Not even poets are up to the task. To a great extent, as Mr. Atcitty observed, you just have to be there.

These points may seem to counsel silence or despair, but to my mind they simply make the project more interesting. You can't exactly make the intangible tangible, but you can make it a little less mysterious, and a little less elusive. When a biologist puts a pin through a frog so she can study it, she ends up with something less than a frog. A lot of information has been lost. For starters, it no longer *does* anything. Much has been lost in the process, but she may yet learn something of value about the animal from the ex-frog that now lies on her table. I think that systematic investigation into happiness can similarly teach us a good deal about the matter, even if much remains beyond description. The challenge lies in bringing a measure of intelligibility if not clarity even to matters that once seemed hopelessly inscrutable. I believe this can be done, to a surprising extent.

Consider what follows the pithed version of happiness: mere shadows playing on the cave wall, perhaps, but a big improvement over sitting in the dark. Or so I hope.

This is a theoretical work. But it is a work in *ethical* theory, and it is no defect in such an effort if it has, as well, some practical import. Think of your fondest childhood memories, or of the things that, to your mind, most make life worth living. What, on your deathbed, do you expect most to regret leaving behind? I suspect that much of your answer will consist of intangibles: things not easily pinned down and named, much less described, and still less measured and quantified. In the progressive era we moderns inhabit, this presents us with a problem: we are busily changing, more like remaking, the world to suit our designs. As a general rule, we do not undertake ambitious construction projects and other major improvements for the sake of an ineffable. . .*je ne sais quoi*. It is hard to build things for purposes you can't name; harder still to get other people to do it with you; and well nigh impossible to get other people to pay for it. By and large, progress and development are driven by tangibles. And if you have a problem with some proposed improvement, you will not likely get far unless you can cite tangible, preferably quantifiable, values in your support. "It just doesn't feel right" tends not to cut it when you are trying to get people to change their plans.

Carried out in these terms, progress can be very expensive. The problem is made apparent in *Hatteras Blues,* Tom Carlson's recent account of development in the traditional island fishing community of Hatteras Village. Economic progress was, at the time of his visits there, moving so fast that soon "an entire way of life would disappear, a commercial system of values based on the sea and a system of community values as old as the Mayflower Compact."[3] Utterly typical of the process, repeated countless times elsewhere, was that "much of what was being lost was intangible—a manner of being, a way of living day-to-day—and what was tangibly being lost was being lost so quickly that it almost seemed a trick of the eye. The W. H. Gaskins house, circa 1860—the oldest house in the village, here today, then, overnight, gone. Bulldozed for someone's septic system." To what end? To make way for garish developments lined with wildly incongruous palm trees and "huge, twenty room McMansions" placed in precarious locations along one of the most storm-swept beaches on the Atlantic seaboard. (In many cases built, apparently, according to the "bigger fool" theory: made not to be used, but to be sold to a bigger fool in a real estate version of hot potato.) The locals detest many of the changes, yet are too independent to organize effectively, an otherwise admirable quality that some fear will be what "gets this village erased." (Though they themselves were substantially complicit.) A developer opines, "F____ 'em! If I want to build a miniature golf course and have fireworks and giant clowns with flames shooting out their asses, I will!"[4]

There is nothing intangible about giant clowns: their value has a fairly precise measure, in dollars. People want them, and are willing to pay for them, knowing pretty well what they will get in return: a predictable dose of amusement, just like the one they got at the last putt-putt golf course. Against such concrete benefits, how do you defend the "feel" of a place, or the inexpressible gratifications of a "manner of being"? (And how many dollars is it worth? Can you seriously answer that question while retaining any capacity to appreciate the values you're talking about?) Particularly when such intangibles are so completely lost on those with no familiarity or affection for the place. I suppose plastic clowns might have a certain *je ne sais quoi* about them, too, just as an old island home built from shipwreck timbers several generations back by your ancestors has its own magic. Maybe. But that isn't why they get built. So instead of a *place*, with a vital, textured life of its own, you just get a bunch of stuff, steam-shoveled in to entertain transient visitors until the next storm washes it away. Variations of the story recur in other domains, including our personal lives. Indeed it is, it seems to me, the story of our age.

This is not a tract of social critique. But I will not be displeased if the discussion contributes something to the appreciation, and hopefully the preservation, of the manifold intangibles that make life worth living.

Acknowledgements

"Never get off the boat." Chef said that in *Apocalypse Now*, after a brief shore excursion in search of mangoes brought him face to face with a tiger. That line stuck in my head for a few years, as I pondered my sanity in choosing such an unpromising topic as happiness for my dissertation. At the time virtually no philosophers were working on the subject—for good reason, we will see—and no one in my department really knew anything about it. Plus, it is not exactly a "macho" subject, the term bringing elves and fairies to mind more than the images of rigorous intellectual engagement that philosophers tend to favor. The philosophy department at Rutgers was known for getting people jobs; but in general it helped if your work connected with something that one of the faculty members, or at least someone in the profession, was working on, or at least knew something about.

Things worked out in the end, due in no small measure to the remarkable generosity of many individuals and several institutions. I am extremely grateful for the assistance and goodwill I have received. Among my greatest debts is to my dissertation advisor, Douglas Husak, who kindly agreed to supervise my research as I got this very difficult project under way. Though I had chosen a notoriously muddled topic outside his own field, Doug's sharp eye and rock-solid judgment saved me from countless errors, and opened up many avenues to explore. It is almost certain that this book would not have come about at all but for Doug's support.

I am indebted as well to the other members of my committee: Colin McGinn, Rob Woolfolk, Steve Stich, and Wayne Sumner. It was in a seminar with Steve that the literature on happiness first caught my eye, and his influence on my philosophical style should be easy to see; I am grateful for his ongoing support. Wayne's pioneering work on happiness made my job infinitely easier; its advance over the previous literature, which frankly was something of a disaster prior to the publication of his book in 1996, would be difficult to overstate. Indeed it is questionable whether I would have succeeded in my project without his generous assistance and shoulders to stand on.

Speaking of "getting off the boat," the supreme award probably goes to Ed Diener, who in the early 1980s, in what must have been regarded as an act of career suicide, left behind a successful research program to take on the then-très-outré topic of happiness. (Outré ain't in it: even toward the turn of the millennium, when the positive psychology movement was getting under way, the hostility to this sort of work within the academy was palpable. To tell people you were working on happiness was to invite what David Lewis aptly called the "incredulous stare." I quickly learned to say I was working on "well-being" or some other respectable-sounding topic.) In fact Ed had tried to study the subject a decade earlier, but his advisor warned him off it, and so—fittingly—he spent his pre-tenure years doing important work on the subject of conformity. It would certainly be an exaggeration to say that Ed single-handedly launched the science of happiness, as various researchers had also braved the odds to do important work on the subject since at least the 1920s, and the pace had already begun picking up when he started his research. But there might not have been *enough* of a science of happiness to get my project off the ground had it not been for the outstanding research and researchers to come out of Ed's lab. (In a recent talk I joked that this field might be termed "Dienerology"—much of his family is in the business as well—but I was only half-joking.) Ed has been very generous and supportive toward this pesky philosopher, so I am doubly indebted to him.

I have also profited immensely from extensive conversations and correspondence with Valerie Tiberius and John Doris, as well as the St. Louis happiness reading group: Anna Alexandrova, Adam Shriver, Matthew Cashen, and Simine Vazire. Valerie's work parallels mine in many ways, and I am hopeful that her work, including an excellent new book, will help to get the psychology of well-being off the ground as a major research area within philosophy. Her very extensive comments on my work, and the great ideas I always seem to get when talking to her, have been invaluable. John Doris, whose book pretty much inaugurated the now-vibrant field of empirically-oriented ethics, has been exploring some similar (and exciting) themes in moral psychology, and I have gotten much wonderful feedback and advice from him. Indeed I owe the title of this book to John, as he suggested I name it after what is now the title chapter. The happiness reading group has also had a tremendous impact on this book, as they very kindly offered to read a draft (and then some) of the entire manuscript, which then was even longer than the book you're now reading. Their careful and penetrating comments, not to mention their support, have been enormously helpful.

A project like this does not happen without considerable institutional support, and I want to thank the philosophy departments and staff at Rutgers University, the University of Arizona, and Saint Louis University. I am especially grateful for the tremendous support I have received at my current institution, Saint Louis University, including a faculty research leave. My departmental chair, Fr. Theodore Vitali, has made sure I had everything I needed and been a wonderful mentor and friend. I must say I did not expect to end up at a Jesuit institution, since my own thinking is decidedly non-theistic, but I am very glad to be at SLU. It is a warm, supportive environment where people take very seriously the idea of making the world a better place, and I probably have more academic freedom here than I would at many secular institutions. Moreover, it seems to me incumbent for ethical theory to engage with people's values as they are, and with human nature as it is. We are, I think, a fundamentally religious species, and most of the thinking about the good life that people have found at all compelling has taken place within religious traditions. It is very helpful to my work, then, to be in an environment where religious thought is engaged with sophistication and understanding, and where there is no "party line"—theistic or non-theistic—one is expected to toe.

Many other individuals have my gratitude as well, for their helpful comments, discussions, or other forms of support. I know I am forgetting more than a few of them, and I apologize in advance. But the names that come to mind include Aaron Meskin, Alan Krueger, Alex Michalos, Alicia Finch, Allen Buchanan, Alvin Goldman, Andrew Pinsent, Barry Schwartz, David Chalmers, Barry Loewer, Barry Ward, Bengt Brülde, Brian Loar, Brian McLaughlin, Christine Swanton, Corinne Gardner, David Rosenthal, David Schmidtz, Eleonore Stump, Elijah Millgram, Eric Schwitzgebel, Eric Wiland, Ernest Sosa, Frank Arntzenius, Frankie Egan, Fred Feldman, George Sher, Gerardo Camilo, Ginny Mayer, Gualtiero Piccinini, Irwin Goldstein, James Bohman, Jerry Fodor, Jim Stone, Jonathan Schaffer, Jorge Garcia, Joseph Neisser, Joe Salerno, Julia Annas, Kent Berridge, Kent Johnson, Kent Staley, Larry Temkin, Lori Gruen, Mark Chekola, Mark Snyder, Martha Nussbaum, Martin Seligman, Michael Eid, Monte Johnson, Ned Block, Neera Badhwar, Paul Dolan, Peter Kivy, Raja Halwani, Randy Larsen, Richard Dean, Richard Easterlin, Richard Lucas, Robert Northcott, robert wolff, Robert Almeder, Robert Biswas-Diener, Robert Morris, Roger Crisp, Ruth Chang, Scott Berman, Scott Ragland, Simine Vazire, Stephen Darwall, Susan Brower-Toland, T. L. S. Sprigge, Talia Bettcher, Thomas Carson, Thomas Christiano, Tim Maudlin, Tony Jack, Ulrich Schimmack, Will Wilkinson, William Morris, William Rehg, audiences at various universities and conferences where material for this book was presented, and anonymous referees for Oxford University Press and several journals.

A special mention is due to Brian Fay, my undergraduate advisor, who gave me early encouragement and helped get me started in the profession. I am grateful as well to Oxford University Press, and especially to my eminently helpful and patient editor, Peter Momtchiloff.

The "long-suffering spouse" award goes to my wife, Elizabeth, who has endured more years of "happiness" than any person should have to bear, and done so lovingly and with grace. She has little patience for philosophy, but she happens to be pretty good at it, and I've benefited a lot from her forbearance and solid judgment. She deserves many years of happiness if anyone does. Our children, Michael, William, and Sarah—the clichés are true; they make it all worthwhile, and have provided many moments of much-needed comic relief and perspective. My in-laws, Carol and Joel, have been steady sources of support for all of us, and I am grateful. And my brother David has been a priceless source of advice and encouragement.

Much of the material in this book is based on previously published work. I am grateful for permission from Wiley-Blackwell Publishing Ltd. to use the following material: Much of Chapter 3 appeared in "What Do We Want from a Theory of Happiness?" *Metaphilosophy* 34(3), pp. 305–29 (2003). Chapter 4 is largely based on material from "Happiness and Pleasure," *Philosophy and Phenomenological Research* 62(3): 501–28 (2001). Chapter 10 is largely based on "Do We Know How Happy We Are?" *Noûs* 41(3): 394–428 (2007). Chapters 6 and 7 are based on, and Chapter 5 contains material from, "On Being Happy or Unhappy," *Philosophy and Phenomenological Research* 71(2): 287–317 (2005).

Large portions of Chapter 5 appeared in "Life Satisfaction, Ethical Reflection and the Science of Happiness," *The Journal of Happiness Studies* 8: 99–138 (2007). Chapter 8 is largely drawn from "Well-Being and Virtue," *Journal of Ethics & Social Philosophy* II:2 (2007). Most of Chapter 9 appeared in "Happiness, the Self, and Human Flourishing," *Utilitas* (2008). Sections of Chapters 1 and 2 are drawn from "Philosophy and the Science of Subjective Well-Being," in *The Science of Subjective Well-Being*, eds. M. Eid and R. J. Larsen. New York: Guilford Press, pp. 17–43 (2008). I am grateful to the publishers of these works for permission to use this material.

With one exception, the chief influence on this book is not a philosopher, or indeed a person at all. It is a place. The reader will learn that much of my childhood was spent on a small, isolated, and relatively undeveloped island, where at the time most residents earned their living from fishing. Following a convention started by my father, who has written about the island, I have chosen not to name it; it is more than well-enough known now already, and I see no need to call further attention to it, and at any rate its name is irrelevant to the points I will make with it. I should clarify at the outset that we were off-islanders, not locals, and that most years we only lived there for about three months of the year. (You could say we "summered" there, but summering is something rich people do. We were very lucky but not, by American standards, rich; to be on the island required a lot of material sacrifices.) It is the only place I've felt at home, indeed the only place I've ever felt like a fully developed human being. The difference being there made to the psyche, at least for some of us, is indescribable, but utterly profound, like being a different person. Part of my great fortune, given my future research interests, was to have had the opportunity to move back and forth between radically different communities, experiencing thoroughly different ways of life. I do not know that everyone from the mainland who spent time there had that experience—a lot depended on what you did when you were there. But if you dropped the mainland ways and wholly immersed yourself in the local rhythms, keeping your mouth shut and your eyes open to the world around you, you could experience a radical transformation of consciousness. You could see the difference in the way the islanders carried themselves, in their bearing and demeanor, compared to the mainlanders. We talked about the differences in inner state a lot, but I do not recall hearing it put very often in terms of happiness. Many of the people I admired most on the island probably spent zero time pondering matters of happiness, and would likely have thought the idea of a book about happiness a complete waste of time. But in retrospect—and this is one purpose of the book—it is clear to me that happiness is precisely what we were talking about. Many of us were never as happy as we were on the island. The excerpt from my father's journals, reproduced in Chapter 6, gives a hint of what I mean. 'Happiness' may not be the first word that comes to mind, but if that isn't happiness, then I'm not interested in happiness.

In the wake of these experiences, some of the more extreme claims people have made about the immutability of happiness, and the destiny written in our "happiness set points," have seemed to me incredible, and plainly false. Your environment, in particular the way of life you engage in, which depends heavily on the environment you inhabit, can make a massive difference in how happy you are. If the empirical research doesn't bear this out—and actually I think the better work does, to an extent—then the research is missing something. Or so it has seemed to me. (This isn't the sort of thing empirically-minded researchers like myself are supposed to say. But we already *know* the measures are imperfect, and if they tell us that, say, a root canal *sans* anesthesia doesn't hurt, we know there's something wrong.)

I am well aware that these reflections, and the similar thoughts scattered throughout the book, will strike some readers as romanticized. This may be true—after all, one theme of this book is that our judgments about our own experiences are remarkably unreliable. But I do not think so, for several reasons. First, I am not alone in recording such thoughts; there is a good-sized literature reporting similar experiences. Second, I was away from the island for many years until a recent visit. During that interval, and during that visit, I got a few "refreshers" in the island mindset which reminded me vividly of the contrast (indeed, one such experience was so stark that it helped convince me to pursue this work). Finally, my father was a writer, and kept very detailed journals of our time there, also producing a book manuscript and an article based on them. As I make my way through those journals, I am struck by how much *better* life on the island was than I remembered it. (If anything he was more likely to write about the bad days than the good ones.) To be sure, we probably had it better than many islanders: fishing was hard work for little pay, and winters could be brutal. But even when working the most unpleasant job I've ever had, my times there were still wonderful. And I think most of the islanders knew it was a pretty good place to be, too. Except for the predictably discontented teens, I don't believe many of them envied the far wealthier, and allegedly "freer," mainlanders at all. Quite the opposite, in my experience. But if the reader doesn't believe any of this, that is fine: I mention it only to illustrate some thoughts that are very hard to convey.

So I want to thank the island, if that makes any sense, and especially the many remarkable individuals who really made it home for us, some of whom would not even make believable fictional characters. To mention just a few: Jo and Esther, an older couple who lived and created art in a marvelous screened porch nestled among the cedars and live oaks (with a tiny trailer for sleeping), and imparted lots of love and wisdom; Jake and Eleanor, who rented us two wonderful little homes on the island and taught us much about island life, Jake taking me gill-netting and bringing me sharks; and especially, Van and Alta, two of the most extraordinarily intelligent and talented individuals I have ever heard of, whose expertise over the years has extended across more domains than I can count. Alta in particular had an almost mystical rapport with crabs, sea hares, fish, magpies, parrots, hummingbirds, raccoons, and heaven knows what else—have you ever seen a *swarm* of hummingbirds?—and was sometimes sought by experts at the Smithsonian or Harvard for her knowledge of corals, mollusks, and other life forms. She was my mentor in the natural world of the island, and while I knew even then that the two of them were pretty special, I had no idea of my great fortune. Someone must write a book about them. All of these people, and many other good friends on and off the island, helped shape the outlook that informs this book.

Of course my greatest debt, though not entirely for the usual reasons, is to my parents, Alice and Ron. My mother, an artist to the bone, fostered my appreciation for the intuitive side of human nature; while my father, a physicist, science educator, and writer, showed me the value of a scientist's, and writer's, analytical eye. In reality, both had a remarkably acute intuitive, empathetic grasp of human affairs, and both had a way with words. More than simply as parents, but as formidable minds, they have shaped my thinking about the matters in this book profoundly. My mother's influence is a bit less obvious, as she tended not to go in for lengthy philosophical disquisitions, her teachings being mainly by the force of her personality. (My father received many requests to write a book about her but never managed to, in great part I think because the task of capturing her in words was so hopeless.) Whereas my father was a good deal more explicit about his intellectual leanings, so much of my own work has basically amounted to adapting and exploring ideas I picked up from him. (Though he had little patience for academic philosophy, and while he seemed to approve of what I am doing here—he described it, jokingly, as "deconstructing the Enlightenment"—this sort of dense philosophical prose was not really his cup of tea.) Anyone perusing his writings about the island will have little trouble discerning the extent of my intellectual debts to him. He was my chief interlocutor, even about philosophical matters. I dedicate this book to them both.

Contents

PART I

FUNDAMENTALS OF PRUDENTIAL PSYCHOLOGY

1

Taking Socrates' Question Seriously

Me, I never saw a definition of happiness that could detain me past train time.

Dorothy Parker

"Just because I don't have the cash for something doesn't mean I shouldn't buy it," says Jane Watson, 29, who carries $8,000 on credit cards and a $438-a-month Saab on her $40,000 income. "I don't think debt is a sin," she says. "I'm living in a style I want to become accustomed to."

"Maxed Out," Newsweek[1]

1. INTRODUCTION

Definitions of happiness are not, in themselves, particularly exciting. Like opinions and a certain rude part of the anatomy, everybody's got one. Not only that, but on the typical definition that treats happiness as a purely psychological affair, you could be happy but not have a good life at all: you could, for instance, lead a sham life hooked up to an "experience machine," à la *The Matrix*, that offers whatever experiences you—who would think they were real—might want.[2] Most people recoil at the thought of permanently plugging into such a machine. Apparently our mental states are not the only things that matter. From such observations one might infer that philosophical work on happiness holds little promise: its subject matter is neither interesting nor important.

Let's test this hypothesis. For starters, set aside the word, which tends to incite no end of tedious quibbles. Think instead about ways of life and what they do for people. Consider, then, two communities, A and B. A typical member of A, on a typical day, is in more or less the following condition: at ease, untroubled, slow to anger, quick to laugh, fulfilled, in an expansive and self-assured mood, curious and attentive, alert and in good spirits, and fully at home in her body, with a relaxed, confident posture. A denizen of B, by contrast, is liable to be: stressed, anxious, tense, irritable, worried, weary, distracted and self-absorbed, uneasy, awkward and insecure, spiritually deflated, pinched, and compressed. The differences, let us suppose, owe mainly to differences in the prevailing ways of life in these communities.

Such communities could, it seems, exist; I believe they actually do. But you need not agree with me on these points; just suppose, for the moment, that there were two communities like these. Which is the better? Without more information, we can't really say. Is A riddled with injustice? Are its people ignorant or corrupt? Are they under another's thumb? Do they live with dignity? How long do they live? What are the bad days like? What are the bad lives like, and how many of them are there? So we need to know a lot more. No matter: I take it to be obvious that community B has a *major* strike against it compared to A. Indeed, it may already be disqualified as a good place to live. (Would you want to call it home?) Whereas A has, in a crucial respect, a great deal going for it. Were you responsible for placing an orphaned child in the community of your choosing, you would *of course* put him in A were other things equal between the two places; indeed, it would take a depraved mind knowingly to choose otherwise. To make it sensible to raise a child in B, when A could just as easily be selected, other things would have to be more than a little unequal.

Were there not a word for the state of mind enjoyed by the people of A, we would have to make one up. Luckily there is one: most contemporary English speakers call it "happiness." Notice that the descriptions of A and B made no explicit reference to happiness or unhappiness. But it should be reasonably apparent that, nonetheless, happiness is precisely what they were about: what A has in its favor is that its residents tend to be happy, whereas the people of B tend not to be. There are other senses to the word, no less legitimate than this, but this is a pretty central meaning—I would suggest *the* central meaning—all the same. Readers who come away from this book unpersuaded of my linguistic proposal are welcome to keep the word and, well, make one up for the psychological condition that will occupy much of our attention in what follows. What matters is the thing, not the word.

As I said, the fact that A's members tend to be happy, and B's not, is not in the least trivial: it concerns one of the chief desiderata of a good life, and of any society that hopes to qualify as civilized. Happiness, thus understood, is not the only thing that matters in the world, nor even in a person's life. Plausibly, human well-being has other aspects, and virtue matters even more than well-being; and beyond these there may be aesthetic and other values to be counted.[3] Let's grant at the outset that many people care too much about happiness and put too much energy into seeking it. It is said that Americans think about happiness an average of once a day, which does not seem obviously to be a good idea.[4] And few things grate on the nerves more than a cad trying to justify his lousy behavior with the plaint, "But I have a *right* to be happy." I will take it as a working assumption that happiness is not a matter of justice or right; the world owes us nothing, least of all happiness. Nor is unhappiness always a bad thing: sadness and other negative emotions all have their place in healthy human functioning. But to say all this is not to concede much: nothing is everything. No one has ever challenged the significance of inquiries into justice, morality, or just about any of the myriad other topics studied in the academy, on the silly grounds that they aren't the only things that matter. Likewise, we should not fault happiness for omitting something that we care about.

There are many interesting questions we can ask about this, the merely-one-of-the-most-important-things-in-the-world. Might B's residents think their lives are going well for them, even if they are not? Maybe they could be satisfied with their lives, or have lots of cheery feelings. Would that qualify them as happy after all? Similarly, we can ask how accurately they assess their own happiness. Might the people of B mistakenly think themselves happy? Perhaps they do not know there is anything missing from their experience of life, or even unpleasant about it. That would be something to know.

A further cluster of inquiries concerns the provenance of these states. Do the people of B fail to be happy despite their best efforts, or because of them? Are their lives unpleasant because they lack what they want, or because they *get* what they want? Another question is which society, A or B, would more likely get the economists' thumbs up. Could it possibly, and noncoincidentally, be B? Do the ideals driving traditional economic thought tend to favor societies more like A, or B? We can also inquire about the nature of the beast that inhabits these communities. What are the psychological needs of this species? How, and in what contexts, are those needs best met? Have the prevailing ethical and political doctrines of our time made reasonable assumptions about these matters? If not, that would really be something to know.

This book is fundamentally a plea for the importance of the psychology of well-being—or what I will call "prudential psychology," following the philosophical practice of using 'prudential' to denote matters of well-being, and the use of 'moral psychology' for the psychology of morality. To that end, I will argue that individuals are less authoritative in matters of personal welfare than modernity has usually allowed. This chapter will explain the nature of our subject and outline the arguments to follow.

Two meanings of 'happiness'

There are two philosophical literatures under the heading of "happiness," corresponding to two senses of the word. In this book, 'happiness' is a psychological term, akin to words like 'pleasure' and 'tranquility'. (See Chapter 2 for a full discussion.) Happiness is usually identified with either pleasure or life satisfaction (Chapters 4 and 5).

Many philosophers instead use 'happiness' as a rough synonym for 'well-being' (e.g., to translate Aristotle's 'eudaimonia'). A theory of "happiness" in this "well-being" sense is a theory of *value*: a theory of what ultimately benefits a person. For this concept, I use terms like 'well-being', 'flourishing', or 'welfare'. Common views of well-being include Aristotelian accounts, desire theories, and hedonism.

I will defend an *emotional state* theory of happiness (Chapters 6–7) against hedonistic and life satisfaction views. But I do not think happiness is all that matters for well-being. Happiness forms a major part of my *self-fulfillment* theory of well-being. Aristotelians reject this view of well-being, but could grant my account of happiness (Chapters 8–9).

2. PRUDENTIAL PSYCHOLOGY: A BRIEF HISTORY

...we must look more closely at the matter, since what is at stake is far from insignificant: it is how one should live one's life.

Attributed to Socrates. Plato, *The Republic* (352d)

Socrates, Plato tells us, posed, and proposed to answer, the question of how one ought to live. Many ethical philosophers since then have taken this as a summary statement of their mandate, and this is now a common understanding of ethical theory's brief: to answer Socrates' question.[5] If we read the modern literature on ethical theory through the lens of this question, however, a further question arises given the narrow focus of most of it on the moral aspects of the good life. Did Socrates misspeak? Or has his query been too narrowly construed? Nearly five decades ago, Elizabeth Anscombe famously took the field to task in a blistering polemic called "Modern Moral Philosophy."[6] Hearkening back to the style of ethical theory practiced by the ancients, her essay inaugurated a welcome revival of interest in the virtues—not just moral virtues, but admirable ways of being and living more generally. This has been an important step toward addressing Socrates' question more fully. Yet simply shifting the emphasis from morality to virtue falls well short of the mark. Most people, when picking up a text with an inviting title such as *The Good Life*, would expect a treatise bearing on the basic questions of what matters in life: what ought to be our priorities; or, again, how ought we to live? What the individual will *get*, on the purchase of said text, is most likely an exposition of the West's long history of less-than-convincing moral theories, the more recent editions with some virtue theories thrown in. Thumbing through the index will probably reveal some entries on "happiness" or "well-being" or "utility," but the associated passages will mostly be brief, occurring mainly within discussions of some theory of morality or virtue, and subordinated to those. Is virtue good for us? What do utilitarians enjoin us to maximize? There might be a few cursory sections on the meaning of life, or Nozick's entertaining experience machine case. But mostly what the reader will have learned is how to *be* good.

But being good is only a part of the good life, as most of us see things. It is utterly ordinary for people to puzzle about what it would mean to live in a sensible manner, to have the right priorities. What animates many people to ask Socrates' question is not worries about morality, but worries about what makes for a fulfilling life, or what it would take for our lives to go well for us. Well-being and happiness, not morality, are probably the first things on most people's minds when they reflect about how they ought to live. They are, after all, largely what makes life worth living. An ethics that proposes to take seriously Socrates' question ought to have something substantial to say about them.

Some modern thinkers have indeed taken an inclusive approach to the good life, recognizing that the fundamental question is how to live, period, and not how to be good. Yet even those writers tend to relegate happiness to the margins. For instance, two eminent scholars of ancient ethics, Julia Annas and Martha Nussbaum, have greatly enriched contemporary ethical thought about the good life, and their writings on the subject are among the most insightful and discerning produced in recent decades. Their work has influenced my thinking on these matters immensely. Yet consider what they had to say about our subject matter in a recent issue of *Daedalus*. Annas writes that:

Being happy is easily taken to be feeling happy . . . a kind of smiley-face feeling. . . . And this kind of happiness does not matter to us all that much once we start to think in a serious way about our lives. As we bring up our children, what we aim for is not that they have episodes of smiley-face feeling, but that their lives go well as wholes: we come to think of happiness as the way a life as a whole goes well, and see that episodes of happiness are not what we build our lives around.[7]

Implicit in this passage, I think, is the suggestion that smiley-face feelings are *all* happiness could amount to if it is purely a psychological matter. And Nussbaum remarks that "Bentham understood how powerful pain and pleasure are for children, and for the child in us"—the idea apparently being that hedonic matters concern nothing more than "the receptive and childlike parts of the personality."[8] Happiness, as we are understanding it here, is a shallow thing for kids and the kids in us. It goes without saying that whatever is going on in the lands of A and B, it is not a superficial or childish matter. I think Annas and Nussbaum would actually agree with me on this; their real target seems to be a popular conception of happiness, which does indeed tend to emphasize superficial cheeriness. But why think that a psychological notion of happiness *must* be like that? Unfortunately, there is not a great deal in the modern literature to counter such stereotypes.

Perhaps the superficiality lies in the way people tend to *think* about happiness and related states, and not in the idea that such matters are of central importance in a good life. This, probably, would have been the view of most ancient philosophers, for whom well-being, including the psychology of well-being, was a major preoccupation.[9] Such thinkers took Socrates' question quite seriously, and tried to articulate ideals of the good life that intelligent persons would, on reflection, find compelling. What they did was not virtue ethics but *well-being* ethics—hence the name "eudaimonistic ethics": their ethical theories were explicitly accounts of eudaimonia or well-being. Virtue and morality came into the picture because of how they connected with the more fundamental notion of well-being, not the other way around. This is precisely the reverse of what we find in the modern literature, including virtue ethics. (Even neo-Aristotelian accounts grounding the virtues in human flourishing are still, in the first instance, *virtue* theories. In fact it is sometimes hard to extract a definite conception of well-being from such theories—a state of affairs that would have been unthinkable for ancient philosophers.)

Ancient ethical thinkers knew that psychology was a key, if not *the* key, to a proper understanding of human well-being. None of the major schools of ancient ethical thought failed to maintain that the good life was a pleasant one, and most took great pains to show how this was so, often developing sophisticated doctrines about the mental aspects of flourishing. While the Cyrenaics espoused a simple form of hedonism centering on the pleasures of the moment, more discerning hedonists like the Epicureans, and perhaps Democritus, held subtler views about the pleasures worth seeking—in the Epicurean case, the "static" pleasures of tranquility or *ataraxia*, and in the Democritean case *euthymia*, which is often translated as "cheerfulness" but may have centered more on tranquility than this translation suggests. (The ideal of *ataraxia* also figured prominently in the work of the Skeptics.) The Epicureans had a lot to say, not just about pleasure, but about the varieties of desire and how to cultivate the proper desires. By contrast the Stoics, who posited virtue as the sole good, and believed pleasure and pain to be "indifferents," even cautioning against seeking pleasure, might be expected to have been more reticent about such matters. But a highly developed psychology of well-being occupied the center of their ethics, partly because virtue for them involved getting one's inner life, particularly one's emotions, in proper order. And despite its freedom from the passions or *apatheia*, the virtuous life was clearly envisaged as a pleasant one involving *ataraxia* and various "good affects" or *eupatheiai*, including a kind of joy (*chara*). It was not a grueling or affectless, "eat your vegetables" affair. They did, admittedly, maintain that one could be *eudaimon* on the rack, so perhaps the sage's life is only normally pleasant. But even the man on the rack could only be flourishing provided that he not let it bother him or in any way disturb his tranquility. Recall the cheerful equanimity with which Socrates, who was widely thought to have come as close as anyone to the Stoic ideal, approached his death. In the words of Crito: "But I have been wondering at your peaceful slumbers, and that was the reason why I did not awaken you, because I wanted you to be out of pain. I have always thought you happy in the calmness of your temperament; but never did I see the like of the easy, cheerful way in which you bear this calamity."[10] This is not an unhappy man.

Plato tries hard in the *Republic* to defend a similar view of well-being, arguing at great length that the unvirtuous must be plagued by psychic disharmony, so that only the virtuous life is truly pleasant. Aristotle moderates such views by identifying well-being with virtuous *activity*, and counting goods of fortune in the assessment of well-being. He too discussed the psychological aspects of human flourishing at length, developing an influential view about the role of the emotions in a virtuous life, but also saying much about the character of pleasure and arguing that the life of virtue is the most pleasant.

It is unlikely that many ancients would have failed to grasp the significance of happiness, as understood here. Admittedly, they seem not to have had a word corresponding to 'happiness', in the psychological sense that concerns us here: '*euthymia*', roughly cheerfulness, or '*ataraxia*', tranquility, may come close in certain ways, but probably neither gets the meaning entirely right; and 'eudaimonia' was an evaluative, not psychological, term corresponding roughly to our 'well-being.' But words aside, the ancients did not consider the subject matter unimportant. If, for instance, studies indicate that certain ways of life are surprisingly unfulfilling or downright unpleasant, this would likely qualify as a significant finding according to any of the doctrines canvassed above. Similarly, society B would not have found many defenders among the Hellenes. To be sure, several qualifications need to be made. First, people can enjoy themselves in questionable ways, for instance in leading lives of passive consumption that Aristotle deemed fit only for "grazing cattle." Hence most ancients would not have considered high levels of happiness to be sufficient for well-being. (Though perhaps its highest reaches are possible only for those leading the best sort of life.) Second, some of the states we associate with being happy, such as giddy elation, would have been thought undesirable by many ancient theorists. Third, many ancients—Stoics and Aristotelians, for instance—rejected the idea that happiness should be our goal. It is, for them, just a by-product or component of virtue—an agreeable accompaniment to the life well-lived. Finally, those same thinkers rejected the notion that happiness could be good in itself, apart from the activities and circumstances associated with it. It was essential that these mental states come about in the right way, at the right time. But none of this shows happiness not to be *important*, and it is doubtful that any ancient school should have taken such a view.

The significance of happiness becomes clearer still when we remind ourselves that a concern for happiness just *is*, ordinarily, a concern for unhappiness as well. No sane individual who cares about matters of health fails to care about *ill* health—and indeed, most "health care" focuses primarily on the negative. Just as health care professions need not be in the business of "positive medicine," neither is the study of happiness especially the province of positive psychology. (To my mind, unhappiness is the more urgent topic; but since its pleasanter counterpart has tended to get short shrift from angst-ridden intellectuals, the positive psychology movement marks a welcome development, and this book is basically a part of it—the dark side of positive psychology, as it were.[11]) 'Health' and 'happiness', along with 'well-being', function not just to denote ideals, but also as blanket terms for general areas of concern, encompassing matters both good and bad.

An interesting thing happens when we get to the modern era: serious reflection on the psychology of well-being becomes relatively scarce, even as accounts of well-being grow ever more psychologized. Indeed, serious reflection on well-being, period, became scarcer in the modern era. The modern literature on well-being is *dwarfed* by the mountain of work on morality and virtue: a recent keyword search of the Philosopher's Index revealed 1,928 entries relating to happiness and well-being, versus 55,876 on morality and virtue—a thirty-fold difference. These numbers probably understate the actual proportion, since many matches for 'welfare' concern different topics, and articles mentioning well-being or happiness frequently do so only in passing.[12] With some notable exceptions, such as Mill, modern ethical theorists seem proportionately to be far less interested in the nature of well-being than their ancient counterparts. Even Utilitarians, who ground their ethics in the promotion of well-being, often understood in hedonistic terms, have tended not to produce great works on the character of well-being or its psychology.[13] Bentham's discussion of pleasure is unusually thorough, but it still is not, for all that, very interesting.

The Lilliputian literature on well-being in turn towers over the all-but-indiscernible collection of writings exploring happiness and other psychological dimensions of well-being. Well-being and happiness are not major vocations for the modern ethical philosopher; they are basically hobbies. If this is not already apparent, then it should be clear enough by the end of this book, if only by the volume of elementary distinctions that will have to be introduced to get our discussion off the ground. The situation may be somewhat better in the continental literature than in the analytic or anglophone tradition in which the present book resides. Writers like Nietzsche and Sartre, for instance, were thinkers about the good life broadly speaking, and not just morality; this doubtless accounts in part for the continued popularity of such authors among the public. But systematic discussion of views of well-being or happiness has not been prominent in that literature; hence, in part, the dearth of references from the continental canon in standard surveys of work on well-being and happiness.

In recent decades, however, researchers in other fields have initiated a major effort to improve our understanding of happiness and other psychological aspects of well-being. After fitful beginnings in the 1960s, this work started to take off with the pioneering research of Ed Diener and others in the 1980s.[14] And the literature has grown explosively in the last decade, particularly since Martin Seligman and Mihaly Csikszentmihalyi, among others, inaugurated the positive psychology movement. Besides positive psychology, we now have the (sometimes overlapping) fields of subjective well-being research, happiness studies, hedonic psychology, eudaimonic psychology, behavioral economics, and neuroeconomics, among others. By now this work is sufficiently well-publicized that I need not enumerate its major findings here; suffice it to say that it promises to become a major influence on public policy and the culture at large. Philosophers too have been attending to these developments, and it is only a matter of time before these matters give rise to a substantial body of philosophical work.[15]

In short, there has been a broad interdisciplinary resurgence of interest in the psychology of well-being. This effectively amounts to a new field of inquiry—what I earlier called *prudential psychology*. Because there are diverse ways of thinking about the psychological aspects of well-being, some of which de-emphasize or go beyond the states encompassed by subjective well-being, it is useful to have a neutral term that can embrace a wide range of approaches. Ancient objectivists about human flourishing, contemporary researchers working on eudaimonic psychology, positive psychologists, "negative" psychologists studying mental illness, and others all have views about the psychology of well-being. They all study prudential psychology. Like 'moral psychology', the term is sufficiently broad and theoretically neutral that it allows practitioners in various disciplines complete latitude in defining their own subspecialties and theoretical approaches to the subject. It is not meant to supplant terms like 'positive psychology', but to place various fields in a broader context that highlights their common interests and significance. It is possible for intelligent people to disagree about the promise of, say, hedonic versus eudaimonic psychology (the former emphasizes the subjectivity and diversity of human welfare while the latter stresses the objectivity and universality of needs). But no one can doubt that prudential psychology is worth doing.

3. THE TARGET: AN ASSUMPTION OF PERSONAL AUTHORITY

Why did philosophical work on well-being and its psychology fall out of favor in the modern era? Such historical questions rarely have simple answers, but surely some credit must go to a shift in views about *personal authority* in matters of well-being. The ancients apparently took it as a given that individuals are not, in general, authorities about their own welfare. Quite the opposite: most ancient philosophers followed Socrates' lead in distinguishing "the many" and "the wise," with the former and much larger class being, basically, dolts. Aristotle notoriously maintained that some of us are so ill-fitted for self-governance that we are better off enslaved, with masters to look after us. Even Epicurean hedonists believed that most of us require considerable enlightenment about the true character of our interests; the pursuit of pleasure, correctly understood, is not at all what most people would expect. The standard economic view of modernity, that well-being consists in people getting whatever they happen to want, would have seemed childish if not insane to most ancient thinkers.[16] Given this sort of background, the richness and depth of ancient thought about human flourishing should come as no surprise: if most of us are badly mistaken about our own interests, then a better understanding of well-being must be among our top priorities. Perhaps it should be the *central* task of intellectual inquiry, as it evidently was among the ancients. Nor should we be surprised if such thinkers paid close attention to the psychology of well-being: our minds are plainly the most important thing about us, yet most of us, according to the ancients, fail to grasp what states of mind are truly worth having and what their role is in a good life.

The spirit of modernity is rather different. Inspired by Enlightenment optimism about the individual's powers of reason and self-government, modern liberals tend to believe in one or another form of the sovereignty or authority of the individual in matters of personal welfare: by and large, people know what's best for them, and tend to act rationally in the promotion of their interests. (I am using 'liberal' in the traditional philosophical sense, for views giving top priority to individual liberties. Many American "conservatives" are liberals in this sense.) We all make mistakes, of course, but not so much that we urgently need enlightenment about our own well-being. What people need more than anything, on this view, is *freedom*. In particular, they need the liberty and resources to pursue their various goals however they see fit. People tend to fare best—and pretty well at that—when empowered to shape their lives according to their own priorities. Call the optimism in question *liberal optimism*, given its association with liberal freedoms.[17]

This sort of view does not eliminate the need for philosophical work on well-being. But it does diminish its importance. People who are authorities about their own good don't need enlightenment; they need empowerment. They need economics, not philosophy. Thus, perhaps, did formal research on well-being pass largely from the philosopher to the economist, who attempts to solve the arcane problems of how most efficiently to get resources into people's hands. Economics, and its attendant focus on our material conditions, became ascendant in the culture and in policy circles. Questions about the character of well-being and its psychology, and the most sensible way to live, have accordingly taken a back seat.

But what if it turns out that people don't have this kind of authority? What if they frequently and predictably make serious mistakes about what matters in life, act irrationally, or otherwise err in ways that undercut their prospects for well-being? What if, as a result, they tend to botch their lives at an alarmingly high rate, in many cases being unwitting pursuers of *un*happiness? It might still seem a good idea to empower people as much as possible to live as they wish; that is another question. But it would probably *not* seem like a good idea to treat the study of well-being and its psychology as an idle intellectual exercise.

The central thesis of this book is that people probably do not enjoy a high degree of authority or competence in matters of personal welfare. We should expect them systematically to make a host of serious mistakes regarding their own well-being. Surprisingly often, people's choices may frustrate their prospects for happiness and well-being rather than improve them. In the pursuit of their dreams, even people blessed with excellent opportunities may less likely succeed than shoot themselves in the foot. Or, at least, bungle the job more often than the liberal tradition's characteristic optimism would lead us to expect. At the same time, I want to reject any stringently objective approach to well-being and affirm that psychological states like happiness are indeed central to it, just as moderns have tended to believe.

In a nutshell, I want to challenge an assumption—call it *Personal Authority*—that is popular among modern liberals, while retaining the basic values of liberal modernity. The assumption claims, somewhat vaguely, that people are highly authoritative about their own well-being: while they sometimes make mistakes, they pretty well know what's good for them and how they are doing, and generally make prudent choices in pursuit of their interests. This should be read as stronger than the mere claim that people's choices are prudent more often than not, meaning rather that people usually *lead their lives*, on the whole, in a reasonably prudent manner. To pull this off requires more than a numerical majority of good choices, since even one bad choice can ruin one's life. The terminology of "authority" should not mislead: I am not disputing people's *right* to make determinations about their own well-being, and indeed the potential for excessive paternalism will be a significant worry raised by this book. We could frame the issue in terms of "competence," but to challenge people's "competence" carries the implication that they are unfit for self-governance, like children.

Personal Authority rests on two claims, which I will call Transparency and Aptitude. *Transparency* holds that well-being is relatively transparent to individuals: what's good for a person is relatively easy for that individual to discern; our interests are not opaque to us. This idea emerges most clearly in the various forms of subjectivism about well-being, which on the broadest construal tells us that what ultimately benefits a person is *determined* by subjective psychological states like desires or pleasures.[18] If what's good for me just is getting what I want, then I probably have a pretty decent grip on what's ultimately in my best interest. But another form of transparency more directly concerns the epistemic accessibility of particular goods that matter for welfare, such as pleasure or happiness, claiming that their nature and value are easily enough known. Intense pain would be a paradigm of transparent disvalue: someone experiencing it will have little difficulty knowing about the problem. Moreover, its sources tend to be readily discernible: it usually doesn't take a genius to figure out which things are going to hurt a lot.

The *Aptitude* assumption is partly a mirror image of Transparency: it maintains that people typically have the psychological endowments needed to choose well given the broad ability to live as they wish, with a rich array of options, that liberals have traditionally favored. Do human beings have the aptitude for living prudently in this kind of environment? An affirmative answer to this question requires both that people's judgments about their interests tend to be often enough right, and that their choices are often enough reasonable given their judgments. Note that the more opaque people's interests are—the less Transparency holds—the higher the bar for Aptitude. Both of these assumptions will be called into question.

4. BROADER THEMES: THREE ERRORS IN THINKING ABOUT WELL-BEING

4.1. The Benthamite error

In the course of our challenge to Personal Authority, several broader themes will emerge. The most important—indeed, my chief purpose in writing this book—is that the psychology of well-being is far richer and more interesting than one might expect from a study of the modern philosophical literature. Theorists can dismiss happiness as merely a matter of "smiley-face" feelings because, by and large, that's about as sophisticated as modern thinking about happiness gets. Our prudential psychology pretty much runs the gamut from frowny-faces to smiley-faces, having progressed very little from Bentham's primitivism. Call this simplistic view of well-being's psychology the "Benthamite error."[19]

4.2. The Platonic error

A second theme will turn up in various forms throughout the book: a more *sentimentalist*, less *rationalistic*, approach to human well-being than one usually finds in the philosophical literature. That is, the book develops an approach to well-being that emphasizes the affective ("sentimental") dimensions of human flourishing, notably moods and emotions, according them greater significance than most views do. I use these terms in a technical, not colloquial manner—I am neither propounding sentimentality nor taking 'rationalism' to be pejorative—but also relatively loosely, designating broad tendencies rather than specific doctrines. In particular, I am not using 'rationalism' to designate views that focus on purely rational insight with no proper contribution from sentiment. Rather, rationalists focus their attentions on high-level, analytic, or "rational" processes in their views of human welfare, particularly agents' considered or reflective judgments, as opposed say to mere feelings, inclinations, or intuitive or instinctual reactions. Sentimentalists, by contrast, assign greater significance to the latter sorts of states. Hedonism, as most commonly understood, would be a paradigm sentimentalist theory. For the hedonist, what's good for you is what is pleasant, *whether or not you think it is*. If your reflective judgment takes a less pleasant life to be better for you than a more pleasant alternative, then you are simply wrong. In this battle, according to such hedonists, sentiment trumps reason. We can distinguish at least three forms of rationalism and sentimentalism regarding well-being, including normative views about the roles of reason and sentiment in the constitution of well-being (as in the example of hedonism) or, second, in the proper governance of human life. As well, there are descriptive doctrines concerning the actual roles of reason and sentiment in determining human behavior. The discussion in this book will problematize all three forms of rationalism.

Rationalism's philosophical roots date at least to Plato, who took human life to be properly governed by reason, and well-being to consist in a well-ordered soul in which reason holds the reins. Much of the philosophical tradition has, in varying ways, followed him in placing reason at the center of well-being; hence I call it the "Platonic error." Aristotelian views of well-being, despite the important role they accord the emotions, are far more rationalistic than hedonism, a point that is most apparent in Aristotle's account of well-being as living according to reason, with reason firmly in charge. Sentiment counts, but only in a secondary role. And so, for the *phronimos* or person of wisdom, nothing could benefit the agent against her own best judgment. If something were to benefit a person against her considered judgment—if this is possible for an Aristotelian—it would represent a serious problem, an abdication by reason of its proper role in guiding human life. It may be surprising that subjectivist accounts of well-being, such as most desire-fulfillment theories, should also be rationalistic. But as we will see in Chapter 9, they may be even more so than the Aristotelian view.

Indeed, already we can see a kind of rationalism in the liberal optimist's description of human beings as highly rational pursuers of well-being. This is, in essence, a democratized version of the Platonic error. Thus does liberal optimism embody a strange admixture of Platonic highbrow and Benthamite lowbrow, marrying a view of well-being as something that even a child could grasp with a lofty account of human rational powers. We simultaneously lower the bar and deem the happiness-seeker an Olympian: anyone can succeed. The arguments to follow will show that the bar is higher (Parts II and III), and the athlete's talents less impressive (Part IV), than liberal optimists seem to recognize.

While this book emphasizes the sentimental aspects of human nature, according the rational aspects a less central place in human flourishing, it is not strongly sentimentalist in the manner of classical hedonism. Our rationality is still quite central to who we are, and a complete account of well-being should probably acknowledge this more fully than hedonism does. This book reflects not a full-blooded sentimentalism but a "dual aspect" approach to human nature and human flourishing, according to which neither reason nor sentiment is properly the sovereign master in either the constitution of well-being or the pursuit of a good life. The idea is closer to shared governance.

I was brought up on a "horse and rider" metaphor of human nature—much like Jonathan Haidt's "elephant and rider" model, but to my mind closer to the right proportions—with reason being the rider, perched atop a somewhat independently motivated horse.[20] The point of the story was that we are divided internally, to some extent irreconcilably, and that an important part of living well consists in learning how to serve both aspects of one's nature well. The horse, in particular, is too easily neglected and yoked to the often quite foreign agendas of the rider, compressing it and grinding it down. (Think, at the limit, William S. Burroughs's spiritually eviscerated "decent church-going women with their mean, pinched, bitter, evil faces." Nietzsche would say that their souls squint.[21]) The influence of such ideas in this book will be plain: in essence, I will be arguing that the rider's role in matters of well-being has been overstated. Little did I realize that what we had been talking about was a folk version of what is now called dual process psychology. We will discuss such theories in Chapter 11.

4.3. The behaviorist error

A further aim of this book is to address the recent empirical work on happiness and related psychological matters. While this research is booming, its significance remains unclear, and it raises numerous philosophical questions. My discussion may seem to counsel skepticism about the empirical research, since I take issue with the empirical literature at a number of points, for instance arguing that self-report measures probably suffer from serious errors, or are misleading, in ways that have not generally been recognized. Yet a major aim of the book is to *support* this research, both by clarifying its weaknesses, noting areas for improvement, and by making manifest the importance of this work. The current science is far from perfect, and none of the researchers in this area would deny it. But it has already turned up a trove of useful information, and promises to uncover a lot more. Yet there continues to be tremendous skepticism about this work in some circles—not reasonable doubts about whether we can always take its results at face value, or whether the evidence is solid enough yet to guide policy. It is blanket skepticism about whether the science ought to be taken seriously at all, say because happiness is supposed to be ineffable or undefinable or unmeasurable. Such claims take grains of truth and inflate them into nonsense, as we will see. I suspect much of it represents a holdover from the inane behaviorism that afflicted much of the academy in the past century, including the economic orthodoxy that currently rules the policy world. I will accordingly ascribe this sort of skepticism to a "behaviorist error," though it should be noted that few people would come right out and endorse behaviorism these days. The reason is that people eventually figured out that behaviorism rested on an epistemology that even physics couldn't satisfy; and since physics is considered a paradigm of science, this meant that a lot of fields must have gone well off their gimbals.

There are alternatives to the science. We can stop thinking about the psychological aspects of well-being, ignoring the daily blizzard of evidence presented to our consciousness, and hope everything works out okay. Or we can think about them, but confine ourselves to anecdotes and armchair speculations. Far be it from me to cast away the armchair; but to dispense with the science would be absurd. The research is extremely diverse, some of it not relying on self-reports at all, and some studies will be more vulnerable to error than others. Some of it garnered a Nobel in *economics*, of all things. And even subjective experience is not so utterly inscrutable that we can't meaningfully study it; kick a friend in the shins and see if you can't divine her feelings. Claims about subjective experience are a lot more testable than string theory, and measurement protocols need not assume that pleasures and emotions can be precisely gauged and boiled down to a cardinal number. So we have to consider the merits of each claim separately, not brush them all off with an undiscriminating wave of the hand.

There may be a further mistake behind the skeptical doubts, namely a tendency to confuse rigor with precision. Any good argument should be developed with appropriate rigor, mustering a sufficiently careful and thorough case for its conclusion. We should not claim to have shown any more than we have in fact shown. I hope the arguments in this book are rigorous enough; there will certainly be enough new distinctions to keep the reader busy. But a rigorous argument need not be *precise*: sometimes the subject matter precludes much in the way of precision, or our aspirations are modest enough that we don't need to be exact. I think both possibilities obtain in this book, and so my discussion will not in general be very precise. Some may see this as a gross deficiency, perhaps not just here but with any inquiry into matters of happiness. It is hard to see why this should be: as long as we manage to advance our understanding of significant matters, that should be enough. In fact I would take the point further: sometimes precision can impede understanding. For part of what we want out of our theories is *fidelity* to the phenomena: accurately representing the reality that interests us. Precision can obviously foster this, e.g., in the successes of physics since the development of calculus. But it can also work against fidelity, since we want not just an exact accounting of reality, but a *full* accounting. And this often precludes a high degree of precision, especially formal precision, since that typically requires an extremely austere representation of reality, abstracting out a few pieces of the puzzle that can be plugged into your equations. The richer the reality you are trying to model, the more of it you are going to have to leave out if you want to keep your model precise. Naturally, this involves tradeoffs, and neoclassical economists (for example) have largely resolved them in favor of austerity and precision, to the point, some would argue, that their theories often fail to model any important slice of reality. The result, arguably, is a very precise but very low-fidelity theory of human welfare and its pursuit. This book is going for a lower-precision but higher-fidelity account.

5. WHY OUR INQUIRY MATTERS

The book's challenge to Personal Authority matters for several reasons. From a purely practical standpoint, there is obviously something to be gained by a better understanding of the psychology of well-being and the human potential for error in this domain. Individually, it may help us to improve the way we live. Collectively, such knowledge may help us to better grasp the advantages and limitations involved in various social forms, and in general to form a more adequate view of the good society. It may also help us to develop policies that better serve human well-being. Generally, we will see many reasons for doubting one of the central assumptions of contemporary political and economic policy—namely, that people's choices reliably track their interests. If people are surprisingly imprudent, and their mistakes are predictable, then policies aimed at compensating for these tendencies might prove more effective than has been recognized. Alternatively, if it turns out that increasing people's control over their lives often yields smaller dividends than expected, then the urgency of advancing that control, say by increasing people's resources or capabilities, may sometimes be diminished. Perhaps it will even tend to leave people worse off in a surprising number of cases. Note that even if people always benefit from having more control over their lives, it will be significant if those benefits prove smaller than anticipated: increasing people's resources or capabilities typically has costs, so reducing the expected benefits of such increases will sometimes tip the scale against doing so.

More broadly, liberal optimism provides the intellectual basis for much of our present form of civilization, centered as it is on the unbridled expansion of individuals' freedom to shape their lives. The possibility that our civilization and way of life are partly founded on a mistake is not, I take it, a question of purely academic interest. Anything that weakens our faith in liberal optimism is bound to have some practical import.

The theoretical significance of our inquiry may be less clear, since the psychology of well-being has not much been on the philosophical table in recent decades, and even among the ancients was largely subordinated to other projects in ethical theory. Yet it seems to me a critical matter for any systematic understanding of the world and our place in it, and hence a central concern for the academy. For we can scarcely claim to possess any such understanding if we do not even understand who or what *we* are; hence the study of human nature has to be among the highest priorities for theoretical investigation. I submit that inquiry into human nature primarily means inquiry into human *flourishing* or well-being.[22] If you want to understand wolves or elephants then among your first questions, it seems, will be "what does it mean for them to flourish?" and "what do they need to flourish?" Surely such questions are not peripheral to an understanding of those species. Are human beings different in this regard? There is no obvious reason why they should be. Suppose they are not: what would well-being-focused inquiry into human nature look like? Presumably it would include a hefty psychological component. Indeed, arguably it would be *mainly* a psychological endeavor, since questions about the intrinsic value of non-psychological goods are liable to be secondary to psychological matters in understanding human nature. Prudential psychology, I am suggesting, should be among the primary concerns of the academy. I do not claim that it is more important for the advancement of human understanding than, say, solving the basic mysteries of modern physics, or resolving the mystery of consciousness. But surely making headway on the mysteries of happiness rates an elevated position on the list.

More traditional projects in philosophical ethics will not likely emerge unaffected by such inquiry. It is possible, of course, to maintain ethical doctrines independently of any psychology, since psychological facts alone may not entail anything about values. But if your ethical or political ideals are to be at all *plausible, achievable* by human beings, *reasonably* applied to human beings, and otherwise compatible with a *good* life for a human being, then they had better comport reasonably well with a correct picture of human nature and human flourishing. This constraint may not be so interesting, if the requirement is easily enough met. But in what follows, we will discuss points that I suspect raise problems for all three of the major ethical theories: Kantian, consequentialist, and virtue ethics, at least in some of their most popular forms. Kantians, for instance, demand a degree of rational governance of life that may not, by the end of this book, seem clearly to be feasible or desirable for human beings; consequentialists wanting to defend a non-repugnant morality and politics typically invoke a raft of assumptions about human nature and what benefits people, for instance in defending liberal restrictions on state paternalism, and these assumptions are not clearly true; and neo-Aristotelian virtue ethicists assert a central role for reason in human nature and its fulfillment, deeming us to be rational animals in a strong sense that, again, will not obviously prove correct. On all these questions I will henceforth be largely silent. (For the record, I endorse none of these theories. That well-being should only be of interest to consequentialists and virtue ethicists is among the more bizarre prejudices afflicting the literature.) Though it is obviously important whether these moral theories are defensible or not, addressing the question with any seriousness would lead us too far afield. At any rate, we've got bigger fish to fry.

6. CAVEATS

It must be emphasized that this book will *assume* some form of liberalism. Even if Personal Authority is untenable, there could—and would, in my view—be compelling moral reasons for preserving liberal freedoms and limiting state interventions in people's lives. We do not treat people with respect by treating them like children, even if that were to leave them better off. What benefits people and what we may do to them are distinct questions. (There is a further question about whether governments could do *better* than individuals at promoting their welfare.) Even so, the political ramifications of our discussion may prove to be substantial.

This book will not be suggesting that people are mostly idiots, as the ancients seemed to think. The point is rather to indicate that well-being is less transparent, and harder for human beings to secure for themselves given their psychological capacities, than we tend to think. It may be—and I think it is—that human beings are quite adept in matters of well-being, but only in contexts where their exercise of control over the shape of their lives is in certain ways constrained, or else assisted by exogenous influences like cultural norms. If people too often act imprudently, the problem may lie not with them but with a mismatch between human nature and the demands imposed by certain environments.

Nor is the point to claim that most people, in Western democracies or elsewhere, are in fact unhappy. Many smart people believe that contemporary Americans and other affluent Westerners are doing quite well, if not flourishing. David Brooks, a perceptive observer of contemporary culture, writes, "the polling...suggests that people are not personally miserable or downtrodden. Their homes are bigger. They own more cars. They feel more affluent. In a segmented nation, they have built lifestyle niches for themselves where they feel optimistic and fulfilled."[23] While we will discuss various grounds for caution on this score, it is not my purpose to refute this sort of claim. Brooks could be right. It will be enough, for my purposes, if people tend to be *too often* unhappy, or at the very least tend too often to judge and choose badly in matters of happiness. In all this we need not assume, implausibly, that people solely or even primarily aim at happiness or well-being in their choices. But that most people take these things to be important for a good life should be uncontroversial.

The focus of this book is theoretical. While I hope its contents will have some payoff in practical affairs, I will offer no practical advice, nor plump for any social or political agenda. At many points I do discuss current social issues and other applied matters. But the purpose is to motivate and illustrate the theoretical points and their possible significance, not to persuade the reader of particular models of living. We would have less need for such excursions were there already a vibrant philosophical literature on happiness, as the significance of the questions would likely be clear enough already. Though the book is mainly theoretical, I have tried to make it accessible to readers outside philosophy. Such readers should not be daunted by occasional excursions into abstruse philosophical issues or technical jargon. Difficult passages can usually be skipped by nonspecialists without significant loss. And though the book is long, its presentation is fairly modular, so readers can usually skip directly to the chapters or sections that interest them.

7. AN OVERVIEW OF THE BOOK

The book has four parts. Part I tries to clarify the theoretical landscape in the psychology of well-being, a crucial task given the vexed nature of our subject. We start in Chapter 2 by charting some important distinctions and setting out the basic positions. Chapter 3 takes up the question of methodology, showing how we can engage in substantive debates concerning happiness and similar "mongrel concepts." I defend a method of "reconstructive analysis" against common approaches like conceptual analysis and scientific naturalism. Crudely, an acceptable conception should be both intuitively plausible and an answer to our practical interests in happiness. This approach enables us to identify the psychological states that matter to us, however ill-defined the ordinary concept of happiness may be.

Part II examines the character of happiness, critiquing the dominant views of happiness—hedonism and life satisfaction theories—which tend to support Transparency, while defending an "emotional state" account that weakens it. Chapter 4 discusses the best-known account of happiness, hedonism. The trouble with this view is mainly that happiness appears to be an emotional and not merely experiential phenomenon, in ways that rule out a hedonistic analysis. Intuitively, one is unhappy (say) by virtue of being *depressed*, not by virtue of experiencing the unpleasantness of depression. Life satisfaction theories identify happiness with being satisfied with one's life as a whole. I reject this sort of view in Chapter 5, largely because life satisfaction appears not to have the kind of significance happiness seems to possess. For instance, life satisfaction attitudes are governed by norms, such as gratitude, that can drive a deep wedge between how satisfied we are and how well we see our lives going for us. Chapter 6 centers on introducing a "default" form of emotional state theory and fleshing out a plausible version of the view, illustrating the sorts of states an emotional state theory should encompass. Chapter 7 develops a particular version of the theory, arguing that a person's emotional condition is composed of two parts: crudely, mood-related affects, along with a variable "mood propensity" that disposes the person to experience certain mood-related states rather than others. To be happy, on this view, is not just to be subjected to a certain sequence of experiences, but for one's very being to manifest a favorable orientation toward the conditions of one's life—a kind of psychic affirmation of one's life. Happiness on such a view is more nearly the opposite of depression or anxiety, whereas hedonistic happiness is simply opposed to unpleasantness.

Part III extends the discussion of Transparency to the theory of well-being. The upshot of this part of the book will be that moderns have been largely correct in thinking psychological states like happiness central to well-being, but wrong to suppose that this confers a great deal of authority on the individual in determining what's best for her. Chapter 8 examines the most interesting rivals to my view, Aristotelian and other theories that cash out well-being in terms of perfection or virtue. The discussion here introduces the notion of nature-fulfillment on which my own view is based, but rejects the strongly objectivist doctrines on which most existing challenges to Transparency have relied. I argue that perfection probably forms no fundamental part of well-being, the popularity of views to the contrary likely owing to an understandable confusion between the notions of well-being and the good life. In Chapter 9 I defend a different type of nature-fulfillment theory centering on self-fulfillment. (This term has unfortunate New Age connotations of self-absorption. But even Nietzsche, by no means a "hug myself" type, arguably held a kind of self-fulfillment view.) The view of well-being is developed by noting that the emotional state theory of happiness reveals a close relationship between happiness and the self: our propensities for being happy or unhappy in various ways of living are important to who we are. This matters, I argue, because it seems important to live in accordance with who we are: well-being consists, at least partly, in self-fulfillment. And self-fulfillment in turn consists partly in fulfilling our emotional natures—in being authentically happy, in Sumner's terms.[24] Since what makes us happy often conflicts with our priorities, subjectivist accounts of well-being are false. I do not claim that this yields a complete account of well-being, a project that will require a more extensive discussion than I can offer here. It suffices to note the centrality of happiness for well-being, and the surprisingly opaque character of well-being.

In Part IV we turn to the question of Aptitude: is human psychology congenial to the optimistic tenor of modern thought about the individualized pursuit of happiness? Chapter 10 suggests a negative answer to this question regarding people's ability to judge their past and present well-being. Indeed, it is surprisingly easy to err even about the present quality of one's experience, for instance because of the importance of elusive affects like anxiety for well-being. Chapter 11 observes that we also tend to make systematic, and often gross, errors in predicting the impact of future events on our well-being, as well as in choosing rationally given the information at hand. These tendencies are probably serious enough to exact a steep toll in human well-being, at least in option-rich environments like those faced by many of us. To support this notion I review several major developments in psychology from recent decades, including dual process psychology, situationism, and evolutionary psychology. I argue that a broad picture of human nature may be emerging that does not sit entirely well with the Enlightenment image of humanity: human psychology may not be well-suited to the highly individualized pursuit of well-being. One upshot, explored in Chapter 12, is that a popular kind of *individualism* about the pursuit of well-being may give way to a more *contextualist* view: human welfare may depend less on individual choice, and more on living in a context that fosters the enjoyment of certain goods, than the liberal tradition has usually assumed. Of course, it is quite another matter whether governments are well-suited to providing such contexts, so a further question is what the book's doubts about Personal Authority mean for politics. I will briefly discuss such matters, but they will largely be set aside for future work.

8. CONCLUSION

Imagine, if you can, a small room, hexagonal in shape, like the cell of a bee. It is lighted neither by window nor by lamp, yet it is filled with a soft radiance. There are no apertures for ventilation, yet the air is fresh . . . An armchair is in the centre, by its side a reading-desk—that is all the furniture. And in the armchair there sits a swaddled lump of flesh—a woman, about five feet high, with a face as white as a fungus. It is to her that the little room belongs . . .

The room, though it contained nothing, was in touch with all that she cared for in the world.

E. M. Forster, "The Machine Stops" (1909/2001)

This is, as I said, a theoretical work. Yet its subject matter seems to me a matter of some urgency, and not just for theoretical reasons. The United States is, by a wide margin, among the most affluent nations in human history, and many Americans enjoy unprecedented freedom to shape their lives—for those individuals, a great success in moral and economic terms. Yet no one ever accused us of "knowing how to live." This is perhaps because, arguably, we don't. Surveys find an overwhelming majority of *Americans* reporting that Americans have badly misplaced priorities.[25] And there is no evidence that Americans grew any happier over the recent decades that witnessed astonishing growth in material standards of living. Self-reported happiness has remained essentially flat, while rates of suicide, depression, and other pathologies have soared.[26]

Concurrently with these developments, and not coincidentally, we have entered what biologist E. O. Wilson calls, for obvious reasons, the Century of the Environment.[27] In coming to grips with that problem, we may have to make significant adjustments in how we live. Surely one part of the equation is coming to a better understanding of human well-being and what we need to flourish. For we need to figure out how to get the most benefit from the least amount of resources, and knowing only the economic side of the equation is not likely to cut it. The daily energy requirement for a human being has historically—well, for ninety-plus percent of human history—been under 5,000 calories. Today's American lifestyle requires the resources of a large community at around 260,000 calories, leaving an ecological footprint nearly twice that of our European counterparts, and several times the global average.[28] Our consumption habits may resemble those of a French monarch more than anything our relations a couple of generations back would have recognized. Some two billion people in China and India are striving mightily to achieve the same. Technological innovation can do a lot to reduce the number and impact of those calories, but we are not likely to get very far if we persist in the notion that our goal is to liberate ourselves from constraint as much as our mortality allows, commanding as many resources as possible. If the massively resourced life is not quite as beneficial as we thought, or even proves sometimes to be counterproductive, that would be useful to know. Maybe we could adjust our goals to yield a good quality of life without leaving our descendants a thermally reconstituted planet of weeds and dust.[29]

Suppose we make it through that bottleneck. Will we be leaving our offspring a civilization that any person with a modicum of perspective and good sense would *want* to live in? The present volume was substantially inspired by my experience growing up, in part, in a tiny island fishing community.[30] Visitors would often remark, as their sojourns on the island came to an end, that it was time to return to the "real world" of the mainland. Even as a child, this struck me as a very odd thing to say. In the world of which they spoke, days are passed sitting at stop lights in an air-conditioned car, arranging one's affairs according to the readings of a little device strapped to the wrist, struggling to do the boss's bidding in hopes of a promotion, and returning home at day's end to takeout pizza and a television-watching marathon in a tidy domicile, thoroughly isolated from the outdoors and cleansed as nearly as possible of all other life forms. I could not understand in what sense such an existence is supposed to be more *real* than living according to the rhythms of the tides and the look of the skies, taking the sun as your clock, catching and killing most of the protein in your diet, knowing intimately the living world around you, and spending your free time not with toys but with other people—taking a midnight sail, or gathering dockside for an evening of stories, songs, and laughter.

I mention the island not as a model for all to follow, but for the perspective it offers. Indeed it was never a paradise, at least not for the locals who took their living from the sea. It could be a hard and sometimes cruel place to live. Even for part-time residents like ourselves, being there meant being a little uncomfortable much of the time—the bugs bit, it was hot, sandspurs caught on the soles of your feet, electricity was a hit or miss affair and television virtually nonexistent, you drank rainwater out of a cistern when you could, and the nearest doctor was a half-day trip off-island. As near as I can tell, virtually all of us, off-islanders and locals alike, loved it. Many of my childhood days were passed on the waterfront with a net, catching specimens for a busy little aquarium I kept—pipefish, filefish, blennies, gobies, barracuda, puffers, seahorses, shrimp, spider crabs, to name a few of the critters that still come to mind. Today, if you can even find an eleven-year-old boy lingering by the harbor, he is likely to be lounging poolside, thumbing away on a portable gaming device or text-messaging distant friends about how boring this godforsaken place is. When he gets home he'll ask his parents, once their headphones are off, to take him to Sea World.

We probably should not be surprised that a civilization dedicated to giving people what they want should have taken such a turn. For the very point of such a regime is to create a world tailored to each person's desires, rendering superfluous, to the extent possible, any need to connect with a reality independent of our own appetites. And so people's lives may come increasingly to be populated by synthetic proxies, shorn of the mess and inconvenience attending all that is human and real. (And by real I do not simply mean "nature." To wander the back alleys of Venice—the real Venice, not the Las Vegas one—is to lose yourself in an ancient and layered reality whose principles are indifferent to your whims. It is a place to be negotiated and appreciated, not consumed.) The result of such a process would, it seems to me, be a world cleansed of many of the gratifications of an ordinary human life. Such an existence could be rich in pleasures—the kinds of comforts and amusements once known only to idle aristocrats—but impoverished in fulfillments.[31]

You might think that if a certain way of life isn't fulfilling, then people with the freedom to choose otherwise will do just that. If people choose the synthetic, then that's their taste; that's what they find fulfilling. For myself, it seems incredible that anyone could find manufactured entertainments, bereft of mystery and texture, as gratifying as the unruly offerings of the non-service sector of the cosmos. But perhaps this really is just a point of taste—and a minor one at that given the manifest benefits of our era, not least the fact that we live decades longer than our predecessors. It may seem that any supposed perils attending the artificiality of modern living are, in the scheme of things, utterly trivial.

The question was taken up some hundred years ago, in a short story by E. M. Forster, "The Machine Stops."[32] The story depicts a future in which humanity has retreated underground, each person occupying a small cell in a vast global hive. Liberated from the primitive need to move their bodies from place to place like animals, individuals communicate with each other, and satisfy their every desire, through an elaborate technological apparatus, including what is essentially a really good internet connection. They don't do manual labor; they share ideas. Though quite busy with this sort of activity, to the point that they have little patience for anything taking more than a few minutes, they are contented. Indeed, they can't imagine why anyone would want to venture to the surface of the earth—or go to see his mother face to face, as the story's refractory hero, Kuno, wishes to do with Vashti, the woman depicted above.

The story is of course a caricature. But I do not think Forster intended merely to entertain. Consider a more familiar example of mass imprudence, American dietary habits. I take it that the present epidemic of obesity and the attendant diseases, such as diabetes, represents less than fully rational behavior. Nor are these developments surprising in light of our innate love of sweets and fats. It also is not surprising that the food industry should have developed increasingly efficient means of capitalizing on this taste, to the point that, as one nutritionist puts it, we may be in the midst of a "national experiment in mainlining glucose." To a growing extent, the American diet consists of highly potent delivery devices for sugar and fat—not exactly "food," as our grandmothers would have recognized it, but junk food.[33] Few of us, I suspect, would regard the shift from breaking bread to mainlining glucose as an improvement in human life.

We have other appetites, and there will be powerful market incentives to cater to them. Technological advances could make us pretty adept at building products that appeal to those appetites, television perhaps representing the first Great Leap Forward along this path. We can at least imagine people choosing someday to spend their lives interacting mainly with those products—a virtual reality of alluring devices for communication, information, gaming, entertainment, and heaven knows what else.[34] Perhaps people would largely retreat to such a world, a "junk reality" as it were, even if it is not more fulfilling. No doubt there would be limits to any such progression, as people will probably always seek token contacts with the outdoors and other human beings. But it seems at least conceivable that a technological civilization could approximate, more closely than we should like, Forster's nightmare.

To many people on the island, that eventuality came to pass a long time ago. Had you, even thirty years ago, referred to a typical "touroid" from the mainland as a "swaddled lump of flesh," or a drone in a colossal hive, you would scarcely have rated a second glance. Such sentiments were not considered radical; they were *clichés*. Nor were they brute prejudices directed toward a sophisticated world the islanders failed to comprehend. Many of them had spent years in the mainland civilization and knew it well; some indeed were quite worldly. Accounts of folks on the island sometimes portrayed them as "larger than life" characters, but this got the proportions backward: they were who they were, full-sized human beings, the contrast lying in the smaller-than-life personas of their mainland counterparts. (The contrast caused me some difficulty back in my mainland schools, since I found it hard to pay much attention to teachers who, to my mind, had far less to teach me than the supposedly backwards people I knew on the island.[35]) Off-islanders like my family who spent most of the year on the mainland could see the transformation into diminished members of the colony ourselves. On returning to the island after a long absence, I watched a pale, lost-looking professorial type trudging awkwardly across the beach and thinking how like Gollum, Tolkien's shriveled creature, obsessed with his Precious, he seemed. I had made many such observations as a youth on the island, but this time I was in no position to observe with much detachment.

There is some irony in this. The extraordinary freedoms enjoyed by affluent mainlanders are supposed to unleash our individuality, yielding a freer-spirited, more fully realized populace. Yet the result could, at least conceivably, be precisely the opposite. Perhaps it is places like the island, with their blend of freedom and constraint, that foster individuality, while the economist's paradise, an ocean of limitless options, perversely spawns legions of Vashtis. That would be an interesting result. It is interesting to note as well that, even in the most hellish of Forsterian futures, people may be able to look back at us and give thanks for all the advantages they enjoy: longer lives, less illness and pain, greater comfort and security, and a host of technological delights we never dreamt of. They will doubtless register satisfaction with their lives, as Vashti does. Should they pity us?

Perhaps these reflections will strike the reader as nostalgic longings for an overrated Tom Sawyer past.[36] But notice, first, that the interesting question is not whether people will be left worse off *on the whole*. It is, more narrowly, whether much of what is best in the world we inherited might be frittered away in pursuit of dubious notions of progress. Squandering your inheritance is stupidity, whether you manage somehow to end up better off than your parents or not. At any rate, you need not share these concerns at all, as my central purpose is not social critique. The important points, for current purposes, are these: first, the mere fact that people so often choose a certain way of life tells us little about its merits, as the following chapters will explain. For we cannot assume that people's choices, even when self-interested, will track their interests. It is perfectly possible that people seeking fulfilling lives will freely choose, en masse, to live in distinctly unfulfilling ways. And even if they do end up better off on the whole than they were before, the price of those gains may be far higher than they realize. Second, and most importantly: *a people armed with nothing better than a smiley-face psychology doesn't stand a chance of answering these sorts of questions.*

The modern era's overriding preoccupation, arguably, has been the betterment of the human condition, inarguably a noble aim. Yet the real focus has been on our material conditions, with far less attention paid to the question of how we are living and what our way of life does for us, or to us. Once it has well enough satisfied the basic constraints of morality, the chief question facing any civilization is: do its members enjoy a reasonable level of well-being? We probably won't get much of an answer to this question if we simply ask what they have got. For human well-being mostly depends not on what people have but, among other things, on what they do with what they've got. A better question, arguably, is this: *do they live in a sensible manner?* A decent response to this question will require us to understand whether their way of life *suits their natures*. And central to that project, surely, will be seeing whether their way of life conduces to their flourishing *psychologically*. If a civilization cannot muster a reasonably affirmative answer to this question, then we might reconsider whether it is properly called "civilized." For if its people do not flourish psychologically, they do not flourish. Period. It is with the psychology, I would suggest, that the really interesting story about the flourishing of these creatures lies.

2

Happiness, Well-Being, and the Good Life: A Primer

I understand the 'New Year' part, but what do they mean by 'Happy'?

Matt Groening

1. INTRODUCTION

There may be a philosophical topic more in need of clarification than happiness, but nothing comes to mind. So star-crossed is this territory that you will be hard-pressed to publish even an article on the subject without dedicating several pages to explaining what you are talking about. Whereupon you can count on a fair proportion of your audience to assume, nevertheless, that you are talking about something else. The trouble, we will see, is that the word has multiple meanings that are not easily distinguished, and which express closely related, and difficult, concepts. Thinking clearly about happiness requires mastering a number of subtle distinctions that frequently confound even professional philosophers. This chapter will lay out the conceptual and theoretical landscape, while the next explains the methods that will be needed to guide our inquiry into the nature and significance of happiness.

The first problem is that even the innocent query, "What is happiness?" frequently fails to be a well-formed question.

2. THE MEANINGS OF 'HAPPINESS'

Most scholarly work under the rubric of 'happiness' centers on two senses of the term.[1] The first usage treats 'happiness' as basically a synonym for 'well-being', or equivalently, 'flourishing', 'welfare' or 'eudaimonia'.[2] The concept of well-being is a normative or evaluative concept that concerns what *benefits* a person, is in her *interest*, is *good for* her, or makes her life *go well for* her.[3] The use of 'happiness' to discuss premodern philosophy almost always takes this meaning, as when it is employed to translate 'eudaimonia.' To ascribe happiness to people, in the well-being sense, is to say that their lives are going well for them. It is to make a value judgment about their lives. This is the most natural reading of talk about leading a happy *life*, as opposed simply to *being* happy. For while being happy seems to be a property of the person, and can sensibly be regarded as a purely psychological matter, most people probably would not say as much about the idea of having a happy life, which plausibly involves non-mental states of affairs as well. Thus you might find it intuitive to say that Nozick's experience machine user could *be* happy, even if his life isn't a happy one at all. The abstract noun 'happiness' often evokes the well-being reading as well, as in "life, liberty, and the pursuit of happiness." We will survey theories of well-being in Section 4.

More commonly, 'happiness' bears a purely psychological meaning, denoting some broad and typically lasting aspect of the individual's state of mind: *being happy*. (Note that the well-being and psychological senses of happiness refer to distinct kinds, not species of a common genus.) This is the standard usage in the subjective well-being literature, and the predominant usage in the vernacular. The dominant views of happiness in this sense are *hedonistic* theories, which roughly identify happiness with pleasure;[4] and *life satisfaction* theories, which equate happiness with an attitude of being satisfied with your life as a whole (this normally involves a global judgment about your life, as opposed to merely having a pleasant experience).[5] In this book I will be defending an *emotional state* account, which emphasizes a person's overall emotional condition, where this is not simply identified with experiences of pleasure.[6] Many empirical researchers employ the construct of subjective well-being as more or less equivalent to happiness; this is essentially a hybrid view combining pleasure, or emotional state, and life satisfaction.[7] I will discuss such views briefly in Chapter 5, but most of Chapters 4–7 will apply in various ways to subjective well-being.

Happiness in this psychological sense should be distinguished from the acute emotion or mood of *feeling* happy; we are talking rather about what is sometimes called the long-term psychological sense of the term. Many would argue that someone could be happy without ever feeling happy, say by achieving tranquility. Using the term in this psychological sense involves no more commitment to matters of value than the use of 'tranquility' or 'depression': one can coherently say that a person is happy even though her life is utterly pathetic. When parents say that they want their children to be "happy *and* healthy," they obviously aren't using 'happiness' to mean well-being. If you seek a friend's advice about your son's future, saying "I only want what's best for him," and your friend says, "then you should encourage him to do what makes him happy," your friend is probably not suggesting, most unhelpfully, that what's best for him is to do whatever is best for him. She is offering a substantive piece of advice. The psychological notion likewise occurs in many ordinary comparatives, as when a student asks herself, "will I be happier as a lawyer or a teacher?" Subjective well-being researchers often make claims about happiness: how happy people are and so forth. These researchers normally do not take themselves to be making value judgments about people's lives when describing them as happy; nor are they in a position, *qua* empirical researchers, to make value judgments. They are simply attributing states of mind.[8]

It should be *patently* clear that much ordinary talk about happiness, even in matters of considerable gravity, concerns not well-being itself but a largely if not wholly psychological concept. To give this claim an informal empirical test, I surveyed 39 students at the start of two introductory ethics courses, before the first class began or any materials were distributed. These were undergraduates at a Catholic Jesuit university who in many cases had already taken philosophy and theology courses with readings in Aristotle and others in that tradition. I presented them with a case of "George," a man who doesn't realize that his family and friends secretly loathe him, and leads a full life in blissful ignorance, replete with pleasure and satisfaction.[9] Was he happy? All but 3 of the 39 students responded either "strongly agree" or "agree somewhat." Yet in six other questions employing terms philosophers tend to use as synonyms for well-being—"life went well for him," "had an enviable life," "was fortunate," "flourished," "had a high level of well-being," and "his life was a happy one"—a majority refused to give an affirmative response in all cases but the "life went well for him" question, the last probably reflecting a reading of the locution as meaning his life went well from his perspective. On the "fortunate" variant, for instance, 18 disagreed, 9 were neutral, and only 12 thought him fortunate. Importantly, on the "happy *life*" question, only 18 agreed, while 17 disagreed and 4 were neutral. That is, almost all students thought him happy, while a majority refused to ascribe well-being to him, and even—on the very same questionnaire—refused to call his *life* a happy one. Though only an informal survey, the results offer some support for my contention about the prevalence of the psychological sense of 'happiness', as well as for the difference between the notions of being happy and leading a happy life. (It also suggests that most of these students are not hedonists about well-being.)

The well-being and psychological senses of 'happiness' do not mark different conceptions of happiness, any more than definitions of river "banks," where frogs live, and the "banks" in which we keep our money, offer differing conceptions of the same phenomenon. They express different *concepts*, and concern different subject matters, altogether. It is likewise a mistake to refer to theories of happiness in the psychological sense as "subjective," in contrast to "objective" theories of happiness in the well-being sense, which again implies that they offer competing accounts of a single thing. When theorizing about happiness, it is essential to keep these issues straight. Just trying to account for undifferentiated intuitions about things called "happiness" is liable to breed monsters—accounts of happiness that address an amalgam of interests relating to different concepts without clearly answering to any coherent set of interests.[10] For example, you might get a theory of happiness as worthwhile enjoyment, where it is denied that this suffices for well-being. Such results can seem confused, like defining banks as places where frogs keep their money.

Summing up: The query "What is happiness?" is not, absent further cues to one's meaning, a well-formed question. One could be asking a variety of things, though in most cases the question will likely have one of two meanings.[11] Roughly:

1. What is this *state of mind* that so many people seek, that tends to accompany good fortune, success, etc.? (happiness in the long-term psychological sense)
2. What is it for my life to *go well* for me? (happiness in the well-being sense)

A crude test for determining what people mean by 'happiness' is given by the case of blissfully deceived George, from the survey noted above. Suppose you were persuaded that George is badly off, despite his pleasure and satisfaction: you feel sorry for him. *Would you nonetheless consider him happy?* If so, then you are very likely using 'happy' in the psychological sense. If not, then you are almost certainly using it in the well-being sense. (Note that it can make a big difference whether you put the question in terms of 'happy' or 'happy *life*'.)

Unless otherwise noted, I will use 'happiness' in the long-term psychological sense in this book. (The main exception being 'happy life' and obvious cognates, which I will use only in the well-being sense, but will generally avoid.)

3. WHY ARISTOTLE DIDN'T HAVE A THEORY OF HAPPINESS

Connecting these points to the philosophical corpus: in the sense of 'happiness' that concerns us, *Aristotle had no theory of happiness*. He had a theory of well-being. Compare the Epicureans, who held eudaimonia to consist solely in the pleasures of tranquility. Despite appearances, we should not translate their 'eudaimonia' as 'happiness' in the psychological sense. For when Epicurus espoused hedonism about eudaimonia, he was not simply making a psychological claim. He was making a claim about value, saying that what ultimately benefits a person is nothing other than pleasure. 'Eudaimonia' meant the same thing for Epicurus and Aristotle: a life that is good for the person leading it. The two philosophers did not have a merely verbal or conceptual disagreement about eudaimonia; they had a substantive ethical disagreement about what sort of life is best for human beings. And while it is possible to trace the history of thought about (well-being) "happiness" by noting that views of *well-being* have grown more subjectivist, such a history does not include contemporary work on "happiness" in the psychological sense, including my own. For that work is perfectly compatible with objectivist views of well-being. Aristotelians can readily agree with Sumner's life satisfaction account of happiness and the suggestion by subjective well-being researchers that most people are happy, since in calling people "happy" those authors make no value judgment about whether they are flourishing. At the same time, Sumner's account of *welfare* as authentic happiness is explicitly subjectivist, and many subjective well-being researchers seem to hold subjectivist views of well-being.[12] On *that* point, and on the value of happiness, Aristotle would plainly disagree.

Obviously, the potential for confusion is great. Many contemporary philosophers use 'happiness' and 'pleasure' interchangeably, at least tacitly endorsing a hedonistic view of happiness. But most of those philosophers would firmly deny the Epicurean thesis that well-being consists solely in pleasure: welfare hedonism, or hedonism about well-being. To maintain a hedonistic view of happiness in the psychological sense does not commit one to hedonism about well-being. Accordingly, the philosophical literature can be singularly unhelpful at times: one writer might endorse hedonism about "happiness" while another denies hedonism about "happiness," without disagreeing at all. John Stuart Mill, for instance, seems to have used 'happiness' in the "well-being" sense, while Roger Crisp has employed it in the psychological sense, allowing that hedonism about happiness in the psychological sense may be false. Yet both authors defend welfare hedonism.

This is an unhelpful state of affairs, but it is easily managed once we recognize the necessary distinctions. It would be helpful if researchers used 'happiness' in the psychological sense where possible, employing 'well-being' or other terms for the well-being notion. While 'happiness' may be hard to avoid when translating historical works, it is possible to use it in translations while reverting to more standard terminology like 'well-being' elsewhere.[13] Confusion can be further minimized by exclusively reserving talk of "happy lives" for the well-being notion and talk of "being happy" for the psychological.

Connecting our discussion with empirical research: Since 'happiness' doesn't even translate *itself* in large swaths of contemporary English, the job of finding equivalents in other languages is bound to be difficult. A term in Chinese might translate 'happiness' in the well-being sense where it means well-being, but not in the psychological sense in which it is used when Americans are asked how happy they are. (I suspect this is the case with whatever word turns up as 'happiness' in fortune cookies.) Suppose you could take the American questionnaire and put it to ancient Greeks. How would you render 'happy'? Not as '*eudaimon*', and in fact it is not obvious that any equivalent existed in ancient Greek. *Euthymia*, roughly cheerfulness, or *ataraxia*, tranquility, may come close in certain ways, but probably neither gets the meaning entirely right. If you ask Americans how happy they are, and Greeks how *eudaimon* they are, you are asking two different questions, one psychological and one ethical. You might get a decent correlation in the answers, but that's because perceived happiness and welfare probably correlate pretty well.

4. THEORIES OF WELL-BEING

Our inquiry into happiness and its value will be clearer if we understand the debates about the nature of well-being. The best-known philosophical taxonomy, offered in 1984 by Derek Parfit, divides theories of well-being into three types: hedonistic, desire, and objective list theories.[14] But since then an important new approach has entered the scene, and an ancient family of theories has gained substantially in prominence. We will, then, distinguish five basic approaches here:

1. Hedonistic theories.
2. Desire-fulfillment theories.
3. Authentic happiness theories.
4. Eudaimonistic ("nature-fulfillment") theories.
5. List theories.

Crudely, hedonism identifies well-being with pleasure.[15] A bit more precisely, well-being consists in a subject's balance of pleasant over unpleasant experience. The central idea is that what ultimately matters for welfare is the hedonic quality of individuals' experience, and nothing more. The chief attraction of this view is that it accommodates the plausible thought that, if anything matters for welfare, it is the pleasantness of our experience of life. And nothing else seems to be valuable in quite the same way. Despite its attractions, most philosophers have rejected hedonism and other mental state accounts, mainly because of experience machine-type worries.

As of now, the theory to beat is the *desire-fulfillment* theory of well-being, also called the preference satisfaction account; for brevity I will usually refer to it simply as the "desire" theory. The dominant account among economists and philosophers over the last century or so, the desire theory identifies well-being with the satisfaction of the individual's desires. Experience machines don't trouble such views, since many of our desires will go unfulfilled in an experience machine. Desire theories come in many varieties, the most important type being informed-desire theories, which restrict the desires that count to the ones we would have given full information (rationality, reflection, etc.).[16] These variants predominate, since many find it intuitively obvious that we don't gain from the satisfaction of desires that are grounded in ignorance or irrationality. Desire theories have a number of attractions, one being that they are extremely flexible, able to accommodate the full range of goods that people seek. But most importantly, they comport with the liberal sensibilities of modernity: what's best for me depends on what I care about, and on such matters I am sovereign. This seems appealingly non-paternalistic.

The third theory, L. W. Sumner's *authentic happiness* view, is meant to rectify the most serious difficulties with hedonistic and desire theories while retaining their emphasis on subjective experience and individual sovereignty.[17] His view identifies well-being with being authentically happy: being happy, where one's happiness is both informed about the conditions of one's life and autonomous, meaning that it reflects values that are truly one's own and not the result of manipulation or oppressive social conditioning. "Happiness" here is something like subjective well-being, involving both global attitudes of life satisfaction and positive affect, though Sumner calls his view a "life satisfaction" account. The root idea is that one's happiness should reflect a response *of* one's own, *to* a life that is one's own, ostensibly ruling out objections about experience machines and happy slaves.[18] And whereas desire theories face the problem of how seemingly irrelevant desires, or fulfillments that don't impact my experience, can affect my well-being, the authentic happiness view incorporates an experience requirement: only what affects my happiness can benefit me.

We turn now to our fourth family of theories, *eudaimonistic* views of well-being. The most prominent variety of these, Aristotelian theories, have stirred considerable interest since the revival of virtue ethics and the rise of the Sen–Nussbaum capabilities approach in political theory.[19] In broad terms, Aristotelian theories identify well-being with "well-functioning," which is to say functioning or living well as a human being: the fulfillment of human nature. This consists, in the first instance, in a life of excellent or virtuous activity, though this is sometimes put less astringently, as a "fully" or "truly" human life. The idea is that we flourish by fully exercising our human capacities. It is not simply a matter of being morally virtuous, although moral virtue is essential to well-being as Aristotelians see it. Aristotelian theories address widespread intuitions about the importance of personal development and leading a "full life" replete with the essentials of a normal human life.

Aristotle's writings are so influential that commentators often use terms like 'eudaimonistic' or 'eudaimonic' simply to denote Aristotelian theories of well-being, or views that emphasize perfection or virtue. But Aristotelians formed only one of the schools of Hellenistic ethics that scholars denote, collectively, as eudaimonistic. Definitions vary, but (ethical) eudaimonism tends to refer to ancient theories that ground ethics in the notion of eudaimonia—the idea being that this is our agreed-upon goal that properly structures our deliberations about how to live, and the theory's job is to determine the nature of this goal.[20] And some ancient eudaimonists, like the Epicureans, denied that eudaimonia consists in perfection. If there was an important feature that eudaimonistic accounts of well-being shared in common, it was the teleological idea that well-being consists in *nature-fulfillment*. Epicureans arguably agreed with Aristotle that well-being involves the fulfillment of our natures as human beings; but they believed that we fulfilled our natures by achieving pleasure.

Thus we might usefully identify welfare eudaimonism as a distinctive approach to well-being, where we start with a conception of human nature or—if we are specifically interested in *self*-fulfillment—the self, and take well-being to consist in the fulfillment of that nature. This sort of approach is not limited to the ancients, and versions of it arguably inform the work of Thomists, Marxists, Hegelians, Mill's discussion of individuality in *On Liberty*, "eudaimonic" approaches to the psychology of well-being, and the work of many other moderns.[21] A eudaimonistic account incorporating a form of authentic happiness as a central element of self-fulfillment is sketched in Chapter 9.[22] It is even possible to found desire accounts and other subjectivisms on a eudaimonistic framework: perhaps the self is defined by one's desires, and thus we fulfill our selves by fulfilling our desires. Eudaimonism merits classification as a distinct family of theories, however, because all share the same fundamental motivation: the idea that well-being consists in nature-fulfillment. Differences arise in their views of a person's nature, and of what it means to fulfill that nature. Subjectivists like Sumner and most desire theorists start from very different foundations, such as the ideal of individual sovereignty.

Finally, we have *list theories* of well-being, which identify well-being with some brute list of goods, such as knowledge, friendship, accomplishment, pleasure, etc.[23] Their appeal derives from the fact that other approaches seem incapable of encompassing a broad range of intuitions about well-being. The elements on most proposed lists do strike many as intrinsically beneficial, so it can make sense to incorporate them in your theory.

5. WELL-BEING VERSUS THE GOOD LIFE

When assessing theories of well-being, it is essential to distinguish well-being from the broader notion of the *good life*. While we sometimes use 'the good life' simply as a synonym for 'well-being', it seems we usually mean a life that is desirable or choiceworthy on the whole: not just morally good, or good *for* the individual leading it, but good, all things considered—good, *period*. To give a theory of the good life is not to characterize some special kind of value, but simply to specify all the things that ultimately matter in life, whether they benefit the agent or not. THE GOOD LIFE functions as an umbrella concept encompassing the domain of values that matter in a person's life, and can be employed within any ethical framework. Since almost no one would deny that it is a good thing both to flourish and to be virtuous, all respectable ethical doctrines will maintain that the good life involves both virtue and well-being, and perhaps aesthetic or other values as well. Kant, e.g., *agreed* with Aristotle that the good life involves both morality and well-being: both values are worth seeking. But unlike Aristotle, he saw these as distinct, and often conflicting, aspects of the good life. Thus Kant allows, along with the Utilitarians and most commonsense thought today, that bad people can sometimes flourish. But being bad, they would not have good lives. We will see in Chapter 8 that Aristotelian and related theories of well-being probably rest on a failure to distinguish the notions of well-being and the good life.[24]

Interestingly, modern theorists tend not to have devoted much effort to comprehensive theories of the good life (at least as such), and indeed the very concept of a good life, in this broad sense, is rarely even distinguished.[25] Usually philosophers employ 'good life' more narrowly, to denote just a morally good life, or a life of well-being. Yet this is not how we normally think about it, say when contemplating whether a deceased friend had a good life. At such times we consider all the values that seem to us to matter in life, whether we are Kantians, Utilitarians, Aristotelians, etc. The relative silence of modern philosophers on the good life, *per se*, may be partly a reflection of liberal optimism: most modern theories focus narrowly on what morality demands of us, leaving the other aspects of the good life up to the individual, whose judgment is presumed to be authoritative in that realm.

6. MAPPING OUT THE CONCEPTS

To get a clearer sense of the relationships among the various concepts discussed here and later, see Figure 2.1 below. The diagram is meant to be as uncontroversial as possible, and should be compatible with all ethical theories and approaches to value. It involves no attempt to depict relative weights or connections between the various values, and any given ethical theory may recognize only some of the goods pictured. Aristotelians will think that one achieves well-being *by* exercising virtue, so that the well-being and virtue aspects of the good life are in fact inseparable. But they should still grant that these are distinct *concepts*, and so the diagram should not offend them. Kantians and Utilitarians should also be happy with the diagram. Finally, note that the chart is divided between "evaluative" and "descriptive" concepts. This way of segmenting matters is not without controversy, but it will serve well enough here. In particular, concepts above the line, evaluative concepts, rest squarely within the domain of ethical or value inquiry. "Normative" theories of their subject matter, such as the theories of well-being depicted, straightforwardly entail value judgments about what *matters*, is *good*, or we have *reason* to do. The "descriptive" concepts below the line seem not to involve values in this way. The nature of a psychological state like excitement seems an empirical matter, not an ethical question. (Health is a trickier case and a matter of ongoing dispute.)

7. WHAT KINDS OF CLAIMS ARE INVOLVED IN THE PHILOSOPHY OF HAPPINESS?

The literature on happiness and well-being often suffers from confusion about the nature of the assertions being made, so we would do well to get clear on these matters before proceeding. The least interesting sort of claim is *linguistic*, concerning the meanings of words. Substantive-seeming disputes are sometimes

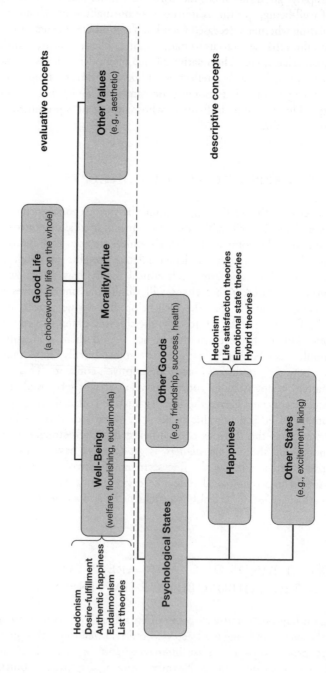

Fig. 2.1. The good life, well-being, happiness, and related concepts, with major theories of well-being and happiness.

merely linguistic. For example: Sumner roughly identifies happiness with life satisfaction; a fan of Aristotle might object that Sumner's account fails to capture much of importance in life—better, instead, to think of happiness as the exercise of virtue or excellence. Is this a substantive objection to Sumner's account of happiness? No: as we saw above, Sumner account of happiness involves no claim at all about what's good for people. So his identification of happiness with life satisfaction in no way conflicts with anything Aristotle said about eudaimonia, and indeed Aristotle could accept Sumner's view of happiness. It is only Sumner's theory of well-being, as *authentic* happiness, that clashes with Aristotle's views.

If an Aristotelian wants to set up an opposition between Sumner's account of happiness—or my own—and Aristotle's account of eudaimonia, she can *only* be making a linguistic claim: that is, arguing that 'happiness' in contemporary English is not really a psychological term after all, but rather a rough synonym of 'well-being'. This point could be defended by noting various facts about the language, and is a perfectly legitimate sort of claim to make (though one I argued against above). But it is still only a linguistic claim.

One reason for the persistent confusion here may be a failure to appreciate the significance of the fact that 'happiness' in its psychological and well-being senses expresses different concepts, not just different conceptions of the same thing. It means that theorists using the term in the different senses cannot be talking about the same thing, so any disagreement they might have about "happiness" could only be verbal. Yet philosophers who clearly *do* have substantive disagreements about a common subject matter are sometimes taken to be using different concepts. Thus, for instance, Aristotle's claim that well-being consists in virtuous activity is sometimes said to be a conceptual claim and, if true, to be conceptually necessary. Whereas Sumner's contention that well-being consists in authentic happiness would likewise be said to be a conceptual thesis. Thus it might be thought that Sumner and Aristotle, given their different views about human welfare, thereby have different "well-being" concepts. Nonetheless, the thought goes, there is some common subject matter—given perhaps by a shared "conceptual core"—about which they have a genuine disagreement. If this were right, then one might similarly infer that, while Sumner's 'happiness' and (the translated) Aristotle's 'happiness' express different concepts, they nonetheless share a common subject matter, about which the two authors disagree. It would thus make sense to weigh their respective merits as competing conceptions of happiness. That this would be the wrong conclusion to draw should, by now, be obvious.

In any event, the "conceptual" reading of the debate over well-being seems itself to be a mistake: neither Aristotle nor Sumner appears to be making a merely conceptual claim about the notion of personal benefit, talking only about ideas. Rather, each makes a quite substantive *value judgment* about what, in fact, benefits a person. The import of this difference is apparent when we reflect on the fact that conceptual claims, unlike value claims, raise no deep metaphysical questions about how they could possibly be true. (At least, no deeper than the sorts of mysteries posed by logical or mathematical claims.) Concepts are just vehicles for thought; by and large, we can take them or leave them. If you don't find it helpful to employ the concept of well-being, then don't use it. But if Sumner's account of well-being is true, then we appear to have an inescapable *fact* about the way things are: what benefits a person, ultimately, is being authentically happy. And the authentically happy person appears to have a certain property: flourishing or being well-off. These appearances might be misleading, but they are nonetheless appearances about *the way things are*. And changing your concepts won't make them go away. Theories of well-being, including Aristotle's and Sumner's, are usually not mere conceptual doctrines; they make substantive normative claims about the nature of a certain sort of value.[26]

Stephen Darwall recently did the field a great service in sharpening the contrast with a book that defends both conceptual and substantive theses about well-being. His conceptual thesis is the "rational care" theory of welfare: roughly, the concept of welfare is the concept of what it is rational to want for someone *insofar as one cares for her*.[27] Well-being ultimately concerns the appropriate objects of sympathetic concern. Thus we can think of the concept of well-being as being given by a conceptual role; i.e., the concept is defined by the role it plays in governing attitudes of caring. Note that the rational care theory tells us nothing about what in fact benefits people; it embodies no value judgment, but merely specifies the character of a concept. Any of the major theories of well-being described earlier could be compatible with the rational care theory. Thus one might agree with Darwall this far, and then ask *what* one ought to want for a person insofar as one cares for him. The desire theorist answers: the satisfaction of his desires; Sumner: authentic happiness; the Aristotelian: a life of virtuous activity; and so forth. Darwall offers a partial answer to this question, arguing for an "Aristotelian thesis" that the best life for a person involves engagement with merit or worth. These are all substantive theses about value.

Notice that Darwall's conceptual claim seems metaphysically rather innocent: few people are likely to puzzle about how such a concept could exist. Just make up a word, stipulate that it means "what one ought to want for someone insofar as one cares for her," and there you go. Things are rather different for the substantive claims: they seem not to be metaphysically innocent at all. For what's to say that there's *anything* one ought to want insofar as one cares for a person? What's to say there are any oughts at all? Maybe the concept applies to nothing, just as nihilists have been trying to tell us. Not so, say the substantive theorists of well-being: the hedonist says that in fact there is something answering to the concept of welfare, namely pleasure. The Aristotelian, by contrast, takes the concept to apply to lives of virtuous activity. Most of us think that some theory, perhaps as yet unheard, has to be correct: some things really are good or bad for us, and the right account will tell us what those things are. (Note that *all* substantive theories of well-being are metaphysically problematical in this way. Even if desire theories cash out well-being in purely naturalistic terms as the satisfaction of desire—revealed preference, etc.—they still involve the value judgment that the satisfaction of desires is *good*, gives us *reasons* to do things, and *ought* to be promoted. And explaining how putative facts like these could fit into a naturalistic worldview is just as hard as explaining objectivist welfare or moral values.)

Call the correct substantive theory of well-being W. The question is, *what makes it the case that W is true?* Clearly, defining words and analyzing concepts won't get us anywhere in dealing with this question. Judging purely by appearances, we seem to be asserting the existence of a property, *being good for*, that applies to whatever things W says it applies to, such as instances of pleasure or authentic happiness or desire satisfaction or virtuous activity or. . . . And this property is *pushy*: it places demands on us, telling us what to do. This is a funny property ("queer," as Mackie put it[28]), and it is reasonable to wonder whether any such property really exists. Alternatively, one might affirm W but try to explain its truth without appeal to funny properties. Maybe pleasure really is what's ultimately good for us, but saying this amounts to nothing more than expressing our acceptance of certain norms—no suspicious properties required.[29] Whatever the correct treatment of the matter, the important point for our purposes is just to see that the nature of well-being really is a *substantive* issue concerning the existence and character of a certain sort of value. Dissecting concepts is not likely to settle it. (The reader might ask just what sort of claim a "substantive normative claim" such as a theory of well-being could be, if not a merely conceptual or empirical claim. An excellent question, which I defer, noting lamely that this is not really meant to be a text in metaethics.)

Let me sum up by returning to Aristotle and Darwall. An example of a linguistic claim here would be to say that 'eudaimonia' and 'well-being' express the same concept. We explain what the concept WELL-BEING is via a conceptual claim, such as Darwall's contention that the concept of well-being is the concept of what one ought to want for a person insofar as one cares for him. Whereas the Aristotelian account of well-being that we know best involves not a linguistic or conceptual claim, but a substantive normative claim to the effect that what ultimately benefits a person is a life of virtuous activity.

Beyond linguistic, conceptual, and substantive normative (or evaluative) claims, we will also be dealing with metaphysical and empirical propositions. Empirical claims—for example, "the sky is blue"—need no explanation. Metaphysical claims are a little trickier; the basic idea is that they concern the true natures of things, and are substantive claims about what the world is like. In giving an account of happiness, my ultimate concern will be metaphysical: the nature of a certain psychological condition, happiness. But most of my discussion will focus on the concept of happiness, the goal (as we will see in Chapter 3) being to reconstruct it in a form that enables us to focus on the psychological states within the extension of the term's ordinary use that answer most closely to our interests in happiness. This will give us a general picture of happiness's nature, the concept serving as a pointer to certain psychological states. But a full account of the nature of those states seems to me substantially to be an empirical question, to be taken up in future investigations. What exactly moods are, for instance, seems impossible to say without leaving the armchair. For even a refined version of the folk concept of happiness, stated only in familiar terms, seems unlikely to specify the relevant psychology with much precision or accuracy. It would be surprising if the folk concept of happiness refers to psychological states that can be adequately characterized using only the crude apparatus of other folk psychological concepts, like belief, desire, etc. A review of the philosophical literature on emotion should illustrate the worry, as much of it attempts to analyze emotions purely in terms of familiar propositional attitudes like beliefs and desires. Such accounts tend to have a distinctly Procrustean air about them, trying to force the psychology into a conceptual framework that, though familiar, may not be well suited to the phenomena. But someone drawn to such a view might argue that it at least offers a crude but useful first approximation of the truth, admitting that a more exact account of emotion would have to be framed in terms that reflect a more nuanced, empirically informed understanding of the psychology.

The emotional state theory of happiness sketched in Chapters 6 and 7 might be regarded in similar terms—essentially as an elaborate form of ostension, pointing to the phenomenon without fully elucidating it—though for the most part it already dispenses with the traditional suite of folk psychological notions. I will take up such questions further in the next chapter.

3

What Do We Want from a Theory of Happiness?

Or how to make a mongrel concept hunt[1]

Happiness serves hardly any other purpose than to make unhappiness possible.

Marcel Proust

1. THE LIMITS OF CONCEPTUAL ANALYSIS

Settling questions about the nature of happiness probably strikes more than a few philosophers as an exercise in futility. Indeed, there may be no question philosophers enjoy hearing *less* than "What do you mean by 'happiness'?" Even once we get past the linguistic hurdles discussed in Chapter 2, we still lack any plausible way of telling a good theory of happiness from a bad one. As someone helpfully put it to me: how are we supposed to play this game?[2]

Traditionally we play the game like this: prefer whichever conception best matches the ordinary concept, or the meaning of the ordinary language term. This is, more or less, the method of conceptual analysis, and it has not proven wildly successful in this realm.[3] The trouble is that the ordinary concept of happiness appears to be neither well defined nor univocal. Indeed, there may be no "the" ordinary concept, but perhaps several, even many. Thus people's intuitions vary widely, even regarding the psychological sense of 'happiness': one person's intuitions may favor identifying happiness with life satisfaction; while someone else's may lean toward a hedonistic account. Still others may feel the pull of both views, or perhaps their intuitions favor some other theory. How do we choose?

Restricting ourselves to the psychological sense of 'happiness' does little to resolve the initial worry. Even here intuitions clash, or are unclear. It is quite plausible that the relevant uses of 'happiness' refer sometimes to this state of mind, sometimes to that, and often don't refer unequivocally to any particular state. It is plausible, in short, that there is more than one psychological state within the extension of 'happiness', as used in the long-term psychological "sense."[4]

This state of affairs is unfortunate. If the notion is indeed as confused as it seems to be, shouldn't we give up on theorizing about happiness and admit that there *is no* saying what, exactly, happiness is? I think such worries are unfounded, and rest on a mistaken assumption that theorizing about happiness can only be about elucidating the folk notion. If that notion is confused, we must remain silent. I want to suggest that we ought not to choose a theory of happiness solely on intuitive grounds: we should consider what's at stake in choosing one theory over another. Are there principled grounds for preferring one theory over others? I shall argue that there are. The idea will be, not simply to describe an ill-mannered folk concept, nor to cast it aside in favor of something else, but to *reconstruct* the folk notion, if necessary dividing it into multiple concepts, with the aim of yielding concepts that will do the work the folk concept should have done in the first place. I will call the approach *reconstructive analysis*.

The situation is analogous to that facing theorists of consciousness. As Ned Block helpfully put it, the lay concept of consciousness is something of a "mongrel concept," a confused mess that is neither clearly univocal nor sharply ambiguous.[5] One response to this situation would be to cease inquiries into the nature of consciousness, declaring the subject a hopeless muddle. That was not the response of Block, nor of countless other investigators who have made consciousness among the most conspicuously "hot" topics in the academy in recent years. And for good reason: figuring out how to fit consciousness into a naturalistic worldview is among the great intellectual mysteries of our time. Solving the acute form of the mind–body problem that it presents could have far-reaching consequences for the way we think about the world and ourselves. To see the problem, you need only be capable of noticing the vast difference between, say, the experience of smelling a rose and the disgusting lump of fatty gray tissue that apparently gives rise to or has that experience. It doesn't much matter what your concepts are like, or whether they are confused: the difficulty is plain to virtually anyone who has both used and looked at a brain, and fussing about conceptual untidiness won't make it go away. If your concepts don't help you deal with the problem, you don't ignore the problem; you fix your concepts. This is exactly what Block does, for instance arguing that within the extension of ordinary consciousness talk lies at least two different types of phenomena: what he calls access consciousness (roughly, "awareness") and phenomenal consciousness (roughly, "what it's like" to smell a rose, etc.). Much research on "consciousness," according to Block, really tells us only about access, whereas the truly deep puzzles relate to phenomenality, which that research does not even address. In short, Block notes that we can distinguish different things within the extension of the term in which we have different interests, and introduces new variants of the concept of consciousness corresponding to them. Whether Block is correct here or not, his strategy illustrates how we can do research profitably about subjects involving confused concepts like consciousness—or, I will argue, happiness.

Just as it would be foolish to cease inquiry into consciousness simply because it involves a mongrel concept, so too would it be unwise to dismiss work on happiness because the concept is, itself, a mongrel.

2. HOW NOT TO BUILD A THEORY OF HAPPINESS, CONTINUED

2.1. Pure normative adequacy

The traditional approach to theories of happiness, conceptual analysis, has already been laid aside. Hedonistic Utilitarians may have implicitly offered a different sort of methodology: happiness is whatever psychological state occupies a certain role in the Utilitarian moral theory—namely the role of utility. Put this way, it is natural that we should conceive of happiness in a hedonistic manner: as equivalent to a subject's balance of pleasure over displeasure. If any psychological state could possibly fill the role of utility, then pleasure is a reasonable candidate. Here, then, is one principled method for deciding on a theory of happiness. It also makes manifest the relevance of happiness for ethics.

This notion does indeed concern the psychological, and not well-being, sense of 'happiness': well-being is not built into the *meaning* of the term, but rather used as a criterion for ranking competing accounts. It is possible that hedonistic Utilitarians have not used 'happiness' in the psychological sense. Suppose, for instance, that Mill were persuaded that radical deception, such as that of an experience machine user, is incompatible with well-being (recall the "George" test in the previous chapter). If he then rejected happiness as the measure of utility, then we could conclude that he indeed used 'happiness' in the psychological sense. If he simply revised his conception of happiness to include states of the world as well as states of mind, then we would know that he was talking about the "well-being" notion. I suspect that some hedonistic Utilitarians such as Bentham were indeed concerned with happiness in the psychological sense, but I will not defend this claim here. Those (if any) who *were* talking about happiness in this sense may not have used principled grounds like the one I suggested to arrive at their views. But let's assume that some Utilitarians have indeed relied on such grounds.

The general idea behind this approach is to prefer whichever notion best fills the appropriate role in moral theory. Call this the *pure normative adequacy* method.[6] This does not seem a promising way to choose a theory of happiness—not because hedonistic Utilitarianism is false, but because the notion of happiness is not a theoretical concept at all. It is not simply up for grabs for moral theorists to use as they please. HAPPINESS is first and foremost a folk psychological concept employed by ordinary people trying to satisfy their own practical interests. Treating it as a purely technical notion risks leaving us with a conception of happiness that no one would recognize as such. We are of course free to use words however we wish. But 'happiness' is one of the central terms in our practical vocabulary. Co-opting it for theoretical purposes is liable to sow considerable confusion unless the theoretical notion turns out, coincidentally, to fit closely with the folk notion. Moreover, it leaves completely unanswered the question of what *happiness*—whatever 'happiness' really refers to—is. Inquiry into happiness ought to be an autonomous line of research. It should not be held hostage to the needs of moral theory.

2.2. Scientific naturalism

A second approach—*scientific naturalism*—might seem more promising, and it is certainly fashionable these days: happiness is whatever scientific discovery reveals it to be. That is, we ought to defer to our best scientific theories of happiness to determine what happiness is. Happiness is a naturalistic phenomenon, and we would be foolish to deny that empirical discoveries about human psychology could teach us something about its nature. But scientific naturalism won't work for happiness: the pretheoretical notion is too ill-defined and covers too much psychological ground for empirical research alone to settle the question of what happiness is. We cannot yet identify any single thing whose essence empirical researchers might hope to discover. Take just two of the candidate theories before us: the hedonistic and life satisfaction views. Pleasures and global life attitudes are awfully different things. What kind of empirical study—other than a survey of folk intuitions—could *possibly* tell us which account is correct? One might as well try performing an experiment to determine whether water is H_2O or a kind of bicycle. We need at least a vague notion of what aspect of our psychology we are talking about before scientific inquiry can reveal its nature.

Scientific naturalism faces another, more serious problem: the concept of happiness is, we saw, a folk notion; 'happiness' is not a technical term for theorists to use as they please. Empirical researchers are no more entitled to co-opt it for their parochial purposes than moral theorists are. And it is quite possible that, left to their own devices, empirical researchers would arrive at a conception of happiness that is not well suited for dealing with the practical concerns of laypersons. Consider the interest that psychologists have in explaining why the human mind works the way it does. One way of satisfying this interest would be to identify types of mental states from an evolutionary perspective, according to their phylogenetic histories. Thus we might identify happiness with a certain class of human mental states along with their homologues in other species (homologues are features derived from some common ancestor).[7] The concept of happiness would thus fail to apply to any creatures without homologous states, however structurally similar their psychological make-up might be. So long as we never encounter such creatures, this may not pose a practical difficulty. But the fact that this is even a possibility suggests that something has gone wrong. From the practical standpoint of ordinary people, and from the standpoint of prudential psychology, the fact that two states are, or are not, homologous is irrelevant. Pain stinks whatever its evolutionary origins. Laypersons don't much care how the mind got the way it is. They care how the mind *is*, specifically in respects that make a difference to their lives.

3. RECONSTRUCTIVE ANALYSIS

Are we reduced to no more principled a method than that of analyzing the folk notion of happiness? No: though the folk notion is not up for grabs, it does not appear to refer unequivocally to any particular psychological category, as I noted earlier. Rather, the folk concept appears to refer variously to different things, often conflating different psychological categories. In ordinary discourse this may pose little difficulty, since we rely on *many* cues to discern what our interlocutors are getting at, including linguistic context, gestures, facial expressions, tone of voice, and so on. Successful communication generally does not require that our terms be precisely defined; ordinary linguistic practice probably tends not to be friendly to philosophical analysis. As a result of such shortcuts in folk psychology there will likely be more than one psychological state we can get away with calling happiness, and intuitions are bound to differ as to which is most credible. The same difficulties will beset empirical studies of lay intuitions, sometimes called *empirical conceptual analysis*.[8] Such investigations can reveal some of the contours of folk concepts and correct for sampling biases inherent in armchair intuition pumping, and I have conducted a couple myself (Chapters 1 and 7). But your results can only be as good as the concepts you are studying, so getting scientific with conceptual analysis is not going to solve the problem.

But we can still ask which of the states within the extension of the unreformed term are most *important*. What conception of happiness would best perform the work we use the notion to do? The question "What is happiness?" becomes "How is happiness best understood given our interests in the matter?" Should more than one conception prove more or less equally satisfactory, we may wish to distinguish further concepts. But there may well be—and I believe there is—a core psychological kind[9] that clearly outstrips the alternatives both in importance and in its fit with the folk notion. Call the concept denoting this kind, if there is one, the *philosophically primary* notion of happiness.[10] This will almost certainly deviate from the folk notion, but only to a point. The aim is to find a concept that does what the folk concept should have done in the first place.

This approach constitutes a kind of analysis, with close ties to ordinary concepts. Its purpose, however, is not to explicate but to reconstruct: reworking rough-and-ready folk concepts to get something better suited to thinking clearly about the matters that concern us. Call it *reconstructive analysis*. It resembles the familiar technique of "reforming analysis," which allows some tweaking, or "paraphrasing," of ordinary concepts to make them more coherent and useful.[11]

But it is less wedded to the ordinary concepts, assuming at the outset that they are likely to need rehabilitation. Pragmatic questions about our interests in a concept thus come in at the ground floor and serve, not just for fine-tuning, but as a primary driver of the inquiry.

Again, the method itself is not particularly new; one can arguably find variations on the theme, either implicitly or explicitly, in recent work by Ned Block and other philosophers.[12] Such an approach could be particularly useful in some areas of intractable dispute, where theorists divide sharply into different camps, as perhaps in debates over the nature of knowledge or practical rationality—debates that have struck some as, at times, tedious marches into the swamp. Often, in such cases, the dispute may chiefly reflect a multiplicity of interests served by the ordinary concept—interests that might be better served by a suite of two or more concepts, as Block contends is the case regarding consciousness.

Some may wonder why we ought to bother with any kind of analysis: who cares what our folk concepts are like? There are two answers to this question. First, *we* care. All of us, being among the folk, employ folk concepts all the time, and most of our questions are framed in terms of them. If you want to know what it is to be happy, then you want to know the nature of something denoted by a folk concept, HAPPINESS. As your understanding of the subject matter proceeds, you may eventually decide to supplement or even supplant this concept with new ones. But first you need some vague grip on what *happiness* could be. By and large, folk concepts are the starting point of inquiry; they provide at least the initial vehicles for thinking about the things we care about.

Second, we are usually right to care about our folk concepts. Not just because we don't have much choice, but because those concepts typically refer to things of significance for us. That's why we employ them. For the most part, folk concepts gain currency and persist because they denote matters of broad and lasting concern. They have been vetted in the crucible of many people's experience, and we use them because, in some sense, they work for us. One reason they work for us is that human beings are extraordinarily discerning intuitive distinction-makers; on a continual basis, we instinctively and implicitly respond to a vast array of important distinctions, most of which we cannot even begin to make explicit. Consider just how richly any normal person is attuned to the countless non-verbal cues offered by her conversational partners. Think of how often one person will sense something wrong or inappropriate with another's behavior or demeanor without being able to say just what it is. And as any ethics instructor knows, people's sensitivity to values far outstrips their ability to articulate them. A good caregiver, for instance, may be utterly lousy at explaining more than a few of the manifold considerations that continuously guide his treatment of the person in his care. But his finely-tuned responsiveness to those considerations is absolutely critical to his being a good caregiver. And such a task as caregiving, which centers on knowing instinctively what really matters, is the sort of thing that human beings are really good at.

Sitting in the philosopher's chair making up theories about what matters, on the other hand, is something we're really *not* good at. In fact we're pathetic at it. (One does not need to teach philosophy and referee journal articles for long to figure that out.) Those who trust theoretical intuitions more than the practical instincts we display in everyday living will not, most likely, be much persuaded. But when it comes to marking the distinctions that really matter in human life, some of us would sooner put our money on intuitive lay practice, and the folk concepts it employs, than on the untethered a priori guesses of cloistered academics.

Our job, then, is to determine what our interests are relating to the folk concept of happiness, and then see which of the possible referents of the term best answers to those interests. The next section lays out the data to be accommodated.

4. DATA POINTS

4.1. The paradigm cases and statements

First, let's get a sense of what the possible referents of the term could be. Consider some paradigmatic cases of happiness and unhappiness:

- *Happiness*: being in high spirits, exuberant, buoyant, joyful, exhilarated, elated, carefree, contented, at peace, at ease, feeling confident and self-assured, feeling "in the zone," being in an expansive mood, delighted with one's life, or blessed with a sense of fulfillment or well-being.

- *Unhappiness*: being depressed, melancholy, despondent, anxious, "stressed out," seething with rage, overwhelmed by fear, worried sick, heartbroken, grief-stricken, lonely, empty, low, burdened with shame, bored, feeling insecure or worthless, feeling spiritually reduced, pressed-upon or "compressed," or deeply dissatisfied with life.

These are, I take it, more or less familiar ways of being happy or unhappy. Or, if some of them are not sufficient in themselves, they are plausibly *constitutive* of happiness or unhappiness: one's happiness or unhappiness is augmented or diminished by virtue of being in these states. The reader is free to add other examples to the list, but I take it to be uncontroversial that all or most of these cases involve happiness or unhappiness. A satisfactory theory of happiness should account for what is going on in these cases.

We can also identify some "paradigm statements": typical statements involving 'happiness' in the long-term psychological sense. The truth value of these statements is irrelevant; the point is to illustrate our interests in happiness by showing the sorts of contexts in which "happiness" talk occurs. Ideally, a theory of happiness will make sense of our use of the language in such contexts, comporting reasonably well with the intuitive meaning and significance of such uses. (At least relative to ordinary conceptions of what is significant.) For instance, the claim, "Most people are happy" seems very significant: if true, it apparently conveys an important fact. If your theory of happiness completely undercuts this appearance, that's at least prima facie a problem. For then (among other things) claims about whether people are happy will turn out to be deeply misleading, seeming to have practical implications that they utterly lack. I will suggest in Chapter 5 that life satisfaction accounts of happiness have something like this result, so that when investigators publish papers about life satisfaction studies under the guise of "happiness," this often has the effect of (unintentionally) inflating the practical significance of their research. Such problems need not be fatal to a theory of happiness—perhaps happiness is a lot less important than people think—but if we can get an otherwise plausible theory that does not make ordinary claims about happiness misleading or uninformative, we should prefer it. The paradigm statements include:

1. Most people are happy.
2. Higher income tends to yield surprisingly small increases in happiness.
3. People in the United States tend to be happier than those in China.
4. Most of all, I want my children to be happy and healthy.
5. You should do whatever will make you happiest.
6. The only time she was truly happy was in her twenties.
7. How is Ernesto? Not very well; he's pretty unhappy.
8. Shelly seems terribly unhappy these days; in fact I think she's depressed.
9. Robert moved back to California, as he was so unhappy living in Boston.

4.2. Practical interests

What are our interests in happiness? Proust notwithstanding, at least the concept has its uses: there are at least four broad functions that the notion performs in ordinary practice. To begin with, we often appeal to considerations of happiness when *deliberating* about important decisions. Someone trying to decide on an occupation will very often ask which option would prove best with respect to happiness: will I be happier as a teacher or a lawyer? Indeed, people often take the impact of their choices on their own, or others', happiness to be the most important factor in their decisions (at least where the decision is significant—people rarely think about happiness when deciding what to order for dinner). Policymakers likewise may consider the impact of proposed state actions on the happiness of their constituencies.

Second, we advert to happiness in *evaluating* or assessing our own or others' conditions, typically to find out or report on how well someone is doing. Thus concerned parents inquire as to whether their children are happy or unhappy. And often the first thing we wish to learn about our friends after a long separation is whether or not they are happy. Interestingly, a credible report of happiness or unhappiness is often if not typically taken to be sufficient grounds for concluding that someone is, or is not, doing well on the whole.

In fact happiness appears in many contexts to serve as a proxy for well-being. On learning that a friend is happy, you may well infer, quite reasonably, that she is doing well. If you find her to be unhappy, you might just as reasonably conclude she is doing poorly. And when deliberating about important life decisions, the judgment that one option will leave you happier normally suffices to settle the question of which best serves your interests. Note that these inferences are defeasible—we are not relying on the "well-being" sense of 'happiness' here: if you find that your friend's husband regards her with utter contempt, and that she would be devastated were she to learn this, you might well decide she's actually quite unfortunate—though happy all the same. This, at least, is how we tend to think about happiness: in ordinary practical reasoning we treat it as so closely aligned with well-being that, for the most part, we can use it as a stand-in for well-being.[13] One reason for doing so is that the notion of well-being is highly abstract and formal, whereas happiness is a more concrete, substantive good, and may thus be easier to assess and discuss. Moreover, assessments of happiness do not involve tendentious value judgments, and so are less subject to controversy.

Many times we appear to be concerned with happiness even when we do not explicitly refer to it as such. To say that one is depressed is simply a way of saying that one is particularly unhappy in a certain way. Indeed, it may well be that *most* talk about happiness does not use words like 'happy'. (I had contemplated the matters discussed in this volume for many years before it occurred to me that I was thinking about happiness.) This makes sense: if being depressed is one way of being unhappy, then we should expect some reports of unhappiness to employ the more informative language of depression. More broadly, the fact that there are many ways of being happy or unhappy indicates that reports concerning happiness will explicitly employ the vocabulary of happiness only when we lack sufficient information to apply more specific terminology, or where we are aggregating the happiness of multiple individuals, each happy or unhappy in different ways. Queries about happiness should tend to rely more on the more general terms, because in such cases we typically don't know in what manner someone will be happy or unhappy. Our interest in happiness appears to far outstrip our use of its terminology.

The third function of the concept of happiness is to aid us in *prediction*. Happiness appears to have deep and far-reaching effects on our psychology and behavior, and this partly accounts for our profound interest in the matter. One's being happy or unhappy should thus license a wide range of predictions. If, for instance, we discover that our friends are deeply unhappy, we can predict that they will be less pleasant and useful companions than were they happy. Such predictions appear to carry forward well into the future, reflecting the fact that happiness has a certain inertia. People who are happy or unhappy tend to stay that way for some time.

Unsurprisingly, happiness also has uses in *explanation*. For instance, that someone is unhappy may explain why he keeps trying to effect major changes in his life—trying out new religions, for example. We can also explain patterns in individuals' emotions and behavior, or particular emotions and behaviors, by reference to facts about happiness or unhappiness. Sometimes the best explanation of a person's inordinate joy over a small gift is that he is happy; of someone's present bad mood, that she is unhappy these days. Puzzled over a friend's inexplicably nasty remark, a person may find some relief in the discovery that the comment reflects no personal animosity, just the friend's general unhappiness.

The notion of happiness performs all of these functions. This is why we care about it. A good theory of happiness ought to respect this fact.

5. CRITERIA OF ADEQUACY

5.1. Overview

At this point it would be natural to draw up particular criteria of adequacy based on these interests, and I have done so in earlier work.[14] But in the context of the present volume it seems more helpful to move directly to a critical examination of the various theories, letting the specific requirements emerge as the argument demands. This will help move things along, and preconceived lists of requirements tend to be drawn up with malice aforethought anyway.

Instead I will mention two quite general desiderata, common to any reconstructive analysis, and say a few things about how they might apply in the case of happiness. These are:

1. Descriptive adequacy
2. Practical utility

5.2. Descriptive adequacy

I borrow the notion of descriptive adequacy from L. W. Sumner;[15] we might also call it "intuitive plausibility." The idea is that a conception of happiness should, at a minimum, be recognizable as such. It should concern something we can at least get away with calling happiness without butchering the language. Ideally, a theory will provide a close fit with our considered intuitions about happiness—at least to the extent that these are relatively uniform—and generate few or no serious counterexamples. More broadly, it should, as Sumner would put it, comport with our experience of happiness. It should "ring true." This does not mean that it has to conform to commonsense platitudes about the matter, or agree with the snap judgments of most laypersons. What seems plausible at first glance may no longer seem so on reflection, and it is our considered intuitions, particularly the strongest and most robust ones, that carry the most weight. It is possible, for instance, that commonsense platitudes about happiness could tend to reflect a hedonistic lay theory of happiness, even where people's *reflective* judgments would tend to converge on a life satisfaction account. The hedonistic platitudes might not hold up under even slight reflection, in which case a hedonistic account may not be descriptively adequate.[16]

The descriptive adequacy requirement is flexible, but only to a point. A theory that flouts too many strong intuitions about happiness risks changing the subject. At a certain point we cease to be talking about anything recognizable as happiness at all. We therefore cease to have a theory of happiness, but have instead a theory of something else. We may indeed wish to change the subject and talk about something else when all is said and done, but first we need to know what *happiness* could be. I have already argued that there probably is no single well-defined concept behind ordinary usage of 'happiness' in its psychological sense(s). But from this it hardly follows that the notion of happiness is free for the taking. The ordinary notion of happiness is not all chaos, and I believe that a sustained examination of the different theories of happiness will reveal far more order than we might have expected.

5.3. Practical utility

Call it "utility" for short. This is just the idea that we should prefer a conception of happiness that vindicates our profound interest in the matter, that best enables us to satisfy our practical, and perhaps theoretical, purposes relating to happiness. Given the status of HAPPINESS as a folk psychological concept, the practical purposes of laypersons take precedence. But theoretical purposes might also count to a lesser extent.

With happiness, foremost among our practical concerns is its evident *prudential value*. Happiness appears to be immensely important for well-being, indeed to be a central aspect of it, and people tend to regard it that way. As we saw earlier, we frequently treat it as a proxy for well-being. This is not to say that being happy must be necessary for well-being, nor that it must be sufficient. Perhaps it is, perhaps not. But happiness appears to be extremely important, and reliably so: being happy seems, with few or no exceptions, to be a pleasant or otherwise prudentially desirable condition. Happiness looks to be far more desirable prudentially than unhappiness. And how happy one is appears invariably to make a big difference for one's welfare. Similarly, differences in happiness seem typically to be matched by comparable differences in well-being. Exceptions, if there are any, appear to be unusual and explicable in ways that do not vitiate the importance we attach to happiness (e.g., limited to atypical circumstances or to people with strange tastes or values). In general, for people who are normally situated, there looks to be no realistic prospect of being lastingly happy yet not being significantly better off for it. Conversely, being lastingly unhappy yet none the worse for it seems not to be a realistic possibility.

This, at least, seems to be how people conventionally regard happiness's value. Other things being equal, we should prefer a theory of happiness that preserves such appearances over one that does not. Such a requirement may seem to undercut the status of HAPPINESS as a non-evaluative, descriptive concept, blurring the distinction between the well-being and psychological senses of 'happiness'. It does not. Compare the notion of pleasure, which is generally considered to be a descriptive concept. It is a problem with a theory of pleasure if it has the result of making it utterly mysterious why anyone should think pleasure important. A theory that has this result, unless accompanied by a very compelling story about why the appearances are mistaken, will likely strike us as having badly missed its target. A good theory of pleasure should, if at all possible, make sense of the appearance that pleasure has a certain kind of value. This is not because PLEASURE is an evaluative concept, but because such a theory is liable to seem neither intuitively plausible nor able to address our practical concerns in the matter.

A tricky question involves the extent to which happiness is supposed to track what *actually* matters for well-being, versus merely what people conventionally *think* important for well-being. The question is how far theories of happiness should be influenced by our theories of well-being. Since the goal is to make sense of people's typical interests in happiness, preserving as far as possible the intuitive significance of the paradigm cases and statements, it will matter to some extent what our view of well-being is like. At the same time, we should not hold theories of happiness hostage to just any old theory of well-being. Perhaps you incline toward a radically revisionary account of well-being, such as a Stoic view on which happiness turns out to have zero or even negative value, no matter how we conceive it. In such a case the prudential value requirement will be impossible to satisfy. For on such a view of well-being, our ordinary practical interests may be deeply misguided. What then? Given again that our goal is to *make sense* of people's typical interests in happiness, preserving as far as possible the intuitive significance of the paradigm cases and statements, we can still think about which account of happiness makes our ordinary interests in the matter seem as intelligible and reasonable as possible. For instance, a Stoic could argue against a life satisfaction theory by claiming that it fails to respect the apparent significance of happiness. For even if (say) a hedonistic account also fails to make happiness something that matters centrally for well-being, it may at least do a better job of preserving that *appearance*. For perhaps the putative value of life satisfaction vanishes given the merest reflection, whereas the seeming importance of pleasure dissipates only under the sort of extensive, rigorous scrutiny needed to appreciate the force of the Stoic position.

5.4. Summing up

On the approach sketched here, the task of giving a theory of happiness amounts to answering the following question:

What kind of psychological state is both plausibly identified with happiness (in its long-term psychological sense) and answers to people's practical interests in happiness?

I noted earlier that there is likely to be more than one thing we can get away with calling happiness. What then? In such a case we will look to whichever account best satisfies the desiderata. If we can plausibly do so, we should simply use 'happiness' to denote the referent of the winning account. If not, then we might distinguish further senses of 'happiness'. But the philosophically primary notion will be the one denoted by the winning account, if there is one.

6. INTUITION AND METAPHOR IN EMPIRICALLY INFORMED ETHICS

The fundamental outlook of the present volume is intended to be thoroughly naturalistic, representing a view of philosophy as more or less continuous with the sciences. The nature of things is taken to be fundamentally an empirical question, and values are conceived in a broadly Humean fashion, as somehow a product of human sensibilities. I will not argue for these assumptions, and most of the discussion will not presuppose their truth; but they do inform the approach. It may seem curious, then, that my arguments frequently trade in "intuition pumps," which empirically-minded philosophers have tended to eschew; and, moreover, that they sometimes rely on oblique, not to say metaphorical, language rather than the crisp, sharply defined terminology preferred in both scientific inquiry and philosophy in the anglophone tradition.

Let me explain, starting with the question of language. The problem arises mainly from the fact that we will be discussing the phenomenology of well-being, along with aspects of well-being that we know about chiefly through their phenomenology. These are, notoriously, difficult matters to talk about. Indeed, they are usually taken to be *paradigms* of the inexpressible, more resistant to articulation perhaps than anything else. The phenomenology of well-being is enormously rich, to put it mildly, leaving even poets at a loss to convey anything more than a hint of it. Part of the problem is that—as will become clearer in the following chapters—the phenomena are often too complex or subtle for the person experiencing them even to apprehend, much less verbalize. But we are handicapped as well by the inherently "lossy" character of linguistic communication: human experience contains far too much information for efficient communication to convey any more than a tiny fraction of it. The process of verbal articulation distills the "blooming, buzzing confusion" of lived experience down to the common currency of shared ideas, using as little of that currency as possible.[17] Most of the information is, of necessity, lost in the transformation. Scientific language is more lossy still, since it trades only in the very narrow coinage of ideas that can be precisely defined, quantified, and measured. For our purposes all of this means trouble, since any attempt to describe the phenomenology of happiness in precise terms will either be extremely fragmentary or extremely long and unwieldy. More importantly, the common currency in this realm, at least in contemporary English, consists of a pathetically stunted vocabulary of terms that typically lack anything like a precise definition.

As a result, it is probably impossible to talk intelligently about the psychology of well-being without resorting, at times, to a more literary mode of discourse that employs picturesque language and metaphor. The idea is to exploit the connotative power of language to direct the reader's attention to phenomena that otherwise we could not talk about at all—the "elaborate form of ostension" I mentioned earlier. This method has drawbacks, since metaphor does not conduce to clarity of thought, much less scientific assessment, and some readers competent in the language may fail to get the connotations and see what we are talking about, in which case we are left at something of an impasse. But the approach can put us on the road to a more exact understanding of matters that otherwise might not get treated at all, helping us to notice and discuss them so that we can study them more carefully and systematically.

The use of intuition pumps will be more familiar to philosophical readers. It is not unproblematical, not least because of sampling bias worries: as noted earlier, the readers whose intuitions are being pumped are not exactly a representative slice of humanity, and even when philosophers' intuitions converge, we cannot be certain that other people, particularly in non-Western cultures, will share them.[18] This is a serious concern, but I will assume here that it is not fatal to the enterprise, letting the arguments to follow speak for themselves. This is partly because human sensibilities seem to me to share enough in common to sustain the practice, partly because I have no idea how to proceed otherwise, and partly for reasons to be sketched momentarily. Still, we will have to bear this limitation of our methodology in mind, asking ourselves whether our intuitions are liable to be widely shared. Better still, when we can, to ask other people, as the experimental philosophy movement maintains.

Intuitional evidence can be defensible partly because the relevant *facts* may connect with, indeed depend on, human sensibilities in ways that at least make it intelligible how our intuitions could be relevant. Some of the facts concern our concepts, and the facts about how we are willing to apply a given term can plausibly tell us something about the nature of the concept it expresses. Similarly, many believe that values depend on, or are otherwise intimately connected with, our sensibilities. If so then again, appeals to intuition may well be relevant. A second point, made earlier, is that we are good intuitive distinction-makers in many realms, particularly when thinking about particular cases as opposed to theoretical claims.

Finally, the present volume reflects a view of ethical inquiry as crucially first-personal: its charge is at least partly to articulate a view of the good life that will strike a reasonable person as, on reflection, an attractive one to lead.[19] This is roughly the approach often thought to characterize Hellenistic ethical theory, except that it is "eudaimonistic" only in method—emphasizing the first-personal concerns of individuals trying to lead good lives—and not in substance: it does not, that is, take an ethical theory to be a theory of the narrower notion of *well-being* or eudaimonia. It is, in effect, a kind of methodological eudaimonism. And on this sort of approach it will be important for many claims about value—at least the values that matter for a good life—to have some intuitive plausibility: an ethical theory is something we have to be able to live with. And an ethical theory that commits us to views we find repulsive, even on reflection, is going to have problems in this regard. (It is possible, of course, to defend an ethical theory one finds intuitively repugnant—perhaps the truth could be like that. But the major ethics journals are not likely to be graced anytime soon by articles with titles like "A Repugnant Ethical Theory Defended.") So intuitive considerations will be a legitimate source of evidence, at least on this sort of approach. Lest a eudaimonistic methodology seem to clash with the idea of philosophy as roughly continuous with science, it should be noted that such an approach is neither non-naturalistic nor indifferent to empirical results. Setting aside the truism that an attractive view of the good life for a human being should comport with the observed facts about human nature, we could look to empirical research for independent support of our reflective views. If, for instance, values are dependent on human sensibility, then we might learn about them either by employing our sensibilities—for example, philosophical reflection—or by putting those sensibilities under the microscope. If neuropsychological research revealed that human beings are robustly wired for deontological values, for instance, then this could provide a degree of support for the idea that some deontological moral theory is *true*, namely by suggesting that only such theories are liable to fit with human sensibilities, to seem intuitively plausible to us.

7. WHAT LIES AHEAD

In the next four chapters I will apply the approach developed here to the main accounts of happiness. Chapter 4 will argue against hedonistic theories mainly on grounds of descriptive adequacy: roughly, happiness is not plausibly identified with pleasure, and the intuitions seeming to favor a hedonistic approach actually point toward an emotional state theory. Chapter 5 contends that life satisfaction theories, while somewhat more promising in terms of descriptive adequacy, cannot make sense of the intuitive significance of happiness. Happiness, on such a view, would be much less important, and important for different reasons, than we ordinarily take it to be. Chapters 6 and 7 argue that an emotional state theory satisfies both the descriptively adequacy and utility requirements. (Chapter 8, which places happiness thus conceived at the center of an account of well-being, will offer further support for this contention.) Happiness is most profitably conceived along the lines of an emotional state view.

PART II

THE NATURE OF HAPPINESS

4

Pleasure

"And does his philosophy make you happy?"

"I have never searched for happiness. Who wants happiness? I have searched for pleasure."

Oscar Wilde, *The Picture of Dorian Gray* (p. 209)

1. INTRODUCTION

One might have thought happiness and pleasure were two very different things. Certainly the temptation to regard the terms as interchangeable is less than overwhelming. Yet the best-known theories of happiness ask us to regard these things as more or less identical: to be happy just is for one's experience to be, on balance, more pleasant than not. This is hedonism in its traditional reductive form, as found in the works of Bentham, Sidgwick, Brandt, and many others.[1] We can distinguish variations on the theme. But the root idea, shared by all hedonists, is that happiness consists solely in pleasant states of mind, or pleasantness itself (and freedom from unpleasantness or unpleasant states, a nicety I will usually omit hereafter).[2]

In this chapter I will argue that hedonistic accounts of happiness are very likely false: they appear fundamentally to misconstrue the nature of the mental states that could constitute anything plausibly called happiness. The argument will largely center on descriptive adequacy, and some may object that hedonism remains superior on grounds of practical utility. I respond to this objection, particularly as it applies to the emotional state view, in Section 6. Since the argument of this chapter rests partly on the claim that alternative theories offer more promising accounts of happiness, much of my case against hedonism will rest with the discussion of those theories, particularly the emotional state view, in Chapters 5 through 7, and 9.

2. WHAT IS A HEDONISTIC THEORY OF HAPPINESS?

Hedonists share the idea that happiness consists solely in a person's hedonic state. The basic schema is roughly this: one is happy by virtue of having a sufficiently favorable balance of pleasure versus unpleasure; and unhappy by virtue of having a sufficiently unfavorable balance of pleasure versus unpleasure.[3] A hedonic balance is "favorable" insofar as it involves more pleasure or less unpleasure, "unfavorable" insofar as it involves less pleasure, or more unpleasure; no value claim is intended by the use of these terms. Hedonists usually maintain that a majority of pleasure suffices for happiness, a majority of unpleasure for unhappiness, but they could place the cutoff anywhere. They can also allow room for an intermediate region in which a person is neither happy nor unhappy. Terms for the hedonic states vary widely, with other formulations referring to enjoyment or pleasant experience versus pain, suffering, displeasure, or unpleasant experience. No terminology is ideal, but I will usually put the view in terms of pleasant, versus unpleasant, experience: what ultimately concerns the hedonist is the pleasantness of our experience. This seems best to express the fundamental ideal and its attractions while having fewer misleading connotations than the alternatives.

The doctrine that interests us is not to be confused with other varieties of hedonism. The *ethical* hedonist, for instance, maintains that pleasure is the only thing worth seeking, while *psychological* hedonists contend that pleasure is the only thing, ultimately, that human beings actually do seek. But hedonism about happiness is most readily confused with *welfare* hedonism, for reasons discussed in Chapter 2: hedonism about "happiness" in the well-being sense just is welfare hedonism. And that doctrine is wholly independent of the view that concerns us here. Epicurean hedonism about eudaimonia, for instance, is a form of welfare hedonism that the arguments of this chapter will leave untouched. (However, this chapter does lay some foundations for the non-hedonistic approach to well-being defended in Part III.) Finally, *axiological* hedonism takes pleasure to be the sole intrinsic good.

As to the nature of pleasure and unpleasure, hedonism comes in two basic flavors, which L. W. Sumner has called internalist and externalist.[4] The former identifies pleasures in terms of a quality intrinsic to all pleasurable experiences. On this sort of view, pleasure is a kind of sensation, feeling, or quality of experience. For instance, what makes a given experience pleasant or unpleasant is a simple, unanalyzable feeling tone that it shares with all other such experiences. Noting the extreme variety of pleasures, externalists deny the existence of any intrinsic property that identifies them as such. Rather, what makes a given experience pleasant is just the subject's attitude to it—whether she likes, welcomes, or otherwise has the right kind of pro-attitude toward it. (Presumably, not just any pro-attitude will do; for starters, it should be based entirely on the experience's intrinsic or felt properties, and not, say, the consequences one expects to follow from it. Moreover, it should be a fairly primitive, low-level reaction and not a detached, reflective evaluation.) Thus any experience can in principle be pleasant or unpleasant, depending on how one reacts to it. A third view of pleasure, related to externalism but importantly distinct, has gained prominence in recent years: the *attitudinal* view of pleasure developed by Fred Feldman.[5] On this account, pleasure is a propositional attitude of *being pleased about* some fact or state of affairs (or, alternatively, enjoying it, being glad that it is happening, or taking pleasure in it). This differs from externalism in that it identifies pleasure not with an experience toward which one has an attitude but a propositional attitude itself, and in taking the object of the attitude to be a fact or state of affairs rather than an experience. To use a pair of examples from Feldman, you might be pleased about the fact that you live in Massachusetts, or take pleasure in the fact that you are tasting beer. The attitude in question is an occurrent conscious episode, but need not involve any kind of feeling or sensation.

In earlier work I followed Sumner's convention of calling the intrinsic view the "sensation" model of pleasure, and externalism the "attitude" model.[6] I will not use that language here, given the potential for confusion with attitudinal views of pleasure, as well as the misleading connotation of "sensation" in connection with internalism: most if not all of the major internalists recognize that sensory pleasures do not even remotely exhaust the class of pleasures.[7]

3. INTUITIVE PROBLEM ONE: IRRELEVANT PLEASURES

3.1. The problem

The most obvious problem with traditional hedonistic theories is that they are too inclusive: all sorts of shallow, fleeting pleasures are made to count toward happiness. Yet such pleasures intuitively play no constitutive role in determining how happy a person is. One's enjoyment of eating crackers, hearing a good song, sexual intercourse, scratching an itch, solving a puzzle, playing football, and so forth need not have the slightest impact on one's level of happiness (though, of course, they may). I enjoy, get pleasure from, a cheeseburger, yet I am patently not happier *thereby*. Conversely for superficial unpleasures. The problem does not concern the intensity of such pleasures: an orgasm may well be intensely pleasurable, yet still fail to *move* one, to make one any happier (consider anonymous or solitary sex). Might the brief duration of the event be misleading our intuitions here? Not likely: it is not just that any particular superficial pleasure seems irrelevant. Even the whole *pattern* of such pleasures over time appears to be. To be sure, we would expect someone who underwent an unrelenting succession of minor irritations not to be very happy *at the end of it all*. But this does not show the irritations themselves to be constitutive of one's (un)happiness; it reflects rather our expectation that these experiences will impact some deeper aspect of one's psychology, such as one's mood. Intuitively, the trouble seems to be that such pleasures don't reach "deeply" enough, so to speak. They just don't *get* to us; they flit through consciousness and that's the end of it.

Note as well that, for any conventional hedonist, a state's contribution to happiness will be proportional to its pleasantness. But some of the superficial pleasures that seem irrelevant are, we saw, *extremely* pleasant: an orgasm, being a paradigm of pleasure, ought likewise to be a paradigm of a happiness-constituting state if hedonism is correct. One need not be a prude to think that even an extended period of orgasmic pleasure would not *ipso facto* yield a paradigmatically happy person. Similarly, a delicious meal can make for a highly pleasant experience without involving a correspondingly pronounced boost in happiness. Even if the hedonist can make out that these cases intuitively involve *some* impact on happiness, she needs more than this: to show that the happiness alters *in step with* the pleasure.

These considerations appear to undermine any hedonistic account of which I am aware. They also demonstrate the error of equating talk of hedonic states with talk of happiness, as many commentators are wont to do. The pleasures of happiness are not the only pleasures to be had, though perhaps they are the most desirable.

3.2. Some notes on attitudinal hedonism

Some readers may not share the intuitions in question. If so, it will I suspect be due to the influence of an attitudinal conception of pleasure: so, for instance, one is pleased at the fact that one is eating a cracker. We commonly speak of being "happy with" or "happy about" this or that, and such talk seems often to concern what Feldman calls attitudinal pleasure. Thus one might, equivalently, be happy about the fact that one is eating a cracker. And so, one might think, one's being happy consists in having enough episodes of attitudinal pleasure—of being happy *with* enough things, and not being unhappy with too many things.

Feldman has been developing attitudinal hedonism as an important new account of happiness in some unpublished work. Being a form of hedonism, it will be vulnerable at least to the arguments in Section 5. And it has substantial difficulties of its own, particularly as a brand of hedonism. First, to put the point crudely, it seems to take the fun out of pleasure.[8] It can be pleasant to drink a beer; yet the pleasantness of that experience does not, it seems, consist in my being pleased at the fact that I am drinking the beer, or that the beer tastes the way it does. Nor does my being pleased about these things seem to be what *makes* the experience pleasant. Indeed, it seems largely beside the point: intuitively, what makes the experience pleasant is *the way the beer tastes*—namely, great. (Externalists might alternatively say something like this: it's that I *like* the way it tastes.) This also seems to be what makes drinking the beer a good thing. The pleasantness and value of drinking a beer, in short, seems to rest with the character of the experience itself, or at least with my liking the beer's taste as such. But the fact that I am *glad* to be drinking the beer, or that it tastes the way it does, might in some other way be a good thing—particularly if, say, I am a connoisseur of beers, or a teenager getting a first sip of the forbidden fruit—but it is at any rate a different matter. (Liking the beer's taste is not the same as liking *the fact* that the beer tastes that way.)

Similarly, the imperative to relieve someone's extreme suffering is not the imperative to relieve her being displeased about certain facts. When illness makes you feel as if your entire body is poised to leap out your throat, the problem is not that you are displeased about the present state of affairs, the fact that you feel that way, or anything else. The problem intuitively is that you simply feel horrible—both the unpleasantness and the disvalue reside in *what it's like* to feel that way. The attitudinal hedonist will reply, first, that what it means to feel horrible is to be very (very, very) displeased about the fact that you feel a certain way, and second, that we answer the imperative to relieve suffering by trying to mitigate the experiences about which we are so displeased. But the first reply simply restates the claim in dispute, while the second misses the point: while the attitudinal hedonist may be entitled to observe that we don't normally answer the claims of suffering by focusing on people's attitudes toward their condition, he still has to say that it is those attitudes that *ground* the claims of suffering. So it is granted that we offer the afflicted morphine rather than a copy of the *Encheiridion*,[9] but we still do so, ultimately, with the aim of stopping the individual being displeased about certain facts. That individual would, I think, beg to differ.

In short, attitudinal hedonism appears not to offer a plausible account of pleasure or its value. As a form of hedonism, it seems deeply problematical. Attitudinal pleasure may still be important in its own way. Perhaps it matters as a kind of judgment about things in our lives, in much the way that attitudes of satisfaction with our lives seem important (see Chapter 5). Henceforth, my discussion will focus on internalist and externalist models of pleasure.

4. INTUITIVE PROBLEM TWO: PSYCHOLOGICAL SUPERFICIALITY

4.1. The alternative theories

Perhaps some *restricted* form of hedonism could suffice: happiness is a matter of pleasure, but only a certain kind of pleasure—"deep" pleasure, maybe, or the Epicurean pleasures of tranquility. This sort of proposal also has serious problems. To show why, I will discuss a couple of alternative theories and explain what distinguishes them from hedonism.

Recall the paradigm cases cited in Chapter 3—for example, profound depression and anxiety on the one hand, and a deep sense of well-being and joy on the other. What is it that makes them examples of happiness and unhappiness? Right away, it seems more than a bit odd to say that these people are happy or unhappy simply by virtue of experiencing a great deal of pleasure or unpleasure.

They certainly are experiencing those. But that is not what constitutes their being happy. If it were, then we might as well add to our list of prototypically unhappy people someone who is experiencing serious chronic pain. No doubt we should expect such a person to be unhappy. But his pain is not his unhappiness, if he is indeed unhappy (perhaps he is a highly disciplined Buddhist monk). It is, rather, the *source* of his unhappiness.

Instead, we would suppose that—him most likely not being a Buddhist monk—his pain *gets him down*. It makes him depressed and irritable, not to mention highly dissatisfied with his lot in life. And it is far more plausible to suppose that he is unhappy in virtue of *these* underlying states, caused by the physical pain. Someone who is depressed, irritable, and dissatisfied with his life is thereby unhappy. One natural proposal, then, is that happiness consists in a person's emotional state: insofar as one's emotional state is basically positive, one is happy. On the most straightforward version of this view, such positive emotional conditions as a predominance of joyfulness, high-spiritedness, peace of mind, etc. would exemplify happiness, while a predominance of their negative counterparts—depression, anxiety, fear, anger, feelings of discontent, etc.—would typify unhappiness.[10] To be happy on this sort of view is not necessarily to *feel* happy. Happiness thus conceived is not a particular emotion or mood at all, but consists rather in a subject's overall emotional state or condition.

This is the emotional state theory. In light of the recent discussion of superficial pleasures, we can safely say that not just any affective states will do. Rather, the relevant states, such as moods, are comparatively deep, or *central*, aspects of a person's affective state. I will not attempt to explicate the notion of a central affective state until Chapter 7, but moods are paradigmatically central. Among other things, central affective states tend to be phenomenally profound, pervasive, and lasting, with far-reaching effects on one's psychology and behavior. (Consider deep sadness.) By contrast, one's mild annoyance at dropping a letter while bringing in the mail is superficial, focused, and short-lived; its effects are limited. It is not central but *peripheral*. We can roughly think of central affective states as equivalent to the class of moods and emotions. Chapter 7 argues that a credible emotional state theory should incorporate, in addition to central affective states such as moods, that aspect of a subject's psychology that *disposes* her to experience certain moods rather than others—what I call a "mood propensity."[11] While counting mood propensities toward happiness would obviously be bad news for hedonism, I will set them aside in this chapter. Suffice it to say that an emotional state view need not be susceptible to the objection from superficiality.

I now wish to mention briefly a different sort of account that one might glean from the paradigm cases. Perhaps what makes someone happy or otherwise is simply her *attitude* toward her life: is she satisfied with it? This, the life satisfaction theory to be discussed in the next chapter, claims that to be happy is to be satisfied or pleased with one's life. Some people's intuitions may favor such a view, and certainly people do sometimes talk about happiness in such terms.

This picture is, I submit, complete: there are no clear-cut cases that fail to conform to one or the other, or some combination, of these views. If one finds emotional state theories implausible, this will be because one's intuitions favor the life satisfaction account, and vice versa. Even if the picture is not complete, we need only grant that one might be happy or unhappy at least partly by virtue of one's emotional condition and/or attitude toward one's life. For even if other things, including pleasure, go into happiness, the hedonistic reduction of happiness to pleasure will fail if any constituent of happiness is not reducible to pleasure. And it is difficult to imagine how any credible theory of happiness could deny that one might be happy at least partly by virtue of one's being satisfied with one's life or being in a positive emotional state. Hedonists must either bite that bullet or insist that one or both states reduce to pleasure. The former option seems preposterous. This leaves only the latter.

4.2. The irreducibility of the alternatives

Interestingly, the life satisfaction account has plenty of philosophical adherents, whereas I am unaware of any philosophical theorists who have even suggested, much less adopted, an emotional state view.[12] Perhaps this results from a mistaken impression that the emotional state view just is a form of hedonism. Then what, one may ask, distinguishes the two? Recall that pleasure is nothing more than having an experience of a certain kind, defined either in terms of its intrinsic qualities or one's attitude toward it. Hedonism thus reduces happiness to the having of such experiences. To say that someone is happy would, on this theory, be to say that his experiences have been predominantly pleasant.

But emotional states are not simply kinds of experiences; nor are they just now-for-now reactions to experiences. Consider the condition of being in a depressed mood: is a depressed mood *merely* a type of experience? The question itself is suspect, like asking whether believing that three is a prime number is merely a kind of experience. Moods are more or less enduring states that consist at least partly in having certain dispositions. Indeed, some of the most prominent accounts of moods take them to be *purely* dispositional, though this probably goes too far.[13] If I am irritable, I am thereby disposed to grow angry, impatient, etc. at relatively minor annoyances; that's just what it is to be irritable. Somebody who was not so disposed could hardly be said to be irritable. Similarly, an individual who is in a depressed mood will likely find little pleasure in what happens, will tend to look on the dark side of things, and may more likely be saddened by negative events. Again, it is not clear what it could mean for someone to be in a depressed mood if she lacked such propensities. This sort of disposition is not just a type or quality of experience. Nor is it merely a kind of con-attitude toward one's present experience. It is also worth noting that psychological accounts of moods and other emotional states typically incorporate the various non-experiential processes that subserve the phenomenology (*inter alia*). Though moods do typically have phenomenal qualities, such properties comprise just one aspect of what is surely a complex psychological state. Moods do not reduce to pleasure, so the emotional state theory is not equivalent to hedonism. (This is even clearer if we incorporate mood propensities.)

Since it is eminently plausible that an irritable or depressed mood—as such, and not merely *qua* unpleasant experience—does constitute a reduction in happiness, we may conclude that happiness does not reduce to pleasure. If one does not think this plausible, then perhaps one's intuitions favor the life satisfaction theory. All the better: being satisfied with one's life is *patently* not just a kind or quality of experience. Neither is it an attitude of the right sort for a hedonistic reduction. For one thing, life satisfaction is a global attitude that concerns far more than one's present experience. Second, it presumably includes appraisals of a fairly detached and reflective sort, such as the belief that one is getting most of the important things in life. Whatever the attitudes constitutive of pleasure, they are surely not so intellectualized as this.

It may be objected that pleasure too is dispositional: it disposes us to say and do certain things, for instance.[14] Indeed, pretty much anything can be said to have dispositional properties in some sense. What's the difference? I do not know how to state precisely the relevant sense in which happiness-constituting states like moods are dispositional, and hope that a better understanding of the psychological mechanisms involved in moods and emotions will eventually allow us to answer the question more exactly. (The discussion in Chapter 7 should help to clarify somewhat.) But we can note some salient differences here, focusing again on the case of moods. First, dispositionality is an essential characteristic of moods, and they are in part *constituted* by their dispositional properties. Whereas experiencing pain may, *per accidens*, dispose me to say "ouch" and other such things, but is not constituted by such dispositions; nor is having such dispositions essential to being in pain. Adherents of externalist views of pleasure might reply that some dispositions are indeed essential to it: pleasure entails wanting, say, and thus essentially involves certain action tendencies or behavioral dispositions.[15] The pleasure of sipping the milkshake makes you want to continue sipping, which in turn consists partly in a disposition to do so; that's at least partly what makes it a pleasure.

Suppose this is right. There is still a clear sense in which this pleasure is a purely occurrent conscious state, whereas irritability is not, being in part a disposition to experience such states. Note, first, that the "wanting" disposition of pleasure is grounded entirely in an occurrent conscious state, and consists in an occurrent tendency to act in certain ways. Whereas a propensity to lash out over minor affronts may be nothing more than that: a propensity, with no occurrent force unless a triggering event occurs. Moreover, pleasure's dispositions are highly localized and stimulus-driven, directed at the object of the pleasure and lasting only as long as the experience lasts. Irritability's dispositions are, or can be, highly generalized, with no particular object; and they can persist long after any particular experience. Finally, irritability consists partly in certain affective, including emotional, dispositions, as well as perceptual, inferential, and other psychological dispositions. Whereas pleasure, as such, seems not to alter one's overall psychic disposition in this way. The "wanting" disposition involved in the milkshake pleasure, for instance, seems basically to be an action or behavioral tendency. It does not seem to constitute a change in the way one perceives, thinks, and responds emotionally to the world.

4.3. Diagnosis

The fundamental problem, I would suggest, is that hedonistic happiness consists of nothing but a series of conscious events: to know that someone is happy on this view is only to know that his recent experience has been mostly positive. So construed, ascriptions of happiness are little more than capsule summaries or histories of subjects' conscious episodes. They purport only to characterize the general tenor of a sequence of experiential events—namely, experiencings and likings (or, on the internalist model of pleasure, just the former). Hedonistic happiness is an essentially episodic and (in ordinary ascriptions) backward-looking phenomenon. But happiness is obviously not just the having of a certain kind of experience, or even lots of them. It is not something that *happens* to a person. It is rather a state *of* the individual, a deeper psychological condition incorporating the more or less stable underlying mental states that *determine*, in part and among other things, the kinds of experiences that will occur. It primarily concerns agents' psychic dispositions, telling us not just about their histories, but also about their current condition and propensities for the near future. It is forward-looking.[16] Being in a certain sort of mood state or emotional condition is such a condition. So, it would seem, is having a certain attitude toward one's life. Experiencing pleasure is not. Hedonism is thus fundamentally wrong about the kind of mental state that happiness is. It appears to commit something of a category mistake.

An important aspect of hedonism's error is that pleasure lacks what we may call causal depth. All appearances are that happiness has deep, far-reaching, and typically lasting consequences for a person's state of mind and behavior. Theories ought to respect this appearance. Causal depth has two aspects. First, causally deep states or conditions are *productive*. That is, they are prolific and wide-ranging in their causal effects. Second, they are in some sense psychologically *deep*: they affect one's psychological condition at a very profound and basic level, in typically lasting ways, and not simply in superficial and transient ways. This is partly a matter of disposing one to have certain mental states rather than others. The pleasantness of our experience may have plenty of causal efficacy, but it does not have causal depth to anything like the extent that our emotional conditions do. Hedonism does little more than skim the phenomenal surface off our emotional states and call it happiness. But happiness runs much deeper than that. This fact will prove significant later.[17]

5. WHY EVEN NONREDUCTIVE HEDONISM FAILS

5.1. A weaker form of hedonism

Some hedonists might grant that happiness does not reduce to pleasure, but insist that the happiness-constitutive states are a species of pleasure in a looser sense: though not *merely* pleasures—not reducible to experiencings and likings—they are necessarily pleasant, and thus conform to what is in some sense a hedonistic account. Call this *nonreductive hedonism*. I want to argue that even this is false: the relevant states need not be pleasant. This raises further difficulties for reductive hedonism as well.

Reductionist hedonism being false, I will henceforth assume that the correct account of happiness incorporates to some extent one or both of the emotional state and life satisfaction views. The first thing to notice is that such a theory might more properly be called an emotional state or life satisfaction account. Be that as it may, a mental state can only be a kind of pleasure in any sense if one's being in that state entails that one is having some sort of characteristic experience, and that that experience is pleasant. Neither life satisfaction nor emotional state satisfies these criteria. This ought to be self-evident as regards life satisfaction: that I am satisfied with my life entails nothing at all about my current experience. Life satisfaction can no more be a pleasure than believing that three is a prime number can. Perhaps it does require one to have pleasant experiences at some point—a feeling of well-being, for instance. But this is clearly not sufficient for life satisfaction to yield anything plausibly called hedonism.

5.2. The dispositional character of moods

Suppose that affective states such as mood are happiness-constitutive. Might these states be construed as a species of pleasure in our looser sense? This is considerably more plausible than a hedonistic reading of life satisfaction. For one thing, we might reasonably suppose that being in a positive, as opposed to a negative, mood just is to be in a pleasant versus unpleasant mood.[18] Yet it fails, for two reasons. First, mood is substantially dispositional, and may occasionally be nonconscious. (Indeed, it is *never* experiential according to the "pure dispositionalists," as we may call them.) Consider irritability, which is presumably (un)happiness-constitutive. The problem is that my irritability need not at every moment impinge on my experience. Sometimes we only discover our disagreeable moods when we find ourselves inexplicably lashing out over some trivial offense. No doubt this is often due to inattention or other failures to notice certain aspects of consciousness. But that is not always the case, and at times one experiences nothing untoward until some provocation comes along and generates a disproportionate reaction.

This seems plain enough as an everyday occurrence, but for our purposes it suffices to note the logical possibility. And surely it is *logically* possible for a bad mood to recede completely from consciousness: a being who becomes temporarily disposed to experience unusually frequent and intense emotions of anger or sadness is thereby in a negative mood, even if some of that time its consciousness remains unaffected. (This is particularly clear if we suppose that this state usually does have the phenomenal character typical of such moods, and that the underlying psychological processes are the same in either case.) Irritability—*inter alia*—does not entail the continuous having of certain experiences. Since it is not a type of experience, it is a fortiori not a type of (un)pleasant experience. (Nor, of course, are mood propensities. My arguments for those in Chapter 7 should reinforce the points made here.)

5.3. Hedonic inversion

La mélancolie, c'est le bonheur d'être triste.

Victor Hugo, *Les Travailleurs de la Mer*[19]

Even where the relevant affective states do manifest themselves in consciousness, it seems that they need not exhibit the usual hedonic properties. For instance, an unhappiness-constitutive affect, such as melancholy, need not be unpleasant, and may even be pleasant. This is clearest on the externalist model of pleasure, but holds as well for any plausible version of the internalist view. While I lean toward an internalist model, it will be convenient to focus mainly on externalism. A major attraction of this account is that we seem unable to identify any feature that all pleasant experiences share, save the fact that we like or welcome them. In principle, it seems, any sensation or feeling can be either pleasant or unpleasant depending on how the subject reacts to it. The sensation one gets when firmly slapped is notoriously liable to be taken as a form of enjoyment or suffering depending on one's predilections and frame of mind. If this is correct, then presumably affective states such as sadness and cheery feelings would be among those feelings that can, at least theoretically, be either pleasant or unpleasant. Yet these states are happiness-constitutive on any credible emotional state account; intuitively, a sad person is unhappy *whether or not* she likes how it feels, whether or not it feels good to her. We would thus be mistaken to classify these states as pleasures of any kind.

We need only the logical possibility of, say, sadness being pleasant to sustain the present contention. Perhaps human psychology rules out certain reactions to certain sorts of experiences. It is doubtful, for instance, whether any ordinary human could find much pleasure in intense nausea. So even if we cannot feel sad without finding it unpleasant, the fact remains that its unpleasantness is only (for the externalist) an extrinsic property of the feeling, and depends on whether the subject *dislikes* the feeling in the relevant manner. There is thus no inconsistency in supposing someone to be sad—hence to that extent unhappy—yet enjoying it.

Perhaps this will be easier to see if we consider a few cases, some of which are not only logically possible but actually rather common. Some people have unusual tastes or values: they *like*, find pleasant, many of the things that ordinary people find disagreeable. For instance, a melancholy person—a Keats, perhaps—might seek comfort in his sorrow, and enjoy wallowing in his own grief. For this sort of individual, his unhappiness *is* his pleasure. (If the reader's intuitions seem to differ here, it may reflect an inclination toward life satisfaction views of happiness, as a Keats might be satisfied with being melancholy.[20]) No doubt this is a somewhat less rapturous pleasure than that available to a normally constituted happy person, but it is a pleasure for him nonetheless. And a tortured artist need not derive any pleasure from the cheerful affects that disgust her (feelings brought on, say, by a shamefully maudlin episode of Barney the purple dinosaur). But one need not be an eccentric to enjoy negative affects or dislike positive ones. Probably all of us have such proclivities to some extent. For instance, many of us like the feelings brought on by reading a sad novel. Likewise, we may take considerable pleasure in the fear and anxiety generated by a suspenseful or scary movie. And sometimes a poignant but particularly fitting episode in one's life, or a Billie Holiday record, can leave one feeling blue, yet not unpleasantly so. (Recall Victor Hugo's observation.) Anger can also be pleasant under the right circumstances, a fact no doubt exploited by demagogues over the ages. Frequently such experiences are bittersweet—pleasant in one respect, unpleasant in another—but often they seem to be pleasant or unpleasant without qualification. Just as with physical pleasures and pains, it appears that any given type of affective state may be eligible for either enjoyment or suffering. If any of the sorts of affective states in question are happiness-constitutive, then nothing plausibly called hedonism can be true.

Perhaps an internalist model of pleasure will seem less friendly to this claim. But internalists—myself included—should also grant my claim: in cases of hedonic inversion, it matters little whether a pleasant instance of sadness differs from an unpleasant one only in terms of an intrinsic hedonic quality, or whether they differ only in an extrinsic hedonic quality. *Qua* affective state type—*qua* sadness—there is no reason to posit any difference at all. Yet this is the only respect that matters on the emotional state view. The issue is not whether the hedonic quality of an affective state like sadness is intrinsic or extrinsic, but whether affective states of a given type can be either pleasant or unpleasant.

If happiness-constitutive affective states need not be pleasant, what distinguishes positive affective states from negative ones? We have several options here, but this question is best postponed until Chapter 7, where we will discuss the emotional state theory in detail. But happiness on any credible view will turn out to be a highly pleasant state in virtually all cases, and certainly all normal ones. There is no need to build pleasantness into the concept itself.

6. PRINCIPLED CONSIDERATIONS

6.1. Objection: only hedonism can preserve happiness's intuitive value

The hedonist may grant that the folk notion of happiness is not hedonistic, and yet deny that this is a real problem for her: for who cares what the folk concept of happiness is? One might think that any value these states have for us is largely if not wholly a matter of their pleasantness. So why not focus directly on pleasure itself? Hedonism does the heavy lifting that its alternatives cannot, and is thus the preferred account despite its counterintuitive consequences, for it best satisfies the "practical utility" constraint discussed in Chapter 3.

The trouble is, hedonism does not simply violate a few intuitions about exotic cases: it appears to get the basic ontological status of happiness wrong. It is not even in the right ballpark. So even if the folk notion of happiness turns out to have no theoretical or practical value at all, we would still have no basis for calling the hedonistic state *happiness*. We can call it happiness if we like, but then we can call it platform shoes or silly string or anything else for that matter.

That said, it would be nice if we could avoid deflationary conclusions about the importance of happiness. Can non-hedonists find grounds for resisting such worries? I think they can, but will consider only the emotional state view here. (We will see in the next chapter that life satisfaction accounts do appear to have deflationary implications.) The basic claim is that, whatever its role in the theory of well-being, emotional state happiness appears to satisfy our practical interests regarding deliberation, evaluation, prediction, and explanation at least as well as, if not better than, hedonistic happiness. The emotional state view thus has considerable substantive appeal even if we reject the account of well-being developed in Part III.

6.2. The predictive and explanatory significance of happiness

Hedonistic happiness cannot fulfill anything like the predictive and explanatory role that happiness intuitively appears to play, and which the emotional state theory seems to allow. As we have already seen, including in my discussion of hedonism's "category mistake," one would have thought that knowing someone is happy would enable us to predict all sorts of things about her future states and behavior. If I know that Gertrude is happy, then I can reasonably expect her to be a more pleasant and agreeable companion than were she otherwise disposed. Such predictions seem to carry well into the future, so that Gertrude's present happiness may warrant expectations of fair companionship a week from now, perhaps even later.[21] It certainly looks to predict such a status for the next few hours. Notice that the predictions licensed are very broad-based: they do not depend on the continuation of her present activity or other experience, but cover just about any activity we care to propose.

Gertrude's hedonistic "happiness," by contrast, does not seem to underwrite such expectations. At best, it might enable us to reliably predict that she will enjoy the continuation of whatever she has been experiencing—and even then only inasmuch as it is the sort of experience that would not soon grow tiresome. Similarly, the fact that she has been liking, versus disliking, what she has been doing or otherwise experiencing says little about whether she will prove a more or less agreeable partner at a game of tennis. Yet the fact that she is in, or has been in, a good mood *does* tell us something about her desirability as a tennis partner for the near future: since moods tend to persist for a while, and since they dispose us to react to situations in characteristic ways, we can expect her to react more favorably to the game than were she now in a bad mood.

It is *possible* to make similar sorts of predictions using hedonistic happiness, but these will be much weaker and more indirect than of those available on an emotional state conception. Thus a predominance of pleasure might weakly predict future agreeability via the role of pleasure in causing positive mood states, or via its status as an indicator of positive mood states. But this is obviously inferior to more direct appeals to the states doing the real work. Indeed, the intuitively correct thing to say about the role of pleasure in this regard is that, in the former case, *one's pleasant experience explains why one is happy*, and in the latter case, *one's being happy explains why one's experience has been pleasant*. Happiness and pleasure appear to stand in a relationship not of reduction, but of mutual explanation. Hedonism obscures this relationship and thus obliterates two perfectly ordinary and seemingly useful forms of explanation. It is not at all clear what, if anything, we would gain in predictive and explanatory power by accepting hedonism over its rivals. By fixing on a state without sufficient causal depth, hedonism not only loses plausibility as a theory of happiness; its errors rob the notion of happiness of much of its usefulness.

6.3. The hedonic value of emotional state happiness

Our emotional states have extremely far-reaching consequences for the character of our lives: how we react to the world, even how we perceive things. They also appear to comprise the single most important *determinant* of our hedonic states. If someone's mood is generally positive and her frame of mind relatively serene, then one wonders how her experience could fail to be largely pleasant. Perhaps she stoically endures chronic and serious pain, but to maintain a truly placid and sunny disposition under such circumstances would require emotional resources not readily summoned for most people. And then we might reasonably suppose that her experience really *is* pleasant all things considered: though she hardly likes the pain, she pays it little heed. (Notice that we would in any event take her to be happy.) Knowledge of someone's emotional state confers substantial warrant for conclusions about the basic character of her hedonic state. And this is not based simply on the causal powers of mood states, but also on the fact that they are themselves deeply pleasant (or unpleasant).

6.4. The role of happiness in practical deliberation and evaluation

One might still think hedonistic happiness more important for purposes of deliberation: what should concern agents when making decisions is less how various options will impact on their emotional states or attitudes toward their lives. What matters is how the options will affect their *hedonic* states. From a deliberative standpoint, it would appear that hedonistic happiness is still more important than happiness as construed by the other theories. Perhaps this is true for some deliberative circumstances. When deciding whether or not to spring for a massage, it seems odd to puzzle over whether it will be fulfilling emotionally, or whether it will make me more satisfied with my life. The real question is whether it will feel good. (On the other hand, it seems more than a little eccentric to fret about whether it will make me *happier*. Which seems like yet another reason to doubt that hedonism offers a credible reconstruction of happiness.)

It is questionable, however, whether the hedonistic notion is more useful for *all* important deliberative situations, especially the ones in which it is natural to consider questions of happiness. These appear mostly to involve issues with far-reaching implications for the quality of our lives. When deciding on whether to take up or abandon a vocation, for instance, we often consider whether we will be happier in that vocation or some alternative. On the hedonistic theory, this amounts to asking which profession would bring the most favorable balance of pleasure over unpleasure. Relative to the alternative theories, is this the most sensible question to ask? It isn't a bad question, but there are reasons for thinking that one may actually be better off asking the emotional state question: which vocation would make me happier according to the emotional state theory? For it is plausible that the better option with respect to the emotional state question will almost invariably be the better option with respect to the hedonic question, and vice versa. If so, then the real issue between them becomes: *which question is easier to answer correctly?* I would suggest that the emotional state question is. The range of pleasures and unpleasures that might result from a career choice is extremely broad and diverse, including innumerable physical, intellectual, and emotional pleasures. Trying to get a grip on one's prospects with respect to these all at once does not seem a simple task in the least. It would hardly be surprising if we tended to overlook or incorrectly weight many of the more important pleasures. But if the emotional state theory takes something like the form discussed earlier, then the relevant states in its case are essentially the class of mood states, broadly construed. Though itself somewhat diverse, this is clearly a narrower and more tractable range of concerns: how will I do with respect to emotional fulfillment, peace of mind, good cheer, high spirits, and perhaps a few other things (which are, no doubt, mostly highly correlated with each other)?

The more limited focus is helpful when the options before us are complex and affect our well-being in a broad variety of ways. This is likely to be the case for any of the most important decisions we make in life, at least where well-being—our own or that of others—is a significant consideration. Indeed, it is plausibly the case with respect to most or all of the circumstances in which we ordinarily appeal to questions of happiness. Emotional state happiness appears, in short, to be what we might call a relatively *efficient* good: it packs a lot of value into a relatively compact, epistemically manageable package.

There are, then, good reasons for thinking that emotional state happiness may actually be more important from the (relevant) standpoint of practical deliberation than hedonistic happiness. If so, then the emotional state notion may well deserve a central place in deliberation, as well as ethical inquiry, *whether or not it deserves to be called happiness*. It certainly is not at all clear that the hedonistic notion ought to occupy a more distinguished position in the pantheon of deliberative goals. Similar points should apply in the case of evaluation: the considerations favoring emotional state happiness as a deliberative good should make it similarly useful for assessing how well individuals are doing: there is less to evaluate, with little loss in value.

It is useful in this connection to note an analogy between the notions of happiness and health, as well as the way we assess the conditions of complex items like cars. (We do, notice, speak freely of the importance of being both "happy and healthy," suggesting that the terms involve similar types of evaluations.) A person's health is not simply the integral of her health-related events over time. It includes those, or some of them at any rate. But it depends mainly on the person's *condition*, her *disposition* in matters of health. It counts against a person's health that she has a massive plaque in one of her arteries poised to break off and cause a fatal stroke or heart attack. Similarly, someone looking to buy a used car, wanting to know its condition, will care about how it runs and looks. But he will also want to know the disposition of the vehicle: can it be relied on to keep running? A car that runs great, but only because a cracked engine block was hastily patched up, is not in great condition: it is liable to die, and soon.[22]

Our concern with how happy a person is similar, it seems to me, to our concerns in these cases: we are interested not mainly in what experiences have been passing through her head lately, but in her basic psychological disposition. (This is not to say that occurrent psychological processes don't matter; for one thing, one's psychic disposition at any given moment will depend substantially on what processes are currently going on, such as her mood.) If we want to know how someone is really doing, we can often do no better than to find out how things are sitting with her at the deepest level.

7. CONCLUSION

A final point: if the account of well-being sketched in Part III proves correct, then emotional state happiness serves as a central constituent of well-being. This of course would lend still more support to the emotional state view and further weaken the appeal of hedonism.

One wonders how so many theorists could have gotten things so seriously wrong. There are probably a variety of reasons for this, but I will mention just two. Most importantly, the hedonistic notion *is* theoretically important. Nothing I have said thus far precludes a hedonistic account of well-being; my target has been hedonism about *happiness*. Hedonistic Utilitarians need not change the substance of their theories on the basis of the arguments given here; they need only grant that their views are not about happiness, in the psychological sense that concerns this book. Their Utilitarianism concerns not happiness, but pleasure. Second, the ambiguity of 'happiness' may have led many theorists astray. Given that it has a prudential sense in addition to the psychological one, and given that many people have found welfare hedonism to be plausible, then we should hardly be surprised if some confusion has resulted. For if 'happiness' just *means* a high state of well-being, and if welfare hedonism is correct, then there is indeed a sense in which happiness is hedonistic: happiness consists in having a predominantly positive hedonic state. But this is not the sense of 'happiness' that concerns us here. Rather, it is the sense in which an Aristotelian would reply that happiness consists in the attainment of human excellence. The current chapter is not in the business of attempting to settle this claim.

5

Life Satisfaction

Tell them I've had a wonderful life.

Wittgenstein

It was a glorious experience.

Moreese Bickham, on his 37 years in a Louisiana prison[1]

1. INTRODUCTION

For as long as anyone can remember, the message from on high was generally some form of "You'll eat it and you'll like it." Or, like Job, you won't. As far as the authorities were concerned, it didn't much matter whether you liked it. The sages who advised us in the betterment of life accordingly tended to focus their efforts on how to bring ourselves to like, or at least stomach, the fetid stew that so often got heaped on our plates. Not so in the age of consumer sovereignty, where the grim creed of yore has slowly given way to a perkier theology of "How may I help you?" The authorities whom we once served now serve us—or so we are told—and our rapidly proliferating needs. Not even college professors can claim immunity to the imperatives of customer satisfaction, many of us having learned from forward-thinking administrators that our job is not to produce an enlightened citizenry but to satisfy our choosy young customers.

In such a society we might naturally expect the *summum bonum* to be the ultimate satisfied customer, the person who is satisfied with her *life*. And indeed, few things are likely to strike the contemporary reader as more platitudinous than that it matters whether people are satisfied with their lives. Some say that this is basically *all* that matters. So entrenched are such notions that consumerism's friends and foes alike tend to embrace them—though it is probably no accident that the historical literature, particularly in the premodern era, appears to place little stock in the idea of life satisfaction. Thus we find many philosophers, including Robert Nozick and L. W. Sumner, taking something as important as happiness to consist largely or wholly in being satisfied with one's life. Sumner goes further, placing life satisfaction at the center of his account of well-being as "authentic happiness": being happy, where one's happiness is solidly grounded both in reality and in values that are truly one's own; deceived experience machine users and brainwashing victims thus don't count as flourishing. The plausibility of this theory hinges on the conception of happiness Sumner employs: a view of happiness as a composite of life satisfaction and pleasure that embodies the agent's overall evaluation of her life. The life satisfaction component of this theory clearly gets the most weight, so that Sumner refers to it as a "life satisfaction" theory of happiness. Other philosophers, like Robert Almeder, go further still, literally identifying well-being with life satisfaction.[2] And in the burgeoning science of subjective well-being, life satisfaction surveys occupy a, perhaps *the*, starring role. Here too we often find 'life satisfaction' used interchangeably with 'happiness'.

Life satisfaction is indeed important, and measures of life satisfaction, or related measures, should remain a major part of research on quality of life. But I want to argue that life satisfaction matters less, and for different reasons, than we tend to think. This along with intuitive considerations makes deeply problematical the attempts to identify happiness with life satisfaction. I will not deny that ordinary talk sometimes employs 'happiness' to denote states of life satisfaction; my point, rather, will be that life satisfaction cannot answer to our practical interests in happiness, so that life satisfaction theories will have misleading and deflationary implications for the significance of happiness. In short, such theories clash with the "utility" requirement discussed in Chapter 3, particularly the idea that happiness could serve as a rough proxy for well-being. At any rate, even the descriptive adequacy of life satisfaction accounts is limited: such views clash with important intuitions about happiness.

My case will center on three arguments. After discussing the putative nature and significance of life satisfaction, I will argue, first, that cases of "cognitive-affective divergence" generate serious counterexamples to the most common sorts of life satisfaction views. Second, there is some reason to doubt whether, as a matter of empirical fact, people actually have attitudes toward their lives that are both robust enough and well-enough grounded in the facts of their lives to have the kind of significance happiness is thought to possess. Third, and most importantly, the idea that life satisfaction should be central to well-being reflects a fundamental misunderstanding about the character of such attitudes. For life satisfaction attitudes are governed by norms that greatly complicate the proper relationship between life satisfaction and well-being. As a result, even people whose lives are going badly for them, by their own lights, can reasonably register high levels of satisfaction with their lives. Such considerations indicate that life satisfaction tracks well-being far less than happiness is thought to, and thus runs afoul of the utility requirement (Chapter 3).

While life satisfaction theories of happiness constitute the chief target of this chapter, our discussion will have a broader and perhaps more important implication: that individuals' judgments about their own lives do not bear anything like the kind of authority that common opinion takes them to. We tend to think that people have more or less well-defined attitudes regarding how their lives are going for them, and as long as they are satisfied with their lives, then they are probably doing well. Perhaps individuals sometimes lack important information about their lives, are self-deceived, mentally ill, or drugged. For the most part we have a pretty good grip on how things are in our lives, and are not impaired in our judgment, and so our verdicts about our own lives should normally be taken as final.[3] If people are satisfied with their lives, then their lives probably are indeed going well for them. This attractive line of thought yields an uplifting conclusion when taken together with empirical studies of life satisfaction, which suggest that the majority of people, in most societies, are indeed satisfied with their lives. For instance, studies usually find at least 80 percent of Americans reporting positive satisfaction with their lives, and often 10 percent or fewer dissatisfied.[4] (Self-reports of *happiness* tend to be even higher; see Chapter 10.) And while some populations tend to report dissatisfaction with their lives, those are in the minority: notably, people living in highly distressed former Eastern Bloc nations, Americans who are homeless or prostitutes, and similarly extreme samples. In an extremely diverse range of societies, and even among very poor people like slum-dwellers in Calcutta, majorities register positive life satisfaction.[5] Which means, on the usual view of life satisfaction and well-being, that most people, in most societies, are doing pretty well. What were the ancients complaining about?

Philosophers and other intellectuals frequently respond to such findings with what can only be described as contempt. (Rare, however, is the curmudgeon prepared to gainsay Wittgenstein's striking claim to have had a wonderful life.) In what follows I will suggest a more charitable interpretation: that most people have good *reason* to be satisfied with their lives. The mistake is in thinking that this tells us much about their well-being. The mistake is an important one: it not only risks leading us to overly optimistic verdicts about people's welfare, it can encourage the trivialization of thought about well-being. If people's opinions about their lives are normally final, settling the question of their well-being, then there may be little to discuss.

Because no author's views are representative of the genre, and most existing accounts are a bit obscure in one way or another, I will focus less on particular authors and more on what I take to be the strongest possible variants of the life satisfaction theory.

2. WHAT LIFE SATISFACTION IS AND WHY IT IS SUPPOSED TO MATTER

Life satisfaction admits of many definitions, so that any critique is liable to meet objections that what it addresses isn't "really" life satisfaction. We must begin, then, by identifying the target notion and considering why this is the right target.

(I will briefly discuss alternative formulations later.) As a first approximation we may define life satisfaction as having a favorable attitude toward one's life as a whole, either at the present time or over some arbitrarily extended duration. (This is very different from the condition of *desire* satisfaction, the focus of desire theories of well-being. Desire satisfaction is not a mental state, but the condition of things actually being the way you want them to.) Opinions vary about the precise nature of this attitude, but typically it is seen as somehow embodying a *global judgment* about one's life taken as a whole: that, all things considered, one's life is satisfactory. Central to life satisfaction for Sumner, for instance, is "a positive evaluation of the conditions of your life, a judgment that, at least on balance, it measures up favorably against your standards or expectations."[6] And a representative example of the scales employed by researchers, for example, asks respondents: "All things considered, how satisfied are you with your life as a whole now...?" (From 1, "dissatisfied," to 10, "satisfied."). Another instrument, Andrews and Withey's Delighted-Terrible scale, asks: "How do you feel about your life as a whole...?" (From 1, "terrible," to 7, "delighted.").[7] The global evaluation embodied in life satisfaction attitudes is important, for reasons to be examined momentarily; hence these questions are distinguished from more specific questions about subjects' satisfaction with particular domains of their lives (work, family, etc.).[8] As well, life satisfaction is probably not merely a plain-vanilla judgment about one's life: we cannot, it seems, reduce it to the bare judgment or belief that one's life is going well, or to perceived welfare. For it is widely thought to involve *affirming, endorsing, appreciating,* or being *pleased* with one's life.[9]

There are several reasons why this might matter. First, thinking your life is going well is one thing, and thinking it is going well *enough* quite another. Some people aren't satisfied with merely good lives. Second, a mere belief lacks weight: it is too thin and intellectualized. When you give someone a gift, you don't just want him to think it a good specimen. You want him to *like* it. Similarly, it seems important for us to appreciate our lives, perhaps because it is a way of being wholehearted in our assessments of our lives. Life satisfaction requires being *satisfied*, not just thinking things satisfactory. A third, related point: being satisfied has motivational implications, at least tempering inclinations to seek major changes in where your life is headed.

Life satisfaction is clearly believed by most to be important. Even among those who do not explicitly identify happiness with life satisfaction, there appears to be a broad consensus that life satisfaction is centrally important for human welfare. Expressions of serious doubt about its significance are few and far between. Still less do we find such doubts among those who do identify happiness with life satisfaction. As we saw in Chapter 3, happiness is generally thought at least to be central to well-being. Indeed, in ordinary practical reasoning we treat it as so closely aligned with well-being that, for the most part, we can use it as a stand-in for well-being. While this practice may ultimately prove misguided, there is no reason to think that those tending to identify happiness with life satisfaction would be inclined to challenge it.

The next question is why life satisfaction is supposed to be so important. Its value is partly hedonic, but this fails to account for why life satisfaction seems distinctively significant. We seem to care about life satisfaction mainly as an *evaluation*: as an ostensibly authoritative verdict on the overall quality of one's life. It seems important whether our lives go well by our standards, and what better measure of this than our own judgments? Note that life satisfaction and pleasure can diverge quite radically, and in fact this is part of life satisfaction's appeal: even dysthymic philosophers could be satisfied with their lives, and thus perhaps achieve a measure of well-being, insofar as they see their pursuits as worthwhile and value such things more than pleasure. Conversely, small-town residents might sometimes be dissatisfied with their lives, longing for the fast life of the city, despite having favorable emotional conditions and leading pleasant lives. This sort of dissatisfaction seems important, at least partly because of what it tells us about how individuals' lives measure up in relation to their own priorities.

The global nature of life satisfaction attitudes also contributes to their appeal: they provide a holistic perspective on our lives, in sharp contrast with the hedonistic reduction of happiness to the mere aggregate of many moments. What matters to us, arguably, is not just having a plurality of good moments, but having a good *life*. And we see our lives as more than just the sum of their parts.[10] Thus the pains suffered in boot camp, or in pursuit of some other achievement, might be seen as a good thing in the context of one's life as a whole. They will at least take on a different significance from the pains considered in isolation, as mere pains.

Having granted the *significance* of life satisfaction as an evaluation, we might ask why such attitudes should be considered *valuable* in themselves, the way happiness seems to be. Offhand it may seem that the value resides, not in the individual's evaluation of her life, but in actually having a satisfactory life. This could be a weighty objection to life satisfaction views. In reply, it could be argued that life satisfaction attitudes are valuable because pleasant, or because of their motivational implications, but neither proposal does justice to the idea that life satisfaction is valuable the way happiness is, and that its value is importantly distinct from the value of pleasure. A better reply would be to say something along the lines of Sumner's view of well-being as (roughly) "authentic life satisfaction," claiming for instance that life satisfaction matters as an essential component of the state of affairs of *leading a life with which one is satisfied*. This suggestion has sufficient plausibility that I will assume henceforth that life satisfaction theorists can tell a prima facie credible story about life satisfaction's value.

3. COGNITIVE-AFFECTIVE DIVERGENCE AND ATTITUDE SCARCITY

Before addressing questions of importance I want to note a difficulty regarding the descriptive adequacy of life satisfaction views. For the life satisfaction theory generates seemingly fatal counterexamples in which life satisfaction and emotional state sharply diverge. On the most natural reading of the view, it is perfectly possible for someone to be satisfied with her life even though she is depressed or otherwise emotionally a shambles. Indeed, this possibility would seem to be an *attraction* to many: the tortured artist might think emotional matters unimportant, or even that it is good to be depressed, and thus be satisfied with her life. Her life is going well by her lights, as she is getting and doing what matters to her. Be that as it may, it is deeply counterintuitive to regard such an individual as being *happy*.[11] This sort of person rejects happiness. Perhaps we can say that she is happy "with" her life, or even that "in some sense" she is happy, but to ascribe happiness without such qualifiers seems perverse. Similarly, someone might be dissatisfied with his life yet not, intuitively, unhappy: perhaps he regrets that he has to live and raise his family in a materialistic society that makes it nearly impossible to live the way he would like to, and thus is dissatisfied with his life. Yet he does not dwell on his dissatisfaction, and for the most part is untroubled, in pretty good spirits, and finds plenty of fulfillment in his work and family. Or, alternatively, match this sort of emotional profile with an inveterate kvetch who rarely leaves Manhattan, and whose favorite sport is complaining. Rarely satisfied with anything, and certainly not with his life, he nonetheless might seem to be happy; at least, it may seem odd to regard him as unhappy.

Such cases may not be the norm, but they probably are not merely the stuff of fiction. While research instruments in this area are still a bit crude, affect and reported life satisfaction are, to be sure, thought to correlate fairly strongly in Western societies. But not so strongly that they cannot diverge significantly. Toward the high end, one study found that daily reports of mood correlated at about 0.66 with reports of life satisfaction using the Delighted-Terrible scale.[12] Reports show much weaker correlations in some other cultures. For instance, Suh et al. found in one cross-national study that the correlation of life satisfaction with positive affect ranged from .09 (India) to .45 (West Germany), and that with negative affect ranged from −.11 (Nigeria) to −.42 (Finland).[13] A second study found *no* significant correlation with negative affect in some "collectivist" countries such as China. But even the stronger correlations found in Western societies are consistent with substantial divergence. For example, one interesting pair of studies found that 42 to 49 percent of those rating themselves as "completely satisfied" also reported significant symptoms of anxiety and related forms of distress.[14] And *6 to 7 percent of the completely satisfied reported that they were "usually unhappy or depressed."*

Cases of severe cognitive-affective divergence point to a secondary, substantive worry we might have about life satisfaction theories: whether attitudes of life satisfaction have a sufficiently strong and broad psychological impact to have the sort of importance we expect happiness to have. Ordinarily, we tend to think that it makes a big difference in a person's mental life whether she is happy or not. While life satisfaction clearly can make a very big difference of that sort, it is not clear that it always does. (Recall the above example of dissatisfaction with life in a materialistic society.) Consider that we often make judgments about how happy or unhappy a person is based simply on observing the individual's expressions, body language, and overall demeanor; this practice presumably reflects a belief that happiness's psychic impact is deep and pervasive. Whereas simply from observing someone over a brief interval it seems harder to tell anything about his attitude toward his life. Life satisfaction seems not to have the kind of psychological significance that happiness is thought to possess.

Proponents of life satisfaction accounts may object that I am construing the relevant attitudes too narrowly. Theodore Benditt, for instance, has argued that to be happy is just to be disposed to *feel* satisfied with one's life when contemplating it.[15] Supporters of such a view might argue that serious divergence will be extremely rare or nonexistent with this kind of satisfaction. The sorts of divergence documented here thus don't count: for the judgments of "life satisfaction" in cases of divergence don't involve the right sort of feeling; they are too intellectualized to count, lacking in wholeheartedness. This move is psychologically implausible: why couldn't a somewhat depressed individual, or a suffering artist, sincerely feel good about his life while contemplating it? Even if such cases were not psychologically possible, they are readily conceivable, which should be problem enough.

The life satisfaction theorist might avoid such worries by stipulating a very strong convergence between attitude and emotional state: happiness as a broad, ongoing sense of well-being. Here the attitude of life satisfaction is not merely wholehearted; it more or less encompasses one's whole emotional state. A problem with this strategy—shared to a lesser extent by Benditt's approach—is that "thick" attitudes of this sort appear to be pretty scarce: while we are sometimes in such states, we usually are not. That is, we typically seem not to have broad feelings of satisfaction *or* dissatisfaction with our lives, to any degree.

This is a problem because happiness is supposed, like pleasure, to be a dimension along which human well-being continually varies: each of us is somewhere on the scale between extreme happiness and unhappiness, and each of us could be more or less happy or unhappy than we presently are. Other things being equal, we try to make choices in life that will leave us happier, while avoiding options that will make us less happy. This is important: if it turns out that we usually aren't anywhere on the scale, because the relevant mental states aren't defined most of the time, then few choices will have any meaningful effect on our happiness. And any effects will be as fleeting as the attitudes themselves. Why, then, concern ourselves so much with happiness? The present proposal appears to have just this result: while sometimes we do have broad feelings of being satisfied or dissatisfied with our lives, such moments appear to be short-lived, mostly occurring when we are unusually reflective. We would probably do well not to make feelings of this sort a central focus of concern when thinking about matters of well-being.

Similar problems of *attitude scarcity* are liable to arise on any view that imposes lavish psychological requirements on attitudes of satisfaction and dissatisfaction: the more it takes to have the requisite attitudes, the less often they will arise, and the less we will be able to assess outcomes in relation to life (dis-)satisfaction. Contrast hedonism: all of us are on the happiness scale at every waking moment, for our experience always has some hedonic character. Every instant we are conscious can thus be assessed in terms of happiness. Not so for (at least) the more demanding forms of life satisfaction. We will see in the next section that attitude scarcity may be a problem even for more modest forms of life satisfaction.

4. ATTITUDE INSTABILITY

The second major worry facing life satisfaction accounts of happiness concerns certain empirical assumptions that underwrite traditional views of life satisfaction's significance. If you think life satisfaction important in something like the conventional manner, then you are probably assuming, as we just saw, that people usually *have* such attitudes—positive, neutral, or negative—toward their lives; that these attitudes tend to be reasonably *well-grounded* in what they take to be the important facts about their lives; and third, that they are fairly *stable,* varying mainly with changes in how individuals' lives are going, and not flighty or fickle. The first assumption is required to avoid attitude scarcity problems, while we need the second and third to ensure that the attitudes have genuine weight as evaluations. Fickle evaluations with little grounding in any important reality are not to be taken seriously.

These assumptions are neither weak nor obviously correct. Suppose that most individuals normally had stable and well-grounded attitudes. If this were the case, then we would expect people to base their reports of life satisfaction on these attitudes. If you ask people how satisfied they are with their lives, they will typically answer by reporting on how they in fact feel about their lives—an easy task. Someone with a determinate attitude presumably will not find herself at sea, or have to work out an answer from scratch, when asked about life satisfaction. She need not have expressly thought about it beforehand, but she won't normally have to construct something on the spot. Moreover, the answer she gives will be reasonably stable and robust, not prone to alter much from one moment to the next. Consider those occasions when we almost certainly do possess attitudes like this, most clearly when we step back and take stock of our lives, feeling firmly that our lives have, or have not, come up to our standards. Deathbed reflections would be a paradigm of this, and it is plausible that the judgments we reach at such times tend to carry a certain authority. At such times, responding to questions about life satisfaction is a trivial matter: just tell them what's on your mind. Similarly, if you ask people what the capital of their nation is, most will simply report what they believe. And in both cases the answers should be fairly robust, not varying significantly with trivial changes in context. This, at least, is what we would expect.

There is some evidence that people usually do not have attitudes fitting this description. In particular, a number of studies suggest that self-reports of life satisfaction are highly sensitive to transient contextual factors, raising doubts about their provenance.[16] These studies find that various particulars of the context in which self-reports are elicited affect the information that is most accessible, as well as subjects' moods. For instance, finding a dime or being given a candy bar shortly prior to questioning can significantly influence people's appraisals of their lives. Similarly, a sunny versus rainy day, a major victory for the local sports franchise, or a somewhat unpleasant testing room can all make substantial differences in how people judge the quality of their lives as a whole—in the case of weather, an average of two points on a ten-point scale. And in one survey of undergraduates, students' reported life satisfaction was unrelated to the reported frequency with which they date.[17] This is surprising, since it seems as though they think of little else. If, however, students are asked about dating frequency *before* the life satisfaction question—raising the accessibility of that information—the correlation rises dramatically, from −.12 to .66. Some aspects of context can have a major impact on life assessments by changing the standards we use. Judgments made in the presence of a handicapped confederate who is not privy to one's response, for example, will be higher than those made in a neutral context: the perceived misfortune of the confederate causes subjects to rate themselves as quite fortunate by comparison. The same effect occurs if questioning takes place after subjects hear a description of past hardships endured by members of their hometowns.[18]

Schwarz and Strack propose the following explanation of these phenomena: reports of life satisfaction are not reports of previously established attitudes but reflect, rather, *judgments* made at the time of questioning. These judgments are "best considered constructions in response to particular questions posed at a particular time."[19] Most often, according to Schwarz and Strack, we consider how we feel at the moment and base our judgment on that. If our current affect is discredited, or if our present affect is mild and other information seems more salient, then we are likely to use a "comparison strategy": use this other information, along with whatever standard of comparison seems most natural at the moment.[20] Such strategies would naturally leave life satisfaction reports subject to influence by trivial factors.

As a result of this sensitivity to context, reports of life satisfaction are said to exhibit low test-retest reliabilities, with responses at the beginning and end of a one-hour interview reputedly correlating at only .40 to .60.[21] In short, this research suggests that reports of life satisfaction are fairly labile. Doubts of this nature have prompted much concern about the utility of life satisfaction research. Schwarz and Strack themselves conclude that "life satisfaction judgments seem too context-dependent to provide reliable information about a population's well-being."[22] And Daniel Kahneman has drawn on these results to press for a shift of resources toward hedonic measures of well-being, notably experience sampling studies, which acquire multiple reports of current affect from each respondent over an extended period of time.[23]

Suppose Schwarz and Strack are correct in their assessment of life satisfaction reports. What would this show about the significance of life satisfaction attitudes? Two possibilities present themselves. First, we might conclude that most of the time, people simply do not *have* the relevant attitudes toward their lives. Usually, there is no fact of the matter about whether, and to what extent, people are satisfied with their lives. Not even roughly, for the concept of life satisfaction does not apply to them. When asked, they have to come to a verdict about their lives, for there is no existing attitude to report on. If this is correct, then we have a serious attitude scarcity problem. This reading of the situation has some plausibility quite apart from the empirical research: when you think about the people you know, is it obvious that most of them are definitely satisfied with their lives, or dissatisfied, or somewhere in between? It is not far-fetched to suppose that people typically do not keep a running ledger of how things are going in their lives.

A second interpretation of the research takes a more liberal approach toward attitude ascription, allowing that someone has an attitude toward something whenever he is willing to offer a sincere judgment about it. Such a policy would yield the result that nearly all persons are somewhere on the life satisfaction scale, since almost everyone gives an answer to life satisfaction questions in survey research, and there is no reason to doubt the sincerity of most such reports. Hence, no attitude scarcity problem. Suppose we grant that people normally do have attitudes toward their lives, even if they have to make a judgment when asked about the matter, then what follows? The natural question is whether such attitudes could be all that important. If Schwarz and Strack are correct, then most people's attitudes toward their lives are unstable and context-sensitive, literally varying with the weather. This would suggest that those attitudes are both *poorly grounded* and more or less *causally inert*. Taking the second point first: if life satisfaction attitudes normally exist only in the anemic sense of being dispositions to form judgments of certain sorts—and highly fickle dispositions at that—it is not clear how much difference they could make in the individual's psychic economy. On such a view, one's being satisfied with one's life would make little if any difference in one's ordinary mental life. This would be an odd result for an account of happiness, since—as we saw in Section 3—we tend to think that it usually makes a massive difference in one's mental life whether one is happy or not. This is not just an intuition: it is substantially why we care about happiness. (Recall also the discussion of happiness's "causal depth" in Chapter 4.) On the present suppositions, however, happiness would not have much of a psychological impact in most cases.

An equally serious worry is that labile attitudes seem not to carry much weight *as evaluations*. If your being satisfied with your life depends substantially on things like finding a dime, then either your attitude is a dubious guide to how things are actually going for you or you are truly eccentric. I once heard a researcher relate a story about his teenage daughter, who reported being very dissatisfied with her life. This was, she explained, because they lacked cable television. Children have been known to think about their lives in silly or obtuse ways, which is why we often don't much care whether they are satisfied with things. If Schwarz and Strack are right, the questionable judgment may not cease with the onset of adulthood.

Summing up: if Schwarz and Strack's account of life satisfaction reports is correct, then life satisfaction attitudes are either too scarce or too poorly grounded and insubstantial to possess anything like the significance happiness is thought to have. Our deep and abiding practical interest in happiness would not make much sense on such a view.

However, the problems may not be as severe as they make out. Some recent work has called their stronger conclusions into question, with some results suggesting that transient factors play a smaller role in life satisfaction reports, that information about important life domains (like family) plays a larger role, and that test-retest reliabilities are higher than Schwarz and Strack found.[24] Notably, Schimmack and Oishi were unable to replicate the "dating study" results, their own study finding no evidence of a significant question-order effect and a strong .40 correlation between life satisfaction and dating frequency.[25] At the same time, Schwarz and Strack's basic "judgment model" of life satisfaction seems not to be in dispute: it appears to be granted that life satisfaction reports reflect judgments made at the time of questioning. And the existence of significant instability in self-reports seems to be well established. The empirical debate concerns whether the context sensitivity is severe enough to undercut the informational value of life satisfaction reports in research on well-being.

This is not the place to settle that debate, but it does seem plausible that life satisfaction measures yield important information about well-being despite the objections raised by Schwarz and Strack. Besides the more recent findings just noted, the context sensitivities may well wash out over large groups of individuals; there is little reason to think that context effects will systematically skew results in one direction or the other. Moreover, self-reports correlate somewhat strongly with other relevant quantities such as reports of affect—and significantly, life satisfaction reports correlate strongly with reported satisfaction with specific domains that people tend to consider important. They do, on average, appear to be substantially grounded in important facts, or at least to correlate well with them. At least within cultures, it is plausible that people reporting higher levels of satisfaction will tend, usually, to be better off than those who do not.[26]

But our concern is not with the use of life satisfaction reports to gain information about people's well-being; it is with life satisfaction theories of happiness. And the challenges to Schwarz and Strack's position do not eliminate the worries I have raised, for several reasons. First, the judgment model of life satisfaction reports, which seems to be granted by all, leaves basically intact the dilemma I noted above: if reports reflect judgments constructed at the time of questioning rather than ongoing attitudes, then either life satisfaction attitudes aren't defined most of the time, or those attitudes are too causally inert to have the sort of impact on our lives that happiness seems to. What life satisfaction researchers claim, *contra* Schwarz and Strack, is that those *judgments*, when elicited, are well grounded in important facts. They may not be fickle, but they may still be insubstantial or non-existent most of the time. Second, there still appears to be a significant effect of context on reported life satisfaction, even if it proves less severe than feared. We may wonder whether evaluations like that are sufficiently robust, carrying enough authority, to have the kind of importance we normally ascribe to happiness. Third, the fact that judgments are consistent over the long term may reflect only that we have consistent methods of fabricating them. We might base them on information that tends to be consistent over time, such as immediate affect. Or we might use consistent rules—for example, "Barring obvious problems or good fortune, always conclude 'pretty satisfied.'" Consistency is not stability. If, say, subjects base their judgments on their immediate affective states, and these states tend to be consistent over time—say, because they are related to temperament—we should expect this kind of consistency even if no attitudes exist. The short-term (e.g., one hour) test-retest reliabilities reported by Schwarz and Strack, taken within the setting of a single interview, are particularly salient here, because they tease out information about the stability and robustness of persons' attitudes, not just their consistency over time. What they suggest is that even a little reflection can easily alter people's reports, raising doubts about their authority. Fourth, it is possible that the correlations between life satisfaction and domain satisfactions to some extent reflect common influences other than the judicious use of domain information to arrive at a life satisfaction judgment. Perhaps both domain and whole life judgments are constructed using similar heuristics, or maybe both strongly reflect the influence of affect—for instance, with people who feel good generally tending to view things in more positive terms.[27] So the life satisfaction reports may correlate well with the right information without being well grounded as evaluations.

Finally, we might conclude that people usually have stable and well-grounded life satisfaction attitudes, but still do not have them *often enough* to meet the requirements of a life satisfaction theory of happiness. Suppose it turns out that one-third of the time, people have no attitude toward their lives: they aren't on the scale at all. It would be surprising, to say the least, to find that people's conditions can only be assessed in terms of happiness about two-thirds of the time, for the rest of the time they are neither happy, unhappy, nor anywhere in between. Alternatively, suppose that one-third of the time people's attitudes toward their lives are so fickle or poorly grounded that, like the teenager pining for cable TV, their evaluations cannot be taken seriously, having little to do with their well-being. Again, it would be odd to say that about a third of the time, it really doesn't matter if people are happy or not.

The points of the last paragraph bear emphasis: given that we tend to employ happiness as a proxy for well-being, a life satisfaction theory of happiness will need to make very strong claims about the prevalence and grounding of life satisfaction attitudes in the general population to avoid highly revisionary and deflationary implications for the significance of happiness. Just being good enough for empirical research on well-being—which hardly needs to be exacting to give us better information than traditional indicators of welfare, like money—is not good enough for a theory of happiness. Think again about paradigm stock-taking moments, like deathbed reflections, where we think long and hard about how well our lives measure up. The verdicts issuing from those deliberations do indeed seem to carry a lot of significance. A problem for life satisfaction theories of happiness is that they appear to assume, implausibly, that people maintain attitudes bearing this kind of weight at all times. Often, when taking stock, what we realize is precisely that our day-to-day ways of thinking about our lives are seriously deficient, in our own terms. Caught up in the hurly-burly of our daily routines, frequently we lose perspective and forget what really matters to us. It is doubtful, at such times, that we maintain attitudes toward our lives that embody those forgotten values.

5. ATTITUDINAL NORMS

Just being alive, having a wonderful family, good friends, watching the sunrise morning after morning—that's what makes me feel good. I think people take their lives for granted. Some just haven't hit that part of their lives where they stop and say, "I am such a lucky person to have the life that I have."

Sgt. Michael A. DiRaimondo, in a letter home from Iraq[28]

5.1. Life satisfaction's norms

We do not know what Sergeant DiRaimondo thought of his life beyond what his letter reveals. But it is not hard to imagine him expressing great satisfaction with his life, warts and all. Neither is it difficult to picture him judging that his life was not going well for him. He was, after all, in the middle of a disastrous and horrific war that would soon cost him his life. The important point, however, is this: he could quite reasonably have been satisfied with his life even when his life, according to his own priorities, was not going at all well for him.[29] And not just reasonably, but perhaps admirably. The fact that such cases are possible comprises part of what may be the gravest difficulty facing life satisfaction accounts of happiness: life satisfaction attitudes are governed by norms that make systematic, often radical, deviations from well-being—by *any* sane measure—both expectable and utterly reasonable.[30] You might, for instance, be satisfied with your life, not because you think things are going well for you, but because that seems to you the most fitting or appropriate way to respond to the life you have. Even the deathbed reflections of a sage are not exempt.

One need not be a subjectivist about welfare to think life satisfaction important. But in this section I will assume that some strong form of subjectivism about well-being is correct: what counts toward an individual's well-being is fixed solely by what she likes or cares about. *I will not assume any kind of objectivism.* We will address life satisfaction where its appeal is strongest.

Granting the subjectivity of welfare does not mean that anything goes when it comes to life satisfaction. As we saw in the last section, even the most ardent subjectivist will want to grant that there's something wrong with someone who views her life favorably on plainly irrelevant grounds, say because three is a prime number. At a bare minimum, our attitudes toward our lives should reflect our priorities and our experience of life. We just saw some reasons for doubting how far these conditions are actually met, but I will assume in what follows that people's attitudes toward their lives do meet them.

Life satisfaction attitudes are governed by norms: they can be more or less reasonable. Call the norms by which to assess life satisfaction attitudes as more or less reasonable *attitudinal norms.*[31] Attitudinal norms include *epistemic norms* such as those just mentioned, according to which attitudes must reflect the facts (in this case, the facts about what we want or care about, along with the facts or appearances about what happens in our lives). No one should be troubled by the fact that epistemic norms like these govern life satisfaction attitudes. If these were the only norms appropriate to life satisfaction attitudes, one might reasonably expect them to track closely, or even be definitive of, human welfare (setting aside other worries I've raised). But they are not: life satisfaction attitudes are not simple assessments of well-being, or otherwise evaluations of a sort that are supposed to correspond straightforwardly to well-being. For they crucially have an ethical dimension: our attitudes toward our lives reflect on our characters, embodying more or less virtuous or unvirtuous ways of responding to our lives.[32] They ought to reflect, not merely how well our lives are going for us, but also virtuous—or more prosaically, appropriate or fitting—ways of responding to our lives. They are therefore subject to ethical norms. So even if life satisfaction attitudes should reflect well-being, they quite appropriately track ethical and perhaps other concerns as well, with the result that inferences from life satisfaction to welfare should be problematical at best. In short, they are not even supposed to track well-being in any reasonably straightforward manner, for the attitudinal norms governing life satisfaction attitudes include not just epistemic but *ethical* norms.

Consider our admiration for driven individuals who seem never to be satisfied. Or how we admire the fortitude or gratitude of those who, like Sergeant DiRaimondo, somehow manage to appreciate their lives, and even embrace them, while facing adversity. The former individuals' tendency not to be satisfied with their lives can be part of what we admire about them, just as the latter's propensity to *be* satisfied with their lives may be part of what we find estimable in them. And someone who expresses dissatisfaction with his life amid great achievement and other manifest blessings, simply because things aren't better still, can strike us as an ingrate or whiner. These examples suggest a couple of points, the most obvious being that our attitudes toward our lives can reflect various virtues and vices, such as gratitude, fortitude, ambition, pride, complacency, smugness, softness, low self-regard, etc.

What this means is that you might reasonably be satisfied with your life, not because it is going well for you, but because you have or aspire to such virtues as gratitude or fortitude.[33] Indeed, you might reasonably be satisfied with your life even when saddled with terrible hardship and a bleak future, and even when you *believe* things are going badly for you.[34] Maybe you're glad just to be alive and able to enjoy even life's smallest pleasures. None of this is to forget the requirement that life satisfaction attitudes be firmly grounded in our priorities and experience of life, for these individuals may still be taking such matters firmly into account. These points already suggest that life satisfaction attitudes should not be expected to correspond neatly to well-being. Such attitudes embody, not just our view of how well our lives are going, but also our sense of how it is appropriate to respond to our lives. Similarly, should you be pleased with the dreadful poem your child affectionately composed for you? Such attitudes should not depend simply on whether things satisfy your preferences.

Complicating matters further is that we have no reason to suppose that norms will impact attitudes *consistently*. The examples we started with make this clear: while one person might emphasize norms of gratitude and thus be satisfied, another might just as reasonably focus on norms of non-complacency, and thus be dissatisfied. Still others may rely on different norms. And so different persons' attitudes will connect with well-being in different ways.

I sometimes refer to people "emphasizing" or "choosing" ethical norms when evaluating their lives, which can make it seem as if we are supposed to be deliberately shaping our attitudes. Obviously, our conduct is not always shaped so self-consciously by ethical concerns. Someone with the virtue of fortitude, for instance, might tend to evaluate her life favorably for a variety of reasons related to the virtue: perhaps her acquisition of the virtue has so shaped her various psychic dispositions that she naturally tends to see her difficulties as nothing to complain about. And even the attitudes of someone with an avowed commitment to fortitude can reflect this commitment in uncalculated ways: simply aspiring to a virtue can alter your desires, perceptions, valuations, etc. so that you become more likely to have the appropriate responses, and this hardly needs to involve thinking explicitly about the virtue whenever the situation makes it relevant.[35]

5.2. Arbitrariness: norms

Not only can different individuals exhibit virtue in different ways; the same individual can at different times emphasize different virtues, and the choice can be substantially *arbitrary*. For there are many ways to be virtuous, and in many cases we lack well-defined personal ideals highlighting particular virtues. The demands ethical norms place on us are, in short, somewhat indeterminate, giving us considerable latitude to determine how much weight to give each. A typical person might, for example, value both gratitude and non-complacency without having any special commitments regarding either ideal. For such a person it can be somewhat arbitrary how much to emphasize each virtue. ("Somewhat": my point is not that life satisfaction attitudes are completely arbitrary, with no reasons at all for going one way rather than another. Rather, they are rationally underdetermined so that, to some extent, it will be a coin toss, or up to the agent's discretion.) This arbitrariness leaves room for the individual to draw on pragmatic considerations, emphasizing whichever virtue seems most helpful in the context. Not only can this be perfectly wholesome, but doing it well may itself mark a kind of virtue. Hence a successful researcher might find it useful normally to stress the value of non-complacency and thus avoid becoming too satisfied for her own good; but when her spouse develops Alzheimer's and requires intense care, this strategy may cease to be functional. She may now find it wiser to count her blessings instead of discounting them. This progression may strike us as not only reasonable but admirable.

Notice that in examples like this the considerations animating the choice of norms actually push life satisfaction in the *opposite* direction from well-being: emphasizing norms that will diminish your satisfaction when things are good, and enhance it when things are bad. (In the paper on which much of this discussion is based, I argue that this is not only possible but probably common.[36] It may have a substantial compressing effect on reports of life satisfaction, dampening the effect of life circumstances on people's reports and exaggerating the evidence for adaptation.)

5.3. Arbitrariness: perspective

Arbitrariness infects life satisfaction attitudes in a deeper way owing to the inherently *perspectival* character of these attitudes. Crudely, whether you are satisfied with your life depends on how you look at it. And there is no uniquely authoritative perspective from which to assess one's life. Each of us can reflect on our lives from any number of different perspectives, each liable to yield a different level of life satisfaction, and it is substantially arbitrary which perspective we take, for the norms governing life satisfaction attitudes underdetermine the matter. Perspective affects our attitudes in several ways, but I will focus on its role in determining the information we attend to and the standards of comparison we use.

Consider an example. Emma, a healthy 64, has recently lost her beloved husband of many years. Several months into her grief, she finds her attitude toward her life vacillating between two extremes. On some days she thinks about her life in relation to those she regards as truly unfortunate, like her divorced friend whose own health is failing and whose children are estranged. (Whereas Emma remains close to her children, all of whom are doing well.) On such occasions she feels genuinely lucky and takes real pleasure in contemplating her fortunes; while her husband's death at 68 was obviously unwelcome, she knows many others have died much younger, and few have marriages as gratifying as theirs. She feels wholeheartedly satisfied with her life. But on other days she reflects more on the enormous gap her husband's passing has opened in her life and wonders how she can go on. The future is a blank. At these times she feels acute loneliness, grief, and anger. She is deeply dissatisfied.

Because she looks at her life from different perspectives at different times, Emma's attitude toward it alternates among highly disparate verdicts. Which is more authentic or otherwise authoritative? Clearly, neither needs be. Both perspectives are fully her own, and both attitudes express responses to her life that are wholly hers, and equally authoritative.[37] Which perspective she takes is, to some extent, arbitrary. (Consider the absurdity of pressing her to settle the matter once and for all: which is it?) And to the extent that she does have reasons for taking one perspective rather than another they will often be ethical or pragmatic, relating to factors like the admirability or instrumental value of taking a certain view of one's life at a certain moment.

We of course are in the same situation—all of us can adopt any of a variety of perspectives on our lives, with no compelling reasons for preferring one or the other, and the reasons we do have often being irrelevant to the question of how well our lives are going. Moreover, all of us *do*: most of us, for instance, assess our lives at one time or another in relation to the lives of those whom we most admire. This perspective focuses attention on how well we are living—are we making the most of our lives, living as well as we could? From this perspective most of us will find our lives wanting, and perhaps be dissatisfied. It may be judgments made from this perspective that Annas had in mind when she suggested that most of us are dissatisfied with our lives.[38] Conversely, probably all of us have examined our lives in relation to the less fortunate and found them to be pretty good (recall the impact of seeing a handicapped person on reports, noted above). This perspective will naturally tend to generate relatively favorable attitudes toward our lives. Doubtless other perspectives are quite common as well. This does not mean some perspectives aren't better than others: epistemic and ethical norms may favor certain perspectives over others. Broader perspectives, for instance, tend to yield more meaningful judgments than narrower ones. Examples might include evaluating things in relation to your immediate concerns—e.g., getting a promotion at work—rather than what really matters in the broader context of your life—e.g., your family. But such considerations will usually underdetermine our choice of perspective. To a great extent, what perspective we take at a given time will be a pragmatic matter, or simply a coin toss.[39]

The effects of ethical norms and perspectives are different, but not unrelated. For instance, a visit to a hospital may induce a shift in perspective, which in turn can direct your attention to the importance of counting one's blessings. Conversely, a person's desire to avoid complacency may lead him to assess his life in relation to his most successful peers.[40] I have not explained just how perspectives influence life satisfaction attitudes. In the preceding discussion they appear to work by altering the standards we use in evaluating our lives: how good is good enough?[41] But there is more to perspective-taking than this, and other ways that perspective shifts can alter life satisfaction attitudes. For instance, our satisfaction with our lives might depend on whether we focus on, say, the entire span of our lives, the current "chapter," the current year, etc. And it is not clear that, say, the "entire lifespan" perspective, or any other, will yield an attitude that is uniquely authoritative regarding our welfare, especially our current welfare.

5.4. Arbitrariness: summary

So life satisfaction attitudes are substantially arbitrary, even from the subjective point of view, due to the arbitrariness of the perspectives we take and the ethical norms that drive our judgments. An additional source of arbitrariness, which I will only mention here, concerns how to add up the various goods and bads in our lives. It is doubtful that our priorities are normally well-enough defined to determine a unique scheme for weighting and aggregating the various things we care about. Any global evaluation is thus liable to be somewhat arbitrary.

As a result of such arbitrariness many of us could, like Emma, just as reasonably and authentically be either satisfied or dissatisfied with our lives. Certainly all of us could at least be significantly more or less satisfied or dissatisfied with our lives than we actually are.[42] Your being satisfied with your life may thus say more about the perspective you are taking, or your values or character, than about how well your life is going. Indeed, *you may reasonably become more satisfied with your life when things are plainly going worse for you*. A diagnosis of cancer, e.g., may induce a shift in perspective that causes you to judge your life more favorably than you did before. You might believe yourself to be worse off than you were; it's just that you look at things differently, and are more appreciative of the good things now.[43]

A similar perspective shift, or perhaps a related shift in norms, might explain one of the more curious results in the empirical literature on life satisfaction. A study of African-Americans found that reported life satisfaction increased during the 1980s even as objective indicators of welfare (like health, education, and income) and self-reported happiness—which tends to track emotional state more closely than life satisfaction—declined.[44] We cannot be sure what explains this result. But one possibility is that the respondents' lives really were getting worse, yet they coped by changing how they looked at their lives, or by focusing on different virtues like fortitude or gratitude. It would be interesting to know whether they really believed their lives had gotten better.

5.5. Norms and perspectives: summary

As I noted earlier, these arguments in no way presuppose an objectivist conception of well-being: they are perfectly compatible with quite strong forms of subjectivism. It may be objected: "But when I reflect on my life and feel satisfied with it, that attitude expresses *my* stance, and so my attitude embodies a response to my life that is uniquely and authoritatively *mine*." Some people may be right in saying this, but not most of us. The objection assumes that we ordinarily resolve the arbitrariness in how we assess our lives by embracing a particular stance, much as an existentialist might commit herself to a certain set of values. But normally we don't *resolve* the arbitrariness at all: we exploit it. Like Emma, we shift stances as it suits us, considering our lives sometimes from one perspective, sometimes from another. Reflecting on our lives in varied ways helps keep us balanced; it helps us to keep things, well, in perspective.

Some may object that issues concerning perspectives and norms don't necessarily drive a wedge between life satisfaction and well-being: those who count their blessings don't just report higher life satisfaction; they really *are* better off. To some extent this is surely true. At the very least, being satisfied with our lives can make them more pleasant and temper the forces of discontent. Moreover, we may find value just in the fact of appreciating the good in our lives: it is good not just to have good things in our lives and know about them, but also to *appreciate* them. (Consider how sad it can be when a person of great talent fails utterly to appreciate her merits, even if at some level she knows about them.) Similarly, there is a connection between life satisfaction and self-esteem, particularly insofar as we feel responsible for the way our lives go, or to the extent that our identities are literally constituted, in part, by our life histories. Such considerations can make it seem like a kind of self-repudiation to be dissatisfied with one's life, and a kind of self-affirmation to be satisfied. Consider this excerpt from a recent newspaper article:

Only two months after Stacey and Justin Smith amassed $20,000 in credit card debt to pay for their May 2001 wedding, Mr. Smith was laid off from his job as a laboratory technician. Ms. Smith said that because of their wedding debt, the couple had to move into her aunt's house to save on rent. They also parted with their two leased cars in favor of sharing a used car, and they enlisted a financial planner to monitor their spending, even submitting their credit card statements for review each month. "Everything was just a mess," Ms. Smith said. *Still, she considers the wedding well worth it:* "It was such a fun day, I didn't care how much we put on our credit cards."[45]

We can readily imagine this woman going on to express great satisfaction with her life. It is tempting to chalk this story up to nothing more than sheer stupidity. But it is arguably an illustration of the lengths to which people can go to affirm their lives, virtually come what may. To regard the wedding as a mistake might feel to her like a repudiation of one of the most meaningful episodes in her life, and thereby, perhaps, a kind of self-repudiation. While her judgment seems obtuse all the same, we can sympathize with the likely motive behind it. In fact we would probably think something wrong with her were she to come *too lightly* to the conclusion that such an important moment in her life was a colossal blunder.

Summing up: happiness is widely thought to serve in many contexts as a proxy for well-being. Yet life satisfaction attitudes are inherently ill-suited to occupy this role, for they are not *supposed* to mirror well-being. The mistake is understandable: we tend to think that individuals have more or less well-defined standards for a satisfactory life, and that life satisfaction attitudes ought simply to reflect how well our lives, as we experience them, measure up to those standards. If our lives meet our standards, it seems, then they are probably going well for us. This plausible view is false, in part because most of us neither need nor have determinate standards specifying how good of a life is "good enough."

A deeper problem is that global attitudes involve stepping back and passing judgment on one's life. Such an act is inherently ethically loaded and dependent on the arbitrarily selected perspective one occupies at the time. As an ethically loaded act, it expresses one's stance toward one's life, and can embody a more or less fitting or admirable way of responding to it. Additionally, the relevant epistemic and ethical norms are open-ended, allowing us to think about our lives from a variety of perspectives. The attitudes we arrive at are thus substantially arbitrary.[46] *These considerations apply even to the judgments of a Socrates at his most reflective.*[47] Accordingly, it is pointless to expect to reach a definitive verdict on one's life—as if one hopes to reach the Pearly Gates and find St. Peter holding aloft a sign declaring one's life a "9.8." Similarly, we should not read too much into Wittgenstein's last words.

If it is problematical to identify life satisfaction with happiness on account of its convoluted relationship with well-being, still more problematical is it to equate life satisfaction with *well-being*, or even a central part of it. To give it a starring role in our conception of well-being would be to misunderstand its nature. Indeed, life satisfaction has a voluntary aspect that makes it a dubious candidate for a major life goal: it is too easy to come by. Thus it is one thing to say "I just want my son to be happy," quite another, it seems, to say "I just want my son to be satisfied with his life." To be satisfied, he can just think of Tiny Tim.

6. SUBJECTIVE WELL-BEING AND OTHER VARIANTS

I have not argued that just anything we might call a life satisfaction theory of happiness has these difficulties. I have assumed throughout the usual understanding of life satisfaction as somehow embodying a global judgment about one's life as a whole. One might try out variations on that theme not really discussed here, such as "reflective" life satisfaction, where what counts is the judgment you would make on reflection, or "perspective-invariant" life satisfaction, where one is satisfied no matter what perspective one takes. But all such views will, I think, be vulnerable to one or more of the arguments mounted above.

Alternatively, we might consider an *aggregative* view of life satisfaction that rejects the need for a global judgment altogether, constructing life satisfaction attitudes out of the aggregate of an agent's attitudes to various items. I will not discuss aggregative views here, save to note a general difficulty they face: any form of aggregation will lack the authority of a global judgment.[48] Indeed, aggregation loses an important dimension of subjectivity: how our *lives* seem to us, as opposed simply to how the various elements of our lives seem to us considered individually. It is not even clear how far we have well-defined priorities taken only individually.

Finally, we might go for a *hybrid* account of happiness, which identifies happiness with some combination of life satisfaction (perhaps including domain or other narrower satisfactions) and either hedonic or emotional state. A "subjective well-being" view of happiness would be a good example (including perhaps Sumner 1996). This may seem an attractively irenic solution in light of our diverse intuitions. I will not discuss such a view at great length, but its difficulties are substantial. First, it is liable to seem like either the marriage of two (or more) unpromising accounts, or of a promising account with an unpromising one. It is not obvious that such a union will yield wholesome results. And people have different intuitions about what counts as happiness, so that no theory can accommodate all of them. Any theory that tries to risks pleasing no one. Moreover, cases in which intuitions seem divided, to some extent pointing toward a life satisfaction view and to some extent favoring a hedonistic or emotional state theory, might seem to offer the clearest support for a hybrid theory. Yet consider the satisfied but suffering artist case: many people will find it counterintuitive simply to call her happy, but there may be some intuitive support at least for the idea that, well, maybe she is happy *in some sense*. A hybrid theory might seem well positioned to handle such a case, but notice that it cannot respect the aforementioned appearance: at most, a hybrid theory could say that she is happy *in some respects* and unhappy in others. To be happy "in some sense" is not the same as being happy "in some respects." It is to be happy in another sense of the term. And it seems at best a distortion to say that the artist is happy in some "respects" but not others. The hybrid theory does not seem to get the right answer even where its appeal ought to be strongest.

A weightier concern is that the various components of any hybrid, such as subjective well-being, matter to us for very different reasons and to different degrees. Telling us, say, that Americans are happier than the French won't tell us whether they are more satisfied, have more pleasant or emotionally fulfilling lives, or both. These are very different sorts of information, with very different implications. While it is helpful to employ blanket concepts like that of subjective well-being to encompass some broad domain in which we have an interest, most purposes may be better served by focusing on more specific psychological kinds, for instance distinguishing life satisfaction from happiness. In measures of well-being, subjective well-being is best viewed, not as a single psychological kind, but as an index of related states.

7. THE UPSHOT

7.1. For the theory of happiness

It is odd that life satisfaction's value is so widely taken for granted, yet so little studied. Even the philosophical literature on life satisfaction tends not to address at any length the reasons we ought to care about it, evidently taking the answer to be obvious. It isn't. Surely the topic merits greater attention than we have been able to give it here, and indeed so poorly developed is the literature on life satisfaction that the conclusions of this chapter must be regarded as somewhat provisional. Perhaps life satisfaction's defenders will be able to articulate versions of the theory, or theses about its significance, that will avoid the difficulties raised here. But at the moment there seems little cause for optimism.

I do not deny that we sometimes use 'happiness' to denote states of life satisfaction. My claim in this chapter is that happiness may not be most plausibly and profitably understood as a matter of life satisfaction: it has serious shortcomings regarding both descriptive adequacy and, especially, practical utility. When empirical researchers present life satisfaction studies as findings about "happiness," this might not represent an abuse of the language, but it is misleading: studies indicating that most Americans are satisfied with their lives are indeed significant; but to put the point by saying that most Americans are *happy* is to suggest something much weightier. In the next two chapters, as well as Chapter 9, I will argue that an emotional state conception of happiness is both intuitively plausible and construes happiness in a way that makes sense of our ordinary concerns with it. If those arguments are cogent, then we would do well to regard the uses of 'happiness' connected to life satisfaction as, at best, secondary. Better, it seems, to distinguish happiness and satisfaction.

7.2. For subjective well-being research

The arguments of this chapter may be thought fatal, not just to life satisfaction theories of happiness and related views about well-being, but to life satisfaction research in the social sciences. This would likely be a serious mistake.[49] It is true that *absolute* levels of reported life satisfaction may offer little information about well-being, given the various ways in which life satisfaction and well-being can diverge. Indeed, my arguments suggest that someone's being satisfied with her life tells us very little about how well her life is going for her, even subjectively. But *relative* levels of life satisfaction across large populations may usually be quite informative, since different groups of individuals may not differ systematically in the ways they generate life satisfaction reports; variations in the norms each individual employs, for instance, may wash out over large samples. Nothing said in this chapter undercuts the supposition that, more often than not, if one group (e.g., the employed) reports higher levels of life satisfaction than another (the unemployed), those individuals' lives are going better for them relative to their priorities.[50] Similarly, you may not be able to tell the temperature from a cheap thermometer that errs by 40 percent; but if you distribute many such thermometers randomly across the United States, they will probably tell you that Florida is a lot warmer than Minnesota.

Though I place emotional matters at the center of my account of well-being (Chapter 9), I will suggest that success in relation to our priorities also matters crucially for well-being. Even if it did not, treating people with respect demands that we pay attention to what they think about their lives when making policies that affect them. At present, life satisfaction measures seem to give us valuable information of this sort. Though the arguments of this chapter do not vitiate such instruments, they do suggest that we seek additional measures.[51] In particular, we should look for instruments that capture the sorts of information that tends to be obscured by the ethical norms driving people's judgments, or that gets overlooked in typical questionnaires. An important recent study, for instance, found no significant difference between the life satisfaction judgments of dialysis patients and healthy controls. Yet other research has found that dialysis patients state they "would give up almost half their remaining years to once again live with normal kidney function."[52] This is an extremely strong preference, and *precisely the sort of information that life satisfaction measures are supposed to provide.* We should try to recover such information, for instance by supplementing traditional life satisfaction instruments with surveys that ask people to list some of the main things in their lives that could be better, how important they are, and how strongly they would like to see improvements in those areas.[53]

The central matter of interest here, it seems to me, is not life satisfaction per se, but something like "subjective values fulfillment"—how well people perceive their lives going in relation to the things they care about.[54] And this chiefly matters, not in itself, but as an *indicator* of how things are actually going in people's lives. There is thus a crucial asymmetry between the life satisfaction and affect components of subjective well-being: affect matters in itself, whereas life satisfaction seems important mainly as an indicator of value. It may be a mistake, then, to think of life satisfaction instruments as simply measuring psychological goods. Their value lies largely in what they ostensibly tell us about people's *lives*, not their psychological well-being.

7.3. For Personal Authority

A broader moral emerges from the reflections of this chapter: namely, that individuals' evaluations of their lives, at least insofar as they take the form of life satisfaction attitudes, do not carry the kind of authority they are widely believed to have. On the one hand, it is doubtful how well grounded the typical person's assessments of her life normally will be. Even given a few minutes' reflection, most of us are unlikely to bring all our important priorities to mind, as well as all the important facts about our lives. We forget things or, being caught up in our current pursuits, lose perspective. At such times—which is to say, most of the time—our assessments of our lives will not have the kind of authority we imagine they possess in those rare moments of clarity, where we can review our lives in broad perspective and with full awareness of what we really care about, such as on the deathbed. Well-being, even for the subjectivist, is hardly transparent to the individual whose welfare is in question. On the other hand, even the best-grounded evaluations of our lives will offer problematic information about how well our lives are going for us, since they are not simply announcements about well-being. Since the act of evaluating one's life itself has ethical dimensions, and since we enjoy wide latitude to assess our lives in various ways relative to what we care about, our attitudes toward our lives will not straightforwardly express how well our lives in fact are going for us.

We ignore these points at our peril. It is commonly thought that someone's being satisfied with her life creates a presumption that her life is, in fact, going well for her. But most people, in most places, are satisfied with their lives. In some places satisfaction may be near-universal. This may lead most people to conclude that they are in fact doing pretty well, yielding perhaps a remarkably contented race. Maybe the conclusion is true; but what if it is not? As Wittgenstein shows us, life has to be pretty grim for a person not to have good reasons for being satisfied with it. (It sure beats the alternative.) Many people may reasonably be satisfied with lives that are not, by anyone's standards, going well at all. If so, it would be a grave mistake to take their assessments—or our own—as final in matters of personal welfare.

6

Emotional State

I have diligently numbered the days of pure and genuine happiness which have fallen to my lot; they amount to fourteen.

Abd-El-Raham[1]

1. INTRODUCTION

Probably most languages have some counterpart to 'happiness' in its oldest meaning, a term for prosperity, good fortune, or "good hap"—roughly, well-being. This is the concept likely invoked at weddings, births, and other major events where we wish, utterly vaguely, for the individuals' lives to go well for them: "May the newlyweds meet with happiness in their life together." Once upon a time, this may have been conceptual apparatus enough for the general lot: the life of enviable fortune tended to be just that—mainly a matter of luck—with little point in troubling yourself about how well you were actually doing in that regard. Moreover, your well-being was at best a secondary concern. What mattered then—and still today in many parts of the world—was less a matter of personal fulfillment and more a matter of your family's material wealth and social standing. You married for cattle, not love, and he who died with the most cows won. If you didn't like cows, or your spouse, tough; no one was asking.

Once we started to regard the individual's welfare as a top priority, and to believe that something could actually be done about it, we needed a richer vocabulary. The problem has been clear since human beings first settled down and started accumulating things: outward prosperity and success hardly guarantee personal flourishing; Abd-El-Raham found this out the hard way, after over fifty years of seemingly unblemished good luck, with little to complain about, left the tenth century Caliph of Cordoba desirous to complain. You can seem to be wildly successful in outward terms and yet fail in achieving a happy life; so too can the seemingly unsuccessful appear to thrive. If we want to promote and assess individual well-being, we will need to focus on more substantive and concrete matters than just formal, abstract notions like well-being or good fortune, since it is not obvious what these things amount to. Since the traditional emphasis on material endowments and public accomplishment plainly fails to suffice, we need concepts bearing on how well these things serve the person: never mind just what you've got or what has happened in your life; how are *you* doing? We need, in addition to concepts regarding the condition of a person's life, concepts addressing the *person's* condition. The concept of health is one such, but it shares with external goods the difficulty that one can easily fare well with it yet still fall far short of flourishing or a happy life. Good health is more or less necessary, but not even close to sufficient, for well-being. Clearly, the missing element here is how all these things relate to the person's inner life: not her physical condition, but her psychological condition. Does the person flourish psychologically? If not, then the person does not flourish at all. If so, then the person probably does flourish—or so, at any rate, it seems. This, if we can pull it off, is a wonderful result: here we have a concrete, substantive good that most of us can agree is, if not sufficient for well-being, then so central to it that we can regard this item as a convenient proxy for it.

What shall the word be for this psychological condition? Since a person's being in this condition (enough of the time) appears almost to suffice for a happy life, why not adapt the familiar term and say, then, that the *person* is happy? And so it makes perfect sense—as it would not given the original meaning of the term—to sharpen our hopes for the newborn infant by expressing our desire that she be "happy and healthy" throughout her days. Now the term is no longer an evaluation of a life, but a description of a person's psychological condition. This is the psychological sense of the word identified in Chapter 2.

The aim of this chapter is to argue, in light of the reflections of the preceding chapters, that this condition is most profitably understood as a matter of a person's emotional condition. I will begin with a default version of the emotional state theory, and then discuss a fleshed-out form of the view, in which happiness is understood as a kind of "psychic affirmation," to illustrate some of the more important types of states that happiness can involve. The next chapter fills in various gaps in the account, and argues that the psychological distinctions that concern us cut across, and extend beyond, the traditional categories of emotions and moods. I sketch the elements of a fuller view that incorporates the new distinctions and show that the resulting account of happiness is coherent and well-motivated. Moreover, it points to important omissions in standard views of human affect, and so should interest emotion researchers and others on that basis alone.

A subsidiary goal of both chapters is to show that the popular "smiley-face" stereotype of happiness, which may seem particularly salient on an emotional state view, grossly distorts and oversimplifies the phenomenon: happiness has a much richer, deeper, more complex, and less obvious psychology than the common image suggests. Cheery feelings matter, and do not deserve the abuse so often heaped on them, but they are a relatively uninteresting part of the story. And much of the story, we will see, is likely to be surprisingly opaque to the individual whose happiness is in question. So elusive, indeed, is the psychology of happiness that I will not even try to offer a precise characterization of it: the theory defended here will be filled in as carefully as I can manage, but a complete account of happiness will require further progress in our scientific understanding of the emotional realm. Certainly a reductive analysis in familiar folk psychological terms, of the sort traditionally favored by analytical philosophers, will be out of the question. Here is an example of what I mean. In "A Theory of Happiness," Wayne Davis offers what he takes to be a hedonistic account, defining happiness as both believing and desiring the propositions one is thinking about.[2] The "happiness function" is:

$$h = \sum_{i=1}^{n} b(P_i)d(P_i), \text{ where } P_1, \ldots P_n \text{ is an enumeration of all thoughts } A \text{ is thinking.}$$

and

$$A \text{ is happy at } t \text{ iff} \quad h_A^t > 0$$
$$A \text{ is unhappy at } t \text{ iff} \quad h_A^t < 0$$

Meaning: "take every proposition A is thinking at the moment, multiply the degree to which it is believed by the degree to which it is desired, add up all the products, and the sum is A's degree of happiness."[3] If the sum is positive, A is happy; if negative, A is unhappy. This is, in significant respects, admirably precise. But it is also the sort of old-fashioned conceptual analysis that rarely yields believable results. As well, the theory is in significant ways imprecise: what is meant, for instance, by 'belief' and 'desire'? These terms cover a lot of ground, and some of the things within their province yield a much less plausible theory than others. And how are the beliefs and desires related? Is the idea that one believes, of the proposition one desires, that it obtains? Or that one desires, of the proposition one believes, that it obtain? Other readings are possible as well. At any rate, I will not so much as attempt this sort of formal precision in what follows.

My arguments will focus not on what it is to *achieve* happiness, but on the more fundamental question of what makes a state *happiness-constituting*: in virtue of what a state makes a constitutive difference in how happy or unhappy we are.[4] This is the crucial issue: for we want to be as happy as we can be, consistently with the other things that matter. The further question of whether we will actually *be* happy, period, is less pressing. It also raises difficulties of its own.

2. FROM PLEASURE TO HAPPINESS

Since the emotional state theory can be seen as an effort to remedy the defects of hedonism, it is worth recapping two of the arguments from Chapter 4. First, it is *psychologically superficial*: it incorporates only the experiential aspect of our emotional conditions. Yet our emotional lives are extremely rich, and do not reduce to their experiential surfaces. They involve unconscious processes of various sorts, and often have physiological components. Recall the paradigm cases from Chapter 3: it is simply not credible to regard them merely as so many experiential episodes. Nor is it plausible to claim that the states listed are happiness-constituting only *qua* pleasures. One is unhappy by virtue of being *depressed*, not by virtue of experiencing the unpleasantness of depression. Happiness has depth that the pleasure theory misses.

The second criticism of hedonism was that it is too inclusive, counting many *irrelevant* pleasures: in its usual incarnations, all pleasures and displeasures are considered happiness-constituting. Yet many pleasures seem trivial or superficial, making no difference to how happy we are. Even intensely pleasant experiences can fail to impact our happiness: notoriously, sexual activity can leave us cold. Sometimes it just doesn't move us. This is one of the hard lessons dealt to the unsophisticated libertine, or the troubled youth seeking to relieve his melancholy through meaningless sexual encounters. Consider also the pain of having one's gouty toe stepped on. Most of us will find unhappiness in such an experience. It is hard not to let intense pain get to you. But someone of a stoic nature may be disciplined enough that such pains don't get to her at all; she maintains her equanimity throughout. Intuitively, her happiness remains untouched.

3. EMOTIONAL STATE THEORIES: THE DEFAULT VIEW

> Happiness in intelligent people is the rarest thing I know.
>
> Hemingway

The distinction between happiness-constituting affects and mere pleasures seems to concern whether a given affect involves one's *emotional condition*. Certain affects, notably "mere" physical pains and pleasures, seem not to be particularly emotional, and need not make a difference in our emotional conditions: they don't get to us. Whereas others, such as the paradigm emotions and especially moods, do seem to alter our emotional conditions while they last. I say "paradigm" emotions because the term 'emotion' ranges extremely widely, including states that seem not to be particularly emotional, or to involve our emotional conditions. For instance, you might be angry with a distant government for some policy you disapprove of, or afraid that this policy will have a bad outcome, yet never *feel* the least bit angry or afraid; your attitudes are purely intellectualized, and would at most implicate your emotional state were you to ruminate on the matter and work yourself up into a genuine state of anger or fear about it. Such notional "emotions" amount to little more than beliefs, perhaps having no affective component at all, and are psychologically very different from paradigm emotions of anger and fear.[5] Thus we are sometimes careful to note that, while we might be "angry" or "fear" something in *some* sense, we are not *genuinely* mad or afraid. It is plausible that states of the latter sort diminish one's happiness thereby, whereas states of the more intellectualized sort do not. (If the reader's intuitions differ, this will probably be due to conceiving of happiness along the lines of attitudinal hedonism, discussed in Chapter 4, or an aggregative form of life satisfaction.) To capture the distinction, we might refer to the paradigm emotions as "passions," but this term may connote too much; I will just call them "emotions" or "emotions proper."

Here is a simple version of the emotional state theory, what we might call the *default emotional state theory* of happiness. It maintains that happiness consists in a person's overall emotional condition, which in turn consists in the aggregate of her moods and emotions. To be happy, on this view, is for one's emotional condition to be, on the whole, positive. That is, the overall balance of one's moods and emotions is positive rather than negative; positive emotions and moods outweigh the negative. As with a hedonistic account of happiness, the emotional state view allows happiness to be assessed over arbitrarily brief or long periods of time. As stated the theory is somewhat vague, but good enough to give us a starting point for further reflection. I will argue shortly for several modifications to this basic schema.

An even simpler form of the theory would count only moods, or only emotions. Without a special account of moods or emotions, however, such a move would be hard to sustain. If being in a depressed, irritable, or anxious mood makes a person less happy thereby, then presumably emotions of profound sadness or anger can as well, and vice versa.

The emotional state theory does not take happiness to *be* an emotion or mood. It is, rather, a *condition* consisting in (at least) the aggregate of a person's emotions and moods, and this can be a complex matter. You can be cheerful and anxious at the same time, for instance. It might be strictly more accurate, then, to call this an "emotional condition" theory, but calling happiness an emotional condition makes it sound like a disease. I will speak interchangeably of a person's emotional state and emotional condition.

It is plausible that some sort of emotional state theory can account for the paradigm cases; this will become clearer in the discussion to follow. Note that the acute emotion or mood of "feeling happy" is just one of the happiness-constituting states. Its role in happiness is grotesquely exaggerated in the popular imagination, doubtless accounting for much of the scorn heaped on happiness by dysthymic philosophers and the like. Intuitively, most happy people don't feel happy most of the time: they may be relatively tranquil, fulfilled, in good spirits, etc. They need not be brimming with giddy exhilaration. Indeed, a plausible form of the emotional state theory could well allow that some happy individuals might never feel happy: one can imagine an Archie Bunker-like kvetch—a New York deli owner, say—who is generally fulfilled and emotionally untroubled, as his favorite sport, complaining, doesn't get him down. He may, despite appearances, be *happy*.

This sort of point comes through well in one of the better literary depictions of happiness. While Hemingway seems to have been no great fan of happiness as such, he arguably left us one of its more compelling illustrations. *The Old Man and the Sea*'s Santiago is not the image of happiness in the "smiley-face" sense, which turns up only briefly if at all, notably at the beginning, where the reader learns that his eyes are "cheerful and undefeated."[6] Yet he is a model of what the ancients called *ataraxia*—tranquility, imperturbability—and Hemingway's exemplar, I suspect, of genuine happiness. Indeed, it is hard to avoid the thought that the author very much envied the Cuban fisherman, who appeared in some ways to be his opposite—unreflective, destitute, bereft of physical comforts, and anonymous but utterly contented and at home in his world, in contrast to Hemingway's own uneasy wealth, fame, and intellectual achievements. (Within a decade of its publication, which quickly garnered a Pulitzer and a Nobel, Hemingway would take his own life. It may seem odd to call Santiago unreflective, since much of the book is taken up with his silent reflections, often perceptive and wise. But even the unreflective have an inner monologue, and all of us engage in some reflection; it is a matter of degree. "Do not think about sin, he thought. There are enough problems now without sin. Also I have no understanding of it . . . Do not think about sin. It is much too late for that and there are people who are paid to do it. Let them think about it."[7] This is not someone you'd expect to find in a Left Bank café clutching a well-worn copy of *Being and Nothingness*.) Santiago's happy disposition shows itself at many points, but I will note just one: despite his poverty, his rotten luck, and tremendous physical discomfort, his sleep throughout is plainly untroubled, characterized by pleasant dreams of watching lions on a beach and the like. The last we hear of him, "the old man was dreaming about the lions," evidently unperturbed, even unimpressed, by the long ordeal that had just culminated in losing a record catch to sharks.[8] Peaceful slumbers are an ancient sign of the tranquil mind, and the scene recalls Plato's depiction of Socrates at the start of the *Crito* (see Chapter 1). Hemingway drives the point home with the jarring introduction of clueless tourists immediately before this. They see the tattered remains of Santiago's marlin and take it for an impressive shark. Santiago's accomplishment will never be known beyond the village.

The emotional state theory bears some resemblance to hedonism, but differs in at least two important respects. In one respect, it is more restrictive, excluding many "superficial" pleasures that fail to implicate our emotional conditions. In another respect, it is more expansive, incorporating our emotional conditions in their entirety, including their unconscious and dispositional components. As well, it regards happiness as fundamentally a different sort of entity: not merely a sum of conscious episodes or events, but a psychological condition. (See Chapter 4.) This point, somewhat cryptic here, will become clearer as we add further flesh to the version of the theory defended in this chapter.

So long as the reader grants the plausibility of some form of emotional state theory, the central aim of this chapter will have been met. But though it is possible for an emotional state theorist simply to identify happiness with the aggregate of an individual's moods and/or emotions, I think there is a more helpful way to distinguish the relevant states. We will return to that question, and discuss other technical matters, in the next chapter. In what remains of this chapter, I want to go beyond the default view and develop the basic schema in more concrete terms, aiming to illustrate the potential richness and depth, and broad appeal, of an emotional state theory. This will also help the reader develop an intuitive feel for the account before plunging into the more difficult territory of the chapter to follow.

4. THE THREE FACES OF HAPPINESS

4.1. Introduction: happiness as psychic affirmation

To fill out the emotional state view more concretely, it will be helpful to start with a broad ideal that can help guide our reflections about the specifics. A natural proposal is to think of being happy as an individual's responding favorably, in emotional terms, to her life—responding emotionally to her life *as if* things are generally going well for her. This usefully parallels the competing ideal of life satisfaction: more or less, the individual's judging that her life is going well enough for her. That is, roughly, responding rationally to her life as if things are generally going well for her. We might say that life satisfaction chiefly concerns the endorsement of the intellect, whereas happiness concerns the endorsement of the emotional aspect of the self (the "psyche," as I will sometimes put it, for reasons to be discussed in the next chapter).[9] Call this condition *psychic affirmation*. In more pronounced forms, we might call it *psychic flourishing*.[10]

The question is what psychic affirmation amounts to. My goal here is to sketch a rough and informal outline of a fuller view, with no pretensions at completeness or exactitude. It will be enough if the reader comes away with some appreciation of the diversity and elusiveness of the states encompassed by happiness. Approaching the matter from a biological perspective, we can ask how it would make sense to design emotional creatures such as ourselves. What sorts of emotional responses would be required? I would conjecture that all emotional states instantiate one or more of three basic modes of affirmative or negative response. At the most basic level will be responses concerning the individual's safety and security: for example, letting one's defenses down, making oneself fully at home in one's life— being in a state of utter *attunement* with one's life, we might say—as opposed to taking up a defensive stance. Next come responses relating to the individual's commitment to or *engagement* with her situation and activities: is it worth investing much effort in them, or would it be wiser to withdraw or disengage from them? Finally, there will be more or less explicit *endorsements* signifying that one's life is not just free of threat and worth pursuing enthusiastically, but positively good, containing things that are to be built upon, sustained, repeated, or sought in the future—as, for example, when one has just achieved a goal or received a great benefit. (Theories of emotion frequently take *all* affects to be of this sort, and accordingly one of my aims is to call attention to other kinds of affective response.) While the three modes of response (arguably) concern progressively less fundamental aspects of well-being, affects of each kind can occur to some extent independently of the others. One need not enjoy security, for instance, to experience something as a positive benefit; on the other hand, the heights of joy may be unreachable for the deeply anxious. We will see as well that some affects appear to instantiate more than one mode of response.

For each of the three modes of response we can identify a corresponding aspect or dimension of happiness.[11] People have disagreed through the ages about the relative importance of these dimensions, so that for each we can identify one or more corresponding ideals that emphasize it. Since these ideals of living have probably arisen in every civilized age, it will be helpful to connect them with the familiar ancient Greek tradition, thus distinguishing Democritean, Aristotelian and Dionysian, and Stoic ideals of happiness. I will discuss them in reverse order, starting with the least fundamental, but most familiar:

1. Endorsement (Democritean)
2. Engagement (Aristotelian and Dionysian)
3. Attunement (Stoic)

Each mode of response encompasses negative as well as positive responses; it will be convenient (if inelegant) to refer to the negative counterparts as "disendorsement," "disengagement," and "disattunement." I will not endorse a particular ideal of happiness, though each dimension is important. And there is clearly more than one way to be happy, as Mill observed in distinguishing two of our three dimensions, writing that "the main constituents of a satisfied life appear to be two, either of which by itself is often found sufficient for the purpose: tranquillity, and excitement. With much tranquillity, many find that they can be content with very little pleasure: with much excitement, many can reconcile themselves to a considerable quantity of pain."[12] (Note also that these ideals can be driven by non-prudential considerations, such as beliefs about what matters for virtue.) But I will suggest that the standard contemporary view of happiness gets the relative priority of these dimensions pretty near backwards: the dimensions listed above appear in ascending order of importance, whereas we find the reverse ranking in the popular imagination.

4.2. Endorsement

My body restore for me.
My mind restore for me.
Happily I recover...
In beauty I walk.
It is finished in beauty.

The Night Chant (a Navajo healing
ceremony for mental illness)[13]

In the present era, the lion's share of attention has gone to the endorsement aspect of happiness, typified by affects along the *joy–sadness* axis, especially those of feeling happy or cheerful.[14] This is—or at least includes—the prototypically American version of happiness, perhaps because it suits the American emphasis on pursuing your dreams. Also, affects along this dimension are the hardest to miss, as we tend to wear them on our faces, in smiles, frowns, laughter, and the like. Even a child can grasp this sort of happiness. The historical literature, by contrast, tends not to emphasize such affects, as we saw in Mill's omission of them in distinguishing the main varieties of happiness. Perhaps this is because such affects can be so hard to sustain: it is difficult to make yourself *feel* happy for any lengthy period of time, at least if you are not already that way by temperament. As with sadness, happy feelings tend quickly to fade. But even among the ancients this sort of ideal seems to have had its defenders, notably in the views of Democritus—"the laughing philosopher"—who apparently held our goal to be *euthymia*, roughly cheerfulness. We know little of Democritus' views, and there is reason to believe that he viewed *euthymia* as more a matter of tranquility than smiley-face feelings. But he has been well-enough associated with ideals of cheerfulness that we might reasonably deem ideals of happiness that emphasize such feelings "Democritean."

While it is easy to overstate the importance of joy–sadness affects for happiness, we should not understate it either; in particular, we should bear in mind that such affects can vary widely in centrality or depth: the profound joy that one's children can bring must not be conflated with a high-fiver's jubilation, or the vacant cheeriness of a shopping mall devotee who finds his life agreeable but has no occasion for real joy. Consider also the Stoic notion of *chara*, joy, among the "good feelings," or the rapturous perception of the world's beauty expressed by the Navajo chant. A shallow cheeriness has its merits, but if that's the best that can be said for your emotional state then it is questionable whether we could sensibly deem you happy.

Other endorsement-type affects do exist, most important perhaps being irritability, which is most naturally contrasted with cheerfulness. The latter, however, appears to fall along the same axis as joy, both being variants of "feeling happy." Irritability appears to fall on a different axis, perhaps one without a positive pole. (Since many emotion researchers regard positive and negative affects as independent rather than occupying opposite ends of common axes, this asymmetry need not be a problem.[15] But nothing important hangs on whether joy and sadness truly fall along a single axis or not.) Other affects, including fulfillment and anger, will be mentioned later. But states along or near the joy–sadness axis constitute the central case.

4.3. Engagement

> I wanted to live deep and suck out all the marrow of life, to live so sturdily and Spartan-like as to put to rout all that was not life, to cut a broad swath and shave close, to drive life into a corner.
>
> Thoreau, *Walden*

A closely related but importantly distinct dimension concerns the individual's engagement with her life: not listless and withdrawn, but energetic and engaged. For one can affirm one's life, not just by giving it a "thumbs up," but by enthusiastically taking up what it has to offer. This can happen even when things are not going particularly well, for instance when struggling to accomplish a difficult goal. There are two ideals associated with engagement, the first of which centers on states of energy or vitality: the *exuberance–depression* axis.[16] A passionate and demanding orchestra conductor, for instance, might be exuberant, even happy, without being obviously cheerful or joyful. I do not know whether the Cleveland's George Szell was like this, but he was evidently quite passionate in living—in his cooking at home as well as in his work—perhaps embodying a kind of exuberance. The mere fact that he was a harsh taskmaster need not disqualify him from happiness. A lot depends on whether his temper often left him deeply unsettled—as seems to have been the case for the mercurial Toscanini—or whether its manifestations were typically superficial and transient, leaving his internal state largely undisturbed.

This exuberant form of happiness is typified in ideals of passionate living, notably in Nietzsche, Goethe, and countless other romantics and artists.[17] I am not sure who among the major ancient philosophers endorsed such an ideal, so I will refer to the ideal as "Dionysian." Proponents of the passionate life frequently claim to *oppose* happiness as a significant value, but I would suggest this owes to an overly narrow understanding of the phenomenon, conflating it with cheerfulness and quietude. Yet there is a real tension here: exuberance or passion often brings in its trail emotional disturbance of a distinctly negative sort, as Stoics, Epicureans, Buddhists, and other ancients were fond of pointing out. The passionate life will normally involve a fair dose of anger, frustration, and sorrow, and so this form of happiness can be hard to achieve without compromising other aspects of happiness. It can thus be a bad bet from the perspective of the individual's well-being. (Though it might be admirable, and thus worth seeking, all the same.) But one need not pursue the passionate life to the Nietzschean extreme: some forms of exuberant living are less risky than others, and many people lead lives of great vitality without plunging themselves into the depths. Exuberance need not entail epic struggles. (Think Whitman's "barbaric yawp," which was not intended to be the howl of a tormented artist.)

A quieter form of engagement than exuberance or vitality can arguably be found in Aristotle's work, and more recently in the notion of "flow" propounded by Mihaly Csikszentmihalyi.[18] This is the state one assumes when fully engaged in an activity, typically a challenging activity performed well. In states of flow, individuals lose all sense of self-awareness, of the passage of time, and are not aware of feeling anything at all. It is nonetheless a highly pleasant state, and clearly a state in which the individual is happy. We might regard its opposite to be boredom. While the other states we have been discussing may seem clearly to involve a person's psychic disposition or stance, flow may not seem like that. But it is: to be in a state of flow is to assume, emotionally and cognitively, a stance of interest and engagement—a kind of psychic coupling with the objects of one's attention. Aristotle does not write explicitly of flow, but his treatment of the pleasures supervening on virtuous or excellent activity clearly resonates (as Csikszentmihalyi notes[19]). Certainly, the happiness that attends Aristotelian well-being—virtuous activity—will include a strong component of flow. We might thus term the idea of happiness as engagement in the sense of flow the "Aristotelian" ideal. (To call it that is not to suggest that Aristotelian ethics centers on promoting flow; clearly it does not.[20] The point concerns the psychological states that tend to be *associated* with Aristotelian ideals, even if only as a by-product of the virtuous activity that really matters.)

The significance of engagement becomes clearest in cases of depression, where the characteristic lethargy and listlessness signals a broad psychic disengagement from one's life. While sometimes disordered and always awful, this sort of withdrawal can sometimes be functional, facilitating major life changes by pulling us out of our existing routines and signaling that our present way of living may not be worth continuing.[21]

4.4. Attunement

Journal notes, August 8.

Sundown on the Pond. A gull is laughing from a perch on a post in the Pond. Now a skimmer glides by, plowing a tiny furrow through the shallows. No permanent mark. Nothing is permanent out here. Sand and water . . . no mark endures save of notion, of idea . . . Here the veil between us and the truth of existence is very thin and, to my mind, can be pierced. These past few weeks, I have settled into mindless existence, with few thoughts and no dreams. My being is effortless, untroubled by pain, unstirred by joy. This being is meditative, with no need of mantras or quiet rooms. Here on the seam between objective and subjective reality no special effort is required to contemplate the merge. When I perceive the gull and apply my perceptual sieves, it is accomplished.

Ron Haybron, *Island*[22]

The third and perhaps most important dimension of happiness is best approached by reflecting on states that fall along on the *tranquility–anxiety* axis. This is not the occasion to plumb the nuances of tranquility, but we might think of tranquility as "settledness": not merely peace of mind or lack of internal discord but a kind of inner surety or confidence, stability and balance, or imperturbability.[23] Whereas endorsement's characteristic appearance is the smile, and engagement's the jaunty gait, tranquility presents itself in the relaxed, easy posture. It is clearly a highly pleasant state, and not simply the absence of disturbance or other feeling. Nor does it rule out states of high arousal or exuberance; indeed, exuberance without any sort of tranquility is liable to be jittery and unstable. But tranquility seems crucial for being happy. Not long ago, during a somewhat stressful period preceding the birth of our twins, I noticed how happy my mood would become while bathing my three-year-old. Yet even during those moments I do not think *I* was happy, for beneath the good cheer ran a distinct undercurrent of anxiety, and I never stopped feeling off balance, unsettled. Hemingway's Santiago, by contrast, is an exemplar of tranquility. (Those of a Nietzschean bent take note: as Santiago makes clear, tranquility entails neither complacency nor passivity.)

So misleading is the conventional understanding of tranquility that it is useful to set that notion aside momentarily and consider the fundamental biological condition that it represents. When an organism is in familiar and safe circumstances, where it has mastery of its environment, it can let down its defenses—dialing down the cortisol, for instance—and confidently engage in whatever pursuits it wishes. It is this condition, in a person, we are concerned with. The Stoics might have said that the individual in that situation finds her life *oikeion*—familiar—to her; she is utterly at home in her life. *In her element.* Similarly, think of the state one assumes when relaxing with a still-close friend after a long separation, particularly if one normally has few close friends nearby. You feel completely at home with that person. 'Tranquility' seems too narrow a term for the condition of psychically being at home in one's life; I will call it a state of *attunement*.[24] In this state a person relaxes and blossoms, living as seems natural to her, according to her internal priorities, and without inhibition. The opposite of attunement, disattunement, is not merely anxiety, but more broadly *alienation*: your circumstances are in some sense alien to you—unfamiliar, imposing, threatening. Defenses go up: anxiety, stress, insecurity.

I will not try formally to define the notion of attunement here, but it appears to have three basic aspects: (1) inner calm or peace ("tranquility" in the colloquial sense); (2) confidence or surety; and (3) openness or expansiveness of mood or spirit, or a sense of freedom (feeling "carefree" being one form of this). To fully capture the notion of being at home in one's life, perhaps we should also add a sense of continuity or fit between self and world—a bit perhaps like the "oceanic feeling" Freud spoke of. 'Confidence' refers to an internal emotional or psychic condition, and bears only a loose relation to one's opinion of oneself. The phenomenon of what we might call "somatic confidence"—feeling wholly at home in one's body—is illustrative. Those who have felt the extremes of somatic confidence know how vastly better it is to have it than not, and how much happier one seems to be when in it than not: think, at the negative pole, of Nixonian awkwardness (the former president seemed to personify a Cartesian dualism of body and mind gone badly askew); at the positive end, the athletic grace of a ballet dancer. This is an important part of what is meant here by 'confidence.' (Is somatic confidence any part of one's emotional condition? I submit that it is: when enjoying such a state one is not edgy or nervous; one's emotional condition is more favorable, and one is happier. You could have stood *behind* Nixon while he thrust his appendages skyward to signal "victory" and known immediately that you were not observing an entirely happy man.)

The term 'attunement' is not ideal; it connotes a state of harmonious coexistence with, or rapt attention to, one's environment. Yet a logger could enjoy this condition whilst clear-cutting the last stand of ancient redwoods; and while someone in a state of "attunement" with her life is indeed likely to have a healthy outward focus, being receptive to her surroundings, being "attuned" to things in the environment is neither central nor essential to it. The attunement in question is broadly emotional, not perceptual.

Among the ancients, the ideal of happiness as attunement seems most naturally to be associated with the Stoics, given the apparent affinity between the present conception of attunement and the Stoics' '*oikeion*,' and more broadly their focus on living according to nature and not being at odds with one's life as it is. To call happiness as attunement a "Stoic" ideal might sow confusion given the common view of the Stoics as joyless ascetics who regarded emotions as a pestilence rather than a central aspect of well-being. While the Epicureans are better known for placing a kind of attunement at the center of the good life, the Stoic resonances seem to me sufficiently compelling that I will call this ideal of happiness "Stoic."

Without going to the Stoic extreme, I would suggest that attunement does indeed form the core of happiness, being not ancillary but quite central to it. Anxiety, stress, insecurity, and related states are not merely unpleasant in themselves; they rob us of much of our capacity for the other dimensions of happiness. Some measure of cheerfulness you might get while suffering from these forms of psychic disattunement, but exuberance, flow, and joy will be hard to come by. Intuitively, a troubled, anxious, tense, or stressed out person—more broadly, someone who does not seem psychically to be at home in his life—does not seem to be happy, however cheerful he might be. This point will prove significant later.

4.5. Attunement, part two: stress and compression

> I distrust the perpetually busy; always have. The frenetic ones spinning in tight little circles like poisoned rats. The slower ones, grinding away their fourscore and ten in righteousness and pain. They are the soul-eaters.
>
> Mark Slouka, "Quitting the Paint Factory"

It is easy to overlook the importance of the attunement dimension of happiness for human well-being, in great part because it does not command our attention like the others do. (I will suggest in Chapter 10 that it may be less conspicuous than other affective states by design.) Consider for example the phenomenon of stress, in the sense of being stressed (this term is vague, but nowadays we all know it well enough that it needs no introduction). It is important to see how deeply anathema this state is to well-being, for it is said to be pervasive in the present culture, yet seems nonetheless not to be taken very seriously. A major reason for this is that it is not usually all that unpleasant—not agonizing like back pain, chemotherapy, or depression can be, and not something we must urgently labor to relieve. It can seem more a nuisance than a great problem. The appearance is misleading, for the trouble with stress lies not mainly in the suffering it immediately involves but in its corrosive impact on the person: it compresses and flattens the spirit and smothers the individual's capacity for pleasure. Stressed individuals get less out of life, for they cannot as easily enjoy, or even notice, what life offers them. The joy of living, the manifold small pleasures that leaven our days—whose importance is readily dismissed, but is never lost on those peering into the grave—are substantially foreclosed when we are stressed. What remains is usually quite bearable, but a lot less worth having.

What of this "flattening of the spirit"? What is meant by it and why does it matter? The phenomenon in question, relating primarily to the expansiveness aspect of attunement, might be termed affective, psychic, or spiritual *compression*. (Though talk of the spirit or soul bears unfortunate connotations of cheap New Age sentimentality, I use these terms in a common secular and naturalistic sense. I mean them to suggest something psychologically deep, intimate, and important to us.) The word may be new but the basic notion, first broached in Chapter 1, should be familiar to any contemporary, and arguably appears in various forms in the works of many writers, notably Mill and Nietzsche. It is easier illustrated than defined: e.g., someone leading a harried life—caught up in the "rat race," as we say—may find himself feeling pressed-upon and confined, like a caged animal, emotionally deflated, small, ant-like—"pinched and hidebound," as Mill memorably put it. (Mill actually used 'compression' to describe the process of making a person like that: e.g., the public's approved "ideal of character is to be without any marked character; to maim by compression, like a Chinese lady's foot, every part of human nature which stands out prominently.")[25] The uncompressed person, by contrast, will feel free, expansive, spiritually enlarged. This is not mere phenomenology: it is how these individuals will seem to perceptive observers as well. To the uncompressed person, her psychically compressed counterparts will seem like "little people," worker bees or ants rather than full-sized human beings—to the ancient Greeks, perhaps, the *mikropsuchoi* (literally, "small-souled").[26] Whereas the uncompressed person is liable to strike others as a "free spirit." The contrast might be seen in comparing our stereotype of, say, an English aristocrat with that of a flamboyant Caribbean islander. Or consider the sharp differences between John Brown, Queen Victoria's uninhibited Scottish servant—or for that matter Billy Connolly, the man who played him in John Madden's film *Mrs. Brown*—and more typical members of a royal court. Uncompression is not exuberance: quieter forms of uncompression exist as well; there is no smallness or compression of spirit in Hemingway's Santiago, or the Dalai Lama. And these are not mere matters of temperament: all of us have experiences of greater and less compression in our lives. You might experience affective expansion when thoroughly engaged in your favorite activity, particularly if it involves physical virtuosity. Surfing does it for some, sculpture for others, trading commodities for still others.

To get a better fix on the idea, it may be useful to indulge in a bit of speculation about how evolutionary processes could favor tendencies toward compression in certain circumstances. (It matters little whether the following story is true: the point is to illustrate what compression involves.) Imagine the predicament of an individual who is in a threatened subordinate position—e.g., is under the watchful eye of a hostile and belligerent dominant figure. One natural response to this kind of situation would be to avoid trouble by keeping a low profile and making oneself as invisible as possible. Hunker down. This is a reactive stance in which one's behavior is driven not internally but by the agendas of others: go with the flow, be agreeable, and don't make waves. What would the emotional aspect of such a strategy be like? We might expect individuals in such a position to be relatively introverted rather than extroverted, to be less likely to be in what we call an expansive mood, to be relatively anxious or prone to anxiety, to be tentative rather than confident, to feel confined or trapped—not liberated—and perhaps to be somewhat flat emotionally. Such individuals might also tend to be relatively petty and selfish—too focused on their own precarious status to care much about others. These are all, I think, among the hallmarks of compression. And we should not be surprised if someone who exhibits these characteristics experiences a certain phenomenology: feeling small, or small-spirited. This is the core phenomenology of compression.

Compression appears to be a response to oppressive circumstances, such as these, in which one's behavior can be neither natural nor free. There appear to be at least two basic sources of compression, each yielding a different form of the phenomenon (which is not to say they cannot combine). First is *imposition* or repression: that is, being in circumstances in which one's functioning is dictated by forces other than one's own nature. Social pressures demanding conformity are an obvious case here (it is ironic, but also fitting, that Victoria's closest confidant should have been a man who personified opposition to the buttoned-down ethos that bore her name).[27] But overscheduled living or struggling just to survive can have the same effect. Second is *threat*, which exerts pressure in a different way: not exactly dictating what one does, but requiring one to assume a reactive and wary stance, anxious and vigilant. In fact all forms of compression seem fundamentally to involve a reactive stance: one's functioning reflects external demands too much, and one's own nature too little. Little wonder that a form of this notion should make its way into Mill's wonderful manifesto on behalf of individuality. Compression is effectively the sleep of individuality. I would suggest that what makes compression so bad is not just that it is not a very pleasant way to be; but that it involves the hindrance of self-expression or self-fulfillment. This intuitively seems like a bad thing, and we will see why that should be so in Chapter 9: well-being consists largely in self-fulfillment. Compression does not seem compatible with that.

Returning to the question of stress, we can see that stressful living often involves both forms of compression: the imposition of having too much to do in too little time, and the constant threat of failing to get things well enough done. Living under a constant bombardment of "insane demands," as Ginsburg put it,[28] and being under continual threat of failure to meet them, tends not to enlarge the soul. Still less if success or failure is judged, not by oneself, but—as often happens in the more anonymous and competitive forms of society—by others whom one may not like or even know.

Of course it would be desirable to define compression in more exact terms; I have been able to do little more than gesture at the phenomenon here. But the sheer difficulty of doing so, or even of pointing toward it with any discernment, is revealing in itself, and rather congenial to the purposes of this book. It illustrates how easily overlooked even central aspects of psychological well-being can be. Probably few people under high levels of compression have had much experience of radically uncompressed living, save in early childhood, and probably few have much notion of the difference, or perhaps even that there is anything missing in the reduced condition. Compression seems easy to live with, however undesirable it may be.

4.6. Summary

Summing up: we have identified three broad dimensions of happiness, each representing a different mode of emotional response to one's life, and each tending to be favored over the others in various ideals of living. The dimensions, and their chief constituents, are (now in descending order of importance for happiness, though not within each dimension):

1. Attunement
    a. Peace of mind vs. anxiety.
    b. Confidence vs. insecurity.
    c. Uncompression vs. compression.
2. Engagement
    a. Exuberance or vitality vs. listlessness.
    b. Flow vs. boredom or ennui.
3. Endorsement
    a. Joy vs. sadness.
    b. Cheerfulness vs. irritability.

The prominence of attunement reflects what we may think of as the stages of flourishing for a creature: the first priority is to establish conditions of safety and security, where the basic needs for functioning are firmly established so that it can make itself at home and blossom—like placing a sapling in fertile soil. The organism is in its element; it assumes a stance of attunement. This established, a stance of engagement will tend naturally to follow, as the creature exploits the situation in the energetic pursuit of its goals. Last comes the stance of endorsement, as the organism succeeds in meeting its goals. Note that the ranking concerns the relative roles of these states in happiness; you could accept it while ranking them differently in terms of *value* or choiceworthiness. A Nietzschean, for instance, might value states of vitality or exuberance over peace of mind, even if this means being less happy.

Naturally, this schema, if illustrative, is a bit oversimplified. For example, I couched compression as a failure of attunement, a kind of psychic disattunement or alienation—it certainly is not a way of being psychically at home in one's life—but it appears to involve the engagement dimension of happiness as well, since the reactive stance characteristic of compression tends not to combine well with exuberance. And states of flow seem to involve a lessening of compression. The example illustrates the interdependence of the three modes of response: affective states will often if not usually involve more than one. This makes sense since a given type of situation may call for a multifaceted response, so that affect types need not conform strictly to the three-mode schema. I will mention a few other examples to illustrate, and to show how some important states fit in the present account of happiness.

Fear is typically thought to involve withdrawal (the engagement dimension), a defensive disturbance akin to anxiety (the attunement dimension), and a negative appraisal of the object (the endorsement dimension).[29] Anger presents an interesting case: it at least involves a negative appraisal, and possibly some defensive disturbance, but it also seems to involve approach tendencies characteristic of engagement. It thus appears, in that respect, to be a *positive* affective state, whilst being negative in others. Though contrary to initial appearances, this seems rather plausible: anger counts against happiness in the obvious ways, but it can also count *toward* happiness to some extent, as might be imagined in the case of a warrior resolutely pursuing a vendetta against a hated enemy, drawing strength from his anger. There can be an aspect of dark flourishing in such a case, for the individual is fully and energetically engaged in the business of living. But we would hesitate to describe such a person as happy on the whole, since there remains a clear sense in which the anger is primarily a negative state.

On the positive side, there is the interesting question of what to make of emotional fulfillment, or feeling fulfilled. This seems a crucial aspect of happiness when we picture its prototypical forms, and we are unlikely to regard as happy someone whose life is unfulfilling. The question merits a fuller treatment than it will get here, but I would venture that fulfillment is chiefly a mixture of attunement and joy (usually muted but deeply felt)—a state that paradigmatically follows on the fulfillment of the heart's desires. We can think of this as taking two forms. At the heights we have the fulfillment of repose, as happens when reflecting on one's great fortune. The more pedestrian variety, the fulfillment of engagement, arises when engaged in activities that well suit our natures. States of flow may sometimes be like this, or perhaps the fulfillment follows them.

It must be emphasized that the preceding taxonomy is intended to be rough and informal, meant to serve as a plausible starting point for further reflection and investigation. The core points, regarding the richness and demandingness of happiness, and the basic character of some of its more important states, could survive even with substantial adjustments to the picture. A rigorous development of the account would need to be put in the context of a more or less complete theory of affect—a project well beyond the scope of this book, and possibly premature given the state of scientific knowledge in this realm. Much greater attention must also be given to each of the states involved in happiness, only some of which have been touched on here. Were there a reasonably mature literature on the subject, we would find numerous journal articles dedicated to each of the many states involved here—significant bodies of work on, for example, the nature and significance for happiness of tranquility, or confidence, or vitality, or flow.[30] For now, a rough sketch will have to do.

In the next chapter we will develop the present version of the emotional state theory in greater detail. First, however, I want to note some advantages of an emotional state approach, illustrating how it can diminish common doubts about the significance of happiness.

5. IS HAPPINESS IMMUTABLE?

If someone still wishes to maintain that happiness is not important, it is hard to know what to say. Neither Nietzsche nor the Stoics, who seem to define the limits of sane opinion in such matters, went that far. It would appear to be a bitter, not to say monstrous, view of human life that denies significance across the board to such things as imperturbability, peace of mind, vitality of spirit, fulfillment, inner surety and expansiveness of soul. If there are those who want to embrace such an ethic, they are welcome to it.

The more interesting questions concern *how* important happiness is, and it is true that happiness is not the only thing that matters in life, or even for well-being. Moreover, it is clearly overvalued by many—those who are all too eager to trade their integrity for the promise of happiness, or who, thinking themselves entitled to be happy, do terrible things to their families, co-workers, or strangers in the name of an imaginary birthright. Others shoot themselves in the foot by valuing happiness so much they forget to put much value on anything else, leaving themselves with no real source of happiness. We should grant that happiness is not as important as some people think it is, and that it ranks firmly beneath virtue in a good life: to sacrifice the demands of good character in the name of personal happiness—or, I would add, personal welfare—can never be justified. We must, above all, act decently, if not well. Or so, at any rate, I am prepared to grant. None of this is incompatible in the least with the aims of this book. Happiness is a matter of central importance for a good life, and an important object of practical concern. To dismiss happiness as a lightweight matter of little import is most likely to be working with a lightweight conception of happiness.

Many other interesting doubts have been raised either about the importance of happiness or about whether we should pursue it. Here I will mention only certain worries about the extent to which our emotional conditions really track well-being. The aim will be not to rebut them fully, but to gesture at the resources an emotional state theory of happiness can bring to bear in addressing them. A familiar concern to those who have followed the empirical literature concerns adaptation and the idea that people have happiness "set points" toward which their happiness naturally tends to gravitate.[31] These set points are said to be substantially heritable, perhaps as much as .80, though .50 is a more widely accepted figure. Recent events, even quite major ones, can move people up or down for a brief period, maybe a few months, but usually they will return to their set point—no more or less happy or unhappy than before. In one of the best recent philosophical treatments of happiness, Elijah Millgram pressed a version of this worry, arguing essentially that happiness functions to track not well-being, but *changes* in well-being. (Peter Railton has been developing a version of this idea, suggesting a "delta meter" model of happiness.[32]) The issues are too complex to address here fully, but it bears noting that most researchers now seem to believe that past claims about the relative immutability of happiness were often overstated.[33] Here I want to note a few ways in which an emotional state view of happiness may be less susceptible to such objections.

One version of the adaptation worry arises in political thought, where happiness is frequently dismissed for being too subject to adaptation, raising the specter of happy slaves and the like.[34] Policymakers should thus focus their attention on other matters, such as the distribution of resources or capabilities. An emotional state view of happiness seems less vulnerable on this count than other theories. For while it is easy to imagine people becoming resigned to oppressive circumstances, even registering satisfaction with their lives or showing the world a happy face, it is not so easy to imagine the enslaved, the solitary homeless, and the browbeaten sweatshop laborer leading *emotionally fulfilling* lives. When reading Martha Nussbaum's admirable depictions of struggling Indian women, 'psychic flourishing' is not the first term that comes to mind.[35]

Second, we should question the standard rationale for expecting strong forms of adaptation to occur—that it usually doesn't make sense evolutionarily or otherwise to feel happy or sad forever after an event, because we need to get on with our lives and deal with them as they now are. Emotions need to facilitate a response to the change and then get out of the way. There is something to this thought, but notice that it chiefly applies to endorsement-type states, which are neither the whole nor even the most important aspect of happiness. If relationships and work and leisure activities improve markedly, and remain so, then why should you gradually settle back to a "set point" level of engagement—ceasing to experience as much flow, and feeling less energetic and alive? Consider, particularly, states of anxiety or stress: if you are living under threat, and things stay that way for a long time, it makes little sense to let your defenses down and cease responding as if you are under threat. So long as they are out to get you, you had best stay prepared; so long as they are not, you should relax and stop toasting your brain and body with stress hormones. The point is not to deny that adaptation occurs with such states. But there is no reason to expect the strong sort of adaptation in such states that we seem to see with feelings of happiness and sadness. It is important to note as well that the empirical research mainly focuses on feelings like these—in the case of self-reported "happiness," indirectly, given the likelihood that people tend to focus inordinately on such feelings when making such reports—or on other measures, like life satisfaction reports, that may also be especially prone to adaptation.[36] (A further limitation of most research, particularly regarding the heritability of happiness, is the homogeneity of the populations studied. To an Amish farmer or San hunter, or the fishermen on the island mentioned in Chapter 1, the affluent Westerners who mostly get studied may seem to be leading pretty near identical ways of life. If all your subjects live in similar environments, then *of course* the role of environment in determining happiness is going to seem limited. It is as if one were to run a series of studies on zoo bears and circus bears, find not much difference in well-being between the groups, and conclude that it doesn't matter very much what environment you put bears in.)

Third, our emotional conditions plausibly tend to be keyed to the general conditions of our lives, not the details.[37] And once our basic needs for health and security are met, they seem to depend chiefly on how we live. Over the long haul, what we have and what happens to us—the sorts of objective variables that tend to get studied—seem to be secondary, typically of little more than transient concern (this is the wisdom embodied in the adaptation literature). If so, then we might expect happiness to seem immutable even if is not: it is hard to change the basics of how we live, at least at the level of individual decision. Consider the sorts of goods that tend to be cited as the main positive sources of happiness: notably, active social engagement, and meaningful activities that are well-matched to your abilities.[38] Such things are not easily changed. If you're lonely, harried, and bored to tears by your work now, you stand a good chance of being lonely, harried, and bored for a long time. And unless you've got the nerve and the ability to make some fundamental changes in how you live, and the wisdom to do it well, there may not be much you can do about it. The fact that your big paycheck, your designer home, your aromatherapy sessions, your personal coach, and your washboard abs have done nothing to make you happier scarcely shows that you've got a brain defect, or that unhappiness is written into your genes. Perhaps these aren't the things you need for a good life.

The pursuit of happiness is not easy. Given that the basic conditions of our lives, and the way we live, are so heavily dependent on our social environment, we may want to look more closely at the societal dimensions of the question. (If this isn't clear yet, it should become so in Part IV.) Even if we are suspicious of using policy instruments to promote happiness, we might at least consider the limits of individual effort, and the importance of context, in shaping how happy we are. Take, for example, recent initiatives to develop and teach methods by which people can make themselves happier. Such efforts can produce very real benefits, and in fact many of the ancients were in a version of same business.[39] While there are legitimate worries about such techniques sometimes reducing to cheap spiritual analgesics, I see no reason why this cannot be avoided.[40] A more interesting question, it seems to me, is how far individual efforts like this are likely to improve human well-being on a broad scale. If the problem lies chiefly in the way you live, and this in turn depends heavily on the kind of society you inhabit, then positive thinking techniques and the like are only going to get you so far.[41]

The difficulty of pursuing happiness is no reason to think happiness a mainly biological or temperamental affair, unchangeable and unconnected with the conditions of our lives. Consider the way that depression has skyrocketed in recent decades. How should we explain this trend? It could be due to some environmental contaminant burning up our neurotransmitters. Or perhaps there is something wrong with the way many of us are living.

7

Happiness as Psychic Affirmation

We are made happy when reason can discover no occasion for it.

Thoreau[1]

1. INTRODUCTION

The last chapter sketched a default version of the emotional state theory on which happiness consists in a person's overall emotional condition. This in turn was understood as the sum of the individual's moods and emotions. To be happy, on this view, is to have predominantly positive, versus negative, moods and emotions. We then filled out this view in certain ways, yielding a "three aspect" version of the emotional state theory on which happiness specifically involves states of attunement, engagement, and endorsement. This was seen as an articulation of a broader ideal of happiness as "psychic affirmation." Here I want to fill out the view in further detail, clarifying both its "psychic" and "affirmation" aspects. We will accordingly focus on two issues: first, the fundamental distinctions in affect driving the inclusion of moods and emotions—and other states, we will see—versus other affects; and second, the "threshold problem": how happy one has to be actually to count as happy, versus not. After addressing these and a few other matters, I will summarize the resulting account of happiness, contending that it is both intuitively plausible and answers well to our practical interests in happiness. Happiness is best understood along the lines of such a theory.

2. TWO DISTINCTIONS IN AFFECT

2.1. Introduction

In the following sections I will argue that existing categories of affect are inadequate, and need to be supplemented. It will help, for starters, to see one of the current taxonomies of affect. A prominent textbook on emotions distinguishes various emotional categories and depicts them in a diagram according to their typical duration (see Figure 7.1, below).

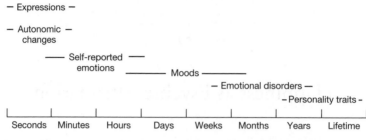

Figure 4.6 A spectrum of affective phenomena in terms of the time course of each.

Fig. 7.1. A diagram of affective phenomena from Oatley and Jenkins 1996*.
*The same diagram appears in the 2006 edition of this text. Used with permission.

Notice what appears between the categories of mood and personality trait: emotional disorders. It is questionable whether emotional disorders belong in the chart, or whether they form a single category of the right sort for this depiction (should depression be lumped together with phobias?). More worrisome is that the diagram, reflecting current practice, recognizes no non-disordered emotional phenomena that are longer lasting than moods and yet less permanent than traits. What about non-disordered depression? Moreover, it supposes that moods sometimes last for months. This is implausible. Do particular moods often persist through sleep? Possibly, but one wonders whether psychologists have failed to distinguish a period in which a kind of mood predominates from one in which a single mood token persists, uninterrupted, for weeks or months.

I want to suggest that we add to the diagram, in roughly the region occupied by emotional disorders, a category of "emotional conditions," for reasons that will emerge in the remainder of Sections 2 and 3. This category includes negative conditions like depression, but also positive conditions like happiness. Thus we incorporate into our taxonomy those relatively prolonged states exhibiting a predominance of moods of certain sorts. This pattern will not be viewed as coincidental but as (at least typically) grounded in states that are more variable than traits, but more stable than moods—mood propensities, I will call them—essentially, a condition that *disposes* one to experience certain moods. And we do not assume that such states are invariably going to be disordered.

To motivate this move let's return to the default view and consider its deficiencies.

2.2. Central affective states

"I have an ear-ache." Do not say "Alas!" And I am not saying that it is not permissible to groan, only *do not groan in the centre of your being*.

Epictetus, *Discourses* (1925, emphasis added)

Stoic philosophers had something of a reputation for making extravagant, not to say unreasonable, demands. But even they recognized that there are limits to what can realistically be asked of us. They did not counsel us, for instance, not to feel pain when hit on the head with a hammer. Instead they told us not to let such things *get* to us, or generate an emotional disturbance. This important distinction, implicit in the passage from Epictetus, seems to have been lost in modern ethical thought. It is implicit in the difference we noted between the class of moods and emotions, on the one hand, and other affects ("mere pleasures"), on the other. But that way of putting it isn't very satisfying, as the class of "moods and emotions" looks to be a conjunction of two different categories, where for our purposes there seems to be a broader category encompassing both. To articulate the distinction in a satisfactory way we will need to depart from the familiar folk psychological vocabulary, as there seems no way to mark it in such terms.

The distinction in question concerns what I have called *centrality* of affect. Some affective states are psychologically deep, or *central*, whereas others are comparatively shallow, superficial, or *peripheral*. The states involved in the paradigm cases from Chapter 3 are central, whereas the superficial pleasures discussed in Chapter 4—amusement or annoyance, physical pain or pleasure, etc.—are peripheral: they seem not, in themselves, to alter our emotional conditions. Nor, accordingly, do peripheral affects appear to be happiness-constituting.

The central/peripheral distinction is well-established, if tacitly, in ordinary talk about our emotional lives. Sometimes we are quite direct about it, noting how deeply something "touched" us, the depth or profundity of emotion it aroused, etc. We also use broadly anatomical metaphors, ranging from the viscerality of "gut-wrenching," upward to "heart-rending," all the way to the ethereality of impacts on one's spirit or soul ("soul-crushing"). A popular song has the singer implore a lover to "satisfy my soul," and it is obvious that he is not simply asking to be entertained or amused.[2] The most interesting class of metaphors used to make the distinction hint at a difference between affective states that do, and do not, constitute a change in the person herself. Thus do we talk of something's not just amusing or annoying you, but "getting to you," "bringing you down," "lifting you up," "moving" you, "perturbing" or "disturbing" you, and so forth. Conversely, something might just "bounce right off you": any emotional reaction you have is small, swift, and quickly forgotten.

These locutions mark a morally significant distinction as well: it is fine to be annoyed at losing a dime, but a person of good character doesn't let such things *get* to her or *disturb* her. Several passages in Hemingway's novel hover around this idea. For instance, "pain does not matter to a man" (p. 84), Santiago "was comfortable but suffering, although he did not admit the suffering at all" (p. 64), and "with his prayers said, and feeling much better, but suffering exactly as much, and perhaps a little more, he leaned against the wood of the bow" (p. 65).

The writer's choice of words here is a bit curious, since 'suffering' suggests pain that bothers the individual; but he apparently means to be describing physical discomforts that do not bother the old man. Consider, finally, that many central affective state terms can be adapted to denote personality traits: thus we have depressive, anxious, serene, cheerful, and happy personalities. We do not speak of annoyed, amused, or pained personalities. Indeed, there seems not even a grammatically correct way to entertain the thought of a personality that tends to experience a lot of pleasure or pain.

This sort of language is not careless metaphor; it signifies a genuine, and important, distinction in our emotional lives.[3] It also hints at a link between happiness and the *self* that does not obtain in the case of (peripheral) pleasure. There appears to be an inner citadel of the self that many affects fail to penetrate.[4] Central affective states seem to constitute changes in us, and are not merely things that happen to us, mainly because they concern an individual's *disposition*. While they last they amount to what are much like short-lived alterations in one's temperament, or personality. For example: to be in an irritable mood is to be, for its duration, less happy than one would otherwise be. For something to cause such a mood is one way for it to *get* to one. And to be irritable is in some sense to be a certain sort of person for that time: a crank, a sorehead, an ill-tempered grouch.

What primarily distinguishes central affective states, I would suggest, is that they *dispose* agents to experience certain affects rather than others. This, indeed, appears to be their essential characteristic: insofar as one's emotional disposition is altered by virtue of being in an affective state, that state is central. If it makes no such difference, it is peripheral. While in a depressed mood, for instance, an individual will likely find little pleasure in what happens, will tend to look on the dark side of things, and may more likely be saddened by negative events. The elated person will exhibit the opposite tendencies. And someone afflicted by anxiety will tend to multiply and exaggerate potential threats, experience greater upset at setbacks, and be more prone to experience fear and perhaps anger. Whereas a more serene individual will tend to take things in stride, see fewer causes for anxiety, worry less about perceived threats, etc. Contrast these states with the clearly peripheral ones: neither the mild irritation expressed at dropping a pencil nor the trivial pleasure of driving past a pretty house appear to have any direct impact on what other emotions one is likely to experience.

We can identify at least four other hallmarks of central affective states.[5] First, they are *productive*: they have many and varied causal consequences—generating other affective states, initiating various physiological changes, biasing cognition and behavior, etc. Second, such states tend to be *persistent*: when they occur, they generally last a while. There is a certain "inertia" to central affective states that peripheral affects seem to lack: they don't vanish without a trace the instant the triggering event is over. Third, the relevant states are often *pervasive*: they are frequently diffuse and nonspecific in character, tending to permeate the whole of consciousness, and setting the tone thereof. They are often said to color our experience of life. Finally, they tend to be *profound*: they are somehow deep, including phenomenally, and often visceral in feel. Though we tend not to describe, say, a mildly depressed or giddy mood as "profound," there is nonetheless a perceptible depth to such states that, for instance, physical pleasures lack. They seem to run all the way through us, in some sense, feeling like states *of* us rather than impingements from without. There is a certain intimacy to our experience even of a low-key mood. Profundity is part of what we have in mind when we speak of something's "getting to" us, lifting our spirits, or bringing about a deep sense of joy, anxiety, etc. Contrast such states with that of orgasm: while manifestly intense, this state may not always feel emotionally profound, at times seeming more a superficial pleasure that fails to move us.

It is revealing that every example of a central affective state described above involves a mood, or something mood-like. I would conjecture that all central affective states are in some sense mood states, and vice versa. Only "in some sense": emotions are not moods, yet many are clearly central: for instance, the emotion of joy that follows on hearing good news, and that of grief felt on learning of a loved one's passing. These emotions are certainly central affective states. Moreover, they are plausibly happiness-constituting. And yet, while not moods, they do appear to be mood-*constituting*: during the episode of joy one's mood is certainly elevated, and during grief it is melancholy.[6] Such peripheral affects as a passing annoyance, by contrast, look to have no direct impact on one's mood at all. At the same time, it is plausible that all moods and mood-constituting emotions are central. Thus we find, apparently, that all central affective states are either moods or mood-constituting emotions, and vice versa.[7] It appears, then, that the notion of a person's emotional condition fundamentally concerns mood-related states.

This conjecture may not survive further investigation. Some of what I would classify as central affective states may not fit the mood picture: anxiety, fatigue or weariness, listlessness, contentment or tranquility, feeling stressed, feelings of vitality, psychic compression, and flow. All of these seem to be affective, and they appear to be central and happiness-constituting. They all dispose us to experience certain affects more, others less. They are also pervasive, productive, persistent, and in some sense profound. And they seem to involve our emotional conditions. Whether these are mood phenomena will depend on our best theory of moods.[8]

The central/peripheral distinction is essentially unknown to the literature, the closest counterpart being a distinction between sensory affects and the very broad category of emotions. As we saw, many "emotions"—for example, being mildly pleased at some extremely minor event—fall, with sensory affects, on the peripheral side of the divide. The result appears to be a tripartite division of affect into the sensory, the notional or intellectual, and the central or "emotional."[9] ('Intellectual' is problematical here, since affects of this sort are often quite automatic and unreflective—for instance, the trivial mental pleasure that occurs when driving past an attractive house.) While affects of the first two types can also be emotional in this fuller sense, they need not be. Interestingly, the conative realm—that of desire—admits of a similar division: urges or appetites (sensory) versus mere wishes or preferences (intellectual or notional), as against longings, yearnings, or the desires of the heart (the "central"). In both cases the central states seem to have a special significance, being in some way more important than the peripheral ones. Regarding central affective states, we saw that they ramify for our characters in ways that peripheral affects do not, and that they seem to involve the personality or self—intuitively, in some non-occult sense, the soul—whereas peripheral affects seem not to. A similar point arises with desires, where it seems important whether a given desire is held merely notionally or intellectually, or is truly *wholehearted*. Some, like Harry Frankfurt, have taken wholeheartedness to be essential for a desire to be constitutive of the self, mirroring our observations about central affective states and the self.[10] The points about desire are interesting, but I touch on them here only to emphasize that the central/peripheral distinction in affect is real and weighty.

I have not been able to draw this distinction as precisely as would be desirable, but it should be clear that some such distinction needs to be made. Hopefully a better understanding of the psychology in this realm, informed by empirical research, will enable a more exact rendering of the distinction. Finding a systematic difference in the neural correlates of central and peripheral affects could be helpful in this regard. It is possible that the distinction will prove to need some revision; it may not be exactly the right distinction to make. But there can be little disputing that *some* such distinction has to be made: the notion of intensity cannot account for the important differences between states like gustatory or sexual pleasure and emotional fulfillment, melancholy, or anxiety. The latter sorts of states palpably affect us in a deeper manner than the former, even when they are less intense, and the difference seems significant.

The contribution an affective state makes to one's happiness is proportional to its centrality, with more central states constituting a larger alteration in how happy one is. Since centrality and pleasantness can diverge—an orgasm is more pleasant, though less central, than a slightly cheerful mood—it should be apparent enough that we cannot substitute familiar notions of pleasantness or intensity for centrality. Notice that to call happiness psychologically "deep" is not to deny that there can be superficial forms of happiness. Since centrality comes in degrees, some forms of happiness are deeper, and others shallower or more superficial *as central affective states*. Peripheral affects are superficial in the stronger sense given above. This raises a question: might the central/peripheral distinction itself be purely a matter of degree? Possibly, but the linguistic phenomena cited above seem to mark a sharp distinction: either something gets to you or it doesn't. And something either alters one's emotional disposition, or one's emotional condition, or it doesn't. If there is not a sharp distinction, then we should apparently have to grant that all affects are happiness-constituting, with "peripheral" affects playing a smaller—apparently imperceptible—role than "central" ones. Not much hangs on the question, so I will set it aside.

2.3. Mood propensities

On a recent visit to Mexico, I emerged from my hotel room one morning to find a member of the groundskeeping staff on the balcony, smiling and waving at something in a nearby tree. Curious to know what had got his attention, I joined him at the railing and saw that the object of his attention was a lovely yellow and black bird that I had not seen before, twittering pleasantly from its nest atop a small palm tree. Delighted to share his find, the man pointed, said "baby," and then directed my attention to the adjoining trees where two other, larger specimens were perched: "mama," and then "papa." "What do you call it?" I queried in fractured Spanish. "Boquillita"—or something like that—he replied, with some authority. (For all I know this meant "stupid gringo," but it seemed to refer to the variety of bird.) With a hectic vacation schedule to attend to, I said goodbye and moved on, while the man remained.

It occurred to me that in the United States one does not often see groundskeepers taking a break from work to delight in the local fauna. The affluent patrons of our hotel could hardly be bothered to do so even while vacationing; I myself had been there for several days without noticing this little family, right outside my room. This fellow certainly did not look like a troubled man: he seemed for all the world to be *happy*. This showed in his bearing, manner, and expressions, and perhaps most of all in the mere fact that here he was, pausing to take pleasure in the world before him—something, to judge from his familiarity with this avian family, he apparently did with some regularity. Of course, it is impossible to draw firm conclusions from a brief encounter with a stranger in a foreign land; perhaps the man was in fact a melancholy poet whose sole consolation was to look at the birds. The telling thing is that it is perfectly ordinary, and often utterly reasonable, to make judgments about an individual's happiness based on the sort of limited information—much of it subtle and unarticulated—that drove my impressions here. This is particularly so when we know the person well. We will return to this point later, since it suggests a major deficiency in traditional ways of thinking about happiness, but for now I want to remark on the nature of the information used here. First, we draw on our extremely rich perceptions of the individual's expressions, tone of voice, and behavior, which carry many clues about his inner state.

Second, and more interestingly, we observe how the individual responds to his environment, the idea being that happy people tend to react to events differently from the unhappy. This effectively amounts to using what psychologists call "mood inductions" to assess how happy people are: life continuously presents us with circumstances that can elicit various moods or emotions—mood inductions, in effect—and we look for clues to a person's condition in how she responds to these situations. If Stan dwells excessively on every piece of bad news, passing over the good, gets inordinately upset over minor irritations, and if his good moods are easily shattered, we will likely suspect that he isn't very happy. In the present case, the fact that the groundskeeper was of a mind to break from his routine and attend joyously to the birds that those of us with greater leisure had not even noticed—birds he had apparently come to know well—seemed to convey something of import about the condition of his psyche. A person who is stressed out, anxious, irritable, or feeling down will generally not act like that.

Note that we do not simply infer what the person's current mood is in such cases—we infer how happy she is in general. Perhaps we infer, first, what the individual's mood is, and then, assuming the mood to be representative, draw conclusions about the person's happiness. That is probably not always, or even usually, the case: for one thing, moods vary too much, so we should be very cautious about assuming any given mood to represent the norm for a person. Second, an individual's response to a situation may not reflect his mood going into it: it is perfectly possible that, before encountering the birds, the groundskeeper was in a neutral mood, or even a bad one; maybe he had just gotten an irritating lecture from his boss. Had the latter been the case, and I knew of it, I would still have guessed him happy; indeed, I would have been *more* confident in that judgment, for it would have been clear that his reaction sprang from something deeper, and more lasting, than merely a passing mood.

But what could this be? The individual's temperament? No: the judgment is not that the person has a happy temperament or personality, but that he is happy. More importantly, the person's current happiness might be uncharacteristic: suppose I had known this fellow well for some years, and believed him to have a somewhat melancholy temperament. This would, again, if anything have bolstered my suspicion that he was happy. Taking this, together with the supposition that he had gone into the situation in a bad mood—and let us suppose in addition that this was my first encounter with him in a long time, so that I had no other information about his present condition—there seems to be only one plausible explanation for my concluding that he is happy: I inferred that his fundamental *disposition* in emotional matters was positive, making him prone to respond to things favorably, just as he responded to this situation.[11] And this I took as fairly strong evidence that he was happy. For normally, given his (hypothesized) melancholic personality, he would have found no joy in it, because he was not normally a happy man. Perhaps things are going his way now.

I would suggest that we very often assess individuals' happiness in just this way: by taking their responses to things to reflect their basic emotional dispositions—running deeper than mere moods—and these in turn as evidence for how happy they are. This could, perhaps, be nothing more than a means of guessing at a person's typical moods, figuring that they will tend to cohere with his basic disposition. But our thinking here does not seem so convoluted as that. Moreover, I have argued elsewhere that when a person's basic emotional condition has just changed radically, we discount most of her moods and emotions of the recent past and base the ascription of happiness primarily on the immediate condition, using her fundamental disposition to anchor the judgment.[12] We seem to take that disposition not simply as a clue to other states, but as itself definitive of at least part of the individual's happiness. It is more plausible, then, to say that the happy person's propensity to experience those moods itself, in part, *constitutes* her being happy: she is happy partly *by virtue of* her propensity to respond so favorably to things.

Let's step back for a moment and return to the emotional state theory as we left it at the end of Section 4.1. At that point we had it that happiness consists in one's central affective states. Even setting aside the preceding points about our ascriptive practices, this seems incomplete: happiness, at least in its prototypical instances, appears to involve something deeper and more continuous. As things stand, happiness is a simple function of one's aggregated moods and mood-constituting emotions. Nothing connects the various affects with each other. The theory thus fails to distinguish cases in which a predominance of positive affect results purely from a fortunate confluence of positive events from cases in which this results from an underlying endogenous condition. Yet it is natural to think of happiness as usually being a lasting condition. Indeed, we might want to explain a given individual's predominance of positive mood as a consequence of his being happy—as opposed to being, say, the result of a series of congenial events.

Consider that one of the benefits of being happy is not just that one happens to experience a lot of positive moods, but that one is prone to experience such moods. Negative events are less likely to generate bad moods. When a bad mood does come along, the happy individual can expect a quicker return to good spirits than someone who is not happy. *The happy person thus exhibits a highly desirable kind of emotional resilience.* This propensity to experience certain moods also enables us to predict the moods of happy individuals; thus we are normally more eager to make plans to visit with friends we know to be happy than with those who are not.

Suppose you learn that a friend has had a hair-trigger propensity for anxiety in recent months (she's struggling to complete her dissertation). Wouldn't you consider her less happy *by virtue of* that fact, quite apart from the anxious moods themselves? Suppose you catch her on a good day, when nothing has triggered the anxiety.[13] Would you conclude that she is, today, no less happy than were she relatively immune to anxiety? When we attend a funeral reception and see grieving family members laughing with old friends, we do not think their unhappiness has completely, if temporarily, lifted. A deeper unhappiness remains. To take a fuller example, consider two friends, Tom and Jerry, both of happy temperament, who take a relaxing vacation at the beach. During their several days together, their moods are generally quite similar and fairly positive, save that Tom is a bit more cheerful, being pleased finally to get away from home some months after a difficult divorce. By and large he is not the least melancholic—most of the time he feels wholly unburdened, laughter comes easily, and he takes great pleasure in catching up with his old friend and conversing with other vacationers. Yet Tom's emotional state remains unusually fragile: on two occasions he inexplicably bursts into tears and weeps uncontrollably. These episodes don't last long, so that Tom's moods are still, on the whole, a little more positive than Jerry's. Is it obvious that Tom is happier than Jerry? The reverse seems more plausible: it appears both that Tom's elevated propensity for sadness diminishes his happiness in itself, and that he is *less* happy than Jerry. It also seems likely that *Jerry* would not consider Tom to have been particularly happy during the trip.

All of this suggests that, beyond the distinction between central and peripheral affective states, a further distinction appears to be required. I would suggest that happiness involves not just agents' central affective states or moods, but also their dispositions to experience moods: their *mood propensities*. Consider, for another example, depression, which is presumably not just a bad mood, nor a series of bad moods. It is rather a broader psychological condition. In typical instances of depression, it is not simply the case that one happens to be in a depressed mood a lot of the time, as if it were a coincidence that one's low mood today mirrors that of yesterday. (Maybe each day began with a separate piece of bad news.) Something deeper is happening. Thus the depressed individual's present good cheer is tarnished by the knowledge that it will soon give way to despair, as if a hidden force is dragging one's spirits ineluctably downward. This sort of phenomenon is quite common with depression, whose sufferers often experience diurnal cycles in their moods (as do non-depressed individuals). To be at a certain point in one's cycle is for one's mood propensity to be a certain way.

To see the distinction, it can help to consider dynamical systems approaches to mood, which conceive of an individual's mood as a point in a multidimensional state space, where each dimension represents a variable parameter.[14] Certain points or regions in these spaces are *attractors*—configurations toward which subjects' moods naturally tend to gravitate (e.g., the attractor for a depressed individual's mood will be somewhere in the region of depressed mood). Moods can deviate from this configuration in response to particular events, but over time they will tend to converge on it. Roughly speaking, an individual's mood propensity is given by the shape of her mood state space: where are the attractors? As her mood propensity varies, so will the location of the attractors.

The importance of distinguishing mood propensities should be clear quite apart from matters of happiness. One use for a variable mood propensity is as a catalyst for either changing or adapting to broad features of one's environment or niche, essentially by varying one's temperament. For instance, an individual who is in a position of social dominance may want to be more confident, extroverted, and prone to positive moods than someone who has lost social status and needs to reassess his strategy while avoiding even more serious losses through fruitless efforts to reassert his former status.[15] Alternatively, it may be adaptive to alter one's mood cycles to match or complement those of the people around one, or to facilitate a change in lifestyle or schedule.[16]

Three points of clarification. As we saw, mood propensity is distinct from a person's personality or *temperament*, which is how she is characteristically disposed to react, emotionally, to various circumstances, at some basic level.[17] Whereas mood propensities vary considerably over time—for example, someone of cheerful temper will sometimes be uncharacteristically prone to melancholy moods, as when a bad relationship leaves her depressed. Second, a mood propensity in the present sense is *generalized*: it involves a tendency to experience positive moods quite generally. It is not object-specific: it does not, in other words, involve a disposition to experience positive moods only in response to particular objects or events, or classes thereof. Thus it is irrelevant to questions of happiness that one is specifically disposed toward cheerful moods when in the presence of one's dog. Rather, one must be disposed to experience such moods in a wide range of circumstances.[18]

Third, some mood propensities seem irrelevant to happiness: say, the tendency toward irritability brought on by a chronic pain in one's toe. Though this may be mediated by a true alteration in one's emotional disposition, we can imagine that such a pain might directly affect mood in the same way that a series of external events might, without any underlying continuity in one's emotional state. In short, we need to distinguish mood propensities that have the right categorical basis.[19] I would suggest that happiness involves, not mood propensity period, but one's *emotionally-based* mood propensity. (For brevity I will usually omit the qualifier.) This is admittedly vague, but the intuitive idea is that mood propensity counts insofar as it is grounded in one's emotional condition. Suppose we could isolate the psychological mechanisms subserving emotions and moods (*qua* affects); call them, collectively, the "emotion system." We could say, then, that mood propensities count toward happiness insofar as they are grounded in the current state of the emotion system. This would exclude toe-pain-based mood propensities. It also excludes personality or temperamental traits: you do not count as happy, say, by virtue of having an exuberant temperament, since you may presently be depressed, and neither exuberant nor prone (now) to be that way.

The notion of mood propensity needs further refinement; we should regard the present formulation as a placeholder, not a finished product. The important point is that we recognize a type of state that is intermediate between moods and traits, which disposes us to experience certain moods and related states, and which plays a constitutive role in happiness.[20] While talk of "emotionally-based mood propensities" may seem recherché, the root idea—that our emotional conditions run deeper, and involve more lasting states, than particular emotions and moods—is not at all unfamiliar. Many would naturally try to explain a case like Jerry's friend Tom in terms of the *unconscious*, deeming him to be the victim of unconscious distress which only becomes manifest at certain times. This sort of psychoanalytic explanation is well embedded in the culture, and it is possible to read the present notion of mood propensity as, at least sometimes, grounded in some such states. Perhaps a completed theory would even replace the notion of mood propensity with ideas of unconscious moods, emotions, or other affects—referring directly to the categorical basis of the propensities rather than the propensities themselves. (Note, however, that such "moods" or "emotions" would be rather different from their "conscious" counterparts, being longer-lasting and manifesting in very different ways. They would also be unconscious in a deeper way than a mood, like irritability, when it lacks phenomenal character. In that case, the relevant state would involve a propensity to *become* irritable, for example, when someone spoils your mood by cutting ahead of you in the checkout line, rather than being irritable.)

3. HAPPINESS AND PSYCHOLOGICAL TAXONOMY

Happiness has two components: first, a person's central affective states, and second, her mood propensity. Or, in more familiar terms, happiness consists in a person's emotional condition. The worry at this point is that the emotional state view might seem to make happiness an ad hoc conjunction of two disparate categories. Why should happiness incorporate just these states? What brings these states together, I would suggest, is their dispositionality: the components of happiness together fix a subject's emotional disposition, at least insofar as this reflects the individual's emotional condition. Indeed, the notion of an emotional condition itself most fundamentally concerns (but is not exhausted by) a person's emotional disposition. Peripheral affects, by contrast, do not in themselves alter a person's emotional disposition. This suggests a theoretical reason to incorporate mood propensities into the account: if happiness concerns us mainly as it involves persons' emotional dispositions, or psychic orientation, then it would be odd to leave mood propensities out. Compare life satisfaction attitudes, which also tend to be conceived as largely dispositional states. Both views see happiness as fundamentally a matter of how the individual stands in relation to her life.

More so than life satisfaction and hedonist views seem to allow, the states involved in happiness have far-reaching effects on how we confront the world and react to things in our lives. As I noted earlier, changes in an agent's central affective states and mood propensity are much like changes in temperament or personality. To be happy is not merely to have experiences of a certain sort; it is also to be configured emotionally in certain ways. Indeed, one's basic psychic disposition seems altered. One is prone to take greater pleasure in things, to see things in a more positive light, to take greater notice of good things, to be more optimistic, to be more outgoing and friendly, and to take chances more. One is also slower and less likely to become anxious or fearful, or to be angered or saddened by events. *One confronts the world in a different way from the unhappy.* Whereas the hedonist regards happiness merely as a state of one's consciousness, the emotional state view takes it to be a state of one's *being.* When you're happy, everything is different.

The present view of happiness circumscribes an important aspect of human psychology, and 'emotional condition' seems less than adequate as a name for it. A more evocative term, perhaps, is 'psyche.'[21] While usually understood as a generic term for the mind, we often appear to employ it more narrowly: it can seem perfectly natural to say that a minor injury was painful yet left the individual's psyche undisturbed or unaffected—namely, if it didn't "get" to her. Similarly, a philosophy student might find an argument in an ethics text persuasive, but only in a very thin, intellectualized sense; her conviction isn't wholehearted, which is to say that the ideas never really penetrated to her psyche. Or a depressed person, on receiving a pay raise or other bit of good news, may be "pleased" about it. But his sentiment amounts to little more than a pleasant thought; his heart isn't really in it, and so the event fails to register in his psyche. Perhaps it is no coincidence, then, that it can seem natural to think of happiness, on the emotional state theory, as a condition or state of the psyche, where this expression conveys some sense of the psychological depth of the phenomenon. (In this sense of the term, 'psyche' seems interchangeable with a common usage of 'soul' to denote, not an immaterial spirit, but the deeper aspects of the mind, which seem to constitute the true self in some sense.) I exploited this point in the previous chapter, referring to happiness as a kind of psychic affirmation or psychic flourishing. Though I will continue this usage, I do not wish to put much weight on it.

4. THE THRESHOLD PROBLEM: HOW HAPPY IS HAPPY?

4.1. Problems with the received view

As I said in the last chapter, the question of what it is to *be* happy is not as pressing as the question of what it is for a state to be happiness-constituting. Yet it is significant: knowing that someone is happy normally licenses an inference that the person is well-off. Whether this holds depends on what the thresholds for being happy or otherwise are. So what are they? The problem is surprisingly difficult, and I will not try to resolve it here fully. (What follows will, however, provide additional support for the emotional state view.) The traditional answer of hedonists is that a predominance of positive suffices for happiness, and a predominance of negative for unhappiness. That is, more than 50 percent positive and you are happy; less than that and you are unhappy.

The received view has many problems. Indeed, it would seem preposterous were it not so widely believed. I will mention a few of the difficulties here. Note, for starters, that it leaves essentially no room for "in between" cases, where an individual is neither happy nor unhappy, but somewhere in the middle. It is intuitively possible, indeed rather plausible, that *most* people are in such a state: not quite happy, but not downright unhappy either. *Comme ci, comme ça. C'est impossible*, according to the received view. This is absurd.

A worse problem is that the received view is extremely undemanding: so long as the negative does not exceed the positive, you are happy. This is happiness? If so, then happiness would not need to be pursued, as it would be hard to avoid: even when life is hard, it is—save for the clinically depressed, those in severe pain, and similarly extreme cases—full of pleasures. (Consider how it is likely to seem from the deathbed.) Much research points to a "positivity offset" such that human beings are wired for positive affect to be the norm.[22] The undemanding character of this view generates numerous intuitive counterexamples. Surely we would not deem happy someone who is miserable almost half the time, even if the total quantity of positive affect outweighs that of the negative. Or take the less extreme case of Sam, who experiences pleasant emotions about 55 percent of the time (around 9 hours of the average day), and experiences negative emotions like anger, fear, or sadness about 38 percent of the time (around 6 hours of the average day). The positive and negative emotions are equally strong. It is not the least obvious that Sam should be counted happy, particularly if we reflect on what it would be like to have that much negative affect. When this case was presented in a brief anonymous survey of 93 students across six sections of an introductory ethics course, administered at the start of the first day of classes, only 38 percent deemed him "moderately" happy (none chose "very" happy). Four percent responded "no opinion," and 58 percent denied that Sam was happy—34 percent rating him "neither happy nor unhappy," and 24 percent calling him "very" or "moderately" *unhappy*.[23] These results must be taken with a grain of salt, of course, given the modest sample size and possible biases introduced by the instrument and setting.[24] One concern is ecological validity, as the use of a "percentage" format may have caused students to rely on lay theories of happiness that do not normally guide their ascriptions. For example, some may have defaulted to a 50 percent threshold as a "logical" place to put the cutoff. Because of this, I suspect the study overstates the proportion of individuals who would ascribe happiness in such a case.

The results suggest that the received view—or even a more modest view that takes a 55/38 split to be consistent with happiness—probably conflicts with lay intuitions about happiness. Most people are not likely to find it plausible when applied to particular cases. In fact some recent work suggests that even a 2:1 ratio of positive to negative affect may not suffice. In an important paper in *American Psychologist*, Fredrickson and Losada argue that healthy functioning or "flourishing" requires at least a 2.9:1 ratio of positive to negative affect, with lower ratios being associated with "languishing." They suggest that this finding may amount to a "breakthrough."[25] Because this is a new development and their discussion too complex to review here, we must be cautious in interpreting such claims. But their findings suggest that we might think of the thresholds for happiness or unhappiness as "tipping points," above and below which we find broad differences in psychological functioning. Happiness and unhappiness might thus be psychological natural kinds. Given the hard empirical questions involved here, I will not put much weight on this model. But I want to note that something in the neighborhood of a 3:1 ratio *intuitively* has considerable plausibility: greater than 25 percent negative moods and emotions seems hard to reconcile with being happy, and indeed it is not clear that the cutoff should not be still lower. Perhaps even 15 or 20 percent rules out happiness. This is bolstered by evidence that very low levels of negative affect—well under 10 percent—may be common.[26]

In any event, tinkering with the percentages seems not clearly to be the right way to go about the matter: in real life, we generally don't bother with computing ratios or integrals of people's affective histories. Instead we look for cues to the individual's basic psychic orientation and base our judgment on that. We saw this to some extent earlier, regarding the examples of Santiago and the Mexican groundskeeper; recall also Plato's efficient depiction of Socrates' happiness in Crito's remarks about the sleeping man's demeanor.[27] We often make snap judgments about an individual's happiness, and often these are well warranted—not because we can quickly determine the ratios or integrals of the individual's affects over time, but because we can quickly ascertain her fundamental condition. Consider a man whose mood is generally cheerful and otherwise pleasant, but only so long as he remains distracted. Keeping himself continually occupied, he experiences far more positive than negative affect. But, when alone with his thoughts at the end of the day, he succumbs to a profound sense of emptiness, despair, and grief. Perhaps he weeps quietly before falling asleep. These moments may be relatively few if he succeeds in keeping himself sufficiently preoccupied, but it is doubtful that anyone would want to call him happy—not because he experiences a lot of negative affect, but because, at bottom, his psyche is a mess. Indeed, it is not even clear we would consider him happy if his distress became manifest only in the guise of fitful, troubled sleep. (Notice that these points lend further support to the inclusion of mood propensities in the account.)

It is worth noting another point suggested by the example: intuitively, some measure of tranquility or peace of mind seems essential for happiness. No amount of cheery feelings could, it seems, make up for a troubled soul. A related point might be made regarding compression and related states. Imagine a formerly exuberant, free-spirited woman who has been caught up in an oppressive, loveless marriage. Making the best of things, she contents herself with this situation and maintains a slightly cheerful mood most of the time, yet is spiritually deflated, tentative, wan, a shadow of her former self. Old friends barely recognize her. It seems odd to think of such a person as happy. This is closer to psychic resignation than affirmation. Consider, conversely, how states of attunement can sustain happiness even in the presence of substantial negatives in one's emotional life. Someone whose basic stance is settled, centered, and untroubled might experience a lot of negative affect, for instance if he is raising small children, while still being happy.[28] Even if his irritation and frustration with the kids frequently impacts his emotional condition, if it does so mainly at a relatively superficial level, so that he tends to get over it quickly and has a robustly favorable emotional baseline, we might consider him happy.[29]

These points reveal, besides the importance of attunement for happiness, that perhaps *no* fixed threshold, in terms of the proportion of positive to negative affect an individual experiences, can yield intuitively plausible results. (Thus we might regard specific values, like the 3:1 ratio, merely as rules of thumb.) This comes out particularly when comparing the way we assess happiness in children and adults. We might readily deem a young child happy, even though she sheds tears at a rate we would find alarming in an adult. Were an adult to exhibit the crying regimen of a three-year-old, even a happy one, we would *not* think him happy. (And if he cried over similarly trivial insults, like a skinned knee, we would suspect a serious mental illness or handicap.) The reason for the different standards is that frequent tears in a preschooler are perfectly compatible with a basically healthy, flourishing psyche; they tend not to signal any deep distress. In a normal adult, crying to such a degree could only mean that something is profoundly awry in her basic emotional condition. We can reconcile the child's tears, but not the adult's, with psychic affirmation.

4.2. Putting the "affirmation" in psychic affirmation

The received view is a mistake. The question now is whether we can arrive at a more plausible account. Here is a tentative proposal. The issue might best be approached by thinking about the role the concept of happiness plays in people's lives. HAPPINESS appears to belong to a family of concepts, including those of health and well-being, that we employ to help regulate the distribution of resources and attention ("condition assessment concepts," we might call them). To say that someone is doing well, for instance, has something like the following practical upshot: generally speaking, we need not worry about the person's welfare. Things in the person's life are broadly favorable, with the negatives being relatively minor. No major problems requiring attention. Certainly we are not saying merely that more things are going well for her than badly. Similarly, saying that someone is healthy amounts to saying that his health is broadly favorable, with any problems being minor. Quite obviously, it is not simply to say that his body is *mostly* in good shape, as though a heart attack, collapsed lung, or gangrenous limb were compatible with good health. And when we deny that someone is doing well or is healthy, we imply, not that things are mostly problematical, but that the problems are substantial if not major: something to be concerned about. To say someone is doing badly, or is unhealthy, is to say that shortcomings in that realm are unacceptably severe and demand attention (insofar as the individual's welfare or health can demand attention at all). In effect, we employ these concepts like the monitoring gauges on a control board: the needle can point to green (good, no need to worry), yellow (tolerable but needs improvement), and red (intolerable, failure). This schema fits well with Darwall's recent suggestion that the concept of welfare is normative for attitudes of sympathetic concern: it is the concept of what one should want for a person insofar as one cares for her.[30] If something like this is correct, then it makes sense for the major thresholds regarding levels of welfare—doing well, not so well, or badly—to reflect the appropriateness of varying levels of concern. We use them to indicate whether concern is warranted, and how urgent the problems are.

The concept of happiness appears to fit the same framework, but applied from the perspective of the agent's psyche: to be happy is to respond emotionally to one's life as if conditions are broadly favorable, with any problems being minor. In general, things are good, with no serious concern required; one's "affective welfarometer," so to speak, is in the green. To be unhappy is to respond as if one's problems are major, threatening even the minimal achievement of one's needs or goals (as the psyche "sees" them).[31] From the perspective of the psyche, substantial change is needed; the affective welfarometer is in the red. This represents an emotional counterpart to life satisfaction: to be satisfied with one's life, arguably, is roughly to see things as going well enough, with deficiencies being minor. No major changes needed. To be dissatisfied is to see things as not going well in general, or to see one's life as having major deficiencies, so that even the minimal attainment of one's standards for a satisfactory life is threatened. Substantial changes required.

What sort of threshold does this schema suggest? It indicates that to be happy, one's emotional condition should be broadly favorable—across the three dimensions of attunement, engagement, and endorsement—with negative emotional states comprising a relatively minor part of the picture. This is the state of "psychic affirmation." Whereas an unhappy person's emotional condition will exhibit negative affect to a major extent, or will fail broadly to be favorable while having substantial levels of negative affect (since "major deficiencies" could involve either major negatives or significant but less weighty—"substantial"—negatives in the context of an otherwise mediocre situation). This is, effectively, a psychic rejection of one's situation. Again, the metric of favorability, and of "minor" or "major," will be heavily weighted toward centrality, and not just intensity or numbers of affects. The intuitive idea is for happiness to embody an emotional response appropriate to good conditions with only minor problems, so one might be happy despite having lots of relatively minor negative affects, since this might be compatible with one's basic emotional condition being broadly favorable.

We might make this somewhat sharper by considering the sorts of affective profiles people exhibit when things are going well or badly for them, at least relative to the values to which their emotional states are sensitive. If a person is emotionally or psychically responding to her life as if it is going well for her, then her basic psychic stance should conduce to sustaining, broadening, and building on her good fortune.[32] Things are good, so spread your wings and take advantage of it. One's emotional condition will not be oriented toward retrenchment, defensiveness, and attempts at aversive or revisionary life changes. The unhappy person, by contrast, will assume an emotional posture characteristic of someone living under unfavorable conditions that call for substantial change. It will conduce to defensive behavior appropriate to living under threat, or to actively seeking (or otherwise tending to promote[33]) substantial revisions in one's life. The question, then, is what sorts of affective profiles are consistent with an emotional posture of *broaden and build*, versus *defend or revise* (the neither happy nor unhappy falling somewhere in between). Empirical research may be able to help us clarify and test this proposal, for instance by examining the emotional conditions of those who seem clearly to be doing well or badly—for example, Fredrickson and Losada's "flourishing" individuals, or those reporting themselves "very" happy who also do well on mental health assessments,[34] versus those grieving the loss of a loved one. Or, alternatively, studying the effects of various emotional profiles on people's behavior and lives: which tend to be followed by significant revisionary or aversive life changes, for instance?

This is still highly vague, but it seems intuitively compatible with the 3:1 (or higher) ratio discussed earlier (as we saw, however, no fixed proportion seems capable of serving in all cases). Certainly the traditional 1:1 threshold looks completely implausible, not to mention utterly arbitrary. There is not the slightest reason to expect that the emotional threshold for responding to major deficiencies in one's life will correspond to the mathematically neat 50 percent mark. This makes no more sense than expecting serious health problems to involve most things in your body malfunctioning.

Note that similar views of the threshold to the one proposed here have been expressed even by writers who appear to accept the traditional 50 percent mark. Kahneman, for instance, writes that "it makes sense to call Helen 'objectively happy' if she spends *most* of her time . . . engaged in activities that she would rather have continued than stopped, *little time* in situations she wished to escape, and . . . not too much time in a neutral state in which she would not care either way." And Mill at one point defined happiness as "an existence made up of few and transitory pains, [and] many and various pleasures."[35] Even these writers seem to have recognized that a bare majority of positive over negative could not plausibly suffice for happiness.

I have not discussed mood propensities in this section. Given the emphasis of this account on the dispositional aspects of our emotional conditions, the purely dispositional mood propensities might seem to merit the heaviest weighting of all. Yet that would likely be a mistake, for several reasons. First, their role in defining a person's overall emotional disposition is remoter, and less salient, than that of emotions and moods. Being anxious alters the way you confront the world in a much stronger and more immediate way than merely being prone to experience anxiety. Both types of state play a role in defining your emotional or psychic stance, but the occurrent processes generally take priority. Similarly, mood propensities intuitively seem less important in defining one's emotional condition than occurrent moods. Finally, mood propensities seem intuitively to be less important in defining how *happy* a person is. For instance, a generally dour individual whose recent good fortune has left her in high spirits would seem to be happy even if her mood propensity remains negative. Though she is less happy than were her affective propensities more agreeable—the slightest setback could plunge her into despair—she seems happy all the same.

We may accordingly wish to distinguish two forms of happiness: one in which the predominance of positive moods and emotions results partly from a positive mood propensity, and a rarer, less stable one in which the predominance occurs despite a contrary mood propensity. We might refer to these conditions as *robust* and *fragile* happiness, respectively.

Rejecting the traditional cutoff for happiness may have important implications. It could mean, for example, that the common view among empirical researchers that most people are happy is false, a point I will explore at length in Chapter 10. Insofar as we think happy people tend to be doing well—and that does seem to be the implication of the "most people are happy" claim—then this change could alter our fundamental assessment of people's well-being. The normative implications of such a claim aren't entirely clear, though we saw earlier that it seems to indicate that concern is warranted. It would at least suggest that happiness should be a higher priority than it would be if most were happy. It is more important to try to improve the conditions of those who aren't doing well than those who are.

5. 'POSITIVE' VERSUS 'NEGATIVE'

What is meant by 'positive' and 'negative' in this theory? A natural suggestion is simply to identify positive and negative with pleasant and unpleasant affective states, respectively. This is clearly the usual, if not universal, practice among psychologists. For our purposes, however, this simple identification will not do. As I argued at greater length in Chapter 4, affective states of the same type usually, but do not always, have the same hedonic properties. Just as one might find a painful sensation pleasant, so is it possible to find pleasure in anger, fear, and even sadness—say, while reading a tragedy. Yet anger, fear, and sadness look to be unhappiness-constituting whether or not they are pleasant.

I will not expend much effort trying to explicate the nature of positivity and negativity as these notions figure in the present account of happiness, since there is little reason to worry that a satisfactory account cannot be given, or that significant confusion will ensue without one. Returning to the paradigm cases of happiness and unhappiness, it seems obvious that in some perfectly ordinary sense the happiness-constituting states are "positive," the unhappiness-constituting states "negative"—and, moreover, that a proper account of this can be given in scientifically respectable terms without relying on value judgments.

A plausible suggestion is that we view the hedonic qualities of affects as just one aspect of a multifaceted psychological response to the individual's situation that also includes approach or withdrawal tendencies, tendencies to influence perception and reasoning in certain ways, physiological (e.g., autonomic) responses, tendencies toward certain other affects or desires (beyond approach/withdrawal tendencies), etc.—taken together, amounting to a response to one's situation *as* a good or bad situation. While affects of a particular type, such as sadness, have a characteristic profile across these dimensions, a given token of that type might fail to exhibit the complete profile. Cases of hedonic inversion would be like this: a case of pleasant sadness retains most of the usual character of a negative emotional response even if it lacks the usual unpleasantness. One will still, for instance, be unusually prone to experience sadness or other negative emotions over other matters, to fall into a bad mood, etc. This is in fact a downside of seeking such pleasures, for they leave you vulnerable, emotionally, and prone to unpleasantness in response to other events. It also explains why such pleasures tend to be short-lived: they tend to promote unpleasures. The general idea, in short, is that positive affective states are those exhibiting enough of a profile of affective response to one's situation as if it is in some way favorable.

Whether some proposal such as this proves correct or not, it should be clear enough that no deep problem lies in the notions of positivity and negativity employed in the account of happiness. As some have observed, we should not simply think of "positive" as good and "negative" as bad.[36] Every type of emotion and mood has its place, and—save for the extremes of depression and other agonies—probably all are desirable to have in some circumstances, undesirable in others.

6. SUMMARIZING THE ACCOUNT

We now have a sketch of a complete account of happiness, a version of the emotional state theory. Fundamentally, the theory takes happiness to consist in a person's overall emotional condition. This in turn has two elements: the individual's various central affective states (roughly, moods and emotions) and mood propensities. Some affects—peripheral affective states, including merely sensory and notional pleasures—are excluded from the account, or at least given very little weight.

The contribution an affective state makes to one's happiness is a function of its strength or intensity and its centrality; mood propensities, given their lesser role in defining one's emotional condition, count for less than central affective states. Centrality in turn has several aspects, most importantly dispositionality: disposing the individual to perceive and respond emotionally to the world in various ways. Happiness on this view most fundamentally concerns an individual's emotional or psychic stance toward her life.

Actually to be happy is for one's emotional condition to embody a stance of *psychic affirmation* in response to one's life: emotionally responding to it as to a favorable life—a life that is broadly going well for one, with only minor problems at most. This in turn involves a broadly positive emotional condition, with only minor levels of negative emotional response. "Broadly positive" means positive across the three modes of emotional response, in descending order of importance: attunement, engagement, and endorsement.

To be happy, then, is for one's emotional condition to be broadly positive—involving stances of attunement, engagement, and endorsement—with negative central affective states and mood propensities only to a minor extent.

Implicit here is a reference to the period of time over which happiness is assessed, with much flexibility; for convenience, I will allow that happiness can be defined over arbitrarily short or long periods of time, though there may prove to be limits at either end.

We should note, before continuing, a further wrinkle in the account. We commonly make an implicit distinction between two "grades" or levels of happiness: being just plain "happy," and being "truly" happy. We often say things like "the only time I was ever truly happy was when I painted," meaning to say nothing more than that such a state was particularly fulfilling or gratifying. I would suggest that standard ascriptions of happiness, or of being just plain happy, concern responding to one's life as broadly favorable or good—psychic affirmation. But sometimes we are in a particularly pronounced state of this sort, a state of optimal functioning: one's life and activities are more or less perfectly matched to one's emotional nature, and one isn't merely happy but positively thriving. One is truly happy. I will call this condition *psychic flourishing*.

7. CAN HAPPINESS BE MEASURED?

Empirical researchers will want to know how to operationalize the points made in these last two chapters, and indeed whether happiness on this view can be measured at all. The short answer, I think, is *yes*, though of course not with great precision. The phenomena are too rich, multifaceted, and resistant to quantification to admit of any precise happiness calculus. But this will surprise no one. The science of happiness was always predicated on the modest notion that scientific methods can improve on armchair speculation. It can give us useful information not available otherwise, and that is all the precision it requires. Close enough for government work is, quite literally, all we need for many purposes, and for many others we can get by with less. (This point is not often enough appreciated, for example, by those who worry that measures of happiness presuppose a hedonistic value theory and are thus vulnerable to experience machine worries. But unless you have an experience machine problem in your polity, such possibilities don't much matter for most practical purposes. Experience machine-type worries do point us toward the need to consider values other than happiness, but they hardly show happiness not to be *important*, as we saw in Chapters 1 and 6. That happiness matters a good deal is not a point of controversy.)

Obviously this is not the place to decide precisely what measures ought to be used, but it will be helpful to gesture broadly at the kinds of instruments that the present view of happiness might favor. Unsurprisingly, the emotional state theory favors affect-based measures, such as experience sampling (ESM), which collects many reports of experience as they happen; and the day reconstruction method (DRM), which elicits detailed accounts of the previous day's experiences.[37] The U-Index, which tracks the proportion of time individuals spend in unpleasant states, may be particularly useful given the disproportionate role of negative affect in determining how happy someone is.[38] These sorts of instruments are presently invaluable, but they do have limitations. For instance, they tend to favor endorsement-type affects, with less effective coverage of the attunement dimension (e.g., stress), which I suggested is the most important aspect of happiness (see, e.g., the Fordyce emotions survey[39]). There also tends to be a "feelings bias" in the measures, so that measures may not be sensitive enough to important dispositional and background states like those related to tranquility or compression. Perhaps the existing instruments can be supplemented or modified to rectify these shortcomings. For instance, ESM studies may be combined with the sorts of multi-item questionnaires used to assess depression or stress, which extend beyond particular feeling episodes to dispositional features of respondents' psychological conditions (e.g., ability to concentrate).[40]

A second concern relates to the extraordinary elusiveness of many of the states involved in happiness. As will become clear in Chapter 10, even ESM studies are likely to miss a good deal of the picture, as we should not expect people to be terribly accurate informants about their emotional conditions. To some extent such errors will tend to wash out over large samples—I will explain in Chapter 10 that self-reports can tell us about happiness even if people have no idea how happy they are—but it seems likely that some will not: that certain sorts of information about people's emotional lives will systematically be underrepresented in our measures.

The examples of communities A and B at the start of this book are instructive: there is a massive difference in quality of life between those communities, and well-being measures ought to be sensitive to that difference. I suspect that current instruments would capture some of this information, but are not yet sensitive enough to convey the magnitude of the difference. Moreover, any self-report-based measures will be susceptible to the influence of norms, as discussed in Chapter 5, making it harder to compare results between populations with different norms. (There we focused on life satisfaction, but reports of affect or happiness will be subject to such norms as well.) It will be helpful, accordingly, to supplement self-report measures with other instruments to the extent possible—facial musculature assessment, salivary cortisol, physiological arousal, brain imaging, etc.[41]

A further avenue is suggested by the incorporation of mood propensities in the present account of happiness. In essence, we might use mood inductions to assess happiness. I suggested earlier that most of us do this informally when making judgments about how happy people are. Investigators might, for instance, see how subjects respond to stressful tasks, the idea being that unhappy people will tend to respond less favorably to such tasks, even if they present as being in good moods at the time. For a bracing example of this technique at work, see Shedler, Mayman et al. 1993 (discussed in Chapter 10); using mood inductions and other methods, this study found that standard depression measures may understate distress considerably. We may want to add mood inductions to our repertoire of well-being measures.

8. CONCLUSION

This emotional state conception of happiness offers a plausible account of the phenomena involved in the paradigm cases, as well as other intuitive cases of happiness and unhappiness. Even apparent exceptions, like deep dissatisfaction with one's life, could largely or wholly be accommodated within this view: what makes that a case of unhappiness is arguably the negative emotional condition we associate with it. Take that away, and it is no longer so clear we are talking about a case of unhappiness. Consider a small-town resident, impressed by television depictions of city life, who believes her environs dull and unsophisticated. Dissatisfied with her life, she wants to get out. Later, having done so, she realizes that her old life was actually rich and fulfilling, with none of the anxiety and loneliness of urban life. She might conclude that, while she had indeed been dissatisfied in her former life, she was nonetheless happy. This theory also accounts for the broad practical significance of happiness: our emotional conditions seem to have the kind of importance that happiness is typically thought to have. We can understand how happiness could be expected to serve as a proxy for well-being.

The theory represents a sentimentalist approach to thinking about happiness, in contrast with the comparative rationalism of traditional life satisfaction views: what matters for happiness is not the individual's judgment or opinion about her life, but how she responds emotionally to her life. These things can, as we just saw, readily diverge, and for good reason: our emotional conditions are sensitive to vast amounts of information that are not even registered by the slow, serial rational processes that largely drive our reflective judgments. They can, as a result, offer a response to our lives that is often richer, more nuanced, and more sensitive to the subtleties of our circumstances than the cleverer but often more ignorant analytic processes are.

This view of happiness also gives the lie to any notion that happiness could be largely transparent to us. While it takes little discernment to figure it out when you feel happy, it takes a lot to figure out how you are doing across the several dimensions of your emotional condition, some aspects of which do not involve conscious or even occurrent states. Many of the relevant states, including numerous moods, are highly elusive and difficult to grasp or attend to. Often we may be little better placed to tell how happy we are than perceptive relations are, and sometimes worse.[42] Indeed, sometimes our best source of information about how happy we are is other people, or observing ourselves from a third-person perspective. Those who have spent much time gaining the perspective of living outside mainstream civilization are liable to find it a truism that many of us may not have a clue how happy, or unhappy, we really are.

> O GENERATION of the thoroughly smug
>   and the thoroughly uncomfortable,
> I have seen fishermen picnicking in the sun,
> I have seen them with untidy families,
> I have seen their smiles full of teeth
>   and heard ungainly laughter.

And I am happier than you are,
And they were happier than I am;
And the fish swim in the lake
　　and do not even own clothing.

　　　　　　Ezra Pound, "Salutation"

PART III

THE NATURE OF WELL-BEING

8

Well-Being and Virtue

Happiness lies in conquering one's enemies, in driving them in front of oneself, in taking their property, in savoring their despair, in outraging their wives and daughters.

Genghis Khan[1]

1. WHAT ABOUT ARISTOTLE?

Part II centered on questions of psychology, specifically the character of happiness, in the long-term psychological sense distinguished in Chapter 2. The emotional state theory of happiness defended there raises doubts about liberal optimism's Transparency assumption, since our emotional lives are surprisingly rich, and much harder to grasp than "smiley-face" stereotypes would suggest. But how important, really, is happiness? Answering this question requires that we turn to the theory of well-being.[2]

Conventional wisdom once took well-being to be an objective affair, something that the masses should not be expected to have a great deal of authority about. Among the more noteworthy ideas in those days was the perfectionist notion that well-being consists, at least partly, in excellence or virtue. The ancient objectivist orthodoxy eventually yielded to the present age of subjectivism, where common opinion has it that what's good for people is, more or less, whatever they say it is. Discontent with subjectivism has been brewing for some years now, driven by a more nuanced understanding of the considerable merits of some objectivist accounts, notably Aristotelian theories, as well as a barrage of criticism aimed at subjectivist views like the desire theory.[3] Indeed, Aristotelian views are now among the chief competitors in discussions of well-being. This is a welcome development, for such work has greatly enriched contemporary reflection on well-being, helping to counter what some of us see as the trivialization of philosophical thought about the good life in the modern era. Whatever the merits of non-subjectivist accounts of well-being, however, it is less clear that the *perfectionism* espoused in much of this literature can be sustained. I will argue that it cannot, using the best-known example of a perfectionist theory, Aristotelianism, to show why. The discussion should concern even those with little interest in perfectionist theories, for a better understanding of the problems confronting Aristotelian perfectionism will illuminate some important points about the nature of well-being and related values.

In the context of the present book, this inquiry is important since Aristotelian theories of well-being probably constitute the best-known and most compelling challenge to the thesis of Personal Authority and its Transparency assumption. But they are generally believed to do so by *rejecting* happiness and related psychological states as values of central importance. As a result they threaten the contentions of this volume both by offering an incompatible alternative to my case against Transparency and Personal Authority and by raising doubts about the importance of the psychological matters that I am claiming to be central to well-being. Beyond that, the approach to well-being defended in Chapter 9, while not Aristotelian, is rooted in the same basic ideal of nature-fulfillment that animates Aristotelian accounts. Extended reflection on the better-known view should make it easier to grasp the rationale for my own account.

We can usefully think of Aristotelian theories as centering on three claims. Our inquiry will focus on the first, *welfare perfectionism*, which maintains that well-being consists, non-derivatively, at least partly in perfection: excellence or virtue—or, in the Aristotelian case, excellent or virtuous activity. Perfection, that is, is a fundamental or ultimate constituent of well-being (non-perfectionists might grant that it can constitute well-being derivatively, say by being desired). For Aristotelians, the perfection in question includes, but *is not limited to*, moral virtue. Perfection is commonly regarded as the perfection of one's nature: being a good specimen of one's kind, for instance, or fulfilling one's capacities well.[4] But I will understand perfectionism broadly enough to include any theory that takes well-being ultimately to consist at least partly in some kind of perfection, excellence, or virtue (or the exercise thereof). Perfection can be construed quite narrowly, in wholly moral or non-moral terms, but all forms of perfectionism will prove vulnerable to at least one of the arguments below.[5] Some contend that Aristotle counted external goods as an additional part of flourishing, distinct from perfection. I have no wish to debate the fine points of Aristotle exegesis here, as I am less interested in the historical Aristotle than in whether a perfectionist view of well-being can be defended. But it seems to me that his view is most plausibly and charitably read as counting external goods only insofar as they facilitate good functioning, and not as distinct contributors to well-being.[6] Roughly, well-being consists in a life of excellent or virtuous activity, or "well-functioning." But the difference should not seriously affect the arguments to follow, for all Aristotelians take well-being to consist at least primarily in virtuous activity.

The second claim, *externalism*, is the denial of *internalism* about well-being. A weaker cousin of subjectivism, which grounds well-being in the person's attitudes, internalism roughly maintains that the constituents of an agent's well-being are ultimately determined wholly by the particulars of the individual's make-up *qua* individual (vs. *qua* group or class member).[7] Something's counting as an intrinsic benefit for a person must depend entirely on what that person is like. It is hard to state the view precisely without wading into controversial metaphysical territory, but internalism may be seen as embodying two root ideas. First, what counts toward my well-being must depend on what I am like. My welfare must not be alien to me, a value that floats down from some Platonic realm and, remora-like, affixes itself to me with little regard to the particulars of my constitution.[8] Second, what counts toward my well-being must not depend on what any other individual, or group or class of individuals—actual or hypothetical—is like. It must be possible to specify the ultimate or fundamental conditions for my well-being without making essential reference to other individuals, or to classes or groups of individuals. (The terminology unfortunately suggests that externalists ground well-being in matters that are spatio-temporally external to the individual, which need not be the case. Note that externalists need not require blindness to individual differences, a one-size-fits-all account. Externalism rules out only *complete* deference to the arbitrarily idiosyncratic particulars of the individual's make-up.) It might be objected that some goods depend on what others are like—my benefiting from friendship, say. But the internalist's claim is not that a person's well-being cannot depend in any way on external factors. It is that something's *counting* as an intrinsic benefit must not depend on such factors. And desire theorists, for example, will say that friendship's status as a good for me depends solely on the fact that I desire it. It forms no part of the ultimate or fundamental conditions for my well-being. A different worry is that it may not be clear how internalism differs from subjectivism. See Chapter 9, where I defend an internalist, but non-subjectivist, account of well-being.

Aristotelian theories are externalist in the intended sense: they ground well-being in facts about the species. What benefits a person is what contributes to her functioning in a characteristically—or fully, essentially, or distinctively—human way. If I would benefit from friendship, for instance, it is (mainly) because human beings characteristically engage in friendships; doing so would thus make for a more fully human life. Absent further explication externalism might seem like an unappealing doctrine, but it may be the Aristotelian view's chief selling point: as Nussbaum and others have recently stressed, the failure of a human being to enjoy or even have the capacity for what we think of as the goods of a full human life can seem deeply unfortunate.[9] A handicap like blindness or the absence of sexual functioning seems a great loss, one that impoverishes a life regardless of the individual's goals, likes, or desires.

The third claim, *welfare eudaimonism*, maintains that well-being is teleological, consisting in the fulfillment of our natures.[10] More or less ubiquitous among the Hellenistic philosophers, including even Epicurean hedonists, this doctrine has attracted many distinguished adherents since then. But in the contemporary literature on well-being, most eudaimonists—I will generally omit the "welfare" qualifier—can be found within the Aristotelian camp.

In this chapter I will argue that perfection probably forms no fundamental part of well-being: perfectionism is false. I will not discuss externalism at any length here, though I believe it too is problematical. However, the third Aristotelian claim, eudaimonism, seems to me correct; and one aim of this chapter is to help pave the way for the non-Aristotelian eudaimonism defended in the next chapter. The discussion has five parts: first, a pair of examples in which well-being and perfection seem not to connect in the manner required by Aristotelian views. The cases themselves will not be entirely novel to readers familiar with the literature, but I will employ them to make some points that have not been widely appreciated.[11] The second part will discuss a different sort of case indicating that Aristotelians face an unwelcome choice regarding the interpretation of perfection: perfection can be understood in a way that supports the desired connection between welfare and morality, or in a way that yields a potentially attractive account of well-being, but not both. Third, I will examine perfectionist treatments of pleasure and suffering, concluding that no perfectionist view can credibly account for the value of pleasure and suffering. Indeed, so unpromising does the Aristotelian treatment of hedonic goods appear to be that it begs for explanation; to this end, I suggest that Aristotelian views may not even be trying to answer some of the central questions animating modern accounts of well-being. In the fourth part, I consider the fundamental character of prudential and perfectionist values and why we care about them, concluding that our interests in the two types of value are very different, so that no perfectionist account of prudential value could succeed. Finally, after briefly addressing a pair of objections, I suggest that Aristotelian and related views have seemed so attractive because of an understandable but serious mistake in the way many of their proponents approach the theory of well-being.

A hazard when discussing matters Aristotelian is that even Aristotle scholars differ sharply on many questions of interpretation, so some readers are bound to object, perhaps correctly, that I have gotten Aristotle wrong on one or more points. I cannot emphasize too strongly that what Aristotle himself thought is entirely secondary to our purposes here. The goal is to see how far well-being can be cashed out in perfectionist terms, and for this purpose Aristotle's views are relevant only because some form of Aristotelianism appears to represent the most plausible form of perfectionism. As well, the case against Aristotelian perfectionism should generalize to other forms of perfectionism, such as the Stoic view. My aim is to attack the most credible form of perfectionism. It will not help perfectionism at all to point out that Aristotle actually held some different, but much less plausible, view than the one I discuss. The question is whether a theory of well-being could be both perfectionist and true.

2. TROUBLES WITH PERFECTIONISM

2.1. Well-being and perfection: cases of intuitive divergence

The most familiar objection to perfectionism is that many find it obvious that some people are, or can be, downright evil and yet, "by any ethological standard of the bright eye and the gleaming coat, dangerously flourishing," as Bernard Williams put it.[12] The Aristotelian has a reply to such worries: a selfish or malicious person with no real concern for others also seems, intuitively, to be leading a stunted or impoverished life. A parent whose child turned out this way would likely feel that the child would have been better off leading a fuller life enriched by the usual moral commitments, even if that life is less successful by narrow Calliclean standards.[13] At least, these are intuitions that many people share, and I will not dispute them.[14]

The problem with such replies is that they can only show that well-being requires a substantial degree of moral commitment, in particular however much is needed for a full and rich life. This leaves room for a considerable amount of immorality: the successful Southern slaveholder who enjoys the approbation of his community and a comfortable existence with a loving family has obvious moral shortcomings, yet it is hard to see in what sense his life must be "impoverished." Why must he be in *any* way worse off than he would be were he more enlightened about human equality? Why must he be worse off than a morally better counterpart who enjoys as much wealth, comfort, success, love, and reputation, but without ever wronging anyone? (We can assume that both are well-settled in their moral convictions, equally convinced of their righteousness.[15]) This point arises with greater force in the case of a brutal warlord like Genghis Khan, who directed the slaughter of tens of millions. He appears to have done so largely with the blessing of his culture's moral code. It is not hard to imagine that his relatively long life, which appeared to be rather successful on his terms, went very well for him indeed. And while his idea of happiness or well-being is not exactly yours or mine, it is difficult to see the grounds for gainsaying it (as a conception of well-being!).[16] Is humanitarian concern for strangers really necessary for a full, rich, or characteristically human life? History offers little reason for optimism on this count.

Some may find it counterintuitive to say that a Genghis Khan could have led a *happy* life. If we do not find it similarly counterintuitive to say that he might have flourished, been well-off, fared well, etc., we should wonder whether this is a linguistic artifact, or whether different normative concepts are in play. I do not particularly share the intuition in question, but neither does it seem wholly foreign, and at any rate some people *do* seem to have the intuition. Are they confused? Yes and no. It can seem odd to call such a monstrous life a happy one, but this is probably because we tend to assess lives for happiness as stories or narratives: was the story of Khan's life a happy one? Well, not exactly, since there was after all so much misery in it. The thing is, the misery belonged to *other people*. He, apparently, did just fine; things seem to have gone rather happily *for him*. (Admittedly, he had a difficult childhood and a propensity for killing anyone whose loyalty he questioned. In any case my interest here is not biographical; should history prove uncongenial to my aims, then we may reflect instead on his lesser known but equally ruthless counterpart, Shmengis Khan, who enjoyed the unwavering support of loving friends and family.) In short, intuitions about whether someone's life was happy may be misleading, since the fates of other actors might impact the story in ways that don't affect the well-being of the central character.

Some may point out that we cannot plausibly say Genghis Khan had a *good* life. True enough, but that's neither here nor there. While we do sometimes use 'the good life' to denote well-being, the most natural understanding of the expression concerns a life that is desirable or choiceworthy, not just for the individual's benefit, but all things considered: *good*. And a life of unchecked savagery is not by anyone's lights—save the savage—a choiceworthy one. Now this could be because, as Aristotelians hold, such a life is not good *for* the agent. But no one not already convinced of welfare perfectionism is likely to say that. Most contemporaries will say, as Kant does, that such a life could at least conceivably serve the agent's interests, but that it is nonetheless an undesirable way to live because it is *wrong*. The good life, on such a view, involves both well-being and, distinctly, virtue. This is not to deny that large strains of commonsense thought see considerable interdependence between welfare and morality ("honesty is the best policy"). But this is a far weaker claim than the Aristotelian makes, and at any rate is not a matter of universal agreement ("nice guys finish last").

A failure properly to distinguish the notions of well-being and the good life can also explain a further reply that might be made against my arguments, namely that no decent parent would wish a life like Genghis Khan's for his child.[17] This is true, but why should anyone think our concerns for our children are exhausted by their welfare? I want not merely for my children to be well-off or flourish; I want them to be good people and conduct themselves well, *whether or not it benefits them*. In fact this seems more important than their well-being.

There are good reasons, then, to doubt that flourishing requires perfection, and even that vice must in any way reduce an individual's well-being. I now want to consider a different sort of case indicating that a life of greater perfection need not involve greater well-being. Now Aristotelians can happily grant that virtue does not always benefit us, since a virtuous act can impede future virtuous activity, say by crippling or killing the agent. But there are other cases that Aristotelians cannot manage so easily. Sumner has pressed this point with his example of a talented but miserable philosopher who ends up much happier leading a laid-back existence that made far less use of his abilities.[18] Intuitively, the philosopher is much better off quitting the profession; yet his life exhibits far less perfection. We thus seem to have a counterexample to perfectionism. Perfectionists can make two replies to this argument. First, Aristotelians hold that virtue requires taking pleasure in one's activities, so they would deny that the unhappy philosopher truly exhibits perfection. Second, it also seems intuitively plausible that the philosopher has made a *mistake*; he has not acted well in choosing a profession so ill-suited to his nature. Hence it is not even intuitively the case that he exhibits a high level of perfection.

Neither reply cuts much ice: the first because Sumner need not claim that the philosopher is fully virtuous, just *more* virtuous than he would have been otherwise; and Aristotelians can only put so much weight on the importance of pleasure for virtue before their account of virtue begins to look ridiculous. (If I wash a leper out of compassion and duty but take no pleasure in it, is my action *wholly* unvirtuous, no better morally than if I had washed my hands instead? Aristotle did not take the ridiculous view of virtue in any event: failure to experience the requisite pleasure would mean you are merely continent, which falls short of virtue but is better than nothing.) If Sumner is right that the philosopher's life *intuitively* involves greater perfection, then Aristotelians deny his claim only by reducing the plausibility of their account of virtue. (And this is not an area where the Aristotelian view is supposed to be counterintuitive; indeed, the role of pleasure in Aristotelian virtue is one of the main things people find *attractive* about the account.) This points to a general difficulty for perfectionist views of well-being: they need to solve simultaneously for two variables, maintaining credible theories of *both* well-being and virtue. But moves to preserve their account of one can easily undermine their view of the other. The second reply speaks more directly to Sumner's challenge, but is not clearly correct: even if we grant that the philosopher chose badly in entering his profession, we might still maintain that his subsequent activities exhibited greater perfection than they would have otherwise, and even that his life as a whole involved more perfection. But a different example should bring out the issues more clearly.

Consider then the case of a high-ranking career diplomat for the UK, Angela, who is contemplating an early retirement at the age of 62: having served her country with great distinction for many years, Angela has come into a good deal of money through some canny investments and a bit of luck. She has all but decided to retire with her husband to a villa in Tuscany, and could do so very comfortably on her earnings. (They have a number of good friends in the area and it would bring her much closer to her daughter and grandchildren, who reside in Milan.) She correctly envisages that a life there would be tremendously satisfying, occupied largely with good company and food and drink, walking the countryside, and catching up on her reading. In short, kicking back and just enjoying life. It would certainly be a welcome and much-deserved respite from her demanding career in diplomacy: while rewarding in its own way, the schedule is hectic, and by now she has had enough of it. Before she can settle on her plans, however, a political crisis arises overseas and she is asked to take an important post where her considerable wisdom and skills would be of great use. It is hoped that Angela's efforts would help to avert a bloody conflict over the next several years. There are others who could do the job, and her efforts could well fail, but no one could fill the role as well as her. Naturally, the assignment would be taxing and heavy on travel, and frequently involves dealing with unwholesome individuals about matters of extreme gravity, often calling for a fair measure of anger and indignation on her part. (As Aristotle observes about courage, virtue isn't always pleasant on the whole.) But the experience would not be grueling, or even unpleasant on the whole, as she does take pleasure in doing what she does best. Moreover, it would not be *so* taxing that she cannot spend some time with family and friends, and otherwise achieve a modicum of leisure. Yet it would be far less pleasant than the alternative.

From Angela's perspective the decision is pretty near a coin toss: she could reasonably go either way. Thus she could refuse the position with no regrets: she has already sacrificed much in service to her country, and she has learned that in this line of work one has to be able to carve out some personal space and say no even to important requests, for important requests come along all the time. No one would dream of begrudging her the comfortable life she had begun to set before herself. Yet she accepts the assignment, also without regret: the stakes are high enough that she feels they are probably worth it. She goes on to serve admirably and with a good deal of success in sustaining the peace, but another six years pass before she can take her retirement, which lasts five relatively sedentary but agreeable years before a massive stroke suddenly takes her life. (A time and manner of death that would have been the same had she not taken the job.)

Has Angela acted in her interest? Is she better off having taken the job instead of retiring? This seems deeply implausible: while she arguably fares well in either scenario, she would clearly have been better off taking the early retirement. It would be much more pleasant, she would be substantially happier, and she would be pursuing the sorts of activities that most appeal to her and, at least at this stage of her life, bring her the greatest satisfaction. (Things might have been different earlier in her life, when she lived for her work, which then involved greater novelty and conflicted less with her other priorities.) And yet the Aristotelian must presumably say she *is* better off having taken the job. For by any reasonable measure, the diplomatic assignment involves greater perfection: it is obviously more virtuous, more admirable, and remains so over time—this is not a case of virtuous sacrifice that inhibits future perfection. And the position involves a greater degree of human functioning; she more fully exercises her capacities, functioning more fully *qua* human being than she would as a retiree. While the life of pleasant retirement has its own perfections, there is no credible sense, non-moral or otherwise, in which Angela, or her activities, would exhibit more excellence on the whole if she retired. There may perhaps be certain areas of human life—personal relationships, leisure, the pursuit of personal goals—in which the early retirement would involve greater functioning. But it cannot reasonably be maintained that her job would leave her impoverished in any of these areas. Note also that putting so much weight on non-moral excellence would be hard for conventional Aristotelians to sustain. (Compare an immoral "renaissance man," highly talented, cultivated, and erudite, with a moral saint whose non-moral capacities and achievements are modest. Most contemporary Aristotelians would presumably want to recommend the latter life over the former, yet it is not clear they can do so if non-moral excellences get too much weight relative to the moral.[19])

In taking the job, Angela chose the path of greater excellence and virtue, a life that more fully exercised her capacities as a human being. But she was not securing or promoting her happiness or well-being. She was *sacrificing* it. This is a problem for Aristotelian accounts of well-being, and any other views that see perfection as the sole or primary constituent of human flourishing. While my argument has not addressed the role of external goods in Aristotelian views, it should be apparent that Angela has not been particularly unlucky in her allotment of the goods of fortune; quite the contrary. Aristotelians who wish to secure an intuitively plausible verdict in Angela's case would have to put a lot of weight on external goods—more, it seems, than even the most extravagant interpretation of Aristotle's views could sustain. It is hard to see how one could place that much emphasis on external goods and still maintain the idea that virtue is the primary and controlling factor in well-being.

2.2. What is perfection? An internal problem

I now want to consider a case that raises internal difficulties for the Aristotelian, forcing an unwelcome choice in the interpretation of perfection. Frank learns that the parents of Dennis, a severely autistic child with cerebral palsy, have suddenly died. While he has long been a friend to Dennis's family, their friendship has been only moderately close. The child, with no relations willing or able to care for him, is to be moved to a state facility that will provide tolerable but impersonal institutional care. Frank, a successful artist and happy bachelor, decides to take Dennis in and give him a real home, and assumes the daunting task of caring for him. Though he gets some help from volunteers and hired assistants, his caregiving responsibilities are often grueling and sharply limit his ability to socialize or pursue other activities; he is able to earn a living (doing more commercial art that is less challenging and rewarding) and not much else. But that is what he expected and he tends to Dennis lovingly and without complaint, and takes great satisfaction in the knowledge that he has given him a far warmer and more stable home than he would otherwise have had. Had he not taken custody of Dennis, he would have continued developing his craft according to his passion, leading a highly active social life involving deep friendships, and pursuing his hobbies of sailing, chess, and playing bass in a jazz combo. That life too would have been very satisfying and much more pleasant (and it too would have involved substantial concern and caring for others, including some philanthropic work, but of a far more pedestrian variety). While he would have felt badly about Dennis's fate, he would hardly have been wracked with guilt at not adopting him.

I take it to be obvious that Frank has acted virtuously, substantially more so than if he had decided not to take in the child. It also seems clear that he would have been a good deal better off not doing so. But the more interesting question is what the Aristotelian should say about this case: does Frank's life involve greater perfection? On the one hand, it does involve greater virtue: it is more admirable. On the other hand, it involves a lesser exercise of his human capacities: his functioning is sharply constrained and inhibited. We could, of course, decide to place such tremendous weight on the range of functionings he does achieve that we conclude that he really is exercising his capacities more fully than he would have otherwise. But this seems strange and unmotivated, yielding a highly moralized and narrow conception of human functioning that denigrates the many other valued functionings Frank achieved in his bachelor life. Intuitively, he functions more fully—more fully in the sense that allows us to think of Aristotelian well-being as *flourishing*—in the life not pursued.

There seems to be a deeply problematical tension within Aristotelian views between two aspects of perfection: *admirability* and *actualization*. When we think of well-being as excellent activity or perfection, do we mean activity that is admirable or virtuous, or activity that actualizes the agent's potential as a human being, that develops and exercises characteristically human capacities? These are different matters, and a plausible account of one may not be a credible account of the other. The problem is that Aristotelians need an interpretation of "perfection" that yields credible views of *both* admirability and actualization. Cases like Frank's suggest that this is not possible: either perfection tracks actualization, which would respect our intuition that Frank would have been better off not taking in the child, or it tracks admirability, which would preserve the traditional association of Aristotelian flourishing with virtue—but at the cost of generating highly dubious verdicts about the well-being of people like Frank.[20] And more worrisome for the Aristotelian, the attractive metaphor of "well-functioning" seems largely to go out the window, so sharply does it discount the exercises of our other capacities.

2.3. Pleasure and suffering

A crucial task for any theory of well-being is to give a credible accounting of the value of pleasant and unpleasant experiences, especially suffering. For nothing else is so plainly central to human welfare, to the extent that many have concluded that nothing else ultimately matters. So strong a claim may well be false, of course, and we may want to qualify pleasure's value in various ways. Thus many of us would not want to lead a life devoid of unpleasant experiences, and sometimes we even value unpleasant experiences. Moreover, certain pleasures are degrading or immoral and may thus be bad all things considered (which is not necessarily to say they aren't good *for* their bearer—that might be why you find them objectionable). Yet we can pile on all the qualifiers we like and still recognize that pleasure is one of the central goods in life. Suffering, conversely, is one of the central evils. Any theory that can't make sense of such platitudes has a lot of explaining to do.

The commonsense view of pleasure is that it is good because, put crudely, it *feels* good. Likewise, suffering is bad because of what it is *like* to suffer.[21] This supposition may well prove false on reflection, but it seems at least an accurate statement of the pretheoretical appearances. The further an account of pleasure strays from it, the less convincing it is likely to be.

What do Aristotelians say about pleasure's value? They certainly do not deny that it *has* value, or rather that the right sorts of pleasure have value. Aristotle even suggests at times that a kind of pleasure is "in some way the best good," though only in a highly qualified sense.[22] When it is objected that their account of well-being assigns too little weight to pleasure, Aristotelians frequently observe that their view takes flourishing to be necessarily pleasant, sometimes seeming to think that this settles the matter. It does not: their view needs to value pleasure *for the right reasons*, and to handle non-ideal cases as well. Exactly what Aristotle thinks about the nature and value of pleasure is not an easy question, and I will not try to answer it here. (Again, it doesn't much matter what he thinks: the question is what a perfectionist can plausibly say about pleasure.) But I will assume that pleasure's value derives, on an Aristotelian view, from its connection with virtuous activity.[23] This idea permits at least five interpretations. The first two I will pass by with little discussion: on the one hand, the behavioristic idea that pleasure just is unimpeded (virtuous) activity, as in "his digging was his pleasure"; and on the other, the claim that pleasure's importance consists in its role as an indicator of value. Both notions may be true to some small part of the story, but as complete accounts of pleasure and its value they are, for obvious reasons, wildly implausible.

A third interpretation maintains that pleasure matters because it "completes" an excellent activity.[24] This too seems hopeless as a full account of pleasure's value. For apparently pleasure is merely a necessary component of virtuous activity, and its value reduces entirely to its role in "completing" such activity. It thus contributes to our lives in much the same way that choosing the fine for its own sake, or doing so from a firm disposition, does: one's activity won't count as virtuous otherwise. And suffering is bad because it renders one's activities incomplete or otherwise defective, undermining their excellence. This is a very strange idea (stranger still if we interpret 'perfection' to put the weight on admirability rather than actualization). The notion that pleasure actually matters *simply* as a cog in the machinery of good functioning is so far removed from the appearances that it is hard to know what to make of it. Is the suffering of young leukemia patients bad simply because their functioning is inhibited? One might have thought that an excellent reason to restore functioning to patients is to alleviate their suffering, not the reverse. (Painkillers can also inhibit functioning.[25])

A related interpretation construes pleasure as itself a kind of virtuous mental activity. To have a pleasant experience is (to some extent) to function well psychically; it is a kind of psychic perfection or fullness of being or actuality. And suffering is a kind of psychic ill-functioning or diminution of being.[26] This proposal would allow the Aristotelian to explain how the cheap pleasures of a passive consumer, leading the life of "dumb grazing cattle," nonetheless have *something* going for them. While such a life is markedly inferior to one of rational excellence befitting a human being, it at least permits the fulfillment of our lower, animal natures. But this account still seems unacceptable, partly because it must sharply discount pleasure's value to maintain a credible account of virtue or excellence. The contribution pleasure makes to our lives seems to far outstrip its role in making our lives excellent or perfecting our being. A further worry is that it departs too far from the commonsense view of the nature of pleasure's value. It is not plausible to claim that the leukemia patient's suffering is bad simply or even mainly because it constitutes a psychic ill-functioning.[27] What does that have to do with the *experience* of suffering? Zombies can have psychic ill-functionings.

A fifth perfectionist option is to construe pleasure as a bonus that accompanies virtuous activity: it "supervenes as the bloom of youth does on those in the flower of their age."[28] *Contra* the bare "completion" view discussed above, pleasure is the icing on the cake, not a merely necessary ingredient like the yeast. (Conversely, suffering must be the spitting on your grave.) One problem with this proposal is that pleasure does not seem to be merely a nice add-on, the icing on the cake: it is, rather, a large part of the cake. It is substantially what makes life worth living, and a very great part of what I imagine the dying regret leaving behind. And the corresponding view of suffering, as merely a final insult (supervening on *what* injury?) clearly fails to square with the reality. Worse, the "bonus" view of pleasure doesn't explain its value at all; it *presupposes* that pleasure is somehow valuable. Why is it a bonus?

In fairness, perhaps no extant theory of well-being can readily accommodate pleasure and suffering, save possibly for hedonism; Aristotelian theories are not alone in this regard. But we can expect our theory at least to come *close*, or to hold out the prospect of someday getting it right. Aristotle himself may have been none too happy with this aspect of his theory, given his repeated attempts to come to grips with it. In any case he was not given to saying stupid things, so it is hard to avoid the thought that we have underestimated the resources of his theory on this point.

Or maybe we have misunderstood its aspirations. Perhaps the Aristotelian claim is rather that, while pleasure is only an ancillary part of our goal in leading good lives—not so much what we aim at as something that comes along for the ride—it is nonetheless a large part of what the virtuous agent hopes or *wishes* for.[29] After all, knowing that your goal is virtuous activity only tells you so much: you then need to know what it means to choose and act in accordance with virtue. That, presumably, means seeing various things other than virtuous activity as preferable or desirable. Other things being equal, the virtuous agent sees pleasant experiences as being more desirable than unpleasant ones, and thus prefers them. Indeed, when thinking about all the things it would be nice to have in life, the virtuous agent can give pleasure a very large role. What she cannot do is see pleasure and other objects of choice as even *potentially* competing with virtue; to pursue these things at the expense of acting well is out of the question. What fundamentally matters, then, is virtuous activity, and pleasure is in a sense worthless by comparison, in the very special sense that it is not to be balanced against the demands of virtue. For in a conflict with virtue pleasure has zero weight.[30] If we construe the Aristotelian view this way then we can see it as having two theories of "value": the main theory, of what should be our goal in life; and a second theory—akin to the Stoic view of indifferents—which concerns the relative weight a virtuous agent will place on the various items that might be chosen or wished for. Such a reading of the Aristotelian project would make it easier to understand not only its popularity but also the success of Stoicism, which can seem downright crazy when viewed through the lens of contemporary debates about well-being.

The problem is that Aristotle never really gives us the second theory; evidently it cannot be specified, but can only be embodied in the practical wisdom of a virtuous agent. (Or, perhaps, derived from an account of human nature.) But if the Aristotelian approach to virtue is to seem at all plausible, we need an account of how the virtuous agent views matters like the leukemia patient's suffering: we need to be told that the *phronimos* sees the suffering as a bad thing, or at least something to be alleviated, *because of how it feels to the child*. Or perhaps for some other reason, such as that the child wants to be rid of it: as long as it turns out that the *phronimos* sees the child's suffering as bad for reasons that are both credible and consistent with a reasonable account of virtue. If the preceding arguments are cogent, the *phronimos* will *not* see the child's suffering as undesirable merely for perfectionist reasons. If she considers it bad simply because it indicates illness or poor character, for instance, we will be compelled to reject the account of virtue that proclaims her to be virtuous. Whether this sort of approach can be made to work is a good question, but I will say something more about it later.

2.4. Well-being as a success value

There seem to be no compelling grounds for holding welfare perfectionism: perfection, excellence, or virtue probably forms no fundamental part of well-being. If perfection does seem to be a great benefit for most of us, this is probably due to its relation to other things, like pleasure or success in relation to our values. Or, alternatively, if perfection is fundamental to well-being, then it plays a smaller and very different role from that posited by Aristotelian accounts.[31]

These conclusions have been reached mainly by reflecting on a variety of intuitive points, but now I want to consider a deeper, more fundamental flaw—one that suggests, moreover, that even more modest forms of perfectionism will not work. Sumner charges that perfectionism results basically from a confusion, failing to see the difference between perfectionist and prudential value.[32] In particular, the concept of prudential value is indexical, relativized to the agent, whereas the concept of perfectionist value is not like this. That charge seems too strong: most perfectionists are probably aware that 'perfection' and 'well-being' express different concepts. What they claim, without confusion, is that the two types of value are tightly connected: individuals achieve one type of value *by* achieving the other. Welfare consists in perfection. But while perfectionists seem to be innocent of conflating distinct concepts, I would suggest they have erred about the character of perfectionist value and well-being, respectively. If we properly understand their significance, we will not find it plausible to maintain that one is constituted by the other.[33]

The perfectionist's fundamental mistake lies in not recognizing that well-being is what we might call a *success* value: it concerns the success of an organism in achieving its goals.[34] This is a very abstract and formal claim, compatible with most accounts of well-being, and that is how it should be. The relevant goals might be understood in the obvious way, in terms of the individual's aims or desires, or more broadly. Thus we might refer to the desires one would have given full information or otherwise ideal conditions. An organism's tendencies for growth and development might also be taken to specify goals (one way in which an objectivist view might fit this schema). Goals can also be found in propensities for positive and negative response: pleasure, pain, happiness, satisfaction, etc. For one way to achieve success, broadly construed, is to attain a state that one welcomes or responds to favorably, even if one had not previously sought it—an *ex post facto* success, so to speak. (If this seems strained, consider how a designer might go about implanting goals in an organism. One option is to build in desires or propensities for functioning in ways that aim at the goals. Another is to build in the right evaluative propensities—tendencies to respond favorably to things that promote the achievement of those goals. This will be especially useful insofar as the designer cannot predict what those things will be in advance, and hence cannot build in tendencies to seek those things directly. By contrast, simply giving the organism the *capacity* to achieve the requisite goals would not be a way of giving it those goals.)

That well-being concerns success can be seen in the fact that actions aimed at improving individuals' welfare are naturally described as "helping," "aiding," or "assisting." We see it also in the ordinary conception of well-being as a matter of an individual's "interests." And it would be hard to understand the appropriateness of sympathetic concern for shortfalls in welfare, much less Darwall's plausible suggestion that welfare is normative for care, if we did not also suppose that well-being somehow concerns the individual's goals.[35] How can we commiserate or sympathize over something that in no way relates to the individual's goals, is not at all rejected or disliked by any part of the individual, and which the individual cannot even be brought to care about? Similarly, the peculiar *in*appropriateness of an emotion like *schadenfreude* seems essentially connected to the broad notion of success. It would make little sense to take malicious delight in someone's vices unless one saw them as somehow frustrating the person's goals.

Perfection, by contrast, bears no necessary connection to anything that can plausibly be viewed as an organism's goals: for one can achieve a perfection, at least to some degree, merely by fulfilling a capacity, even if one hasn't the slightest desire for it, could not be brought to desire it, is in no other way oriented to seek it, and even if one responds with nothing but pain and revulsion toward it.[36] Indeed, one's perfection, as understood by most perfectionist theories, can depend on the fulfillment of capacities one doesn't even *have*, and can't have. It is very hard to see how this sort of perfection could count as succeeding in one's goals, understood as loosely as you like. The problem is that perfection is not a success value but a *performance* value, a type of value that concerns doing things well or being a good example of one's kind. Perfection is normative not for attitudes of caring or sympathetic concern, but for attitudes of *admiration* or deploring, or approval and disapproval.[37] To conceive of well-being or flourishing in terms of perfection, then, is to engage in an inescapably Procrustean enterprise: we will invariably be able to imagine cases in which excellence meets nothing that could be considered among the individual's goals, or where the degree of excellence attained outstrips the degree of goal-attainment.

Our interests in well-being and perfectionist value are fundamentally different: they answer to different concerns. Think about *why* human beings should care about such values, as all healthy persons seem to. What is their role in human life? A proper treatment of this important question should connect with the growing body of empirical research on the domains of value recognized in different cultures and their functions.[38] But here are some preliminary remarks. Prudential value, at least in the case of well-being, apparently relates to the universal problem of deciding how to distribute resources and attention among those we care about, including ourselves. When does a given individual require assistance or special care? Who needs it most (and least)? Who has more than they need? Who has given up the least, or most? Such questions naturally relate to individuals' goals—again, broadly conceived—and what they need to reach them. It would be odd to answer them mainly by reference to individuals' excellences, and I am unaware of any society in which people normally settle such questions that way. This is probably because perfectionist values are not suited to such questions. They concern a different set of problems that face social creatures such as ourselves: the problems of affiliation, including the establishing of relationships and enforcement of norms, that confront groups of individuals trying to live together given disparate abilities and agendas. Who should we trust, befriend, or marry? Who should we avoid? Who should we emulate? It should be unsurprising that a value concept oriented to answering these kinds of questions would be ill-suited to addressing the concerns of well-being—helping us decide who needs help and so forth. For these questions bear only tangentially on the individual's goals: for the most part, our interest in these questions has no bearing on the individual's goals, needs, or interests. We are more interested in *other* people's needs.

Perhaps the Aristotelian will be unmoved by the preceding account of prudential and perfectionist values. But then we are owed a competing account of well-being's value: if well-being isn't fundamentally a success value, then what sort of value is it, such that a perfectionist account of it would make sense? Some writers, like Hurka, have simply denied that we need a distinct category of prudential value: why not say that perfection is good, period, and be done with it?[39] What's to be gained by distinguishing *good* from *good for*? It is not clear what else one can say.

2.5. Accounts of well-being versus deliberative accounts of the good life

Often with philosophical problems, the hard part is just figuring out what the question is supposed to be. Aristotelians have been asking what is in some ways exactly the right question; it just isn't the right question if you're looking for a theory of well-being. Julia Annas writes that "in ancient ethics the fundamental question is, How ought I to live? Or, What should my life be like?"[40] This eminently reasonable question is arguably approached, at least in Aristotle's writing, by thinking about our ultimate goal in life: each of us seeks to lead a good life; what, then, is the nature of our target, so that we may succeed in hitting it?[41] In short, what is our ultimate goal in life? The question invites us to take up a certain perspective, a first-person perspective from which we think about what our ultimate priorities or goals in life should be; call this the "goal-setting" perspective.[42]

From this standpoint a perfectionist view like Aristotle's can seem highly appealing: surely we ought, above all, to act well; and perhaps nothing is worth seeking if that means acting badly. Such a view seems all the more plausible when we observe that it need not preclude acting on ordinary reasons of "self-interest" such as that something would be pleasant, healthy, etc., since acting well presumably includes choosing well with respect to such things. As I noted earlier, this view also makes sense of the otherwise curious—to some of us bizarre—idea that pleasure does not really matter all that much in itself, being merely a by-product that accompanies the achievement of what is truly worthwhile. Even today one often hears such ideas, including from ordinary folk with no commitment to Aristotelian doctrines. And the reason, I am suggesting, is that those who endorse them are focusing on something like the goal-setting perspective: thinking about the role goods like pleasure should take in setting our priorities in life. While pleasure can seem centrally important even from this perspective, it need not: many decent and intelligent people have thought it inappropriate to make pleasure one's aim in life.

The problem is that, in approaching the theory of well-being from this perspective, we have effectively changed the subject. To ask how we ought to live, or what our priorities in life should be, is equivalent to asking for an account of the *good life*, in the broad sense mentioned earlier: the sort of life that it is good to lead, not just for one's own sake, but period. Or, more exactly, it is to ask for an account of the good life taken as a goal (we will see the reason for this qualification shortly). As a result, 'eudaimonia' seems in Aristotle's writings to fill two roles: on the one hand, it appears to be a rough synonym of 'well-being', a notion that concerns what benefits a person; this is pretty much the conventional understanding of the term. On the other hand, it is claimed to represent whatever it is that would constitute an ideal life, a life that is most choiceworthy, and thus occupies a role akin to the broad understanding of 'good life'.[43] Thus Annas tells us that "for Aristotle it is trivial that my final end is eudaimonia," for the notion of eudaimonia just is the "notion of living our life as a whole well."[44] And eudaimonia "in ancient theories is given its sense by the role it plays; and the most important role it plays is that of an obvious, but thin, specification of the final good."[45] But if we begin our inquiries with this understanding of eudaimonia, then we are effectively *stipulating* that eudaimonia is equivalent to the good life. Any account of eudaimonia that cannot credibly explain what it means to live one's "life as a whole well" is simply a non-starter.

Since modern theorists of well-being generally are not even trying to give accounts of what it is to live well, they are just not in the same game as Aristotelians and other proponents of eudaimonistic ethics. Indeed, probably most of them, like Kant, would expressly deny that well-being is a good measure of a life lived well, since they think it perfectly possible for a bad person, living badly, to flourish. More generally, anyone who believes well-being not to be the measure of a good life, being only a part of it, are not just wrong according to the Aristotelian view—the way, say, they take Epicureans to be wrong. Rather, they reject a fundamental presupposition of the inquiry, and so aren't invited to the party at all. We should not be surprised, then, that Aristotelians and their critics, notably subjectivists about well-being, so often seem to end up talking past each other, and that they frequently regard each others' views with bafflement, if not outright contempt. But this is, to some extent, the wrong comparison: Aristotle and other ancient eudaimonists were fundamentally concerned to recommend a certain way of life. And while—for example—Kant's subjectivist view of well-being differs radically from Aristotle's account of eudaimonia, the two philosophers actually recommend rather similar *ways of life*, in that both accept strong doctrines of the primacy of virtue. Of course, there remain substantial differences, for instance in Kant's advocacy of a far sterner, more moralistic conception of the good life than Aristotle.

The mistake here—in effect, trying to give a theory of well-being by asking what the good life is like—is quite understandable, and it is not surprising that many discerning observers should have made it. To begin with, the goal-setting perspective obscures the differences between well-being and the good life: when we imagine what true happiness or success would be for ourselves, what we picture tends to be precisely the sort of life we deem to be ideal on the whole. When thinking about our ultimate goals, the good life tends to be indistinguishable from the life of well-being. Similarly, we are unlikely to see profit in pursuing a way of life seriously at odds with our considered convictions about the best way to live, period. If you value honesty as a moral virtue, for instance, it would likely be prudent for you to make honesty one of your priorities, simply because people living at odds with their own values tend not, even by their own lights, to flourish.

Where Aristotelians go wrong, in short, is in approaching the theory of well-being via the wrong question: what is my ultimate goal? The natural way to answer such a question is to offer a *first-person comprehensive ideal*. But any theory of well-being that takes such a form is liable to suffer from a host of problems. Insofar as we are asking for a *comprehensive* ideal, which is to say an ideal that encompasses everything desirable in a life, we are really asking for a theory of the good life. And as I have suggested, Aristotelian theories are fundamentally theories of the good life that have been dragooned into service as accounts of well-being.

The other aspects of the approach are problematical as well. Insofar as a theory centers on an *ideal*, or target, it risks being unable to handle non-ideal cases well; in general, it is much easier to say what an ideal life is like than to give criteria for assessing the many ways in which ordinary lives like Angela and Frank's fall short. And as we get away from perfect lives the various components of an ideal life will often seem intuitively to diverge, as virtue and pleasure (*inter alia*) do in Angela's case. The dual roles of Aristotle's 'eudaimonia' likewise come apart, with the "good life" aspect tending intuitively to stick closer to virtue and the "well-being" aspect tending to track pleasure and other traditional prudential goods. Insofar, finally, as the theory aims to provide a *first-person* ideal, it is liable to neglect aspects of life that are important yet not appropriately aimed at by the individual whose life it is. This could be because they lie beyond the individual's control (e.g., you can ensure you act well, but not that a good outcome follows); because they are most fittingly objects of third-personal concern (e.g., concern for the suffering stoically endured by a loved one); or because the goods in question tend to be the by-products of other things that are more wisely or appropriately aimed at (e.g., pleasure accompanying worthwhile activity). Such points are largely why the Aristotelian treatment of pleasure gets as much traction as it does. Along with the limitations of ideals, they are also why I have qualified the Aristotelian's fundamental concern as with, not the good life *simpliciter*, but rather the ideal of the good life that should guide our deliberations.

As I said, Aristotelians are in some ways asking exactly the right question. Indeed, contemporary ethics arguably suffers from a handicap of its own in not taking that question more seriously than it does. One might expect that the question of how we ought to live would be central to any serious philosophical ethics. Yet modern ethical theorists tend to address the question piecemeal, looking narrowly at the moral side of the equation, or the prudential side, or at some other aspect of the good life. Or, in the case of the Utilitarians, so inflating the moral side of the equation that it gobbles up everything else, resulting in a theory that is probably impossible to live with. It is a virtue of the ancient tradition that it takes seriously the task of helping people deliberate wisely about their priorities in life, and it is no coincidence that even today many people skip the modern literature and turn to the ancients for philosophical guidance about how to live.

My arguments in this section suggest that Aristotelian and other ethical theories in the eudaimonistic tradition may be founded on a confusion.[46] But perhaps such theories are not fatally flawed so much as miscast. For if we recast Aristotelian theories, not as theories of well-being, but simply as deliberative accounts of the good life—that is, accounts of the ideal of living that ought to guide our deliberations—then they may seem a lot more compelling. Indeed, the broader canvas of ancient eudaimonism may prove more compelling, and less alien, on such a view (revisionary though it is). You could grant everything said in this chapter and still accept Aristotle's views about the primacy of virtue, and the importance of activity, in the life well-lived; you just wouldn't think they amounted to a credible theory of *well-being*. Indeed, you might even want to supplement Aristotle's account of the good life—which, as I noted earlier, is notoriously underspecified on many questions, like how we ought to view the suffering of our loved ones—with a subjectivist account of well-being, or perhaps the account defended in Chapter 9. Whereas the Stoic emphasis on the individual's internal state, rather than activity, insulates their view from worries about how we can make *activity* our goal given its dependence on the goods of fortune. And again, we would still need to know about those indifferents: which are preferred, to what extent, and why. A conventional account of well-being may be needed here. Even Epicurean hedonism could retain its appeal on this sort of reading: for those who believe we are only capable of seeking pleasure, the Epicureans offer a psychologically realistic yet attractive view of the good life by showing how the pleasant life requires discipline and the traditional virtues. I do not know if this sort of rehabilitation of ancient eudaimonism can be made to work—the treatment of well-being would obviously be revisionary. But it seems an avenue worth exploring.

3. CONCLUSION

The diagnosis offered here is meant to illuminate the mistakes that I suspect have made Aristotelian *perfectionism* seem plausible to many of its supporters—or at the very least, to articulate the best motivation I can think of for accepting the view. I am not claiming that all Aristotelians have approached the theory in the suggested manner, or that this is the sole or even best reason for being an Aristotelian about well-being. For example, one attraction of Aristotelian accounts of well-being is a kind of naturalism they seem to embody: starting with a general schema for thinking about the flourishing of any living thing, we develop our account of specifically human flourishing by looking at our specifically human natures. We thus situate our view of human well-being in a broad theoretical framework that illuminates much else besides. (And for Aristotle, at least, this picture integrates with a still broader comprehensive metaphysics.) So regarded, Aristotle's account of well-being doesn't seem first-personal at all.

All of this, I think, is compatible with the diagnosis proffered above: it is perfectly possible, and I think likely, that Aristotelians, and probably Aristotle himself, have approached the theory of well-being from more than one direction. One possibility is to begin from a third-personal naturalistic perspective that leads to the idea that eudaimonia is our ultimate goal in life, then switching to the first-person "goal-setting" perspective. In any event, I would suggest that the naturalistic perspective, while arguably one source of the Aristotelian view's allures, is not the perspective that gives perfectionism its primary appeal. Aristotle's metaphysics may have helped to motivate his perfectionism, but many contemporary Aristotelians don't buy the metaphysics. Nor is it clear how thinking about human beings as organisms, in the context of plant and animal flourishing generally, compels us to accept perfectionism. There is indeed something appealing about the idea that goodness in a lion consists in perfecting its nature *qua* lion.[47] But is it so obvious that lion *well-being* consists in being a good lion, or in the exercise of liony excellence? Perhaps it does so consist, but this idea is not nearly as compelling as another. For what the naturalistic point of view does motivate, I would suggest, is welfare *externalism*: an organism flourishes insofar as it enjoys the goods characteristic of its kind. And very many people find it sad or unfortunate when an animal's life is devoid of some major part of a normal or full life for its species—for instance if a lion is never able to hunt. The problem, intuitively, is not lack of perfection—not being a good lion or exercising the virtues proper to lions—but "missing out," failing to enjoy one or more of the elements of a full life for a lion. Similarly when a person is born blind, retarded, etc. Such intuitions have considerable force for many people, and as I noted earlier may constitute the strongest support for Aristotelian accounts of well-being. But this support appears to be for Aristotelian externalism, not perfectionism.

In all this I have not tried to deny the importance of perfection or excellence. Indeed this seems a matter of first importance, more important even than well-being in the achievement of a good life. What I do deny is that *well-being* fundamentally concerns perfection. In fact welfare perfectionism seems in a way to discount the importance of perfection by subsuming it under well-being: perfection matters not *simpliciter*, but because it is at least partly constitutive of flourishing. (And of course it cannot be more important than flourishing.) But it seems more plausible to say that perfection matters, period—whether it benefits us or not.

9

Happiness, the Self, and Human Flourishing

It may even be held that [the intellect] is the true self of each, inasmuch as it is the dominant and better part; and therefore it would be a strange thing if a man should choose to live not his own life but the life of some other than himself. Moreover . . . that which is best and most pleasant for each creature is that which is proper to the nature of each; accordingly the life of the intellect is the best and the pleasantest life for man, inasmuch as the intellect more than anything else is man.

Aristotle[1]

1. INTRODUCTION

Our excursion into Aristotelian approaches to well-being served several purposes, one being to counter a major source of doubts about the importance of happiness. At the same time, recognizing the considerable force of the Aristotelian position may soften support for the main alternative, the various forms of subjectivism. This is useful, since popular notions of the transparency of well-being, and hence personal authority in such matters, draw much strength from subjectivism. Finally, the approach to well-being that I want to develop here centers on an old idea most commonly associated with the Aristotelian paradigm, welfare eudaimonism: grounding well-being in some ideal of nature-fulfillment. Because contemporaries tend not to think of psychological states like happiness in such terms, our investigation of Aristotelian eudaimonism should help the reader to see the deep historical roots of the basic approach I will be defending. There is nothing exotic about it.

The primary aim of this chapter is positive, namely to defend, at least provisionally, a partial account of well-being that accords a central place to happiness. Negatively, my chief target will be, not Aristotelianism, but *subjectivism*. Subjectivism can be understood in any number of ways, but here I conceive it in the manner that seems best to explain the popularity of such theories (roughly following L. W. Sumner).[2] Subjectivist theories of welfare assert the sovereignty of the individual about her own well-being (what Richard Arneson aptly calls the thesis of "agent sovereignty"): her own priorities determine what sort of life makes her best off. Nothing can make you better off that goes against your all-things-considered (informed, etc.) preferences, desires, or judgment. The appeal of such a view lies mainly, it seems, in the plausible idea that by deferring to subjects' own judgments we respect their status as autonomous agents. We seem thus to avoid a kind of paternalism. Non-subjectivists, by contrast, confront a formidable objection: "Who are you to say what's best for *me*?" A further attraction is that subjectivism seems to respect the "internalist intuition" that an agent's well-being must connect appropriately with her motivational structure. The main impetus behind this intuition is put nicely by Connie Rosati, who writes (citing Peter Railton) that "an individual's good must not be something *alien*—it must be 'made for' or 'suited to' her. But something can be suited to an individual . . . only if a concern for that thing lies within her motivational capacity."[3] Subjectivist theories include happiness-based views like Sumner's, which focuses on subjects' evaluations of their lives,[4] but most subjectivists these days subscribe to desire theories, especially informed desire theories. Subjectivism does allow for some kinds of error, such as inconsistency, but not for fundamental errors in one's values.[5] While subjectivists need not claim that well-being is transparent to the agent, their commitment to agent sovereignty constrains how far they can reasonably move in the direction of opacity. The less transparent your theory makes well-being, the more susceptible you are to the "Who are you to say?" objection about paternalism. In any event, the common notion—pervasive among economists—that people typically know what's good for them clearly gets much support from the dominance of subjectivism.

Happiness would seem to be a paradigm subjectivist good. But this appearance, I will argue, is false: while subjectivists like Sumner correctly give happiness a central role in well-being, the value of happiness is not easily accommodated within a subjectivist framework. In fact happiness proves to be a source of *counterexamples* to subjectivism. The best accounting of happiness's value requires, instead, a eudaimonistic, and non-subjectivist, conception of well-being. The type of eudaimonism I have in mind centers on the idea of *self-fulfillment*, which I understand as a specific form of nature-fulfillment: the fulfillment of the *self*. While sharing the eudaimonism of Aristotle's views, we will see that my approach departs from the Aristotelian mold in important ways.

The central contention of this chapter is that happiness—or rather, "authentic happiness"[6]—has intrinsic prudential value as an aspect of self-fulfillment. This is because happiness bears a special relation to the self: the facts about what makes us (authentically) happy partially define who we are, our selves. (Happiness is understood here along the lines of the emotional state view defended in Chapters 6 and 7.) The main argument will be intuitive, centering on a pair of cases to be presented shortly. After drawing out the relevant conception of happiness and its relation to the self in Section 3, I present two further arguments in Section 4. The first concerns the inability of hedonism to account for happiness's value, and the second contends that the self-fulfillment view enables us to solve a pair of difficulties confronting Sumner's authenticity constraint. Additional support is offered in Section 5, where I elaborate on the notion of self-fulfillment and sketch a view of well-being in which happiness plays a central role. I will not defend a complete theory of well-being here, and for that reason regard my conclusions as provisional.

2. THE INTUITIVE ARGUMENT: TWO CASES

Consider a young man, Henry, who has a passion for model trains. Henry has the opportunity to go into business with a profitable model railroad shop at which he knows he would be happy. Yet he decides, after careful reflection, to purchase a farm.[7] He has good reasons for the choice: he imagines—correctly—that he would make a fine farmer, and finds the prospect of working the land highly attractive: he sees an elemental appeal to being outdoors and getting his hands dirty, dealing with matters of human survival, and living in close contact with an independent reality. Nothing made-up about it, and none of the degrading political maneuverings and double-dealings of the professional world. Finally, he desires the extra money it would bring, as it is a highly profitable venture. Henry goes to work on the farm and succeeds admirably. He is, in short, successfully carrying out a thoughtfully chosen plan of life. (We can assume that he fulfills his other major aims: marrying a woman he loves, having happy and healthy children, etc.) I will stipulate that his plan of life is consistent with what he would choose were he fully informed, reflective, and rational (in the sort of minimal sense employed in informed-desire theories).[8]

The trouble is, Henry is deeply unhappy, and has been since taking over the farm. Though he would prefer to be happy, he thinks such matters overrated: a small, and ultimately dispensable, part of the good life. Life isn't supposed to be fun. Besides, he's pursuing a noble calling: happiness is small potatoes by comparison. (He reads a lot of Tolstoy.) But a few of Henry's old friends see things differently: he chose the wrong line of work. In spite of his ideals, working the land is not an activity that moves, inspires, or fulfills him. It has the opposite effect. It's not that he hates everything he does; again, he thinks it worthwhile, and it pleases him when his crops do well. But the only time he comes alive is when he indulges in his hobby. *That's* what turns him on.

Henry could still go into the model train business, and he knows that he would be far happier if he did. But this is an option he does not take seriously: after all, he's successfully pursuing a lifelong, and surely worthwhile, dream of working a farm. And model railroading, he thinks, is an amusing but somewhat frivolous hobby. This is not to say that he believes a life running the shop would be completely pointless; he recognizes that such a life would still be meaningful and worthwhile. It's just that he considers farming to be *more* worthwhile, a better choice. Further information and reflection would not change his mind.

Consider also the case of Claudia, an attorney. Claudia too has chosen a life of unhappiness, in her case because she prefers wealth and social status to happiness, and she found lawyering to be the most efficient means to these ends. She has succeeded, amassing great hordes of money, acquiring the finest luxuries, and earning the envy of her peers. But work at the kind of prestigious firm that meets her needs is, for her, stressful and emotionally unfulfilling. As a result she is short-tempered, stressed out, anxious, and mildly depressed. She could be happy in other pursuits, such as teaching or painting, which she would see as perfectly meaningful and worthwhile. Yet such happy-making activities do not bring her the riches and social prominence she desires. She does not regret her choice, and would not accept a life of average means and standing for any amount of happiness. As with Henry, her choice does not depend on errors in reasoning, factual ignorance, or thoughtlessness: these are her values.

Intuitively, Henry and Claudia have chosen professions that do not suit the kinds of people they are. There are ways of living that make them happy, and farming and lawyering, respectively, are not among them. Such facts comprise an important part of who they are, their natures or selves. Were their constitutions altered so that very different things made them happy, they would be very different people.

The question is whether, by living in conflict with their natures, Henry and Claudia have made a mistake. I would submit that they have: their values are misplaced. Intuitively, they assign too little importance to their happiness. I think their more perceptive friends would, quite plausibly, say that they are living in conflict with who they are. This mistake is prudential: they would be *better off* happy. And the mistake concerns the value of happiness as an aspect of *self-fulfillment*: living in a manner that conforms to the sort of person one is, permitting the fulfillment of the self. We ought not to live in conflict with our natures, or at least the aspect of the self involving happiness, without good reason (e.g., a weighty moral reason). If this is correct, then happiness is, in an important sense, an objective good: it is good whether one values it, or would value it given all the facts etc., or not.[9]

This criticism of Henry and Claudia resembles what we say of someone who lives in a kind of self-imposed bondage, such as a man with a great love and talent for painting who chooses to do something which he has neither the inclination nor any special ability to do, such as accounting, simply because it is more "respectable." We are liable to think his choice a poor one, and not simply because he lets his talent go to waste. We may think that his way of life needlessly frustrates the expression of his nature, of who he is. Think also of the repressed, dutiful Victorian daughter living as she is told. Or a gay man struggling to lead a heterosexual life. (Homosexuality is notoriously criticized as unnatural, a point often used against nature-fulfillment theories of well-being. Yet it is far more plausible to say that it is the gay man leading a heterosexual lifestyle who lives contrary to his nature. Notice that this is not, as we tend to suppose, due mainly to the frustration of his desires. For if he would be no happier given their satisfaction, we would not likely see him as fighting his nature in any problematical way.)

It may be objected that we can handle these cases without invoking the vexed notion of the self: Henry and Claudia have simply erred in taking the less pleasant route, or they aren't really getting what they want.[10] I will address the first objection in Section 4.1; whereas the second assumes too much about their psychologies: the mere fact that Claudia would be happy, say, as a teacher, doesn't show that she *wants* to be a teacher at all; perhaps the thought of teaching never occurred to her. Nor must we imagine that she has a burning desire to engage in the sorts of activities that teaching (etc.) would entail. We can more easily envision that Henry's heart's desire is to run the model train shop, but again this assumption is dispensable. The information about happiness suffices to ground our intuitions in these cases; we do no not need to make further inferences about Henry and Claudia's desires to see the problem. The notion of the self is indeed somewhat obscure, and we will need greater clarity about it before a self-fulfillment view of well-being can be fully vindicated (I will say a bit more about it later). But we are not likely to be rid of the notion anytime soon: ideals of self-fulfillment have been with us for at least as long as the philosophy of well-being has, and such ideals strike very many people as deeply compelling. And the literature on the self is vast, spanning a variety of disciplines and ideologies: people seem to care very much about what defines them as the distinct persons they are, and this concern informs much philosophical work in other realms. For example, it is not obvious that we can make sense of autonomy or freedom of the will without some conception of the self. If we employ the notion elsewhere, why deny it to the theorist of well-being? Particularly if, as I am suggesting here, no other notion will do the job. What would be odd, in fact, would be to maintain that the character of the self, of who one is, could be important in other domains but not in thinking about what is good for us.

Readers worried about the specifics of these cases are free to change them. Those who think farming sufficiently worthwhile to justify Henry's misery should imagine him in some other, less estimable profession. Note that even such skeptics should grant the crucial point: that Henry, mistaken or not, is *worse off* than he would be running a train shop. I focus on Henry only because, *pace* Claudia's case, our intuitions are less likely to be clouded by feelings of disapproval that have nothing to do with the matter at hand. In fact our inclination toward his choice, considered apart from its effects on his happiness, is probably favorable. I chose examples involving the choice of an occupation because such choices are especially helpful for illustrating the relevant phenomena. But the point is quite general. A relationship can go poorly, for instance, because one's partner is not well suited to one's nature: there's nothing wrong with him; he just doesn't make you happy.

My criticisms of Henry and Claudia require that they have, or had, alternatives that would make them significantly happier. They might have been incapable of greater happiness in any line of work, for instance if their values were sufficiently strong and deeply ingrained. But we need not assume their values are like that: few people made unhappy by their way of life have such rigid and narrowly oriented constitutions and values that they could not have been happier living in some manner other than the one of their choosing. I have also assumed that the happier options would strike them as worthwhile and meaningful, for we will see in Section 5 that well-being probably also depends on such factors: gains in happiness can fail to make us better off if they require deep enough conflicts with our commitments. My contention is not that Henry and Claudia's desires and values are *irrelevant* to their welfare; only that happiness is part of the story, and can trump such factors when they conflict.

We have, then, some grounds for thinking happiness important to who we are and, for this reason, to well-being. In Section 4 we will consider two further arguments for this point. First we need some explanation of the notions of happiness and the self and how they relate to each other.

3. HAPPINESS AND THE SELF

3.1. Happiness and the self: initial considerations

To recap the view defended in Chapters 6 and 7, to be happy is roughly for one's emotional condition to be broadly positive with only minor negatives, embodying a stance of psychic affirmation. This condition has two aspects, namely the individual's central affective states—roughly, moods and emotions—along with her mood propensities. For simplicity, I will not focus on mood propensity in what follows, though it clearly enhances the significance of happiness for the self. On this view, happiness is not merely a state of one's consciousness. It is more like a state of one's being—not just a pleasant experience, or a good mood, but *psychic affirmation* or, in more pronounced forms, *psychic flourishing*.

What is the value of being happy according to the present theory? For starters, it is pleasant. Yet attempts to account for happiness's value in purely hedonic terms seem to miss something. They do not account for the appeal of criticizing hedonism on the grounds that it is psychologically superficial. It seems important to note the psychological depth of happiness, the fact that it involves more of our psychologies than just their phenomenal surfaces. *Why?* The answer lies mainly in the connection that happiness makes with the self.

Return to the central/peripheral distinction. Everybody knows about this distinction; we just don't call it that.[11] But we employ it regularly, as when talking about things that do, or do not, *move us, get to us, bring us down, lift us up*, or *bounce right off us*. (Recall as well the "satisfy my soul" lyric noted in Chapter 6.) Central emotional reactions somehow constitute temporary changes *in* us, and are not just things that happen *to* us. Indeed, changes in emotional state, particularly mood propensity, are tantamount to temporary changes in personality: they alter the way we perceive things, how we evaluate things, the inferences we make, how we react (emotionally and otherwise) to events, what we desire, our physiology, and so on. (Compare how someone is when depressed with what he is like having fallen madly in love.) Suitably extended changes in emotional state can quite literally amount to differences in personality: a once dour person may now be high-spirited, a serene individual may become anxious, etc. Peripheral affects, by contrast, have few if any such implications: your chronic backache might cause you to be an irritable person. But the pain does not constitute a change in personality, in who you are. It is something that happens *to* you. (And which, if you can, you will not allow to *get* to you. The stoic strive to remain unmoved by the unpleasantness of their pains. The language here is interesting: we say "I *am* happy," versus "I am *experiencing* pleasure"—i.e., more or less, "Pleasure is happening to me." Such talk appears to construe happiness as a property of the person, and pleasure as something that impinges on the person.[12])

The central/peripheral distinction appears to be quite important, relating not only to the phenomenology and causal role of affect but to the character of the self. Consider how a normally happy person might react to a bout of depression: "This just isn't me; I feel like I'm not myself anymore, like a different person has taken over my body." Interestingly, chronic sufferers of depression sometimes find the happiness brought on by a successful course of antidepressant therapy to be deeply unsettling. They may discontinue the therapy altogether. This phenomenon, called "uplift anxiety," reflects a feeling that one is naturally an unhappy person, and that one is no longer oneself. Essentially, it is anxiety over the loss, deep alteration, or displacement of one's identity. One must either embrace a new identity or go back to being depressed. To the best of my knowledge, people do not undergo identity crises when relieved of chronic pain.

3.2. Concepts of the self

What is meant by the self? I am not concerned with the question of reidentification of individuals over time—the problem of "personal identity."[13] I am interested rather in those aspects of us that are important to making us the distinct individuals we are, that are important to understanding *who* we are, and not so much *which* individuals we are. I am not denying that these questions are related, but they do seem different. Suppose we believe that personal identity consists in nothing more than physiological continuities, or that it is a primitive relation. We should still be concerned with the "thicker," more substantive notion of the self that interests us here. Explaining this idea clearly is difficult, but it should become intelligible enough in what follows.

We can distinguish at least four broad notions of this thicker self. We might, for instance, distinguish a person's "social identity," where this is a matter of how others see the individual, or the individual's social role. Second, we might focus on certain morally or ethically important aspects of who a person is: her "character." Third, there is an individual's *temperament*: whether, for instance, she has a depressive, cheerful, extroverted, etc. temperament. Fourth, there is a family of notions pertaining to a subject's self-understanding or self-conception: the understanding of herself that is implicit in the way she sees or thinks about her herself, her life, her ideals, her projects and commitments, and her relationships to society and other people. This is what we typically have in mind when we speak without qualification—as I will in this chapter—of a person's "identity." Examples include the concepts of "ideal identity," "practical identity," "self-esteem identity," "narrative identity," etc.[14]

If the contentions of this chapter are correct, the self has at least one further aspect, which I will call a person's "emotional nature." With qualifications to be noted in the next section, to have a certain emotional nature is to be disposed characteristically to be happy in certain circumstances and not others.[15] Our emotional natures are partly determined by our temperaments, but not wholly: our desires, values, characters, and habits of thought, perhaps among other things, also have a role. (Although, as Henry and Claudia illustrate, our values are sometimes less significant for our natures than we might expect.) As I am arguing in this chapter, our propensities for happiness are not merely a part of our natures; they are more specifically a part of *who we are*: the self.[16] Our propensities for physical flourishing or pleasure, by contrast, seem not to be part of who we are,[17] though they plausibly constitute a part of our natures. We can put the difference this way: the fact that certain ways of living are healthiest for me, or bring the most physical pleasure, plausibly determines some aspect of my nature: the sort of creature I am, we might say. It's simply my nature to be made healthier by exercise, and to find the taste of broccoli pleasant—that's the sort of creature I am. But these things seem not to affect *who* I am: I would not be a different *person* if a sedentary life were best for my body, or if broccoli tasted awful to me. Changes in these respects would not, in general, engender identity crises.[18]

The term 'emotional nature' bears an unfortunate connotation, namely that our emotional make-up is more or less permanently fixed. The notion of emotional nature, as I understand it here, requires no commitment about such matters.[19] But the idea that a person's emotional make-up is set in stone, much less innate, is deeply implausible. Our propensities for happiness clearly evolve over time, depending heavily on social and cultural factors as well as our particular values, among other things. And there are many ways to fulfill one's emotional nature. Indeed, one might reasonably embark on a plan to *change* one's emotional nature, say by undertaking to become a cellist, and thus to be made happy by the things that tend to make cellists happy (like playing the cello well). This sort of example poses no difficulty for my view: our emotional natures will still constrain the options that make sense for us.[20] If you do not have the right sort of nature to begin with, or do not go about training as a cellist in the right way, your plans may fail. Some people aren't cut out to be cellists, because they lack talent, patience, or simply can't find satisfaction in it. So while we can alter our emotional natures, we must attend to the limitations imposed by our existing emotional make-up (which itself, note, is partly a product of our values, past choices, etc.). A further limitation comes in the form of the authenticity constraint, discussed in the next section: we can alter our emotional propensities through brainwashing or surgery, but such methods will only make self-fulfillment harder to attain. Indeed, they amount to ways of corrupting or destroying the self.

3.3. Authenticity and the role of happiness in self-fulfillment

Self-fulfillment consists at least partly in the fulfillment of our emotional natures: roughly, in being happy. "Roughly," because some forms of happiness, like that of the deceived or brainwashed, are problematical. Could such individuals really be flourishing? This is implausible. But so is the idea that one could attain self-fulfillment in this manner.

Sumner has recently proposed a novel means of handling such worries while retaining a central role for happiness in welfare. He argues that well-being consists in *authentic happiness*: being (well enough) informed and autonomous in one's happiness.[21] He explicitly identifies happiness with life satisfaction, but his view is better understood as a hybrid that includes pleasure—conceived along the lines of a preferred experience theory—as well. Happiness amounts to having all-around favorable attitudes toward one's life: finding one's life to be satisfying.

Sumner contends that well-being has to be subjective, reflecting the subject's point of view and priorities. Happiness as he conceives it arguably meets this criterion in the standard case. But what if our happiness is based on complete ignorance of our circumstances? What if we evaluate our lives favorably only because we have been brainwashed or manipulated? In both sorts of cases our happiness arguably fails to be a response to our lives that is truly *ours*. In cases of the former sort, it is not really our lives to which we are responding, but an illusion: we aren't adequately informed. In cases of the latter sort, the values that ground our attitudes are not truly our own. It isn't really *us* responding to our lives: our happiness is not autonomous.

There seems to be something deeply right about Sumner's notion of authentic happiness. I would like to co-opt the notion for my own purposes, substituting the emotional state conception of happiness for his, and allowing that well-being has other aspects even as happiness remains central: self-fulfillment requires authenticity.[22] I would suggest refining the autonomy constraint to allow that happiness need not be rooted in autonomous *values*; it may instead reflect, say, one's temperament. Autonomy presumably does require, however, that one's happiness *not* be based on values that are manipulated or otherwise non-autonomous. The activities that ground one's happiness should likewise be autonomous: a free-thinking slave might have autonomous values, but any happiness she might achieve nonetheless seems less than fully authentic if it is grounded in activities that aren't autonomous. For her happiness reflects a life that is not really her own. Authenticity also seems to require proper functioning, at least within broad limits: someone whose brain is pathologically stuck on "happy," no matter what happens or what she thinks, is not credibly viewed as authentically happy. Such happiness is more like that of the *soma* eater. (In severe cases where the self is badly disrupted it may not be clear what *could* count as authentic: some people lack well-formed selves.)

Authenticity arguably has a further dimension, beyond the information and autonomy requirements, namely *richness*. Briefly, the authenticity of one's happiness increases, other things being equal, to the extent that it is grounded in richer, more complex ways of living. For such ways of living more fully express one's nature. Someone might conceivably be happy, for example, leading the impoverished life of Rawls's grass-counter.[23] The choice to lead such a life could well be autonomous, say as a means of making happiness easier to come by. But there is not much of *him* in such a way of life, for he isn't really doing much of anything—indeed, his happiness reflects a stunted version of himself. Whittling oneself down in this way hardly seems a path to authenticity. A more authentic life—a life more fully expressing *his* nature, his individuality—would have him fully engaged in the business of living, with all the richness of an ordinary human life. And the resulting happiness would, it seems, be more authentic as well.[24]

This characterization of authenticity is admittedly somewhat cursory. But I am not trying to articulate a complete account of well-being here; further precision can wait until we have a broader theory to guide our reflections.[25] In fact the definition of authenticity is best left somewhat vague, since we should allow room for dispute about what counts, for instance, as being autonomous. Just insert the conception of autonomy that seems most credible to you, and you will likely get the reading of authentic happiness that strikes you as most promising.

With the notion of authenticity in hand, we can add the necessary qualification to our characterization of emotional nature: to have a certain emotional nature is to be disposed characteristically to be authentically happy in certain circumstances and not others. The fact that I would be happy with a frontal lobotomy does not seem important to who I am.

We can now state the central claim of this chapter: well-being consists partly in authentic happiness—in "emotional nature-fulfillment." More specifically, authentic happiness has intrinsic prudential value as an aspect of self-fulfillment, which in turn constitutes at least part of well-being. This value, moreover, is objective in the sense that it benefits you whether you want it, or would want it after reflection, or not. This might seem a weak claim, but it rules out virtually all extant theories of well-being.

3.4. Is there really an emotional self?

Some readers may balk at the very idea that mere affective dispositions could be central to who we are. Won't it seem to Henry as if his unhappiness reflects an alien part of him? *He* wills that he live in a certain manner, and he succeeds. Yet his emotional nature rebels; it does not reward him with the happiness he expects. From Henry's point of view it may seem that *he* is not, even partly, a set of emotional dispositions, but is rather the entity doing the willing. And these emotional dispositions are thwarting *him*. Discussing the phenomenology of choice, Korsgaard writes: "When you deliberate, it is as if there were something over and above all of your desires, something which is *you*, and which *chooses* which desire to act on."[26] Whether this self is something over and above your desires, or is itself constituted by certain desires, it certainly seems distinct from your emotional propensities.

Such appearances are exactly what we should expect given the distinction between emotional nature and identity. Our felt sense of who we are concerns the latter, happiness concerns the former. One's emotional nature need not be perceived as part of the self. Moreover, *consider how it will look to Henry's friends.* Those who know him well enough may not think his unhappiness the result of anything alien at all. On the contrary: his unhappiness very much reflects who he is. The problem is not that his true self is being thwarted by alien forces erupting from the nether regions of his psyche. It is rather that he is blinkered, insufficiently appreciative of his own nature. He is living in conflict with who he is.[27] If anything, his friends may see his snobbish *values* as alien, the impositions of a sometimes tyrannical intellect. (This is clearer still in Claudia's case.)

If all this is right, then matters of affective make-up are far more significant than we tend to suppose. Why hasn't this putative fact gotten more recognition? Mainly, it seems, because "mere" matters of emotional constitution are seen as little more than parameters that limit the range of our realistic options in life, much as the facts about how tall or intelligent one is are among the brute facts one must accommodate when planning one's life. A rational agent had best take such factors into account when deciding what to do, but this is not because they have any special value. It is just that *she won't get what she wants* otherwise. Typically we very much want to be happy, and so we shall need to consider the facts about what makes us happy when deciding what to do. Traditional subjective theories of well-being, like the desire theory, can readily accommodate this phenomenon. But what if someone doesn't consider happiness to be particularly important? This is among the questions raised by the cases of Henry and Claudia, and subjectivism is less plausible here. There is, I suspect, a second reason for the neglect of our emotional natures: a naïve assumption that happiness neatly tracks the extent to which we are getting what we want. What makes us happy is getting what we want. Some writers have clearly made this assumption: the switch from happiness to preference as the gauge of utility among economists was substantially premised on the belief that preference satisfaction could serve as a proxy for happiness, which they found too difficult to quantify and measure.[28] In short, we have tended either to ignore the emotional self altogether, or to consider it significant only as a potential obstacle to the satisfaction of our desires.

4. FURTHER CONSIDERATIONS FAVORING THE SELF-FULFILLMENT VIEW

4.1. The argument concerning hedonic value

Someone might grant that Henry made a mistake but dispute my diagnosis. We might think Henry's error consists simply in having chosen a needlessly *unpleasant* life. The mistake is purely hedonic. Notice that this proposal makes pleasure out to be an objective good: we are better off with pleasure whether we want it or not. This implication is actually quite plausible: it is not as if we *make* pleasure good in wanting it, as if pleasure were itself neither good nor bad—as if our preference for pleasure, rather than displeasure, were arbitrary. I do not mean arbitrary in the sense that there could be no explanation of any sort for it. The idea is rather that, if pleasure is not intrinsically good, then we ultimately have no more reason to like it *qua* experience—for the way it feels—than to dislike it. We could just as well have been constructed to want experiences of extreme nausea or depression rather than massages and happiness, and *there would be no non-instrumental reason for preferring the one constitution to the other*. This is hard to believe.[29]

Even if we grant the objective value of pleasure, that cannot be the whole story, for three reasons. First, peripheral displeasures, such as physical pains, do not seem to invoke the same intuitions. We might think it irrational for someone to choose a life of discomfort involving back pain without good reason. But we would not be especially inclined to describe such person as living in a way that conflicts with who she is, except insofar as the discomfort makes her unhappy (perhaps she is stoic and doesn't let it get her down). Our criticism of Henry, by contrast, resembles what we say of repressed artists and the like, as I remarked in Section 2. Hedonism seems false to our understanding of these cases. It is not just that Henry's experience is unpleasant. More pressing is that *his very being* seems to be in rebellion against his way of life.

Second, the kind of disvalue involved in Henry-type cases does not neatly track the hedonic disvalue. Intense back pain can be more unpleasant than a mildly depressed mood, even if you somehow manage not to let it get to you. Yet we are much more likely to consider gratuitous inflictions of negative emotional states as involving conflicts with, or the suppression of, our natures. The disvalue of unhappiness tracks not only the intensity of the displeasure, but the centrality of the affective states involved as well.

Third, if Henry's problem were merely hedonic, we could fix it by giving him a pleasure pill or brain implant, were such treatments available. Such measures would confer *some* benefit, namely by making his life more pleasant. But they would not solve the fundamental problem, which intuitively is that his nature is unsuited for farming. Indeed, they would seem to make him worse off, as the resulting happiness would be a sham. At least his present unhappiness is *his*. My account can explain this: however little Henry fulfills his nature as an unhappy farmer, he would fulfill it even less by unhinging his mind from reality.

4.2. The authenticity argument: Sumner's problem

I now want to argue that the present account of self-fulfillment enables us to solve two difficulties that confront Sumner's theory of welfare: the authenticity constraint sits better with my view than Sumner's. The most serious problem is that Sumner seems unable to give a plausible account of how authenticity affects the value of happiness.[30] Is the value of happiness *wholly* conditional on authenticity? This is not credible: surely you are better off as a happy brain in a vat or brainwashing victim than as an unhappy one. Certainly you are better off in one respect, as we just saw: your experience is more pleasant. In fact the hedonic value of happiness appears not to be affected at all by considerations of authenticity. In what way, then, is your well-being compromised? This is hard to say. Inauthentic happiness is not prudentially worthless, nor is it simply bad. It appears to be mixture of good and bad. Sumner's theory seems unable to account for this, save perhaps by ad hoc stipulation. If happiness is valuable not just hedonically but also as part of self-fulfillment, however, then we can plausibly account for the significance of authenticity: whereas happiness's hedonic value is untouched by inauthenticity, its value *qua* self-fulfillment is undermined in proportion to the shortfall in authenticity. In short, we cannot achieve self-fulfillment insofar as our happiness depends on ignorance about our lives, on being mindless tools, or on other forms of inauthenticity. Self-fulfillment is manifestly incompatible with lacking autonomy, at least on some reasonable views of autonomy. It also rules out being badly deceived about the conditions of one's life, for self-fulfillment is not credibly viewed as a solipsistic ideal that concerns only the state of the individual. It involves an individual's leading a life that suits her nature. Even with other animals, where we commonly assess well-being in terms of the fulfillment of the creature's nature, we do not think such fulfillment supervenes entirely on the state of the individual: a happy "wolf-brain in a vat" is liable to strike us as pathetic, failing badly to fulfill its nature. Likewise, self-fulfillment for me requires my responding favorably to *my* life, not a mirage.

Sumner's account has another difficulty: reconciling the authenticity constraint with his subjectivism.[31] Suppose I live under a totalitarian regime that has indoctrinated me to venerate its leaders and accept the state's values. I might be happy, yet inauthentically so: my happiness is not autonomous, for it depends on the acceptance of values imposed on me through manipulative practices. This is a problem. Is it a *subjectivist* problem? It is not a problem from the subjective point of view: I wholeheartedly endorse my values and way of life. I see nothing wrong with my circumstances. This affirmation may persist through reflection and exposure to the facts. You might call my attention to my lack of autonomy, the inauthenticity of my happiness. I might agree with you on this, but then say, "so what?" I do not *value* autonomy or authenticity. As far as I am concerned, these are the decadent values of a pathologically individualistic society. Leave me alone.

It is worth considering what is to be done with someone like me. Deprogramming seems the only route to enlightenment. Sumner writes of the "individual sovereignty which characterizes a subjective theory" of well-being (1996, p. 160). Yet his own theory denies that the individual's own best judgment, even when well-informed, is always sovereign.[32] This sounds a lot like an objectivist claim. (Consider how it will sound to the heteronomous agent.) Sumner will, of course, deny that it is really one's *own* judgment at all when autonomy is lacking. To the agent, however, it seems for all the world like it is his judgment, that it really reflects *his* values. The only way to make sense of Sumner's contention, it seems, is to see it as appealing to an objective conception of the self: the agent's judgment does not reflect his *true* self—who he really is, as opposed to who he takes himself to be. Or the self he would be were he not so benighted. This should not sit well with the subjectivist, who will normally want to resist appeals to "true selves" that differ from the selves we take ourselves to be.[33] While there is no formal inconsistency in basing a subjective view of welfare on an objective view of the self, the conjunction is unnatural. We shall doubt whether the theory of well-being is reasonably considered subjectivist.

The point is not to quarrel over the word 'subjectivist'. It is that an authenticity requirement seems to run against the basic rationale of Sumner's approach, which stresses the agent's point of view and priorities, and the importance of individual sovereignty with respect to the agent's own well-being. At any rate, it is doubtful that his response to the heteronomous agent offends subjectivist sensibilities significantly less than my response to Henry and Claudia. In both cases we override the agent's own best judgment, and in neither case do we recommend a way of life that the agent, once in it, will find onerous. Quite the opposite.

In short, Sumner appears to make authenticity an objective good. The worry is similar to a charge sometimes leveled against existentialists: despite their protestations to the contrary, they do posit at least one objective value, namely authenticity. You must be authentic whether you like it or not. It also resembles the complaint some have made that the strong information requirement demanded by informed desire theories of well-being raises skeptical worries about the significance of welfare: why should I care what I *would* say if fully informed, which is to say very different from my present condition? That isn't *me*, the person actually making the choice.[34]

The objective value of authenticity is a problem for Sumner's view, but not mine: authenticity is necessary for self-fulfillment, which is objective to begin with, and rests on the sort of objective account of the self that we need. By taking happiness to be objectively valuable as part of self-fulfillment, we can accommodate the authenticity constraint. This provides considerable support for the account I have been defending. Indeed, what originally seemed a problem for it is actually a virtue: for now we can say what is wrong with, say, a happy *soma* eater. This individual's happiness doesn't reflect who she is. Her way of life does not embody self-fulfillment.

Interestingly, the authenticity constraint also seems to explain what's *right* with many cases of antidepressant use. Recall the discussion of uplift anxiety in Section 3.1. More common, I gather, is the reverse: "Finally, I'm really *myself*." What's going on? Intuitively, many such cases seem not to involve inauthenticity: we do not begrudge these individuals their newfound happiness, perhaps because we see the depression as a genuine disorder; the drug simply restores proper functioning. So the happiness is authentic enough, at least in some cases, and what the patient's testimony reflects is the phenomenology of self-fulfillment.

More authenticity is not always better. Sometimes we do not want to know all the facts. Sometimes we are happy to maintain certain minor illusions, particularly about our loved ones. (Do you want to know *everything* about your parents?) In fact there is considerable evidence that happy people typically have inflated opinions of themselves, are unrealistically optimistic about their prospects, and otherwise see the world through rose-tinted lenses.[35] Indeed, it is sometimes claimed that the only people who have a realistic sense of themselves may be *depressed*, or suffer from low self-esteem. This may seem problematical for my view. On the contrary: the present view can explain our ambivalence about these phenomena. Insofar as our happiness depends on illusion, it is less authentic, hence less valuable with respect to self-fulfillment. But insofar as we are happier, our experience is more pleasant, hence better in that respect. It stands to reason that small departures from perfect authenticity—minor illusions—may be justified by a significant hedonic payoff in some cases. We trade a little bit of authenticity for a sum of pleasure. So we may be better off for it, but there is a cost nonetheless.

5. TOWARD A SELF-FULFILLMENT THEORY OF WELL-BEING

I will not defend a full-blooded account of well-being here. But it will help situate my claims about happiness if we have a rough picture of the ideal in question. Self-fulfillment, again, is a eudaimonistic ideal, a species of nature-fulfillment. Many moderns find the teleological structure of welfare eudaimonism objectionable, but numerous commentators have recently emphasized that teleology in ethics need not rely on any metaphysical teleology. What we count as the relevant "nature" may well reflect our ethical outlook, and cannot simply be read off "the facts."[36] One possibility is that value is somehow a projection of human psychology, and that the mind projects value onto the world according to a teleological paradigm. We see things as having "natures," and see value in the fulfillment of those natures.

The idea that some sort of nature-fulfillment is intrinsically valuable has a very broad appeal: eudaimonistic ideals can arguably be found among not just the ancients and their followers but Thomists, Marxists, Nietzsche, the existentialists, and humanistic psychologists like Maslow and Rogers, among many others. Whereas ancient and medieval thinkers tended to focus on our generic natures as human beings, the modern era has taken an inward turn, emphasizing the peculiar psychological constitution of the individual person: the self. Because it is easy to characterize certain ideals of self-fulfillment in wholly ateleological terms, self-fulfillment may play a far greater role in modern accounts of well-being, even among subjectivists, than is generally recognized. This is arguably the case, we saw, with Sumner's view. And it is questionable whether desire theories of human welfare would be so popular if we did not also tend to think that our desires, understood broadly to include values, ideals, and the like, are important to who we are.[37] In satisfying our important desires, we find self-fulfillment. Indeed, perhaps the only popular account of well-being that seems not to rest on an ideal of nature-fulfillment is the pleasure theory: welfare hedonism. Here the value seems brutely phenomenological. Yet there have even been hedonistic forms of eudaimonism: Epicureans grounded their brand of hedonism in nature-fulfillment, holding that we are, at bottom, pleasure seekers.[38] And Mill is perhaps our most eloquent spokesperson for self-fulfillment, as we find in his paean to individuality in *On Liberty*. Other hedonists, like Sidgwick and Brandt, have rooted their views in a type of desire theory, and hence may have relied implicitly on the notion of self-fulfillment.

It is worth noting some points of contrast between the variety of eudaimonism suggested here and its Aristotelian relatives. Theories in the Aristotelian tradition are perfectionist and externalist, conceiving of nature-fulfillment in terms of the proper exercise of our distinctively human capacities. The present view, by contrast, is non-perfectionist and internalist, grounding nature-fulfillment in the arbitrarily idiosyncratic make-up of the individual. Insofar as virtue benefits the individual, it does so via its connection with other goods, such as the agent's happiness. (For the record, I regard this connection, though contingent, as fairly strong: by and large, virtue tends to be good for us. But our chief reasons for being virtuous are not prudential.)

The present account also differs from Aristotelian views in positing a less intellectualistic view of human nature, placing a greater emphasis on its affective dimension as something that matters independently of its connection with reason.[39] But this is not a romantic irrationalism. The claim, recall, is that happiness has intrinsic prudential value as a *part* of self-fulfillment. A full-blooded account of welfare would likely incorporate goods other than happiness, depending on how we view our natures. Obviously important in this regard—so important that it tends to be conflated with the self—is a person's identity. And it is highly plausible that self-fulfillment will involve, not just being happy, but success as well in relation to those commitments that define who we are and lend meaning to our lives. Consider, for instance, the role that one's spouse has in giving meaning and structure to one's life and sense of self.[40] We might claim that welfare consists partly in the appropriate fulfillment of this role: how well the narrative of one's life goes depends, at least in part, on how things go with respect to the commitments that shape one's identity. The loss of one's spouse vacates a crucial ("narrative") role in one's life: one's life loses meaning, and a part of the self is lost—a phenomenon no doubt reflected in the common observation among the bereaved that it is as if they've suffered an amputation. This seems a prudential loss quite apart from its effects on one's happiness. (Eventually one may adapt and stop grieving; but the vacancy remains.) Such phenomena indicate that we should consider incorporating identity-related fulfillments into an account of well-being as part of self-fulfillment. We could perhaps call it "narrative role fulfillment."

The view that emerges roughly reflects a familiar understanding of the self, on which it has an emotional aspect and a rational aspect. (While the "rational" aspect obviously has an emotional dimension, and might even be defined partly in terms of emotion,[41] our reflective concerns—for example, a commitment to vegetarianism—are quite central to our identities. And what we reflectively deem to be unimportant to us tends not, barring self-deception, to be important for our identities.) This chapter may be viewed as arguing for a more central place for the emotional self in our view of human flourishing: self-fulfillment is not simply a matter of living up to our ideals, achieving our goals, etc., but also of living in accordance with our emotional natures. And sometimes the demands of the emotional self will have normative primacy over those of the rational. While these two aspects of the self are deeply intertwined and overlapping, they require separate attention. The upshot is that some improvements in happiness, even authentic ones, may not make our lives go better for us on the whole. For they may deprive our lives of too much meaning.[42] Why aren't Henry's and Claudia's cases like this? I have assumed, first, that Henry and Claudia would be *much* happier in different occupations: we are not talking about taking happy people and making them a little happier, but taking patently unhappy people and making them happy. Second, I have assumed that they could lead lives that make them happier *and* are perfectly meaningful.

The suggested addition of identity-related fulfillments may not yield a complete account of well-being. For there might be further aspects of the self to consider, and there are subpersonal aspects of human nature that may beg for inclusion. For example, we might conclude that well-being consists not just in the fulfillment of the self's two parts, but also in the fulfillment of our subpersonal, "nutritive" and "animal" natures: health or physical vitality and pleasure.[43] (It may thus be strictly inaccurate to call this a "self-fulfillment" account. Yet self-fulfillment remains quite central to the view, and distinguishes it from better-known forms of eudaimonism.[44])

To arrive at a complete account of well-being will require a broader theoretical framework, one that can among other things explain what counts as an individual's "nature" in the relevant sense. Why do propensities for happiness count, for instance, and not the appetites? But these remarks should help to situate my contentions about happiness, illustrating the sort of place happiness might occupy in a fuller theory of well-being.

6. CONCLUSION

The central aim of this chapter has been rather modest: to establish, at least provisionally, that happiness has intrinsic prudential value as an aspect of self-fulfillment. And the arguments for this claim have themselves involved fairly modest claims, notably that at least part of well-being can be characterized in terms of self-fulfillment, and that the facts about what makes us happy are important to who we are. These contentions seem quite plausible, and not particularly shocking. But they have led us to some interesting places. I will close by noting three of them.

As I noted at the outset, the allures of subjectivism result mainly from the thought that objectivist alternatives both violate individual autonomy and make our well-being something that is alien to us. But I have argued that one reason for the objective value of happiness is precisely that it is *not* alien to us: it is deeply bound up with the self. Subjectivism seems necessary to avoid alienation only if we assume certain narrow views of the self—views that, I have argued, are false. And as the discussion in Section 4.2 suggests, ostensibly subjectivist theories themselves face worries about paternalism insofar as they are prepared to override subjects' considered judgments about their lives.[45] Most such theories are so prepared—and must be, if they are to be at all plausible. Do we all, then, fail to respect autonomy? It is hard to see why: we avoid paternalism and treat people with respect not by *agreeing* with their judgments about their lives, but by taking those judgments seriously—whether we agree with them or not.[46]

Second, our discussion has pointed us toward an ancient approach to well-being that in the recent literature has been overwhelmingly dominated by the followers of Aristotle. But welfare eudaimonism can take many forms, some—like the Epicurean variety—diverging widely from the Aristotelian paradigm. There is something deeply appealing about the basic idea of grounding well-being in the fulfillment of our natures, and this root notion deserves more attention. We may find, as I have tried to indicate, that the most promising form of eudaimonism bears a stronger resemblance to the subjectivist accounts favored by moderns than we might have expected. The view suggested here takes a middle path, one that promises greater critical power than subjectivist theories can offer without imposing the stringent—some would say alien—demands that make Aristotelian eudaimonism so hard for many contemporaries to accept.

Third, the present view of well-being marks a turn away from a kind of *rationalism* that has arguably characterized most recent thinking about human welfare, one that places tremendous weight on agents' reflective judgments about their lives. As I noted in Chapter 1, Aristotle's view is rationalistic in the intended sense: to flourish is, for him, to lead a highly reflective life of excellence with reason firmly in charge. Subjectivists also privilege reflective judgment, though naturally according a less demanding standard: if the idea is to show respect for individuals' autonomy by making people the ultimate authorities on their own welfare, then agents' reflective judgments about their lives will naturally need to bear a lot of weight. Pleasures or cravings that the individual does not, or would not, endorse on reflection cannot be allowed to trump the individual's own best judgment. Subjectivism thus embodies a kind of rationalism: it makes well-being strongly dependent on the part of us that reasons, deliberates, and reflects. (Accordingly, most subjectivists, particularly informed desire theorists, include a rationality constraint. Why should even *I* regard my judgments or desires as authoritative when they are self-defeating or otherwise blankly irrational?)

The view defended in this chapter takes a more *sentimentalist* approach to thinking about well-being: human flourishing depends substantially on the verdicts of our emotional natures, to a significant extent independently of what we think about our lives. There is a large part of well-being, in short, that hinges on matters of sentiment, needing no stamp of approval from reason. Of course I have not denied an important role for reason in a fuller account of well-being, so that a complete view would likely have both sentimentalist and rationalist elements (in contrast, say, to hedonism, which in its canonical forms is a wholly sentimentalist approach). Nor have I suggested that reason and sentiment can be wholly separated; perhaps sentiment always has some rational element and vice versa. But it does appear that our reflective judgments do not bear the sort of authority regarding our welfare that many of us take them to.

This concludes our discussion of the Transparency claim. Part IV turns to the other aspect of Personal Authority, the Aptitude assumption. While moderns have been right to place psychological states like happiness at the center of well-being, the character and value of these states can be surprisingly elusive. We should not assume that matters of personal welfare are at all transparent to the individual. The potential for error is great. Indeed, it should by now be easy at least to imagine people settling, en masse, for unfulfilling lives. The question now is whether, given the facts of human nature, such a result is anything more than a bare possibility.

> "I want you to come and see me." . . .
> "But I can see you!" she exclaimed. "What more do you want?"
> "I want to see you not through the Machine," said Kuno. "I want to speak to you not through the wearisome Machine." . . .
> She replied that she could scarcely spare the time for a visit.
> "The air-ship barely takes two days to fly between me and you."
> "I dislike air-ships."
> "Why?"
> "I dislike seeing the horrible brown earth, and the sea, and the stars when it is dark . . ."
>
> E. M. Forster, "The Machine Stops" (1909)

PART IV
PURSUING HAPPINESS

10

Do We Know How Happy We Are?

On some limits of affective introspection and recall

. . . we are giving you total, dictatorial authority over the account of how it seems to you, about *what it is like* to be you.

Daniel Dennett (1991, p. 96)

By definition, the final judge of someone's subjective well-being is whomever lives inside that person's skin. "If you feel happy," noted Jonathan Freedman . . . "you are happy—that's all we mean by the term."

David G. Myers (2000b, p. 57)

. . . with respect to his own feelings and circumstances, the most ordinary man or woman has means of knowledge immeasurably surpassing those that can be possessed by anyone else.

Mill, *On Liberty*

1. INTRODUCTION

Never mind what it's like to be one of Professor Nagel's bats. I want to know what it's like to be *me*.[1] This is a real question, not a joke, because there are good reasons for doubting that any of us have a firm grasp on the quality of our experience of life, in particular its affective character. Possibly, many of us are profoundly ignorant about such matters, to the point that we often don't know whether we are happy or unhappy, or even whether is our experience is pleasant or unpleasant. This, at any rate, is what I will argue in what follows.

Consider an illustration. Glen has, for the last twenty years, run a successful machine shop in Detroit. His formative years were spent on his family's ranch in Wyoming, where he thrived. For most of the last few decades, however, he has been fairly unhappy, afflicted by a low-grade but steady mix of depression, anxiety, and stress. Not that he paid it much mind: when his sister, a therapist, first inquired about his feelings, his response was dismissive. "What in the world kind of question is that? Who gives a goddamn how I feel? If you have to know, I suppose I feel fine. Got nothing to complain about. Yeah, sure, I'm happy."

He has since mellowed a bit, growing more receptive to his sister's inquiries, but his basic response never changed much: for the most part he would report, sincerely, that he was happy—although he still didn't think that any sensible person would give much thought to such frivolous matters.

Now Glen finds himself on a ranch near his childhood home, this time for an extended visit with an old friend. The experience is revelatory: back on his old stomping grounds, reimmersed in the activities that engaged him as a youth, it is as if he has transformed into a new person. He experiences real joy for the first time in years, but more than that he feels a tremendous surge of vitality and expansion of spirit. He feels *free* and *big*; by contrast, his usual self, and most of those back in the city, now strike him as tiny, compressed, and shriveled up, like ants. He instinctively resumes the confident posture and stride of his youth, and at day's end slips easily into a deep, untroubled sleep. He now realizes that what had previously seemed like happiness was anything but—not because he didn't understand what happiness is, but simply because he was oblivious to the character of his emotional condition. This becomes more apparent still when he returns home to Detroit and gradually resumes that unhappy state. Sadly, the memories of his experience on the ranch fade, and with them the recognition of what he is missing. Once again, he considers himself happy.

I want to suggest that there is a little Glen in all of us. Our powers to assess our own happiness—specifically, our affective states, including their hedonic character—are weaker and less reliable than we tend to suppose. We are, in short, vulnerable to what I will call—for want of a better name—"affective ignorance," or AI. AI can involve two sorts of epistemic failure: ignorance about our past affect ("past-AI"), and ignorance about affects we are currently experiencing ("present-AI"). The central claim of this chapter is that widespread, serious errors in the self-assessment of affect are a genuine possibility—one worth taking very seriously. That many of us may be badly mistaken even about our *experience* of life is, I think, an interesting claim in its own right. If we are sound judges of anything, it seems, it would be about what our lives are *like* to us. But we will see that the reflections to follow have a number of other implications. For example, they identify a number of difficulties for the use of self-reports in research on well-being and on consciousness (though one aim of this chapter is to lend *support* to the use of self-reports by reducing uncertainties about their limitations). My arguments also have implications for our understanding of consciousness itself, but I will not treat those questions here.[2] Most importantly, the discussion ramifies for our understanding of human welfare and its pursuit: an important component of the Personal Authority thesis, the Aptitude assumption, is called into question. We should be concerned about our competence at assessing, and hence pursuing, happiness. I will set aside further explanation of the Aptitude assumption and its significance for Chapter 11.

Few contemporary researchers believe us to be perfect judges of our affective states. Yet it is unclear that anyone has recognized just how far off we can be.[3] Some of the more extreme forms of present-AI, in which we are essentially blind to hedonically important aspects of our experience, have yet to gain general recognition, if anyone has noticed them at all. (I find that most people respond with stark incredulity when first told of them.) One of the most prominent researchers in this literature, Timothy Wilson, recently published a fascinating book called *Strangers to Ourselves,* detailing how shockingly little we seem to know about our own minds.[4] And yet the chapter discussing AI does not mention that the more serious sorts of errors detailed below are even possible. Moreover, a recent paper by Wilson and Daniel Gilbert defends the accuracy of self-reports of present affective states by claiming that "if [the respondent] is candid and articulate, then one can make the case that his verbal report is unimpeachable."[5] Consider also a growing body of work on "unconscious emotion," including Wilson's book, that documents affective processes that putatively occur outside of consciousness; the idea that some of these phenomena actually *are* conscious, yet fall outside introspective awareness, seems not, for the most part, to have been taken seriously.[6] Finally, a couple of the studies cited below as possible examples of present-AI seem to read as though the authors felt it necessary to come up with any explanation of the data *other* than that subjects just didn't know how they felt. (In at least one case, one gets the distinct impression that the authors suspected precisely this, but feared even mentioning the possibility.) I do not think that what follows will merely be stating the obvious.

While I will cite a variety of empirical results in support of my contentions, these results will often be open to varying interpretations. For the most part, my case will be intuitive. Readers worried about the reliance on intuitive considerations should bear in mind that such arguments form a perfectly respectable part of scientific practice. A standard way of evaluating proposed explanations of experimental results is to ask whether any alternative explanations of the data seem plausible. The list of potential explanations that get taken seriously never depends solely on the data; to some extent we must rely on our best judgment. Accordingly, my goal is to sharpen our judgment about the possibilities worth taking seriously in this realm.

To keep the application of our discussion as broad as possible, I will be largely neutral between an emotional state and a hedonistic conception of happiness: for immediate purposes, we can think of happiness as consisting in pleasant affect.[7] Problems of AI will be significantly worse on the emotional state theory developed earlier, since much of the story takes place beneath the threshold of consciousness.

I will not try to catalogue every possible source of AI, but will focus only on some of the more interesting varieties. Thus, for instance, I will set aside worries about self-deception, as well as problems of misidentification, where subjects are fully aware of their affects and their phenomenal qualities but classify them incorrectly (say by misapplying the concept UPSET to a case of anger).[8] Nor will I discuss problems with self-reports not bearing on AI, for instance when subjects edit their reports to suit the social circumstances. We begin with present-AI.

2. IGNORANCE ABOUT PRESENT AFFECT

2.1. Elusive affects

Paradigm affects like being gripped by terror, writhing with pain, or giddy with elation seem pretty hard to miss. We probably are pretty good judges, at least in broad terms, about these and many other affects. And we seem to be particularly observant immediately following a sharp change in affective state, where the contrast highlights qualities of our states that may otherwise be less obvious. (This phenomenon plays a significant role in a number of the arguments to follow.) But some affective states are more elusive than the paradigmatic ones, particularly moods and mood-like states such as anxiety, tension, ennui, malaise, or the pleasant state of "flow" that comes with losing oneself in challenging and rewarding activities. They may exceed our powers of discernment even while they are occurring.

How is this possible? Consider, first, why paradigm affects like strong emotions or intense pains are so hard to miss. Most obviously, they are intense. But more interestingly, they are relatively focused states, having a more or less specific object or (phenomenological) location: one is terrified of the spider crawling up one's leg, elated over getting the job of one's dreams, or feeling pain in one's freshly stubbed toe.[9] Such affects are thus comparatively easy to attend to. To discern a pain in your toe, for instance, you need only attend to your toe—and even this will typically happen automatically, given that stubbed toes have a way of calling attention to themselves. Similarly, if you are feeling uneasy about visiting the dentist, you can attend to your unease simply by thinking about your impending appointment and noting how that feels—something that, again, tends to happen all by itself. But if you are feeling uneasy *in general*, about nothing in particular, to what do you attend? This feeling attaches to nothing in particular; it just forms a part of the background to your experience of everything. You must, then, attend to a diffuse background phenomenon that pervades every aspect of your experience—not impossible, but a bit like attending to the air around you. There isn't much to grab hold of.

The same seems true of moods in general (and perhaps other affects as well, but for convenience I will focus on moods). Unlike emotions and sensory affects (namely, physical pleasures and pains), moods have no particular location or object. (If they have an object at all, it is everything, which phenomenologically is pretty much like having *no* object.[10]) They are also highly diffuse, pervading the whole of one's consciousness. They are, moreover, comparatively diaphanous, offering us not so much distinct objects within the field of consciousness as alterations of the field itself, coloring the entirety of our experience. Finally, moods tend not to be very intense. They are usually low-key affects that do not call attention to themselves the way that, say, sensory pains do.

Yet moods are quite central to the experienced quality of our lives, far out of proportion to their grip on our attention. A vague sense of malaise might easily go unnoticed, yet it can sour one's experience far more than the sharper and more pronounced ache that persists after having stubbed one's toe. Likewise for depression, anxiety, and related mood states, at least in their milder forms. Consider how a tense person will often learn of it only when receiving a massage, whereas stressed or anxious individuals may discover their emotional state only by attending to the physical symptoms of their distress. Presumably being tense, anxious, or stressed detracts substantially from the quality of one's experience, even when one is unaware of these states.

So elusive are some moods and mood-like states that whole classes of them may fail to register in our collective awareness. Many distinctions in moods surely remain to be made, but two in particular are worth noting. The term "flow," for one, has yet to enter the popular vocabulary, but we can all recognize this important phenomenon once it is described. This, as I noted in Chapter 6, is a state of total absorption in an activity, normally an activity that is challenging yet not too difficult, and which is perceived as worth doing. (And which is being done well.) The athlete experiences flow when she is "in the zone," as does the novelist lost in his work. Flow is often described as having no phenomenology, since we are not aware of feeling anything while it happens. (Thinking about how one is feeling typically ruins the experience.[11]) Yet it clearly does feel like something, since it is manifestly a pleasant state. Indeed, some researchers argue that it is a crucial element of happiness.[12] But the very existence of flow has largely gone unrecognized. Talk of things like being in the zone suggests a faint awareness of the phenomenon, but the very absence of a word indicates just how faint that awareness is.

A related phenomenon arises in the case of Glen. Recall the "expansion of spirit" he experienced when visiting his friend's ranch: a sense of freedom and inner enlargement, of being uncaged and allowed to grow to full size, of being *alive*. His workaday existence in Detroit, by contrast, left him feeling "pinched and hidebound,"[13] tiny and ant-like, drawn-in and shriveled up like a pea—compressed. This is what we called compression in Chapter 6, and it isn't pleasant. While it rarely gets noticed, it is arguably quite common. Indeed, those who have undergone experiences like Glen's might see compression as more or less ubiquitous in our society.

Why would moods and related affective states be so elusive? This is no place to develop a theory of moods, but a plausible conjecture is that moods function to govern our responses to the general circumstances of our lives, whereas emotions and sensory affects constitute responses to specific stimuli.[14] Suppose this is correct. Thus, for instance, anxiety may serve in hostile circumstances to make us vigilant and primed to respond to threats. For this purpose it is not essential that anxiety command our attention. On the contrary: its very point is to keep our attention available to focus on whatever problems may arise, wherever they occur. The disgust felt when drinking spoiled milk, by contrast, will prove fruitless if it does not focus the mind rather sharply on the issue at hand. Because it is so narrowly directed and involves one's full attention, the feeling of disgust should not be particularly hard to notice. A generalized anxiety, being utterly diffuse and leaving one's attention free for other matters, may be comparatively easy to overlook—precisely because it is supposed to be.

Let me take this a step further and suggest why we might *expect* the chronically anxious often to seem like, and think, they're happy. The reason is that anxiety may be able to do its job of making us more vigilant and so forth without rational processes being aware of it at all—indeed, with the agent thinking everything's just fine. If so, then it may be adaptive in many situations to be anxious while *believing* that one is happy, and more generally *presenting* oneself as happy. For overt displays of anxiety project weakness and vulnerability, whereas displays of happiness send the opposite message. It isn't hard to see the advantage, in many circumstances, of being highly prepared to deal with threats while projecting a relaxed and confident demeanor. (Perhaps Americans are experts at this.) Similar remarks may apply to a variety of other elusive states, like being stressed, or depression or compression, and perhaps mood in general. In short, some problems are best handled by subrational processes, leaving reason out of the loop if not downright misled.[15] If this is right, then such states may not serve the informational function performed by emotions and sensory affects. (Note that this would eliminate an important rationale some have posited for hedonic adaptation in relation to such states: that affects must diminish with time to free up attentional and other cognitive resources.[16])

An interesting further conjecture is that elusiveness should tend *not* to attach to affects associated with universal facial expressions like the "basic emotions" of sadness, feeling happy, anger, fear, contempt, disgust, and surprise.[17] Such emotions clearly serve important signaling functions: they try to make themselves known, at least to others. Plausibly, it would be most adaptive for such emotions to be known to their bearers as well. If you are displaying anger to a big fellow before you, for instance, you might want to be clued in. Perhaps not coincidentally, then, the elusive states we have discussed do not seem to involve canonical facial expressions. They seem not to have the kind of signaling function served by the basic emotions. Maybe, at least for some of them, their work is best done in secret.

These remarks are of course speculative. But they are not implausible, and seem broadly consistent with what we know about mood.

2.2. Adaptation to persistent affect

Everyone knows that we often adapt to things over time: what was once pleasing now leaves no impression or seems tiresome, and what used to be highly irritating is now just another feature of the landscape. Could it also be that some things are lastingly pleasant or unpleasant, while our *awareness* of them fades? I would suggest that it can.

Perhaps you have lived with a refrigerator that often whined due to a bad bearing. If so, you might have found that, with time, you entirely ceased to notice the racket.[18] But occasionally, when the compressor stopped, you *did* notice the sudden, glorious silence. You might also have noted, first, a painful headache, and second, that you'd had no idea how obnoxious the noise was—or that it was occurring at all—until it ceased. But obnoxious it was, and all the while it had been, unbeknownst to you, fouling your experience as you went about your business. In short, you'd been having an unpleasant experience without knowing it. Moreover, you might well have remained unaware of the noise even when reflecting on whether you were enjoying yourself: the problem here is *ignorance*—call it reflective blindness—and not, as some have suggested, the familiar sort of inattentiveness we find when only peripherally aware of something.[19] In such cases we can bring our attention to the experience easily and at will. Here the failure of attention is much deeper: we are so lacking in awareness that we *can't* attend to the experience, at least not without prompting (as occurs when the noise suddenly changes).

There is some empirical evidence that persistent noise can degrade the quality of our experience in ways that escape our notice. In a recent study of office noise, physiological and behavioral measures of stress were significantly higher in subjects who had worked for three hours in a simulated office with low-intensity noise (55 dBA) than in subjects assigned to a quiet office (40 dBA). Noisy-office subjects showed elevated epinephrine levels, made half as many ergonomic adjustments to their workstations, and were markedly less persistent in efforts to solve difficult puzzles afterwards. Yet the researchers were surprised to find *no* differences in reports of perceived stress—specifically, reports about the extent to which subjects felt "bothered, worried, relaxed, frustrated, unhappy, contented, [or] tense."[20] Plausibly, the noisy-office subjects had adapted somehow to the conditions, and saw nothing amiss. By contrast, an earlier study involving a much briefer noise exposure, and subjects who were much less experienced at office work, *did* find differences in perceived stress. It seems likely that given enough time, the experienced office workers used in the newer study ceased to notice the unpleasant effects of the noise. Yet it also seems plausible that the noise affected not only subjects' physiological responses and behavior, but the hedonic quality of their experience as well: they experienced more stress, had a less pleasant time of it, than they would have without the noise.[21] Other interpretations of the data are of course possible. But setting aside matters of health, *which group would you prefer to be in?* Would you be indifferent? (Cases like this make a good test of the skeptic's convictions, since matters of welfare are at stake. Those who deny that we can have phenomenality without knowing it should presumably be indifferent to such a choice.)

Attentional adaptation, as we might call it, probably extends to persistent affect quite generally, at least where the affect is not especially intense. Take two people, one who is newly depressed after a long period of happiness, and another who is equally depressed, but has been like this for some years. Is it really plausible that both individuals will judge their experience equally unpleasant? Rather, the freshly depressed person will probably be much more vividly aware of the awfulness of her predicament; the long-depressed individual, by contrast, will likely have gotten more or less used to his suffering, and perhaps no longer notice it at all. Perhaps he has even come to regard his depressive baseline as a normal, not unpleasant, state of being.

Much has been written in recent decades about a "hedonic treadmill": we adapt to many changes in our lives, so that we tend eventually to wind up no more or less happy than we were to begin with (see Chapter 6). But given the heavy reliance of these findings on self-report measures, and given the likelihood that adaptation is sometimes at least partly attentional rather than hedonic, these findings may prove to be exaggerated. In short, we may be substantially on an attentional treadmill, and not merely a hedonic one.[22]

2.3. Attentiveness and discernment

There is no reason to suppose that we are all perfectly, or equally, attentive and discerning observers of our own affect. Surely the Dalai Lama notices things about his emotional state that would have completely escaped John Wayne. We can't all be introspective Prousts, and probably very few of us are. The problem that arises here is not simply that some affects are elusive, or become so through adaptation, but that a given affect can elude some people and not others. And insofar as one is relatively inattentive about one's affective state, or an undiscerning observer of what one does attend to, one is liable to be comparatively ignorant about the quality of one's affect.[23]

This sort of problem may be particularly acute for those raised in cultures that discourage emotional introspection. I have been told that my relations of a few generations back would not have *understood* an inquiry into their emotional states, much less figured them prominently in their assessments of their lives. Be that as it may, the preoccupation of present-day Americans with their feelings is clearly more pronounced than it was in the pre-war years, perhaps to a fault. It would not be at all surprising to find that self-reports of affect among Americans are more accurate now than they used to be. They may also be more accurate than those of individuals from so-called "collectivist" cultures, such as those of many Asian countries. Such cultures place far less emphasis on emotional states inasmuch as communal concerns are believed more significant than personal ones.[24] Thus judgments of life satisfaction in collectivist cultures have been found to draw less on affective state than judgments in individualistic cultures, and in some countries—like China—may not correlate with negative affect at all.[25] It is hard to believe that people in any culture are that indifferent to how they feel. Perhaps people in countries like China are less accurate observers of their inner lives than Americans are, precisely because they assign a lower priority to such matters.

Consider a study that compared self-reports of emotion with autonomic nervous system (ANS) activity patterns among American and Indonesian (specifically, Minangkabau) subjects after they had been instructed to engage in various emotional expressions such as smiling and frowning.[26] The American subjects were much more likely to report experiencing the corresponding emotions, even though ANS profiles were the same between the two groups. It is possible that the Minangkabau refused to apply the emotion concepts in the absence of the usual eliciting circumstances, a hypothesis offered by the authors. Yet the fact that some Indonesians *did* report emotion experiences indicates that their emotion concepts permit emotion ascriptions in the absence of appropriate eliciting factors. A more plausible interpretation, I would suggest, is that the Minangkabau *had* the relevant emotional experiences, but weren't able to identify them without the usual external cues.

2.4. Scale norming

How pleasant would you say your experience is, on a scale of one to ten? Your answer to this question will depend, not only on what you take your experience to be, but also on where you draw the lines between good, neutral, and bad, as well as on the range of possible experiences you are comparing it against. What counts as a ten, or a one? Different people will answer differently, and your answer today may differ from the answer you would have given a few years ago. A Manhattan debutante may consider a day without her cell phone about as bad as it gets, while a crippled resident of Manila's trash dumps is liable to have rather different standards of unpleasantness. In short, people can use widely varying scales when rating their experience, a phenomenon known as *scale norming*. Thus one person's ten might be another's six.[27]

Scale norming may strike the reader as a mere technical issue regarding measurement techniques. But its existence has nothing to do with empirical research methods, and generates a quite serious—and probably widespread—form of AI, namely ignorance about the *relative* quality of our experience. For one thing, it undermines interpersonal—and *intra*personal—comparisons insofar as we aren't sure whether two individuals, or two time-slices of the same individual, are rating their experience using similar scales. More importantly, scale norming suggests that we often fail to recognize how our experience rates in relation to the possibilities. To the extent that this happens, we don't know what we're missing, and therefore don't know how good (or bad) what we've got is.

Consider someone who has been more or less depressed for years. Even if she knows she's depressed—a large "if"—she may well be so deprived of great pleasures that she simply cannot comprehend the vastness of the gap between her present state and happiness. She may, in other words, fail utterly to recognize how unpleasant her lot is. Conversely, someone who has led such a sheltered life that he has had few occasions for real suffering may have little comprehension of just how pleasant his experience really is. Probably all of us have experienced corrections of such misapprehensions, for instance when visiting a hospital.

As these two examples suggest, scale norming can be a source of adaptation. Insofar as this happens, then we have a second AI-based reason for thinking that hedonic adaptation may be less extensive than self-reports would suggest: for these reports may reflect a kind of "scaling adaptation," in which subjects' scales change over time. Lasting changes in hedonic state may thus be obscured by adjustments in the scales we use to rate our experience.

2.5. Affect-type bias

Affect-type bias has received little if any attention, but may profoundly impact the quality of our self-assessments. The idea is that some types of affect are more likely to be considered than others when judging the quality of our experience. When judging how happy we are, for instance, we may focus primarily on affects that fall along the joy–sadness dimension rather than on those, say, along the anxious–calm dimension. And we may do this even if we believe that the latter sorts of affect are just as important for happiness as the former. Such biases might reflect societal or personal tendencies to regard certain affects as more representative of the affective realm, of happiness, or simply as more important (but for reasons other than their hedonic quality). Alternatively, biases might arise simply because some affects are more elusive than others. Classic emotions like joy, sadness, fear, or anger tend to be easily identified and labeled, and hence may be relatively likely to be considered in our reflective assessments.[28] We probably cannot say the same about more diffuse states like anxiety, tension, ennui, malaise, flow, or compression. One possibility worth taking seriously is that such biases frequently cause self-reports to overlook states, like anxiety and stress, that are crucial to the experienced quality of our lives—even if we are aware of them while they are happening, and even if we are reporting on our immediate experience.[29] Inasmuch as stress is often said to be one of the hallmarks of our age, our primary measures of happiness may be, at least in that respect, overly optimistic.

Affect-type biases may constitute a third AI-based source for some of the findings on adaptation, along with problems of elusiveness and scale norming.

It is likely, as I noted in Chapter 6, that hedonic adaptation tends to be more pronounced with some types of affect than others. For example, we may adapt more with states of joy and sadness than with states of anxiety or tranquility.[30] If so, and if affect-type biases make us less likely to figure the latter states in self-reports of happiness or emotional state, then we might appear to adapt completely to circumstances that in fact leave us lastingly more or less anxious. The adaptation research might, then, be skewed by a tendency for individuals to focus on certain types of affect at the expense of others.

2.6. Expectation effects

To the extent that we find it difficult to render judgments about how happy we are, or about the quality of our experience, we might rely somewhat on our *expectations* concerning how we should feel, or are likely to feel, given the circumstances. A groom on his wedding day might fail to come to grips with the complexity of his emotions and think himself filled with pure joy, mainly because that's how he is supposed to feel, and how he imagines any newlywed must feel. Similarly, if a researcher comes and asks you, Bill Gates, how happy you are, you might sincerely claim to be *very* happy, in great part because you are, after all, the wealthiest human being on the planet. So naturally you must be happy—who wouldn't be?—and insofar as your own introspection doesn't yield obvious answers one way or the other, you may conclude that, yes, you are indeed quite a happy fellow. And someone who just lost a pet might overrate her unhappiness because she came into the situation believing she would, or should, be miserable.

Such reasoning need not be explicit, of course; more likely it would involve the sort of processes that occur when we confabulate memories of past affect.[31] Indeed, expectations are what drive such confabulations, and expectation effects clearly impact our recall of past affect (and hence can be a source of past-AI as well).[32] What I am suggesting is that they can affect judgments about the present as well. Consider also that we often infer how we feel by observing our own behavior and physiology, as when one recognizes an irritable mood as the best explanation of having put one's computer out the window.[33] Such guesswork will obviously be subject to our expectations or "theories" about affect.

2.7. Can we tell pleasure from pain?

It is one thing to claim that we can be wrong about how pleasant or unpleasant our experience is. But might we even get the *valence* of our current experience wrong? That is, might we mistake pleasant for unpleasant states, and vice versa, even while they are happening? It seems possible that we could, at least with respect to moods. Problems of elusiveness, scale norming, and adaptation might cause us to become so profoundly mistaken about the basic character of our experience that we can't even tell whether it is pleasant or unpleasant. Such mistakes are clearly at least conceivable, given just the distinction between having an experience and being reflectively aware of it, along with the (in principle) fallibility of reflection. Less clear is whether human psychology could actually give rise to them.

Yet this is precisely what appears to happen in Glen's case: though unhappy, he sincerely judges himself to be happy. What might explain this? For starters, his judgments—I will suppose—tend to exhibit a positive bias:[34] despite his gruff demeanor, he has little patience for whining or complaining and tends to look on the positive side of things more than the negative. As a result, many of the negative affects that he experienced are overlooked. Second, his unhappiness consists largely in some of the more elusive affects, such as emotional compression, or being mildly anxious or stressed. He simply never notices them. Adaptation, moreover, has caused him to stop noticing other affects, such as his depressed mood. And affect-type biases lead him to ignore even many of those affects that do fall within his awareness. Nor does it help that he is pretty near the opposite of a Proust as an observer of his inner state: he tends not to think about it at all, and when he does attend to it his perception is crude and undiscerning, like a five-year-old hearing Stravinsky. Finally, the relative homogeneity of his recent experience has caused him to assess it on a truncated scale: what now seems to him like a highly desirable condition would, on the ranch, strike him as a pale imitation of happiness. It seems plausible that, under such conditions, he might believe his experience to be pleasant even when it is unpleasant. And this could be just what he realizes when he suddenly finds himself truly happy. If so, then he has mistaken an unpleasant experience, indeed an unpleasant *life*, for a pleasant one.

People do sometimes take themselves to have had experiences of this nature. (I am one of them.) The only question is whether their retrospective assessments should be taken seriously.[35] Given the many ways such evaluations can go wrong, we should certainly be cautious here. But it nonetheless seems plausible that Glen got the very valence of his experience wrong. Similarly, a chemotherapy patient's good day might be a newlywed's bad day—that is, the very experience that one considers pleasant may be judged unpleasant by the other.[36]

It may seem absurd that we could possibly be unable to tell pleasure from pain. Even if we grant the conceptual possibility, such ignorance might seem utterly alien to human psychology. With respect to pronounced sensory pleasures and pains, as well as emotions, this might be correct. For in such states the pleasure or pain attaches to an object, which makes it easier for us to attend to our feeling. Moreover, we presumably will feel either aversion or attraction (or some other pro- or con-attitude). Thus one way of telling that the fire feels bad is that I very much want to pull my hand out of it. It also helps that the experience is intense and highly localized. But a vague and generalized anxiety, by contrast, can be so low-key, diffuse, and free-floating that it is harder to say how we know its valence. To what do we feel aversion or attraction? Everything? The point is not that moods are altogether hedonically inscrutable. It is just that they offer fewer and less obvious cues as to their hedonic character.

3. IGNORANCE ABOUT PAST AFFECT

3.1. Omission

Errors about the past are less striking than those concerning the present, since no one expects us to have perfect recall. Yet such mistakes can leave us substantially blind about our welfare, since in evaluating our lives we have very little else to go on but our memories, the present being the fleeting thing it is. The most mundane source of past-AI is simple omission: we experience countless affects every day, and there is no way to bring all of them to mind when reflecting on the past quality of our experience. Errors of omission should not prove worrisome as long as we do not omit too much, and are evenhanded about the affects we omit. Yet there is some evidence that we do tend to omit quite a lot, and that our retrospective assessments are anything but unbiased.[37] Affect-type biases and expectation effects, for instance, may be even more prominent when recalling past affect than present, since the relevant information is less accessible.

3.2. Peak-end effects and duration neglect

A number of studies have found that the remembered quality even of a recent experience is strongly biased by the nature of its peak moment—where the intensity was greatest—and by its ending. Indeed, the remainder of the experience seems largely to be ignored. Such "peak-end" effects, as they are called, can cause people to form preferences for *less* pleasant experiences over more pleasant ones.[38] For instance, doctors can improve the remembered quality of a painful medical procedure (a colonoscopy) by extending the procedure, but with a slightly less painful coda. That is, you can make an experience seem less painful in retrospect by *adding more pain*. Not only did this manipulation yield surprising memories of hedonic quality, it also affected future choices: patients given the more painful procedure were more likely to return for another exam five years later.[39] Similar results have been found with a wide range of situations: the peak-end rule appears to govern hedonic recall quite generally.

A corollary of the peak-end effect is that our memories of hedonically salient experiences tend to disregard the length of the episode—*duration neglect*. For instance, a series of colonoscopy studies varied between 4 and 69 minutes in duration; yet the correlation between the duration of the procedure and subjects' retrospective evaluations of it was only .03.[40] Schwarz and Strack suggest in light of this phenomenon that three years of economic hardship may not seem much worse in retrospect than one year if the peaks and ends are about the same.[41] Needless to say, this makes retrospective assessments of experience problematical.

3.3. Valence bias and cross-cultural comparisons of well-being

If the Stones' "(I Can't Get No) Satisfaction" had been written in Yiddish, it would have been called "(I Love to Keep Telling You That I Can't Get No) Satisfaction (Because Telling You That I'm Not Satisfied Is All That Can Satisfy Me)."

Michael Wex, *Born to Kvetch* (pp. 2–3)

At least two further types of bias are worth distinguishing. The first, *valence bias*, or "affect-valence bias," concerns subjects' tendencies to focus disproportionately on either negative or positive affect.[42] This can skew recall of past affect, attention to present affect, and judgments of overall quality of affect. "Kvetches," for instance, are more likely to emphasize negative experiences. (Wex writes: "*Gants gut* [Real good]—if you're not afraid to say it, you have no business speaking Yiddish.")[43] We have all known individuals who seem pretty happy but invariably launch into a litany of woes when asked how they are doing. "Pollyannas," by contrast, focus on the positives. There is considerable evidence that most people, at least in Western countries, are Pollyannas, exhibiting a wide range of positive biases in memory recall and judgment.[44] Lykken and Tellegen, for instance, found that over 86 percent of subjects rated themselves more "happy and contented" than about two-thirds of the population.[45] And people tend to recall positive past events and emotions more easily than negative ones.[46] Insofar as we are Pollyannas, then, we are probably less happy than we think we are.[47]

The potential impact of valence biases on self-assessments of happiness and related matters, notably life satisfaction, would be hard to overstate. In countries like the United States, which notoriously tends toward the Pollyanna end of the spectrum, not to be happy can seem a personal failure, perhaps a sign of poor character; and actually believing as much about oneself, a further sign of defect. American subjects rate happy people as more likely to go to heaven, for instance.[48] In such a culture, there will be plenty of motivation to see oneself as happy, and this is unlikely to leave people's self-assessments unaffected. It would be astonishing if such biases did not have a significant effect on people's judgments about how happy they are. (The special significance of "happiness" for many moderns might explain why self-reports of happiness tend to be higher than those of life satisfaction, since people may be less motivated to avoid low ratings of life satisfaction than of happiness.) Given the variety of cultural norms in this realm, this will make cross-cultural comparisons of self-reported happiness problematical.[49] We shall want to know how far differences in norms—e.g., kvetch vs. Pollyanna cultures—account for observed results.[50]

Several recent studies indicate that such effects may be substantial, though the evidence must be regarded as provisional at this point. In one case, Asian and Asian-American students retrospectively reported lower well-being, both in affect ratings and satisfaction, than European American students, consistently with other research on global self-reports. Yet there were no differences in online reports.[51] In another study, European-Asian life satisfaction discrepancies were tested against a measure of implicit life satisfaction (ILS), which is less susceptible to the influence of norms, as it assesses reaction times to word pairs associating respondents' lives with good and bad attributes (faster reaction times to positive than negative associations indicating favorable attitudes).[52] As usual, European Americans reported higher explicit life satisfaction than Asian counterparts. Yet ILS measures found no differences. (Interestingly, Latin Americans scored the highest in ILS, while being low in explicit life satisfaction.) A third line of evidence comes from a major new study of well-being among women in the United States and France.[53] As one of the authors noted in an earlier paper, global self-reports of well-being tend to be much lower, improbably so, among the French than Americans; indeed, the employed French score about the same as *unemployed* Americans.[54] That paper also observes that self-reported health tends to be much lower among the French, even though they live three years longer than Americans. In fact, reported health among developed countries, which correlates very strongly with life satisfaction, is "completely uncorrelated" with adult life expectancy, prompting the quip that "it is fair to describe national differences in self-reported health, at least among developed nations, as 'reality-free'."[55] Yet the new study's DRM (day reconstruction method) measures, which ask respondents for detailed descriptions of their moods the previous day, found American participants apparently doing *worse* hedonically, for instance spending more time in an unpleasant state (18.8 versus 16 percent).[56] Time allocations in France also favor more pleasant activities, like eating and active leisure, than those in the United States. (Interestingly, child care yields a U-Index among the French—11 percent—less than *half* that for Americans—24 percent—where it is notoriously reported to be among the most unpleasant parts of the day.[57] It is possible that contemporary American culture has managed to turn family life from one of the more enjoyable parts of the day into one of the most unpleasant.) I would suggest that these results reflect, in part, differential valence biases due to differences in cultural norms. For example, American cultural norms probably tend to bias global judgments in a positive direction. (I have been simplifying matters somewhat, as cultures can influence judgments in many ways. Moreover, it is likely that valence biases will also affect judgments of online experience.)

Such norms can vary across other groupings as well, for instance between socioeconomic groups. Perhaps positivity biases correlate with income, with wealthier individuals tending to emphasize positives more than less wealthy persons. Likewise for wealthier nations. This would, of course, exaggerate correlations between income and reported happiness. I suspect such an effect is real, for several reasons: for instance wealth, and the greater opportunities it brings, probably correlates with optimism, and positivity biases generally; second, increasing wealth may increase the associations between unhappiness and personal failure, thus enhancing motivations to avoid seeing oneself as unhappy; finally, wealthier individuals may tend to be more career-focused, hence benefiting more from displays of success and confidence (there were few Eeyores among my wife's classmates in a well-known MBA program, where the pressure to appear happy and unflappable, showing no sign of weakness, was palpable). In fact there is good evidence that happiness, or at least reported happiness, actually promotes later career success.[58] This effect is likely to seem less relevant to peasant farmers than MBAs. It is surprising, in light of such points, that wealth doesn't have a stronger impact on reported well-being than it seems to.[59] We should probably expect a significant positive correlation even if it yielded no net benefit at all.

3.4. Present-affect bias

With *present-affect bias*, finally, the subject's current affective state influences which types of affect are most likely to come to mind. In particular, we tend to recall affects that are congruent with our present state more than those that are not.[60] When in a good mood, for instance, you are more likely to recall similar moods from the past rather than bad moods. The significance of this bias will become clearer later in this chapter.

4. ARE WE AS HAPPY AS WE THINK WE ARE? SOME EVIDENCE OF ERROR

> Standing here in the strangely windless rain, with a rabbit instead of pond pickerel nearby for company, I felt the same way [Thoreau did]. A letting go of sorts, something inside me exhaling deeply. I hadn't realized I'd been knotted inside so tightly: by Mo, her illness, and a sampler of other related suburban worries.
>
> Tom Carlson, *Hatteras Blues* (p. 109)

How pervasive are these problems? A sure answer to this question obviously cannot be forthcoming given present measurement techniques. Indeed, I see no way of proving that some of these phenomena are even psychologically possible, much less pervasive: for the most part, the best evidence we've got relies either on retrospective assessments—"wow, I really did feel lousy"—or on indirect evidence, such as failures of self-reports to correlate with other measures of affect, such as ANS arousal. But retrospective assessments are themselves fallible, and failures to correlate with other quantities might reflect cases of affect (or related states) without the phenomenology.

So my arguments are not conclusive. But again, the primary aim is to establish as a serious possibility that substantial AI is widespread, to the extent that we should be concerned about our ability to assess how happy we are. (Such concern is consistent with the idea that people are mostly accurate about their happiness. Just because you aren't wrong about your happiness *most* of the time doesn't mean you shouldn't be worried that you're wrong *too much* of the time.) In any event, I suspect that my contentions about AI will comport with the experience of many readers. Who among us hasn't at one time or another learned of their emotional conditions only through the testimony of observant friends and family members, or by attending to the physical manifestations of their emotional states, such as muscle tension or gastrointestinal symptoms best left to the imagination?[61] And who hasn't encountered blinkered souls who seemed spectacularly misinformed about their own emotional lives? Probably all of us have known someone who, like Carlson, reported feeling like a huge weight had been lifted off their shoulders, yet hadn't recognized the burden prior to this.[62] In my own case, it seems that anyone wanting to know how happy I am would best consult my wife, as I am often the last to know. (I could, naturally, be wrong about this.)

Looking to the science of happiness, there is good reason to think that self-reports of happiness, at least in many populations, are systematically inflated, and that AI has something to do with it. I want to review some of this evidence here. I noted in Chapter 1 that my case against Personal Authority is consistent with most people being happy. (E.g., people might be happy *despite* high levels of freedom to shape their lives; or perhaps they would be far happier but for their systematic tendencies to err.) But the practical import of my discussion will be enhanced if it turns out that people in countries like the United States are not doing as well as they think.

Among the more striking claims in the subjective well-being literature is the apparent finding that most people, in the United States and most other countries, are in fact happy. This claim is widely accepted in the subjective well-being literature, and given traditional views of happiness it is well supported.[63] There are three main lines of evidence for the idea that most people are happy: first, solid majorities of people report being satisfied with their lives (Chapter 5); second, people typically experience more positive than negative affect, and indeed we seem to be wired for a "positivity offset."[64] Third, most people *say* they are happy. Self-reported unhappiness tends to be very low in most surveys, typically less than 10 percent and sometimes much less.[65] In one oft-cited study, only 3 percent offered negative responses (see Figure 10.1). The percentage of subjects

Here are some faces expressing various feelings. Which face comes closest to expressing how you feel about your life as a whole?

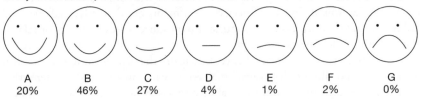

A	B	C	D	E	F	G
20%	46%	27%	4%	1%	2%	0%

Faces and feelings (Andrews and Withey, 1976).

Fig. 10.1. Based on Argyle 2002.

giving the most negative rating in this study was: *zero*.[66] About 93 percent gave favorable responses.

While this instrument is no longer favored, the results are not anomalous. A 2007 Gallup poll found 92 percent of Americans reporting happiness, with only 6 percent "not too happy" (the closest thing to a negative option).[67] Remarkably, *98 percent of respondents with household incomes over $75,000 reported happiness, while only 2 percent proffered "not too happy."* In one of the largest worldwide surveys of happiness, the World Values Survey (WVS) out of the University of Michigan, 94 percent of Americans reported being happy in 1995. (I will focus on this widely cited figure in what follows.) Since even in the best conceivable society we should expect some people not to be happy at any given time—death in the family, incurable disease, foolishness, etc.—this figure indicates we are in the vicinity of a theoretical limit. In terms of percent happy, we may be doing about as well as a society possibly can. Except for Iceland, where 97 percent claim to be happy. In fact a number of countries match or exceed the United States, and Venezuela and the Philippines trail close behind, at 93 percent.[68]

A majority of people may indeed be happy. The self-reports just noted are so relentlessly upbeat that they could be considerably inflated even with most people actually being happy. But it is hard to escape the suspicion that the reported levels of happiness are a little overstated. Before reviewing the evidence on this count, I want to remark on the very real significance of these findings. First, these results are themselves more than a little surprising: few of us would have anticipated such positive responses in surveys. It is plausible, in light of them, that most people regard their lives as a positive good, indeed are satisfied with them, and experience more pleasure than pain or suffering. In fact life surely *is*, for the great majority of people, a great good—even when things are bad. Given traditional philosophical accounts of happiness, all this would suffice to show that most people are happy. So empirical researchers have good grounds for their claims on this point. Yet I argued in Part II that the relevant views of happiness are false: neither life satisfaction nor a majority of positive affect suffices for being happy. Indeed, life satisfaction results are irrelevant, save as crude indicators of affect. So we need to assess the data in light of a more plausible conception of happiness, and in relation to the other evidence we have.

Is it true, then, that all but about 6 percent of the American public are happy, as they claim to be in the WVS? Consider what we find using other methods. Perhaps the best source of data about people's affective lives is the experience sampling method (ESM), which relies not on global self-reports of happiness but on detailed online reports of subjects' experience roughly as it happens.[69] One technique is to distribute electronic devices that signal the subject several times a day to record their feelings at the time. This method is obviously subject to AI, but less so than global measures, particularly given that it doesn't rely on summary recollections of past experience. One important ESM study of 188 European subjects of varied backgrounds used reports gathered over a month through experience sampling (six reports per day per subject). Participants reported feeling either sadness, fear, or anger 22 percent of the time, with the percentage of negative affect rising to 34 percent if we count feelings of "fatigue" (a category that includes stress and exhaustion).[70] If these reports are accurate, the average participant experienced these emotions more than *a third* of the time. This seems rather high. How happy can someone be who spends a third of her day being sad, angry, afraid, stressed, fatigued, or exhausted? The higher figure clearly exceeds Fredrickson and Losada's 3:1 positivity ratio, which I suggested earlier marks a plausible threshold for happiness (Chapter 7). Studies such as this are conventionally taken to confirm the notion that most people are happy, yet they may *undermine* it.

Consider also the aforementioned French-American DRM study. The U-Index—the percentage of individuals' time dominated by negative affect—was close to *60 percent* for the top quintile of American subjects, and in the vicinity of 25 percent for the second quintile; the bottom quintile, by comparison, shows a U-Index of roughly zero, and even the fourth quintile scores under 5 percent.[71] Finally, lower rates of happiness are suggested by measures of psychological well-being from the eudaimonic tradition, which emphasizes multi-item assessments of various aspects of psychological functioning along the lines of mental health surveys.[72] One large study of the adult American population in 1995 classified 26 percent as one or both of "languishing" or depressed, though a more accurate figure given the way depression was assessed would be about 22 percent.[73] Only about 17 percent were rated as "flourishing." There are interesting questions about the meaning of these terms, but it would be very bad news indeed for these measures if they were classifying very many *happy* people as "languishing" or "depressed."

Now consider some indirect evidence. Notice, to follow up on the preceding research, that the rate of self-reported unhappiness is in the neighborhood of many estimates of the rate of *depression*. The present rate of depression appears to be about ten times that of a century ago. Interestingly, it is also said to be five to ten times that found in today's Amish—who live much like our predecessors a century ago did—and this is one of several reasons for thinking the measured increase genuine.[74] Estimates of depression range upwards from 2 percent of the population at any time, and a recent study reports a current (one-month) prevalence of major depression alone of 5.2 percent.[75] The one-year prevalence cited in one major study, the NCS, was 10.3 percent; the average depressive episode lasts about six months.[76]

The depression figures may themselves be considerably understated, as AI can infect depression measures. These instruments rely on subjects' self-reports about various questions that are transparently aimed at assessing mental health, and hence are subject to both AI and a possible lack of candor. In a remarkable series of three studies by Shedler, Mayman, and Manis, such instruments were compared with the judgments of clinicians and physiological measures (heart rate and systolic blood pressure reactions to various psychological stressors such as counting backwards). The investigators found that a *majority* of those rated healthy by the scales were deemed to be distressed—as opposed to mentally healthy—in clinical evaluation.[77] In one of the studies, for instance, 16 of 74 subjects were rated genuinely healthy by both the Beck Depression Inventory (BDI) and clinical evaluation, whereas 21 of those rated healthy by the BDI were judged distressed by clinicians.[78] Referred to as "defensive deniers," the latter group of individuals also exhibited much higher coronary reactivity in response to stressors than those rated healthy by the standard scales and clinicians, and as much as *double* the reactivity of those rated as distressed by both other measures. They also scored higher in verbal defensiveness during the psychological stress tests, and panels of undergraduates in one of the studies offered evaluations of the subjects that were similar to those of the clinicians. (The proffered explanation, corroborated by other studies, is that suppressing and concealing mental distress is costly, both psychologically and physically.[79]) It may be that the clinicians overestimated distress, and that some of the less extreme cases of distress might qualify as happy, or at least not unhappy.[80] But the corroboration from the physiological data, along with the highly negative appraisals for some of those classified as defensive deniers, strongly indicates that some, and possibly even most, of those rated as healthy by the self-report-based scales have serious deficiencies in their emotional conditions.

Turning to other forms of unhappiness, many people appear to being experiencing high levels of stress—40 percent of Americans in one survey, for instance, said their jobs are "very or extremely stressful."[81] The American Psychological Association reports that 47 percent of Americans are "concerned" about the level of stress in their lives, 15 percent are "very concerned," and 43 percent suffer adverse health effects from stress.[82] A recent news report claims that "half of all heads of household are too tired to put much time or effort into evening meal preparation."[83] And 42 percent of a random sample of 3,400 workers told researchers they felt "used up" by the end of the workday.[84]

Anxiety: it is estimated that about 3.1 percent suffer a generalized anxiety disorder (GAD) in a single year.[85] The one-year rate for all anxiety disorders, not counting specific phobias, is over 9 percent.[86] With comorbidity of GAD and major depression (MD) being about 60 percent, the one-year prevalence of GAD without MD was 1.3 percent. This suggests, then, that nearly 12 percent of the population has one of these two disorders in a given year. Assuming, conservatively, that the rate of these disorders at any given time is half that, we arrive at a rough estimate that close to 6 percent of the population has one of these two unpleasant conditions at any point in time. This, note, is about the same as the population of *all* non-happy Americans in the WVS. Another source, drawing on ECA data, claims that anxiety disorders afflict 6 percent of men and 13 percent of women in a six-month period.[87] Significantly, anxiety appears to be much worse than several decades ago: reported anxiety in adult and child populations increased nearly a full standard deviation between 1952 and 1993, and American children in the 1980s typically reported higher levels of anxiety than *psychiatric patients* in the 1950s.[88]

Other disorders also rate a mention. The rate of substance abuse disorder in a one-year period was 3.8 percent, and impulse control disorders occurred in 8.9 percent of the population.[89] Only about 45 percent of individuals with one disorder have more than one, so these figures are not entirely overlapping One of the largest studies of mental health found that nearly half of Americans can expect at some point to suffer a psychological disorder, usually emotional, and typically starting in childhood.[90] And overall the one-year rate of mental illness was said to be 26.2 percent—over a quarter of the population. You can reasonably question whether this many people actually have mental *illnesses*, are clinically depressed, etc. Indeed, I think there are weighty concerns here about treating ordinary, healthy unhappiness as if it were a disease. But it would be hard to maintain that most of these individuals are happy. (A focus on misery can be particularly useful given the introspective limits discussed in this chapter: sufferers may be relatively sensitive to problems that most of the population can absorb or adjust to well enough not to notice, and so can function as canaries in the coal mine.)

Some may be happy only because they are medicated. In 2006, antidepressants were reportedly prescribed for about 11 percent of American adults under the age of 44.[91] A study by the CDC a few years earlier found 8 percent of adults reporting the use of antidepressants in just the last month.[92] Among non-Hispanic white women, the figure was *13 percent.* Anxiety medications are also popular, with one industry source citing 8 million prescriptions filled in the United States in September 2006 alone.[93] This translates, conservatively, to about 2.7 percent of the entire population receiving such drugs in a single month; the actual rate of adult usage is almost certainly higher.[94] Additionally, there were over 4 million prescriptions for sleeping pills in that month, and nearly 3 million for stimulants, mostly for ADHD. We do not know what proportion of these individuals were happy, but it is questionable how many would have been happy without their pills.

Restful sleep has long been recognized as a sign of happiness, and troubled sleep a sign of the reverse. Estimates of insomnia in the American population are cited in one source as ranging from 10 to 34 percent, and a large health study found that 17.4 percent reported regularly having insomnia or trouble sleeping in the past year.[95] (The DSM-IV defines insomnia as a complaint about sleep at least three times a week for at least a month.) A recent commentary notes an estimate that 30 to 45 percent of the population at any time has a sleep complaint, while 10 to 15 percent have chronic insomnia.[96] Americans report getting an average of about seven hours of sleep a night, down from about nine hours in 1900. Yet a study that tracked the actual sleep behavior of 669 participants found an average of only 6.1 hours of sleep per night.[97]

Now consider loneliness. We are an intensely social species, and in many societies exile is deemed comparable to, or worse than, death. Yet as of 1994, about 12 percent of American adults lived alone; in a 1990 Gallup poll, over 36 percent of Americans reported feeling lonely.[98] In 2004 a widely-cited study found that Americans averaged only two confidants—individuals with whom they can discuss important matters.[99] Nearly half have no more than one confidant. Over half have no friends in whom they can confide, and *a quarter of Americans have no confidants at all.* These breathtaking figures, if correct, signal a dramatic weakening of social networks just since 1985; for example, the percentage having no confidants more than doubled, from 10 to 24.6 percent.

I will mostly spare the reader the dispiriting evidence regarding youth in the contemporary United States, such as the 17 percent of Princeton and Cornell students who practice forms of self-abuse like cutting and burning themselves, or the nearly 10 percent of American undergraduates who report having "seriously consider[ed] attempting suicide" in the last year.[100] But in light of our broader concerns in this book, it is worth mentioning the recent studies by Luthar and Csikszentmihalyi suggesting significant *inverse* relationships between socioeconomic status and well-being among American teenagers.[101] Referring to a nationally representative study of over 800 teenagers, using the gold standard of experience sampling, Csikszentmihalyi writes: "Children of the lowest socioeconomic strata generally report the highest happiness, and upper middle-class children generally report the least happiness."[102] And in one of Luthar's studies, tenth grade girls in an affluent suburb, with paradigmatically open futures, registered clinically significant symptoms of depression and anxiety at remarkably high rates—in each case, 22 percent. These rates are significantly higher than typical for American teens, indeed three times higher in the case of depression. It is not known how many more were subclinically unhappy.

It is basically impossible that 94 percent of Americans are happy. Clearly, many Americans are not happy, and indeed many are plainly unhappy. No doubt some of those unhappy people fell through the cracks and are not represented in the figures above. We should take seriously the possibility that very many people are substantially mistaken about how happy they are. This in turn may reflect erroneous views about the nature of happiness or other causes besides AI. But we cannot dismiss the possibility that AI plays a major role in leading many of us astray about how happy we are. We must allow that AI may be causing many of us to make serious errors about the quality of our lives.

The phenomena canvassed here are not recondite perceptual quirks; they threaten to undermine our authority about some of the most important things in our lives: the fundamental goodness or badness of our experience of life may be something that systematically eludes us. So much of our upbringing aims to facilitate the empathetic capacity to see what it is like to walk in other people's shoes. Yet we may often be distressingly blind about what it is like to walk in our own.

5. WHY SELF-REPORT MEASURES STILL MATTER

I fear that the discussion of AI may lead some to conclude that empirical research on happiness is more or less worthless. Setting aside the fact that such research is highly diverse, some of it not subject to AI, this would be a serious mistake. Indeed, a principal aim of this chapter is to *reduce* skepticism about such research, as well as other uses of self-reports of affect in empirical studies, as in the search for neural correlates of consciousness.[103] For there is already considerable doubt about the value of self-report measures, based largely (I believe) on an inchoate sense that such measures are subject to considerable error. The best reply to such worries, it seems to me, is to get clear on just where errors are liable to arise, replacing inchoate fears of an epistemic boogeyman with specific areas for concern. Those who want to challenge a given result will no longer be able simply to dismiss it. They will need to give an argument, showing where exactly we have reason to doubt the study's validity.

One reason for limiting skepticism is that self-reports could be informative even if profound AI were *ubiquitous*—indeed, even if no one had a clue how they felt. For self-reports can actually gain reliability from present-affect biases: such biases skew self-reports toward subjects' current affective states, and might do so even if the subject has no awareness of those states. People who feel good may be more likely to see their situations favorably, even if they don't realize how they feel. In short, self-reports can convey information about affective states even when subjects don't know about them. Thus someone whose emotional condition is favorable will tend to offer more positive appraisals of her state even if she isn't aware of the relevant states. Averaged out over large samples, we should expect even the reports of utterly benighted individuals to correlate significantly with how happy they are.

Granted, other problems, including other sources of AI, might obscure the salutary effects of present-affect biases. But for these to cause worry we need some reason to think they are systematically skewing reports in a certain direction. For another point to bear in mind is that AI-related errors will often wash out over time, or over large samples. When you are assessing your own happiness, *any* errors are liable to lead you astray, so AI is much more worrisome. But for researchers studying large populations, many mistakes—e.g., a tendency to report being happier on sunny days—can be set aside as random "noise," as they will tend to cancel each other out.[104]

While self-reports may be useful guides to happiness even if we had no idea at all how we felt, this is obviously an extreme assumption. Even Glen surely knows quite a lot. We can readily imagine that he normally knows when he is feeling particularly lousy, or playful, when he is angry or elated, and so forth. And that he typically can tell his better days from his worse ones. So while he fails to see a lot of important things about his emotional state, and mistakenly thinks himself happy when really unhappy, he could still tend *on average* to recognize it when he is happier, and when he is less happy. Thus an entire society of Glens, with an obscure and fragmentary awareness of their happiness, may well yield a good deal of useful information in surveys asking them how happy they are.

Significantly, a variety of studies indicate that self-reports do correlate reasonably well with happiness. For instance, there are substantial correlations between self-reports and other measures of affect, such as facial expressions, testimony of friends and family, and physiological measures.[105] People reporting greater happiness tend to live longer and healthier, fare better in a variety of domains, and have better immune response.[106] Note that self-reports could correlate perfectly with happiness yet still be systematically skewed—for example, everyone might think themselves twice as happy as they are. So these points offer more support to correlational and relative results than to claims about absolute levels of happiness.[107] When I draw on self-report data in this book, I will focus chiefly on claims about relative happiness, and at all times with an eye toward possible defeaters, such as differences in norms or introspective accuracy. Consider the finding that unemployment has a strong effect on happiness, which has been replicated in a range of studies.[108] So long as we have no reason to think that AI afflicts different groups of subjects differently in this case, it should not worry us in relation to such claims. And it seems unlikely that the differences in reported happiness between employed and unemployed individuals are attributable solely to differences in the accuracy of their reports.

While these points offer little comfort to individuals trying to assess their personal welfare, they should temper skepticism about the science. Self-reports do give us useful information about people's happiness. But that doesn't mean they can't be terribly inaccurate in important ways. It doesn't mean that most people aren't, in stark contrast to self-reports, *unhappy.*

Ironically, introspection may often be more useful in scientific contexts, and for those who rely on empirical research, than for the conduct of our personal lives. For the same reason, AI could yield a peculiar reversal of Mill's confidence about the privileges individuals enjoy about the contents of their experience. Mill claimed that individuals tend to know their own affects better than anyone else does. In a sense this is obviously true. But suppose, for the sake of argument, that most people mistakenly think themselves happy. Even if they are the best judges of their *specific* feelings, it may be that well-informed officials have a better grip on how the population feels, in general, than the individuals taken in aggregate do. So, for instance, state officials might know that the average person isn't happy, while the average person mistakenly believes herself so.

6. CONCLUSION

The primary contention of this chapter has been that the possibility of serious, widespread AI should be regarded as a live hypothesis. We cannot assume that people are reliable judges of their own affective states. In fact I suspect something stronger: that pervasive AI is not just a possibility, but the reality. As I noted in Chapter 1, most of my youth was spent shuttling between an undeveloped island, where my family spent part of the year, and a mainland home in Ohio. This afforded a Glen-like experience twice yearly, when we made the radical transition from the "mainland" mindset to the "island" mindset and back. The perception many of us had on the island was that mainlanders were by and large a tense, small-souled, and thoroughly domesticated lot—not necessarily wretched, or perhaps even unhappy, but nothing like the perpetually jolly folk depicted in self-reports of happiness. That at any rate was how we regarded the "touroids" who descended on the island like visitors from space, and for that matter how we regarded *ourselves* once the yoke of mainland respectability had reasserted itself (at least until we had been away from the island long enough for the contrast to fade from memory). These impressions could of course be somewhat romanticized. But I am hardly the first to record such thoughts.

There is a family I know—I will call them the Robinsons—whose members are remarkably loud. They are warm and intelligent people, but the din from their constant shouting and thumping is, for the unseasoned visitor, difficult to bear.[109] The Robinsons, on the other hand, seem to have no idea there's anything at all unpleasant or odd about it. Those who know them tend to see things differently: however hardened their sensibilities might have become, their household is almost certainly an unpleasant place for the family too. It is worth pondering whether contemporary Americans might not tend to be a little like the

Robinsons: oblivious, and more or less inured to, a noisy, obnoxious, stressful, and spiritually deflating way of life.

> She made the room dark and slept; she awoke and made the room light; she ate and exchanged ideas with her friends, and listened to music and attended lectures; she made the room dark and slept. Above her, beneath her, and around her, the Machine hummed eternally; she did not notice the noise, for she had been born with it in her ears. The earth, carrying her, hummed as it sped through silence, turning her now to the invisible sun, now to the invisible stars.
>
> E. M. Forster, "The Machine Stops" (1909)

11

The Pursuit of Unhappiness

I don't need any of this! I don't need this stuff, and I don't need you. I don't need anything except this [picks up ashtray] and that's it. . . . I don't need one other thing, not one—I need this! The paddle game, and the chair, and the remote control, and the matches, for sure. . . . And this! And that's all I need. Except the ashtray, the remote control, the paddle game, this magazine and the chair. I don't need one other thing.

Navin R. Johnson, *The Jerk*[1]

1. INTRODUCTION

For most of the living world, the good life is mainly a matter of context. Given the right setting and a good dose of luck, most organisms tend to do well, or at least to succeed in their terms: that's basically how they're wired. Conversely, put a typical creature in the wrong setting and—good luck or no—it is lost, pretty much guaranteed a quick death. For perhaps the majority of life forms, almost every place on earth is "the wrong setting" (a fact that gives zookeepers no end of headaches). Not so, it seems, for *Homo sapiens*, a species so adaptable that its members can flourish just about anywhere, probably including space. This is not because they are hard to kill, like cockroaches and rats, but because they are *smart*. Though rather needy in purely physical terms, these tropical primates have a remarkable talent for engineering whatever environment they find themselves in to suit their purposes. They are "ecological engineers," to use Kim Sterelny's apt expression.[2] Impressed by their seemingly boundless ingenuity, many of them, at least in the brief era leading up to the twenty-first century, have thought that their species largely *transcends* context. For its members really need only one thing: freedom, including the resources needed to pursue their goals. Give them that, and they'll take care of themselves just fine (*modulo* of course bad luck and the occasional mistake). If an individual needs something that can be gotten, she will typically figure out what that is and either secure it for herself or enter into cooperative arrangements with others—community, for instance—to get it. Given, that is, sufficient freedom to make of her life what she will. Whether the primates are correct in these beliefs remains to be seen, as their brave experiment in freedom is still getting under way at the time of this writing. While their attempts at civilization-building have tended to meet with mixed results, there is cause for optimism in the astonishing gains in longevity and the standard of living that were achieved for a large portion of the species in the decades preceding this inquiry—due in no small measure to the progress of freedom.

The idea that freedom is what human beings fundamentally need to have their best shot at flourishing is a central tenet of modern liberal thought (Chapter 1). Since it is indisputable that human beings are in some sense a freedom-loving species, an important question is how "freedom" is to be understood here. Liberal modernity has tended to view freedom primarily as self-determination, floridly conceived: to a first approximation, the ability to shape our lives in accordance with our own priorities. This conception gets its most eloquent sustained expression in Mill's justly admired *On Liberty*. Here is a recent statement of one of its central elements. Defending a child's right to an "open future" in a discussion of Amish educational practices, Joel Feinberg writes that an "education should equip the child with the knowledge and skills that will help him choose whichever sort of life best fits his native endowment and matured disposition. It should send him out into the adult world with *as many open opportunities as possible, thus maximizing his chances for self-fulfillment.*"[3] The implication is that freedom, including having a wide array of options, is good for us. A life rich in options is, in fact, our best bet for attaining well-being. While we may not be geniuses, we still tend to know what's best for us and how to get it. Moreover, many would add, we tend to do rather well when empowered to live in the manner that seems best to us.

Such appears to be the spirit of the modern age: a spirit of optimism about the individualized pursuit of well-being, founded in Enlightenment trust of the individual and her powers of reason. Since "Enlightenment optimism" is vague, additionally encompassing epistemological and historical views, and since the optimism in question concerns the effects of certain freedoms associated with liberalism on well-being, I called it *liberal optimism* (Chapter 1). Liberals need not be optimists in the present sense; besides weakened forms of liberal optimism there is room for liberal pessimism as well as, in between, what we might call liberal sobriety. Yet one does not often hear it suggested that the ideal of empowered and unfettered living is, from a prudential standpoint, a bad thing, or merely the least bad option of a sorry lot. You certainly won't hear it from many economists.

Liberal optimism is obviously appealing, but it rests on some non-trivial assumptions. Here I want to consider the plausibility of liberal optimism's chief psychological doctrine, which I will call the *Aptitude* assumption. Roughly, Aptitude maintains that human psychology is well-adapted to environments offering individuals a high degree of freedom to shape their lives as they wish. We have the psychological endowments needed to do well, indeed best, in such environments by choosing lives for ourselves that meet our needs.

In this chapter I will discuss recent work in empirical psychology that raises significant doubts about Aptitude. This research challenges Aptitude via a *Systematic Imprudence* thesis:

Human beings are systematically prone to make a wide range of serious errors in matters of personal welfare. These errors are weighty enough to substantially compromise the expected lifetime well-being for individuals possessing a high degree of freedom to shape their lives as they wish, even under reasonably favorable conditions (education, etc.).

Others have made similar claims in recent years, but usually the worry is narrower, or concerns general questions of rationality, without addressing the question of overall lifetime well-being.[4] Note the emphasis on a *wide* range of errors: our tendencies to eat badly or save too little money are well-known, but they are usually—certainly by most economists—considered to be exceptions to a general rule of rational, prudent conduct. If Systematic Imprudence is correct, then the truth of Aptitude becomes at least an open question. Liberal optimism consequently rests on a questionable view of human nature: we may not be well-equipped for the individualized pursuit of happiness, perhaps even tending unwittingly to be pursuers of *un*happiness when we possess the freedom to fashion our lives according to our own designs.

The central contention of this chapter is that the individualized pursuit of well-being is probably substantially undercut by systematic tendencies toward imprudence: the Systematic Imprudence thesis is very likely true. This in turns suggests that a key assumption of liberal optimism, Aptitude, may well prove to be false. I will not be claiming that the Aptitude assumption is in fact false or unwarranted. The point is rather that we should take this possibility seriously. The truth of Aptitude should be considered an open question. A secondary aim is to sharpen our grasp of the remarkably bold psychological assumptions underlying much modern thought about human nature, the good life, and the good society.

I will assume in what follows that people are pretty smart: like other life forms, human beings are quite good at what they do, which includes the use of their formidable rational powers in the promotion of their interests. The question is whether "what human beings do" should be understood in the first instance to include fashioning lives for themselves in the sorts of option-rich environments traditionally favored by liberals. The discussion will also assume that happiness, understood along the lines of the emotional state theory defended earlier, is centrally important for well-being. But it would make little difference if we accepted any of a wide variety of theories of welfare. Depression, anxiety, and other forms of unhappiness tend not, on any popular view, to be associated with flourishing. In any event much of my case applies to prudential goods other than happiness, and to choices not aimed at promoting the individual's happiness. And again, I do not intend to challenge liberalism; the question I want to examine is how well-equipped we are to *benefit* from certain freedoms. Our moral entitlements are another matter.

2. THE TARGET: LIBERAL OPTIMISM'S APTITUDE ASSUMPTION

To speak of an "Aptitude" assumption raises the question, aptitude for what? The idea is roughly that we have the psychological equipment needed to secure our well-being when empowered to live as we wish—when, that is, we enjoy a very broad kind of self-determination. Let me explain. The standard liberal ideal of self-determination has narrower and broader aspects. Narrow self-determination roughly concerns freedom from the predations, whims, or domination of other people—in one sense of the term, autonomy. This includes the "basic liberties," the rights to non-interference and democratic participation that, among other things, commonly underwrite constitutional guarantees. Such liberties might be enjoyed by individuals who have little scope to shape their lives, say because they live in an isolated community with limited resources. The preservation of such freedoms arguably constitutes the essential core of liberalism. But liberal moderns typically cherish, in addition, a much broader form of self-determination centering on freedom in the sense of having a wide range of *options*, specifically effective rather than merely formal options. Call this *option freedom*, as distinct from other types of freedom such as autonomy or non-interference, though I will often omit the qualifier. Option freedom can be understood in a variety of ways, but we need not commit to any particular formulation here.[5] I will assume that the options must not be indisputably worthless or utterly trivial; probably no one will think that our freedom is meaningfully enhanced by the option to be boiled in eleven different kinds of oil, or to choose among a million styles of shrink-wrap for their aspirin.

According to the liberal ideal of broad self-determination, people will enjoy sufficient option freedom that they confront an option-rich environment—or, to take a cue from Feinberg's notion of an open future, a situation of *unbounded choice*. The idea is that individuals face an effectively limitless array of significant options spanning many, perhaps most, domains of life, thus affording tremendous scope for people to pursue arbitrarily varied, and often quite creative, ways of life.[6] "Effectively" means that this is how it seems to the agent, or perhaps how it will seem to the agent assuming she is reasonable. (We might prefer the latter formulation since one possible type of error is failing myopically to recognize how much freedom one really has.) Upper-middle class American communities might constitute a paradigm of this sort of environment. An environment might offer many significant options in life without qualifying as unbounded; many working class communities might be like this. Situations of unbounded choice shift our focus from trying to pick the best item from some menu to imagining what we most want and then setting out to realize that alternative. Call the associated ideal of self-determination *unbounded self-determination*. (Note that broader forms of self-determination need not be stronger than narrower ones. For instance, it is possible to infringe people's basic liberties without seriously reducing their options.)

We can distinguish degrees of boundedness or unboundedness, with isolated agrarian or hunter-gatherer communities representing a narrowly bounded choice situation, and lower-middle class urban communities being more broadly bounded. A further distinction concerns the "hardness" or permeability of the bounds: growing up in a factory town, you might face a pretty simple default choice situation, with relatively narrow bounds, in that you are expected to stick around and enter one of a few occupations. Yet those bounds may be "soft": given a passion for philosophy, say, a motivated individual can leave town and seek her fortune in academia.

The focus thus far on boundedness is incomplete, since options ideally should be not only unbounded but *unburdened*: as easily pursued as possible, consistently with the goods to be attained. (Difficulty is essential to the realization of some values.) So the liberal ideal of option freedom involves *unbounded and unburdened* choice and self-determination. This point is important, for example, because societies can burden choice through incentives, social norms, and the like without actually limiting options. But I will usually set it aside for convenience.

The question of Aptitude, then, is this: is human psychology well-adapted to managing arbitrarily high levels of option freedom? Specifically, Aptitude claims that:

> *Given (roughly) the greatest possible option freedom, and otherwise reasonably favorable conditions, individuals will tend to choose prudently, so that most can expect to do well over the course of their lives, and better than they would given less freedom to shape their lives.*[7]

If Aptitude is false, it does not follow that people tend to do better given limits on their option freedom, or that the unbounded society is not the best environment for human welfare. While that is one possibility, it may also be that most people don't do well under *any* circumstances—the liberal Utopia may not make anyone very happy, but other arrangements are worse still; call this "cruel world liberalism." (I do not know how many commentators have explicitly claimed that people do *well* given lots of option freedom, but the sentiment is clearly widespread among liberal moderns.) Another possibility is that people don't need to be prudent to benefit from high levels of option freedom: perhaps individual needs are highly idiosyncratic, so that even the imprudent benefit from having lots of options, or the inherent or collective benefits of option freedom suffice to make it our best bet despite our tendencies to err. This we might call "Clouseau liberalism." I take it that any of these results would be interesting, and surprising to many.

To assess the plausibility of Aptitude, we can ask the following questions:

1. Do people know how happy they are, and were in the past?
2. Do people know what will make them happy?
3. Do people choose well given their beliefs?

Aptitude requires a reasonably affirmative response to each of these questions, skepticism about happiness aside.[8] I discussed the first question in Chapter 10, so here we will focus on the second and third. I will sometimes discuss these matters in terms of rationality, but I do not wish to put much weight on any particular conception of rationality.[9]

To keep things manageable, I will discuss only a few of the many relevant phenomena that have been documented. Even a cursory examination of that work should make it apparent that, if anything, the following arguments understate the magnitude of the problems. (And I will set aside the most obvious sources of mistakes, such as myopia and weakness of will.[10]) Because the literature in this area is still young and rapidly developing, I will not claim the empirical research discussed below to be definitive; most of the results should be regarded as provisional and subject to revision in light of future research. But they were chosen in part because they are liable to seem fairly plausible once they are pointed out.

The Aptitude assumption is not implausible. But neither is it trivial. Consider the sorts of choices that people living in the unbounded society have to get right if they are to achieve good lives. They must choose well concerning, among other things: what to do for a living, whom if anyone to settle down with, whether to have children, how to raise them, how to balance work and personal relationships, whom to seek friendships with, how to participate in community life, how to spend their leisure time, what if any hobbies to pursue, where and in what sort of community to live, how to manage their material wealth and prepare for the future, how to care for their health, what if any place religion will have in their lives, what kind of education to pursue, how and in what ways to develop their talents, etc. In most of these areas, human beings traditionally have had little or no choice. In some of these areas, a single mistake can ruin one's life. (Thus the economist's idealization of agents as rational choosers may be seriously misleading for predicting individual well-being even if it yields fairly accurate predictions of behavior. If your choices are utility-maximizing 99 percent of the time, then someone might reliably predict your behavior by assuming you to be a utility maximizer. But that other 1 percent could wreak havoc with your *life*, which is basically the point of literary tragedies.)

The task is demanding. Are we up to it?

3. PROBLEMS OF PREDICTION AND CHOICE

She generally gave herself very good advice (though she very seldom followed it).

Lewis Carroll, *Alice in Wonderland*

3.1. The impact bias

Let's begin with prediction: do we know what will make us happy? Are we, in short, good at *affective forecasting*? There is good evidence that we are not.[11] The most serious difficulties noted in the literature relate to adaptation. With most events, large and small, we tend to adapt quickly, probably within a few months, and return to our prior level of happiness (or misery, as the case may be).[12] This is the well-known phenomenon of hedonic adaptation. I argued earlier that claims about adaptation may often be exaggerated (Chapters 5, 7, and 10). But there can be no question that hedonic adaptation is a very real phenomenon, and that many events have surprisingly little effect on our long-term happiness.

The problem is that affective forecasts tend to overlook adaptation. When predicting how an event will make us feel, we typically imagine what it will be like at the time of the event and then project this feeling long into the future—far longer, in general, than it will actually last. This tendency has been found in numerous studies covering a wide range of matters, including tenure decisions, romantic breakups, election outcomes, being rejected for jobs, sports events, etc.[13] A likely cause of many such errors is that forecasters overlook the fact that we tend quickly to take successes for granted and to move quickly past failures, rationalizing them in various ways or changing our priorities so that they come to seem less important. It is natural, for instance, to think about events in relation to our present commitments; but of course this will lead us astray insofar as those commitments are liable to change.

While researchers have tended to focus attention on neglect of specific mechanisms of adaptation, like "ordinization" or the "psychological immune system," we can set aside such particulars here and simply regard the current phenomenon as *adaptation neglect*. This in turn results in an *impact bias*, and is indeed the most prominent source of this bias.[14] The impact bias is a broad tendency to overestimate the enduring emotional impact of future events. This tendency is deeply problematical for the pursuit of happiness. Adaptation neglect, for instance, makes us prone to exaggerate the importance of monetary outcomes for our happiness, since financial gains typically yield only short-term emotional benefits. Employers who offer generous signing bonuses know well what they're doing: the recipients may picture themselves reveling in their windfall, not recognizing that the joy will soon fade.

The impact bias has many sources, but I will note just one other. The *isolation effect* is a kind of framing effect, where the way we represent an event alters our perception of it. In this case people contemplating alternative scenarios tend to isolate distinguishing features of the options, and disregard features shared in common.[15] In affective forecasting, this can cause us to exaggerate the differences between our options, leading us to believe the choice more important than it really is. For example, college students in one study were asked to forecast their overall level of happiness in the following year if they lived in dormitories they deemed desirable or undesirable.[16] The students predicted they would be much happier in the desirable housing, when in fact it made little difference which housing they received. The error arose because the subjects framed the choice in a way that focused attention solely on the physical aspects of their housing, features that tend to have little impact on happiness. What they overlooked, evidently due to an isolation effect, were the great commonalities between their prospective living situations (such as that their friends would room with them in any event). Thus a second study found that students primed to think about other features of their situations, such as the social aspects, predicted smaller differences in their happiness between the alternatives. Continuing the real estate theme: anyone familiar with recent home-buying trends in the United States should have little difficulty seeing the practical upshot of the isolation effect. It may explain, in part, why many affluents find themselves glumly contemplating the dim financial prospects brought on by their half-furnished McMansions. By fixating too closely on the differences between their options, people forget how similarly their options will affect their lives. Hence they can sacrifice too much to get the "better" option.

3.2. Positive illusions

If we are unrealistically optimistic in predicting outcomes, we will tend to make some bad choices. There is considerable evidence of a general tendency toward *positive illusions* in thinking about ourselves and our lives, raising serious concerns about our ability to make important life decisions wisely. At least three types of positive illusion contribute to this worry.[17] First, we tend to have inflated opinions of ourselves: most of us are above average, in most respects, in our minds. Thus, for instance, most people have been found to rate themselves more favorably than observers do on various personality measures. And people tend to see positive personality and other attributes as more descriptive of themselves than most people, and negative attributes as less descriptive. Most of us think, for example, that we are above-average drivers.

Second, we tend to overestimate our control over outcomes. For example, subjects tend to believe that they have more control over a roll of the dice if they personally throw them than if someone else does. Third, most people are unrealistically optimistic, believing their futures to be brighter than the evidence warrants. Thus we typically think ourselves more likely than our peers to experience pleasant events, such as liking our first job or receiving a good salary, and less likely to experience negative ones, like having difficulty finding a job or being involved in a car accident.[18] We also tend to overestimate our performance on future tasks, more so to the extent that we see the task as important to us. And our predictions of the outcomes of a wide range of tasks correspond less to what is really likely than to what we desire, or see as socially desirable.

Few will be surprised to learn that people sometimes overestimate their virtues, or take an overly optimistic view of their prospects. But what is striking is how pervasive these tendencies appear to be. Taylor and Brown argue that they are prerequisites for mental *health*: if they are right, then just about everyone appears to view the world through positive illusions except the depressed, or those suffering from low self-esteem. Perhaps we are better off with them than without. (George Will recently observed that minor-league baseball would scarcely be possible otherwise.) But positive illusions clearly pose difficulties for the pursuit of happiness. Doubtless they lead many of us to make poor financial decisions; economist Robert Frank observes that "most of us have an unwarranted, not to say preposterous, degree of optimism regarding our own future well-being."[19] Thus, he suggests, we may underestimate our risk of serious illness and so be unwilling to buy health insurance. Perhaps a similar excess of optimism causes many youths to seek careers as practicing attorneys despite hearing horror stories about the widely alleged miseries of the profession: they may figure they'll be among the lucky few who find happiness in it.

There has been some debate about whether positive illusions are cultural artifacts peculiar to certain societies, particularly Western ones, and not universals of human psychology. There is indeed good evidence that certain cultures, notably East Asian ones, exhibit positive illusions less than in the United States and other Western nations, and in some cases not at all.[20] But studies have found evidence of such biases—for example, the "better than average" effect—even in the most disputed cultures such as Japan, and some investigators report that positive illusions in such cultures focus on different attributes, namely those valued in such "collectivist" societies.[21] One possibility is that tendencies toward positive illusions are indeed universals of human nature, but that cultural norms can moderate, neutralize, or even reverse them, as well as influencing the domain over which they operate. Were there such tendencies, we might *expect* some cultures to embrace norms of modesty and humility to maintain social solidarity. It would be useful to know if there are any societies lacking such norms which also fail to exhibit positive illusions.

In any event, it is likely that at least some positive illusions will not pose difficulties for the pursuit of happiness in some cultures.[22] One thing to note is that this does not help those in the other cultures. But more importantly, doubts about the universality of positive illusions probably *strengthen* my case. For the cultures exhibiting diminished positivity biases are also collectivist cultures that reject liberal ideals about the individualized pursuit of well-being. You might avoid certain positive illusions if you keep reminding yourself that, as they say in Japan, "the nail that stands out gets pounded down."[23] But such an outlook is not likely to find many fans among liberal optimists. Positive illusions appear to correlate with the extent to which a society embraces the ideals characteristic of liberal optimism. So it is questionable whether cultural influences on positive illusions could provide support for the liberal optimist. Indeed, they probably make things worse: the liberal's individualistic emphasis may well exacerbate positive illusions.

3.3. Lay rationalism

Here's the thorn in my side—I never did care for Faulkner's *Plowman's Folly*—I enjoy plowing. Just this past year the [Soil Conservation Service] technician told me, in all seriousness, that if I'd join the no-till crowd I'd be freed from plowing, and then my son or I could work in a factory. . . .

I failed to get his point.

David Kline, an Amish farmer[24]

Lay rationalism is a tendency to base decisions on "rationalistic" attributes, such as economic values, rather than "soft" attributes like predicted experience or happiness.[25] Roughly, the idea is that we often choose options that fare better according to "hard" criteria like monetary payoff, even where we predict that those options will be *worse* for our experience of life.

Consider a suggestive early study, where undergraduate students were asked to imagine that they had just received a graduate degree in communications, and that they were considering one-year jobs at two different magazines.[26] Magazine A offers them a job paying $35,000, but other workers with the same experience and training at that magazine receive $38,000. Magazine B, on the other hand, offers a lower salary of $33,000, but the co-workers earn only $30,000. Half the students were then asked "Which job would you take?" The other half were asked "At which job would you be happier?" Even though 62 percent of the subjects judged that the lower-salary, higher-relative-position job at Magazine B would make them happier, 84 percent of the subjects chose the higher salary job at Magazine A. A crucial gap in this study, however, is that subjects might have guessed that the extra money earned at Magazine A would yield greater happiness afterward, or outside the workplace.

But a series of studies by Christopher Hsee et al. indicates that this was not likely the case.[27] In a variant of the Tversky and Griffin study, for instance, they confronted subjects with a choice of taking a job with a small (100 sq ft) office or one with a larger (170 sq ft) office, where the smaller office involves a similarly qualified co-worker getting a same-sized office, but the larger office has a co-worker receiving an even bigger office. While only 34 percent of subjects predicted greater happiness in the larger-office job, 57 percent chose to work there. Another study manipulated which variables were seen as hard or soft; researchers asked students imagining they were shopping for a stereo to choose between two equally expensive Sony models, based on two attributes (e.g., "richness" or "sounding powerful"). For each of two groups, one attribute was labeled "objective," the other "subjective." In particular, "power" was called objective in one case and subjective in the other. In each group, a larger number of respondents predicted that the stereo faring better on the "subjective" attribute would yield greater enjoyment, while larger numbers *chose* the "objectively" superior model.

Why should people's choices be biased toward "hard" qualities in this way? A major reason may be that such decisions are easier to justify. Subjects in a further study were instructed to imagine making a hiring decision. Those who expected to have to justify their decision to themselves later exhibited greater lay rationalism than those who did not.

The potential of lay rationalism to subvert human welfare should not be underestimated: probably the most important things in life, beyond the bare necessities of existence, tend to be intangible or "soft," and hence at a disadvantage relative to "harder" factors.[28] Thus one's choice of an occupation may tend to depend excessively on matters like income rather than how rewarding it will be, or how worthwhile. Lay rationalism could help us to explain the prevalence of materialism without having to claim that people overwhelmingly have materialistic *values*: for the most part, the values people endorse in surveys are decidedly non-materialistic.[29] Indeed, there appears to be a massive disconnect between people's values, at least in the United States, and the way they live. It may simply be that our most important values, like family, friends, and personal happiness fare poorly in rationalistic terms next to money, possessions, and the like. And so our choices fail to cohere with our values.

One of the persistent mysteries of development, at least for many of those who have seen it in action, is why so many people seem eagerly to trade decent, or at least tolerable, situations for bad. Why, for instance, do some indigenous people freely abandon a functional way of life for the alcoholic, fetid desolation of life below even the bottom rung of civilization's ladder? Why do some towns gladly embrace tourist development, only to find themselves demoralized and alienated, bereft of the close-knit community and meaningful work that once sustained them? Doubtless such appearances are often the product of wishful thinking by outsiders who romanticize the lives of people in less-developed communities. But genuine cases of such mistakes are not, I think, uncommon.[30] Lay rationalism cannot be the only factor behind such mistakes, but it may be particularly salient: for the compensations of development are nothing if not conspicuous. There is nothing intangible or mysterious about the allures about greater wealth, health, and high-tech amusements, or convenience and physical comfort. Whereas the benefits enjoyed by many non-urban peoples are often difficult even to articulate—a supportive community and family life, freedom from hurry and the compressing forces of a sprawling civilization, an engaging and meaningful relationship with the land, and the quiet pleasures of exercising skill in a wide range of life-sustaining tasks. Indeed the latter tend to be invisible, as they are in the pleasures of engagement or flow, which preclude attending to how one feels (Chapter 6). We should not be surprised if a species of lay rationalists might tend to go for the more tangible sorts of goods, even if the rewards are smaller. It would be hard to justify choosing greater inconvenience and discomfort, or less wealth, simply because the attendant way of life somehow—you can't really say how—seems more fulfilling.

In Malaysia some years ago, a psychologist visiting a rural village was shown an elaborate machine devised by a local inventor, which the villagers proudly demonstrated for their guest.[31] It was a mill, which in the course of a few minutes hulled enough rice to supply five or six families for a meal. Normally it would take a half hour for those families to hull as much rice—a vigorous daily task for the women and girls who do it, using a large mortar and pole. In a half hour, the psychologist estimated, this machine could supply the entire village with a day's rice. Yet the machine lay idle: they did not use it, save to show it off. The psychologist, who had been raised among such peoples, surmised that this was because the women clearly *enjoyed* hulling the rice, singing and laughing as they worked, and would miss the ritual if freed up to do . . . what? Their lives were not rushed; they didn't need a time-saver. Yet how many people in like circumstances would refuse such a convenience? To the lay rationalist in us, such reluctance to be liberated from work is liable to seem insane.[32]

3.4. Combined effects

I have discussed lay rationalism, the impact bias, and positive illusions as distinct phenomena, but we should bear in mind that they might exhibit perverse synergies when taken together. Lay rationalism, for instance, may tend to privilege risky goods at the expense of sure things, an example being wealth versus relationships. Often you get the latter more or less by default—just hang around and be a decent friend, sibling, etc. Whereas monetary success is usually a much riskier venture, and most people who set out to get rich don't even come close. This might not be such a problem if we tend to assess our odds of success, and the nature of the payoff, reasonably well: our rationalistic bias would be tempered by the recognition of our dim prospects and the fast-decaying rewards of a triumph. But of course we aren't like that: we tend to think we'll beat the odds and that we'll be lastingly happier when we do, so that our positive illusions and impact biases *encourage* us to place the stupid bet that our rationalistic inclinations laid out for us, thus magnifying their impact. Lay rationalism might also generate harmful asymmetries in loss aversion (see next section): given a general bias toward tangible goods, we might tend to frame tradeoffs between tangible and intangible goods as gains when trading intangibles for tangibles (e.g., giving up family time for income), but as losses when giving up tangibles in favor of intangibles (e.g., giving up income for family time). It may be no coincidence that we call the latter sort of tradeoff "downshifting," the former "moving up."

This small sampling of biases does not even come close to exhausting the hurdles our brains present to us in the pursuit of happiness. But together they indicate that we may be biased to pursue goods that do little to advance our well-being over the goods that really do benefit us, and that such biases are encouraged by inflated views of our chances for success.

3.5. The Jerk and Larson's cow: or why people remain in bad situations

The best evidence that people make reasonable decisions in conducting their lives might seem to be the fact that they so often choose to stick with those decisions: if their lives are so bad, why don't they change things when they have the chance? I will discuss some good reasons for doing so in the next chapter. Here are some dubious reasons, starting with *loss aversion:* giving losses more weight than gains in choice, for human beings have a strong aversion to loss.[33] A great deal has been written on loss aversion, and since the basic idea is already familiar to many, I will note just one study here. In a classic illustration of this phenomenon, subjects in one group were given a choice between receiving a coffee mug or a sum of money, namely the minimum amount of money they would prefer to the mug; subjects in a second group were given a mug and then asked how much money it would take to get them to give up ("lose") the mug. Whereas subjects in the first condition valued the mug at a median of $3.12, those in the second group valued it at $7.12.[34] In short, subjects put a higher premium on avoiding a loss (giving up the mug) than on achieving a gain (acquiring the mug). The effect is quite general, and extends beyond monetary scenarios. And it can shape important life decisions. An overworked professional who wants to "downshift" to a less stressful and more rewarding, but less lucrative, line of work may find this choice inordinately difficult: it would mean giving up many possessions, social standing, etc. And while these things may not strike her as particularly important in the abstract, or in prospect, they will loom large in her decision-making as losses, to the point that she may lack the nerve to make the change. Like Steve Martin's Jerk, we often find that giving up things entails difficulties well beyond their value.

While losses might tend to impact our happiness more than gains to some extent, loss aversion appears primarily to be a phenomenon of choice rather than outcome; there is no evidence that it affects happiness to anywhere near the same degree.[35] Loss aversion could be simply a forecasting phenomenon: we predict that losses will hurt more than gains will benefit, and choose accordingly. But our aversion to losses may be more basic to choice than that, and at least somewhat independent of our forecasts.[36] As with our would-be downshifter, we may recognize that giving up certain things would be for the best, yet be unwilling to pull it off.

A second reason we might expect people to acquiesce in less than desirable circumstances concerns the processes driving their evaluations of their lives: people's evaluations of their lives probably exhibit a positive bias in most cases. Our general tendency toward positive illusions would be one reason to expect this: given that our perceptions of ourselves and our futures tend quite generally to be excessively rosy, it would be surprising if we did not tend to apply a similar tint to the stories of our lives. Such biases could both dampen adaptation to positive events and enhance adaptation to negative events, even transforming them into positive events, as happens when we end up recasting a failure or setback as a good thing, say because it made possible some of the goods we now enjoy. Consider how often we hear people say things like "it was all for the best," or "even so, I wouldn't change a thing." In fact the motivation to make the best of a bad situation, and cast our lives in the best possible light, appears to be strong and pervasive.[37] Nobody wants to think her life a pathetic failure, and most people are probably willing to go to great lengths to cast their lives in a favorable light—a factor, no doubt, in the high levels of reported life satisfaction across cultures (Chapter 5). Perhaps this tendency is not universal, given that some cultures make a sport of complaining, and even frown on professions of happiness. But even an inveterate kvetch could very well, when pressed to set aside the wisecracks and make an honest assessment of his life, admit that his life is actually pretty good—*keynehore*.[38]

This sort of positivity bias need not involve an illusion, or indeed be unreasonable at all, given the norms governing the way we think about our lives (Chapter 5). People can reasonably register satisfaction with their lives even in times of great hardship, because evaluating our lives is an ethically loaded endeavor that reflects on our characters, so that a reasonable judgment isn't simply a matter of how well we are doing. Think of how bad one's life would have to be that one could not reasonably endorse it, and even take pleasure in reflecting on it. Imagine that you are a highly sought-after attorney, wildly successful in your professional accomplishments and material possessions, but struggling also with loneliness, chronic mild depression, and a brood of selfish children forever bickering over the fortune you've accumulated. Must you be dissatisfied with your life? You might reasonably feel that so to regard your life would make you a soft, weak-minded, and ungrateful fool. This is the life you've chosen and made for yourself. Indeed, it may seem a kind of self-repudiation, and hard to reconcile with a healthy degree of self-regard. (Thinking yourself or your life a failure when the facts do not compel you to do so might involve an unseemly lack of self-regard.) And so you may, without error, affirm your life.

Another factor in cases like this may be a kind of *retrospective lay rationalism*: a tendency when reflecting on our lives to give excessive weight to "hard," quantifiable, or otherwise easy-to-justify factors like material success, accomplishment, and social status. I know of no empirical tests of this idea, but it seems very likely to be a factor in people's assessments of their lives. For one is less likely to complain when the only grounds for it are not so conspicuously significant, or are relatively intangible—a vague sense of malaise, ennui, emptiness, alienation, loneliness, estrangement from loved ones, etc. Yet such intangibles make up a great part, if not the lion's share, of well-being.

"Wendell . . . I'm not content," says Gary Larson's bejeweled cow to her husband, a bull, who watches television from his comfy chair as she sips a martini. Yet for all the splendor she may have an excellent point. Any outwardly successful person who senses that things have somehow come up short risks feeling a bit ridiculous, like Larson's cow, if he pursues such doubts very far.

I would conjecture that the norms concerning life satisfaction attitudes, coupled with lay rationalism and a broad tendency to accentuate the positives when thinking about ourselves and our lives, exert a strong upward pressure on most people's attitudes toward their lives, so that people will tend to exhibit higher levels of life satisfaction than well-being, and in general will be less dissatisfied than we might expect given their quality of life.[39] As a result, people may often remain in less desirable circumstances despite the existence of better options.

3.6. Why people may not want what they need

Question: if people aren't getting what they need in their present circumstances, wouldn't they at least *recognize* it? We have seen numerous reasons to question this idea, but I want to raise a more general challenge to it: why should we think that our needs would invariably advertise themselves to us? An obvious reply is that we would be poorly designed creatures indeed if we were not generally motivated to seek out what we require. Call this—the idea that human beings are normally motivated to pursue what they need, in proportion to the degree of need—the *needs/motivation congruency thesis*. There is good reason to doubt this thesis. The reason is that, in the environments in which we evolved, some of our needs would have been met either automatically or otherwise independently of our efforts. There would be no point in having motives to seek them, since it would make no difference to our enjoyment of them. To take a physiological example, there is good reason to think that young children need exposure to various pathogens and allergens to get their immune systems "trained up"; modern children raised in relatively sterile suburban and urban environments, lacking adequate exposure of this sort, thus tend to be more vulnerable to allergies and asthma, among other things. There is no inherent motive for children to seek what they need in this regard (as such), probably because there was no need for such motives in our evolutionary forbears: their world was plenty dirty.

Perhaps there are psychological counterparts to this phenomenon, such that we are not motivated to seek some of the things that are important for happiness, because there was no need for our ancestors to seek them. Or, alternatively, that we are *insufficiently* motivated to seek, given their importance for our well-being. Thus, for instance, we may be inordinately motivated to seek material goods and social status compared to relationships, meaningful activity, or engagement with environments offering the richness of stimulation of the natural world, because our ancestors might have tended to get the latter automatically, while the former took considerable effort to achieve. (Compare our appetites for ice cream versus spinach.)

The point is a crucial one, because it indicates at least the possibility that important psychological needs could generally go unmet without people being either aware of the deficit in their lives or motivated to do anything about it. Or, at least, that people's motivation to satisfy those needs tends to be far too weak given the stakes, with the result that they systematically sacrifice their interests in the pursuit of more trivial goods. Conceivably, a people's way of life could be grossly unsuited to their natures, at great cost to their happiness, without them having any idea what they might be missing.

4. ASSESSING THE THREAT TO APTITUDE

4.1. Are these harmless quirks?

I take it to be obvious that these phenomena are not merely peripheral concerns of little more than academic interest. While no one expects us to be perfectly competent seekers of happiness, the sheer mass of potentially weighty difficulties suggests a darker picture than we might have anticipated. It may be objected that the problems discussed in this chapter could easily be corrected by educating people about them. Certainly such knowledge can help, but it is a staple of the literature that most of the difficulties that have been documented are deeply ingrained in most people's psychologies, so that even specialists in this research, who ought to know better if anyone does, tend to exhibit them.[40] Moreover, careful reflection is costly and relatively infrequent, with most behavior being automatic and intuitive. You might, say, avoid positive illusions when coolly deliberating about a career choice.[41] But such choices typically take place over extended periods of time, and rarely depend solely on moments of calm reflection. Even if you realize, when thinking carefully, that you will probably be just as miserable as most associates at the prestigious law firm you are considering, you may still tend most of the time to envision yourself among the happy minority, and end up taking the job despite your better judgment. At any rate, even where the suitably trained can eliminate a given error, the benefits of an open future are not normally thought to accrue only to those who receive a lot of special training.

Another possible cause for optimism is the oft-cited evidence that most people are in fact happy. But we saw in the last chapter that the evidence for pervasive happiness is, to say the least, uncompelling. Rates of mental illness *alone* exceed those of reported unhappiness, and surely most unhappy people are just that—unhappy, not mentally ill. And beyond that there probably lie the far larger ranks of those in between: not quite unhappy, but not happy either—*feh.* Indeed, we saw some reason for thinking that *most* people are not happy, though the case for this is more speculative.

Insofar as people are not as happy as they might be, how much of this owes to the sort of imprudence we have been discussing? This of course cannot be answered with any precision. But as Daniel Gilbert dryly observes, "the average American moves more than six times, changes jobs more than ten times, and marries more than once, which suggests that most of us are making more than a few poor choices."[42] We may also find it instructive to note that in the late 1990s, when the economy was booming, the average American household carried $7,000 in high-interest credit card debt; the savings rate was zero (and is now negative); and one family in 68 filed for bankruptcy.[43] We reportedly work, on average, more hours than a medieval peasant, enjoying a leisurely pace of life only compared to our Dickensian recent past.[44] The United States divorce rate, at around 2 percent per year, has more than doubled since 1960. Yet the greater ease of exit from bad relationships has met with a decline in marital satisfaction. Only half of fifteen-year-olds live with their biological father. (Reflect on that figure for a moment. This is a social *disaster*, on a par, arguably, with serious material poverty.[45]) Americans watch an average of over 4.2 hours of television a day.[46] And 75 percent of college freshmen say that being financially "very well off"—not just comfortable or secure—is their primary objective in life.[47] About the same percentage reportedly expects to become millionaires.[48] Almost 20 percent of Americans reportedly think they already belong to the richest 1 percent and a further 20 percent believe they will in the future.[49] Given the way many Americans eat, that future may be pretty short, or at least unpleasant: some 60 percent of us are overweight, with at least a quarter obese, and a recent longitudinal study found that close to 90 percent of young to middle-aged adults can expect to become overweight; about half will become obese.[50] Help may be on the way: a Harris poll of potential parents in the United States found that over 40 percent would like to genetically engineer their children to "upgrade them physically" and "to make them smarter."[51]

Such is life in our strange Utopia, where almost everyone thinks they are happy.

4.2. The results in broader context: converging developments in psychology

Now suppose that nature's real purpose for you . . . were that you should survive, thrive, and be happy—in that case nature would have hit upon a very poor arrangement in appointing your reason to carry out this purpose! . . . In short, nature would have taken care that reason didn't intrude into practical use and have the presumption, with its weak insight, to think out for itself the plan of happiness and how to get it.

Kant, *Groundwork*, Paton trans. (p. 6)

The psychological phenomena charted above are not outliers, a collection of interesting but isolated trivia. They are just a few of *many* related effects that have been documented in the recent literature on heuristics and biases in human judgment and choice. Placed in the context of three other developments in psychological research from the last few decades—evolutionary psychology, dual process psychology, and situationist psychology—this work is part of a broader corpus from which a fairly coherent picture of human nature may be emerging. That picture may depart substantially from the dominant images of philosophical lore. On this view, we probably should not expect human beings to possess much aptitude for unbounded living; if such a way of life benefits us, it may largely be *in spite of* our cognitive endowments, not because of them. In this section I will sketch an outline of the view in question. There will be little argument in defense of this view; the point is not to convince the reader of an account of human nature, but to offer a plausible background story that could situate the findings discussed here in a broader context. Insofar as that story does seem plausible, it will give us further reason to doubt the Aptitude assumption.

We can approach the first development, evolutionary psychology, with a natural objection: how *could* we fail to be competent at securing our well-being? Natural selection hardly tends to be kind to massive prudential ineptitude, the objection goes, and the simple fact that we made it through the Darwinian sieve might seem to indicate that most of us somehow manage to conduct our lives pretty well, at least from a self-interested perspective. In fact it is not clear how far we should expect evolutionary processes to select for prudent behavior, since natural selection ultimately favors not prudence but fecundity, broadly speaking: inclusive fitness. The male peacock would be better off without an elaborate tail to drag around and attract predators, but no matter: the tail serves the genes, not the bird. Similarly, it might have been adaptive for early human males to have more or less as many mates, and children, as they could manage; but success in that endeavor may not have made their lives simpler, or them happier.[52]

But let's set this caveat aside and suppose that evolutionary forces did indeed yield a fairly high degree of prudence in our Pleistocene ancestors. While there may be some important exceptions, such as our oversized libidinous urges, this supposition does not seem implausible. Human beings, on this assumption, are pretty good at promoting their interests in the sorts of Stone Age settings they evolved to deal with—the "Environment of Evolutionary Adaptedness," or EEA, as it is called in the evolutionary literature.[53] It does not follow that human psychology is well-equipped to manage other sorts of environments, such as the option-rich societies that concern us here. How sanguine should we be on this count?

Consider that virtually all of human history, between 90 and 99 percent of it depending on when you start counting, has taken place within hunter-gatherer societies. And whatever "post"-hunter-gatherer evolution might have occurred has had only some 10–12,000 years to work its magic, with the great majority of that taking place within highly traditional agrarian societies that are not exactly paradigms of the liberal ideal. From a biological perspective, we are basically a hunter-gatherer species. Of course, the mere fact that we evolved in a certain kind of environment does not even come close to showing that we cannot flourish in very different circumstances. Organisms often manage to thrive in circumstances differing from those they evolved to inhabit, and human beings are a particularly adaptable species. On the other hand, we do not have merely *a* difference between hunter-gatherer and option-rich societies: we have a *vast* difference, in ways that matter, in the demands these environments place on people. Hunters have nothing like the power we enjoy to shape our lives. They probably do not, in any meaningful sense, form life plans of their own at all. They cannot choose friends and partners from a large pool of candidates; select an occupation from a virtually limitless array; decide which of many leisure activities to pursue; or move to California or New York or Paris or the jungles of Papua New Guinea; convert to a new religion; fashion their own religion; decide on their moral principles; set out to become an artist, a monk, or a captain of industry; and so forth. It is questionable that they often have to make important life decisions concerning complex matters they know little about, as we do when deciding on an occupation. Indeed it is doubtful how far most hunters make long-term plans at all.[54] By and large one takes life as it comes and lives the way everyone else lives, leaving it to many generations of collective experience and decision to have given the answer to Socrates' question: how should I live?

Compared to our predecessors, we need to be able to devise and pursue a much more extensive and varied set of plans ranging over much longer periods of time, solving simultaneously for many more variables—including novel ones not even known to our parents—predicting and tracking their evolution and interactions over weeks, months, years, or even a lifetime. We must sustain longer chains of prudent choice in pursuit of more complex hierarchies of goals. As well, we must reason effectively in a more diverse array of domains (such as deliberating about our values). In stark contrast to the conditions in which we evolved, life in the unbounded society requires setting one's own priorities and successfully pursuing a complex and varied set of goals that will, over the course of a lifetime, satisfy both the individual's diverse priorities and, of course, the individual himself. In accomplishing this, the agent must effect a three-way convergence of his motivations, his emotional make-up, and his arbitrarily diverse priorities. And all these things must come together, often with little advice or precedent from others, with a very low serious error rate. Happiness takes many choices; unhappiness needs only one.

Should we expect individuals optimized for Pleistocene lifestyles to come equipped for unbounded living? We should wonder whether any life-form could be up to the job: the sort of "bounded" rationality we have been discussing in this chapter is not simply a fact about our little primate brains; it is a fact about any kind of brain we could possibly hope to encounter in nature. So numerous and complex are the decisions human beings must make, even in the constrained circumstances of the EEA, that cognitive shortcuts will be inevitable no matter how smart we are.[55] True, we do pretty clearly possess a potent domain-general capacity for reasoning well about virtually anything that isn't too large or complicated for us to grasp. That's how we know the problems discussed in this chapter are problems. But—as I will explain a bit further below—this capacity is limited: slow, resource-intensive, capable of dealing only with very limited amounts of information, and prone to performance errors, with an unsure grip on our motivational structure (indeed perhaps more often *in* the grip of our motivational structure). We need the shortcuts, and some other source of motivation, to take up the slack. The trouble is that the shortcuts and motivational tendencies we evolved appear to have been designed to deal with fairly specific sorts of problems, most of them short-term problems. And while we share some of the problems confronting our hunter-gatherer ancestors, such as detecting cheaters in social exchange, the overlap in environmental demands is—to put it mildly—less than complete.

In short, our important choices in life must accomplish a remarkable harmonization of many factors that are utterly removed from the conditions of the Pleistocene world, while at the same time being relatively immune to heuristics and biases and motivational tendencies better suited to that world than our own. It is possible that our evolutionary endowments will transfer effectively to life in the unbounded society, so that we are well-adapted for this sort of situation despite its gross novelty. Hunter-gatherer societies are themselves quite varied, for instance, contending in many different ways with a wide range of physical and social circumstances, so perhaps the adaptability that served us there will do the same for individuals in option-rich societies. This is possible. But it does not seem likely, and the burden of argument lies with the liberal optimist who wants to assert it. (Indeed, the interesting question seems not to be why we make so many mistakes, but why most people blessed with open futures manage to survive into old age. Judging by the frequency with which parents in option-rich communities must rescue their adult children from their own blunders, the answer may be that most people manage to stay alive only because they live in a society in which the basics of survival require very little skill.)

It may be helpful to reflect on one of our better known tendencies toward imprudence: our propensity to overindulge in sweets and fats, to the point that it basically kills many of us. We have evolved a formidable sweet tooth and "fat" tooth—a sensible disposition in light of the dietary constraints facing our Pleistocene ancestors. Perhaps human beings have evolved other "teeth" as well—such a "stuff" tooth or a "status" tooth—that cause us to seek certain things even when doing so threatens our interests. Readers skeptical of evolutionary arguments in this realm should note that my central argument here is quite modest, and hardly adaptationist: my point is that we have little evolutionary reason to expect high levels of prudence in contemporary environments. If you doubt we have evolutionary reason to expect much of anything about human psychology, all the better: for then we *really* shouldn't expect people to have special talents for navigating option-rich environments.

Looking beyond evolutionary arguments, is there more direct evidence that human psychology actually *is* that way, beyond the heuristics and biases documented earlier? There is, from two broad lines of research. According to the first, dual process psychology, rational decision seems to play a surprisingly humble role in the conduct of human life.[56] While the field remains very much in development, there appears to be widespread agreement that human mental processes broadly involve two different systems (or sets thereof): first, the analytic or reasoning system, which subserves explicit or "conscious" thought, slowly processes information in a resource-intensive, serial, rule-based manner, often involving language, and is under voluntary control; and second, the intuitive or automatic system, or systems, which operate quickly, holistically, and automatically. They are not under the direct control of the analytic system. They also comprise the lion's share of our mental lives, and are the prime movers of most of our judgment and behavior, at least proximately. A variety of studies, for instance, have found that we frequently confabulate explanations of our behavior that have nothing to do with why we really acted—and we are not in on the joke.[57] (Our subjective impression that rational processes tend to drive behavior may be skewed by the fact that the analytic system, wherein our inner monologue occurs, effectively holds the microphone. Studies of split-brain patients—where for instance the language-using hemisphere sincerely avows pure love for the patient's spouse while the right hemisphere evinces unambiguous dislike—offer some chilling evidence to this effect.[58]) And our explicit ideals can have depressingly little to do with our behavior; for example, one study found that non-African American subjects primed with subliminal exposure to pictures of African American males tended to get much angrier after a subsequent computer failure than those shown Caucasian males—and that the intensity of the reactions bore no connection to the views about race that subjects expressed in a questionnaire.[59] If the general picture suggested by this body of research is right, then we should expect many choices to depart from the classical canons of rational deliberation, often conforming instead to the sorts of heuristics and biases, such as loss aversion, that characterize automatic processing. (The heuristics and biases research is sometimes taken to fall under the umbrella of dual process psychology, which is possibly misleading, since it seems possible that some biases reflect the characteristics of rational rather than automatic processes.)

Notice that this much is compatible with the idea that reason is nonetheless the usual and proper determinant of the *important* choices we make. Perhaps the analytic system sets the basic agenda, leaving it largely to the automatic systems to handle the details. This remains a live hypothesis, but some researchers doubt that it is the right picture. Jonathan Haidt, for instance, depicts the relationship between the two systems using an "elephant and rider" metaphor, with the elephant corresponding to the intuitive system and the rider representing the reasoning system.[60] The elephant dwarfs the rider, who will have a hard time getting the elephant to do anything it doesn't want to. Still, one might think that the rider is basically in charge. Yet Haidt points out that the analytic system is a recent—and still somewhat buggy—evolutionary innovation, appended to a basically intuitive brain that previously managed pretty well without it. The analytic system, he suggests, gives us a tremendously useful tool for performing certain tasks. But, at bottom, its job is to enable a basically intuitive organism to do those things: the rider, Haidt argues, exists to serve the elephant. Put another way, it's not that intuition is a tool that a rational creature often employs; it's rather, to put it crudely, that reason is a tool that a basically instinctual creature often employs to accomplish certain ends. For the most part, the intuitive system sets the agenda.

I do not claim to have given a convincing argument for this notion, and Haidt's own arguments for it are not decisive. (In fairness, he is writing for a wide audience, and it is not clear what a conclusive argument for such a broad conclusion could look like.) While some elements of his account may be overstated somewhat, and the question is likely to remain in dispute for the near future, it is not at all implausible that something in the neighborhood of this view is correct. We should take the possibility seriously. And if this view is at least in the right ballpark, then we should expect even people's important decisions to be shaped substantially by the workings of the automatic systems rather than rational deliberation, perhaps reflecting the kinds of biases discussed in this chapter. While it may be possible for reason to assert itself and make rational deliberation, unskewed by our varied assortment of biases and heuristics, the determinant of our major decisions, this will at least be an uphill battle.

Returning briefly to the evolutionary perspective, we can see how such a division of cognitive labor might have made more sense for our ancestors than for us: for the hunter contending constantly with the natural world, the automatic systems' speed and holistic processing of vast amounts of information would be crucial to daily survival. Explicit deliberation would have its place, to be sure, but probably a more limited place. Fashioning a life of one's own in an option-rich society, however, probably requires far more deliberation and planning, placing much stronger demands on the analytic system. Offhand, it seems plausible that this mode of living is more analytically-oriented than the hunter's way of life. (It is not uncommon for those who have lived close to the land to remark on the extraordinary cognitive differences between that existence and life within urbanized society, for instance talking about a shift to the "animal" mind in the former case, as contrasted with the "calculating" mindset one acquires in the latter. The former also tends, perhaps not coincidentally, to be characterized as much more gratifying, not to mention more fully "human," brutish metaphors notwithstanding. Indeed, making the shift to that mindset can seem as if previously idled cylinders in one's psyche have suddenly begun to fire. I have not heard anyone say this of the transition to civilized life.) If the sort of option-rich living favored by liberal optimists does indeed rest more heavily on analytic processing than the hunter-gatherer mode of life, then, again, we might expect a host of errors to arise that were not much of a problem for early humans: the distribution of cognitive burdens would differ substantially from what we evolved with, placing greater weight on the slow, information-poor, psychologically burdensome, and error-prone analytic system than it was designed to bear—indeed, effectively putting it in charge of designing our lives, something it never did in our evolutionary ancestors. This roughly amounts to putting your fate in the hands of the neural equivalent of a British sports car: capable of delightful feats, but not necessarily the most reliable way to get to the office.

Complementing the dual process model of human psychology is the situationist paradigm in social psychology. Made prominent in the recent literature on virtue theory by philosophers like John Doris and Gilbert Harman, situationism maintains that human behavior depends far less on matters of personality and character than we tend to suppose, and far more on external features of the situation. Paradigm studies in this tradition include the Milgram research on obedience, the Stanford Prison Experiment, Darley and Batson's work showing the effects of hurry on "good Samaritan" behavior, research on the "bystander effect," and Isen's study showing the impact of finding a dime on helping behavior.[61] This represents only a tiny fraction of the literature, but the general moral is this: human behavior is extraordinarily sensitive to situational factors, particularly social factors, so that such influences can easily motivate us to act in ways having nothing to do with, or worse conflicting with, our express priorities. Some have even argued that matters of values, character, and personality play a relatively small role in explaining most behavior, though this is controversial and to my mind implausible. While moral behavior has gotten the most attention, there is no reason to think situational influences are limited to that: doubtless the effects are quite general. Stated crudely, how we choose to live may depend substantially if not mainly on who we're with, not who we are or what we care about.[62]

Situational effects can neutralize the benefits of option freedom insofar as we tend not to take advantage of our freedom. (Which may be why many people do as well as they do.) A more worrisome possibility is that situational effects may compound some of the issues raised in this chapter: they may, for example, tend to intensify lay rationalism, adding external pressures in that direction to our internal tendencies. It is also possible that unbounded societies would tend to generate pernicious situational effects of their own, say by weakening communal bonds and thereby subjecting people more to unhelpful influences from strangers—for instance, increased concern for conspicuous markers of status and other behavior aimed at securing approval from relatively anonymous others. Such processes could, ironically, yield greater homogeneity among persons in some respects as the heterogeneity of their options increases (see the end of Chapter 1).

Situationism is essentially an extension of dual process psychology, since situational effects are highly automatic, unmediated by rational processes. It thus strengthens the dual process case for a less rationalistic view of human nature. From an evolutionary perspective, it would make sense for hunter-gatherers to be highly sensitive to their environment, responding to many cues without recourse to slow and clumsy rational processes. It makes good sense as well for people to be delicately attuned to others around them, constantly adapting themselves to fit with their social situation. Human beings have to be capable of getting along with virtually all other members of their species, since they have tended to live in close quarters with each other, with little choice over their companions. So the sort of strong character that would resist Milgram situations might not have been adaptive on a large scale. Situationism suggests that we are quite thoroughly social creatures, more so than most of us would like to think.

These points suggest a more *sentimentalist* and *communal* view of human nature than we tend to find in the liberal tradition.[63] Liberal thinkers, and many philosophers before them, have tended to stress the individual's rational deliberations as the fundamental and proper guide to human life, properly lived, thus taking a view of ourselves that is in an important sense both rationalistic and individualistic.[64] If something like the story sketched here proves correct, then we may need to rethink common assumptions about the nature of the beast we are dealing with. (Of course one might accept this description of human nature while deeming it irrelevant to ethical claims about how we *ought* to live. But the resulting ethic is not likely to be very attractive.)

This may seem to paint an unflattering portrait of human nature. Aristotle's view it is not, but it bears remarking that the "rational animal" of philosophical lore does not obviously constitute a more dignified portrayal of ourselves. Suppose we really are fundamentally rational beings whose natures are best fulfilled by planning and executing our lives as seems best to us on reflection—more or less on the model of the gods. In essence, we have the intellects of third-rate divinities. (Or fourth rate, to judge from the spectacular ineptitude most people show at philosophical reasoning.) It is not clear how this image is supposed to be inspiring: at least the other animals are *good* at what they do. Perhaps we should fix our attention instead in a more terrestrial direction, at our animal heritage. From this perspective, our rationality may still be in some ways—for instance, morally—the most important thing about us. But it appears to be a fragmented, biologically messy affair pieced together from the available resources to cope with particular sorts of problems, and fitted into a primate brain with lots of other agendas. It is neither a third-rate nor a fourth-rate version of the all-purpose deliberative instrument envisioned by so many. That seems to be the wrong way of looking at it altogether. The human mind is not necessarily faulty or underdeveloped; it might be extremely effective within its natural domain. But it probably was not designed to function on the model of a lesser deity. To cast aspersions on our intellects for failing to do *that* well may be like faulting wolves for hunting in packs.

None of this proves that we are not amply equipped to thrive in the sorts of option-rich environments favored by liberal modernity. But I don't need to prove it: for our purposes it suffices to make the idea just plausible enough that it becomes an open question whether human nature is congenial to the speculations of liberal optimism. And the idea that we are prone systematically to make serious mistakes in the individualized pursuit of happiness should not be regarded as an esoteric possibility, much less an outright fiction. It should be the default view.

In fact it has been, for virtually all of human history. The question of Aptitude is not new, save perhaps in the extreme form that liberal optimism poses it. Probably all cultures have considered it, and outside of modern liberal societies the uniform answer has been resoundingly negative: to stray from the tried and true path in life, even within the relatively undemanding confines of a highly bounded society, is not just to violate the norms of one's tradition. It is to court personal disaster. Probably most traditional cultures include, in the repertoire of stories handed down across the generations, cautionary tales about the woes destined to befall the youth who veers too far from the ancestral ways. Liberal societies, by contrast, tend to favor a more optimistic and inspiring kind of tale. Exemplified in any number of children's movies, this sort of story exhorts the individual to cast off the bonds of tradition and make her own path in life. To which, perhaps, should be added a coda: good luck; you're going to need it.

5. CONCLUSION

It is difficult to produce direct scientific evidence of the costs of imprudence. But there is abundant indirect evidence that human beings tend to commit a wide variety of serious, predictable errors regarding their well-being. While I cannot claim to have established the Systematic Imprudence thesis conclusively, it is, I think, well-supported: systematic imprudence very likely makes a substantial dent in the well-being of most people living in option-rich environments. In turn, the Aptitude thesis looks increasingly dubious: perhaps it is true, but its truth certainly is not obvious. The idea that human psychology is well-adapted to unbounded and unburdened living cannot be taken for granted. At a minimum, we clearly tend to make a variety of *predictable*, often serious, errors in the conduct of our lives.

In this chapter I have effectively been arguing against a certain picture of human nature, and in the last section suggesting an alternative view. It is hard to argue for an account of human nature. For one thing, it is not entirely clear what an account of human nature is, except that it is not the sort of thing that lends itself to demonstrative proof or decisive arguments. But it is easier, and may seem wiser, to approach the question piecemeal, taking one piece of the puzzle at a time: we may not be able to give compelling arguments for a view of human nature, but establishing the existence of a particular phenomenon like loss aversion can be done with a fair degree of rigor. Why not stick with those more tractable questions?

The reason is that our basic decisions about how to live, and our views of the good society and the sorts of policies that make sense for us, often depend on broad assumptions about what we are like: an image or metaphor of the human animal that establishes various presumptions about the ways of proceeding that are liable to seem fitting for us. The liberal optimist's view of human nature, embodied most plainly in mainstream economic thought, has helped to create a set of very strong and pervasive presumptions about the value of certain freedoms for human welfare, and in turn about the kinds of policies and social forms that tend to promote well-being. Even if you could point to a particular psychological quirk, like loss aversion, and thus raise doubts about a certain policy, you would not have challenged the basic presumption that put that policy on the table, and which made the job of challenging that policy very much an uphill battle. So long as the broad picture of human nature remains in place, it will retain the momentum and the decisions it favors will largely continue to get made. If that image is false or misleading, then, we need to tackle it head-on; the piecemeal approach won't work. We need to look at the evidence on hand and try to assemble a more convincing picture, one that better fits the observed facts. This will be a messy affair, with much uncertainty and few conclusive arguments. But there is no reason to think we cannot mount arguments about such matters with any rigor at all, or reasonably draw interesting conclusions about what a defensible view will have to look like. The extravagant assumptions informing liberal optimism should not enjoy immunity from challenge. I have been suggesting that these assumptions may in fact be wrong; we cannot take them for granted.

Perhaps liberal optimism's psychological assumptions will turn out not only to be wrong, but *really* wrong. We may, in the fullness of time, conclude that our civilization is founded on a fundamentally mistaken view of human nature and what we need flourish. As if a misguided zoo established a habitat for tigers with the idea that they were dealing with dingoes. The correct response to such a discovery would not, in the first instance, be to pore over our tax and regulatory schemes in the hopes of correcting for this or that cognitive bias. We should want, rather, to rethink how it makes sense for creatures like us to live.

12

Happiness in Context

Notes on the Good Society

The only way that economists know that utility has increased is if a person has more options to choose from, and that sounds like freedom to me.

Edward Glaeser

No . . . we do not mind when others call us Sakai [slaves]. We look at the people down below—they *have* to get up at a certain time in the morning, they *have* to pay for everything with money, which they have to earn doing things for other people. They are constantly told what they can and cannot do. . . . No, we do not mind when they call us slaves.

A Sng'oi tribesman[1]

1. INTRODUCTION

My father once watched a fisherman, a resident of a traditional island community often mocked by outsiders as backwards and primitive, construct a skiff approximately eighteen feet in length—cutting, shaping, and fitting the numerous pieces together to form a handsome, seaworthy craft. All by eye and memory, using hand tools only. This is an astonishing, but for such fishermen perfectly ordinary, feat requiring a degree of intelligence, discernment, and judgment far surpassing anything we see in other animals. There is nothing backwards about someone who can do that, and on that island there were not many stupid people (stupid people tended quickly to become dead people). Yet the fisherman's knowledge was largely inexplicit and inarticulate; he could have said something of what he was doing, but much of what he knew about building that boat he "just knew." So too was most of the other knowledge traditionally required to survive in the often harsh environment of that island: among many other things, how to build and maintain a home that won't wash away in a hurricane or winter storm, how to repair your tools and machines, how to handle a boat in rough seas, how to read the sea and skies and predict the weather, how to extract a livelihood from the sea, what are the character and habits of the local wildlife, and how to instruct your children in all these matters. This was human rationality in one of its highest expressions, richly employed in context and not stripped down, denatured, and reduced to pure abstract reasoning. Those islanders knew their business and were perfectly capable of looking after their interests. Though modestly schooled, they excelled in a way of life that imposed stringent, complex, and wide-ranging cognitive demands, requiring an exceptionally broad deployment of their human capacities.[2] They were, as much as the members of any community you are likely to meet, *capable*, and competent in matters of substance and worth.

All creatures have limitations, and a good part of wisdom is knowing one's own. Even the cunning Ulysses knew himself to be perfectly capable of sealing his own doom, and had himself tied to the mast. The islanders were good at what they did, arguably because what they did is the sort of thing human beings are *supposed* to be good at. Given a decent upbringing, children born on that island—the one I first mentioned in Chapter 1—could expect to become fully competent, and reasonably prudent, members of that community. But put kids in an affluent mainland community where you can live comfortably without even being able to feed yourself, indeed without being good at much of anything, and tell them "the world's your oyster, live however you want," and you have changed the equation on them considerably. Put them in a "posthuman" world where you can engineer the germline of your descendants to suit your lifestyle, and purchase technological enhancements to increase your physical and mental powers and longevity, and you have changed the game on them altogether. Who knows what will happen? Except that, as should now be clear, there is a good chance they will not use such radical freedoms well. Yet this is where liberal optimism, with its ideal of unbounded self-determination, is leading us.

The islanders, by contrast, lived under considerable constraint, which had its disadvantages. But they were also, in another sense, remarkably *free*. By and large, they lived life on their own terms, answering to no one but themselves, the sea, and the people they cared about. These were people for whom 'government' was typically a form of invective, and indeed beyond the largely unwelcome intrusions of outside agencies there was no government and no meaningful regime of laws in place. The county did employ a couple of deputies, mostly it seems to keep up appearances and deal with unruly tourists. But an official who tried to intrude too deeply in island affairs bore some risk of simply disappearing. These were a stubbornly independent people who neither wanted nor needed the government to come in and manage their lives, to make them happier or for any other reason. A decent politics ought to honor that spirit in people.

But most of us no longer live that way. We have become profoundly dependent on a vast global civilization that requires—to put it mildly—a Byzantine apparatus of laws and government and corporate bureaucracies to administer. The robust form of self-reliance exhibited by the islanders is, for the great majority of us, a remote fantasy. We have outsourced most functions of living to distant proxies, and immense state and non-state enterprises shape our lives in myriad ways. Most of us can no more liberate ourselves from such influences on our well-being than we can leap over the moon. And while this new order brings many benefits, providing much comfort and physical security and allowing us much more choice in our lives, the relatively novel and non-trivial cognitive demands it imposes make it in some ways much more hazardous. We live in a world increasingly awash in Sirens, while we steadily unravel our bindings.

The chief goal of this book has been to challenge common views about personal authority, among other things revealing the importance of a better understanding of well-being and its surprisingly rich psychology. This challenge clearly has the potential to impact our thinking about the character of the good society, and in this chapter I want to survey some of the more important possibilities. We will, first, consider questions about option freedom's dividends for well-being, in particular whether the doubts we have raised about Personal Authority should translate into doubts about the extensive benefits of high levels of option freedom assumed by liberal optimism. I will suggest that they may, and that a more cautious "liberal sobriety" may be in order. An obvious suggestion at this point is that this bolsters the case for government policies aimed at promoting happiness and well-being. Indeed it does, but government interventions raise hard moral and practical questions of their own, and I will not treat them at any length here.

A more fundamental question needs to be addressed. It concerns human prudential ecology: the sorts of environments that conduce to human flourishing. Do human beings tend to fare best when individuals have the greatest possible freedom to shape their lives according to their own priorities, or do they tend to fare better given social or physical contexts that influence or constrain people's choices in certain ways, thus favoring particular goods or ways of living? The former view we might call *individualism* about the pursuit of well-being, the latter *contextualism*. The disagreement here is not in the first instance a political question, since it is quite another matter whether governments can effectively or permissibly influence or limit people's choices in the desired manner. The question is broadly ecological. In this chapter I want to suggest that the individualist orthodoxy, embodied in liberal optimism, may well be false: we should take seriously the possibility that human beings have environmental needs that are best not left entirely to the individual's discretion. Even as adults, we may need an obliging social and physical context to help shape the way we live. And the successful pursuit of happiness may be less an individual affair, and more a matter of living in the right social and physical context, than the modern tradition has normally assumed. While my focus will remain on happiness, it will make little difference what account of well-being one holds for the arguments to follow. In general, a social form that tends to frustrate happiness is unlikely to promote well-being on any sane view of the matter. My arguments will necessarily be somewhat programmatic; my aim is to get a certain view on the table, not to definitively establish it.

2. LIBERAL OPTIMISM AND THE BENEFITS OF OPTION FREEDOM

2.1. Liberal optimism and its commitments

The notion of liberal optimism was left somewhat vague in Chapter 1, since the overall focus of the book on Personal Authority, emphasizing the surprisingly rich and elusive psychology of well-being, did not require anything more specific. But in this chapter we want to focus on the benefits of certain sorts of freedoms, and this will require a more specific formulation of liberal optimism. The liberal optimism that interests us here is quite standard among liberals, so we might call it "default liberal optimism about human welfare." It will be simpler, however, just to call it "liberal optimism." Liberal optimism consists of several related claims. Roughly:

LO1. People tend to fare best when they possess, more or less, the greatest possible freedom to live as they wish. Exceptions will be marginal. Ideally, people will face circumstances of maximally unbounded and unburdened choice.[3] (This will later be termed "individualism.")

LO2. More freedom in determining the character of one's life is almost always better, in terms of average well-being, with exceptions representing a fringe of special cases.[4]

LO3. The benefits of option freedom are not marginal but *major*. A great increase in option freedom will typically yield large gains in well-being.

LO4. Individuals are almost always better positioned to make choices concerning their well-being than anyone else, aside from limited resources and matters of special expertise.

LO5. People not only do best in conditions of unbounded choice; they tend to do pretty *well*.

LO6. Option freedom benefits individuals primarily through the successful exercise of their own agency. This is because it enables them to tailor their lives to their particular needs.

These claims appear to be widely accepted, not just among libertarians and economists but on the left as well, as we see for example in egalitarian political theories emphasizing the promotion of resources or capabilities.[5] While left-liberals often evince hostility toward consumer culture and the sorts of options it proliferates, this typically reflects a belief that consumerism's options are trivial, doing little to enhance our powers of self-determination. These skeptics rarely express similar doubts about the value of giving people more latitude in deciding weightier matters like occupation or lifestyle for themselves.

Liberal optimism is quite a strong doctrine. Some might think I have made it too strong, but something like the above formulation is needed to account, not just for some common arguments against state paternalism, such as Mill's in *On Liberty*, but also (among other things) for the very strong presumption favoring increases in people's option freedom in the liberal tradition.[6] (Recall the earlier quote from economist Glaeser, and David Brooks's remarks in Chapter 1.) Because liberal optimism makes such bold claims, it should still be possible to mount a reasonably rigorous examination of it even though the issues here are large. Such an examination is important, since liberal optimism provides crucial support for major policy decisions, including development policies driving radical transformations of *other* people's societies. Liberal optimism is also tied to widely shared views about human nature and the good life.

We have seen that liberal optimism rests on the Personal Authority assumption targeted by the previous chapters. But it depends on two other assumptions as well, and these might to some extent compensate for the weakening of Personal Authority. The first assumption is that the individualized pursuit of well-being is, on whole, collectively benign; call this *Benign Composition*. It might even be highly beneficent, for instance if the invisible hand of the market proves potent enough. The other assumption is that having lots of freedom to live as you wish tends to be, on the whole, inherently benign: simply having choices is not in itself particularly costly. Call this, somewhat awkwardly, *Inherent Benignity*. Taken together, then, liberal optimism's assumptions are these:

1. Personal Authority
    a. Transparency
    b. Aptitude
2. Inherent Benignity
3. Benign Composition

Perhaps the other assumptions, Inherent Benignity and Benign Composition, can vindicate the liberal optimist's vision of the good society despite the problems we have seen with Personal Authority. The question here is whether people need to be prudent to benefit from high levels of option freedom. Maybe liberal optimists should give up just the idea, embodied in LO6, that high levels of option freedom promote well-being mainly by empowering individuals to shape their lives to better suit their needs. The chief benefits derive instead either from the collective impact of many people having such freedom, from the inherent advantages of having such freedom, or both. I will not try to rebut this proposal in any detail, but we should briefly examine the prospect that Inherent Benignity or Benign Composition might rob the preceding discussion of much of its force in thinking about the good society.

2.2. Inherent Benignity: the inherent benefits of option freedom

> The tourists approached the ticket booth with a feed-me attitude. They expected a benevolent Nature. They wanted assurances that they would see whales, good whales. They wanted guarantees for the weather, for their satisfaction, and they needed to be back in time for dinner reservations.
>
> Justin Tussing[7]

Let's take the individual case first: Inherent Benignity. A weak form of this assumption maintains only that freedom's inherent downsides do not outweigh its inherent benefits. The claim will have to be stronger than this if it is actually to provide positive support for liberal optimism. There are several good reasons to think option freedom inherently beneficial. For starters, it can involve greater privacy and reduced pressures to conform to parental and social expectations.[8] It may promote a liberating sense of optimism and possibility. Moreover, there is good evidence that having a sense of control over one's life is an important contributor to happiness.[9] This clearly indicates a benefit of option freedom, but the relevant sense of control tends to center on people's daily activities rather than the basic features of their lives, so it is not obvious that people with relatively modest option freedoms, like the islanders described at the start of this chapter, could not do rather well on this count.[10] Finally, there might be intrinsic benefits simply to being the architect of one's own life, or to chasing after one's dreams. But again, we must not exaggerate the support this sort of claim could offer for liberal optimism (recall the case of the fishermen).

Inherent costs also increase as our options grow richer.[11] First, making decisions takes *work*—gathering information, deliberating—and the more options we have, the more work it can take. (And the more *anxiety* it can provoke.) Second, with greater choice comes greater *expectations*. We expect a better result when we have more say, and so are more easily disappointed. Third, the possibility of *regret* increases with choice: more options means a greater chance that you had better alternatives than the one you chose. Fourth, our *responsibility* for outcomes in our lives increases. While this can be nice if we choose well, it can make bad outcomes worse: no longer is it merely a bad result; it's your fault. And even a "merely" good outcome can be cause for self-reproach when options are rich enough that you expect something better. Fifth, a perceived excess of options can result in *decision avoidance*, so that people opt out of choices where, given fewer possibilities, they might have obtained significant benefits. Finally, a plethora of options can weaken the *commitments* that give meaning to our lives insofar as we find it easier or more tempting to quit them, or relax our grip on them, in the hopes of something better.[12] These problems are not necessarily minor, and indeed a review article in *American Psychologist* discusses them under the heading, "The Tyranny of Freedom."[13]

I will note just a few of the studies illustrating the limitations of having a varied menu of choices. One study, of undergraduate job-seekers, found that students applying for more jobs got higher-paying positions, yet experienced more negative affect in the process and wound up less satisfied with their jobs.[14] Another study found that shoppers were much more likely to buy jam when offered only six varieties rather than thirty; they tended to be significantly more satisfied with their purchases as well.[15] It's only jam, but there is no reason to think that the effect won't scale up. Other research finds that employees are less likely to avail themselves of an employer-subsidized 401(k) plan when given more plans from which to choose.[16] There is some evidence that people often express ambivalence about even the idea of having choices, particularly those who appear to have had fewer options in life. A recent study asked undergraduates to pick three adjectives describing what the word 'choice' means to them.[17] Whereas students with college-educated parents were more likely than others to cite 'freedom,' 'action,' and 'control,' students whose parents did not go to college were more inclined to mention 'fear,' 'doubt,' and 'difficulty.' Schwartz has suggested that the explosive increase in options for recent Americans is the primary force behind a massive surge in depression rates. With more choice, he argues, has come declining social cohesiveness, increasing expectations, and an increased tendency to blame ourselves for unsatisfactory outcomes—a style of attribution that is well-known to contribute to depression.[18]

We have been focusing on how people deal with particular choices involving lots of options. But unbounded living could also affect our psychologies in broader ways, for instance generally impacting individuals' cognitive styles. Recall the point made in Chapter 11 about the way situations of unbounded choice enable us to focus more on what *we* want rather than on our circumstances. This is part of the appeal of unbounded choice, as it holds out the prospect that we can better attend to our needs. But it may also involve tradeoffs. For it might engender a far-reaching psychological change whereby people's attention shifts inward, toward themselves rather than their environment. One possible downside of such a shift is that it may encourage a ruminative cognitive style that, like the tendency to blame oneself for bad outcomes, is associated with depression.[19] Another is that people who focus more on their wants may tend to be more needy and in that way vulnerable. Third, it could make people less attentive to their environment, reducing their capacity to enjoy the moment and appreciate things as they are. These are speculative remarks, but we cannot dismiss these possibilities out of hand.[20] Future empirical study may well reveal systematic changes in cognitive style when people's options increase—at least across certain thresholds—and they may not be wholly advantageous. Perhaps some such psychological shift is connected to popular stereotypes of the consumer society's denizens as being like Tussing's tourists: oafish, grasping and self-absorbed, seeing the world as something to be served by, not reckoned with or appreciated on its own terms. (A tourist visiting our fisherman's island walked into a store and, having heard that the locals possessed a distinctive dialect, barked a command: "Speak!") Such a mindset may not conduce to getting the most out of life.[21] Indeed, it is pretty near opposite what many ancient thinkers recommended as a path to tranquility: tempering one's desires and conforming oneself to the world rather than viewing it as a resource for the gratification of one's desires.

Such prescriptions sit poorly with another aspect of unbounded choice: the enhanced perception of contingency that comes with greater options (or even the perceived possibility or expectation of greater options). That is, simply knowing about alternatives to one's situation can transform the inevitable to the evitable. That's the point, of course, but it is harder to be contented with one's circumstances when there appear to be many alternatives, and when one's hardships seem unnecessary. (Recall the earlier discussion of lay rationalism and positive illusions, which can amplify such disgruntlement.) In one anthropology documentary, a traditional slash-and-burn farmer of the Yucatan Maya struggles to do the best thing for his two young sons, giving them the option either to continue farming or to leave their settlement for the city of Merida.[22] While the members of the community hardly seem unhappy—relaxed and quick to laugh and joke—farming the Yucatan is, to put it mildly, hard work. So the allures of the city are substantial. After an abortive initial foray to the city, one son returns and apparently stays there to work. The other son elects to stay behind and take up his father's vocation; but he is clearly torn, and his heart isn't in it. (What possibilities have I passed up? Why am I toiling in the blazing sun when I could have a factory job?) It may well be that the city offered a better life for both sons than their father enjoyed. The important point is that the son who chose to follow in his father's footsteps was very likely worse off than his father, who apparently never faced that choice; he certainly seemed less contented. Indeed, he probably would have been better off never having had the option to leave in the first place. One reason to give up the old life for a new one in the city is simply that *knowing* about the city can make life worse in the country. Development's burgeoning possibilities may gain people's assent partly by poisoning the well.

2.3. Benign Composition: the collective benefits of option freedom

According to Benign Composition, the joint impact of many people seeking their goals in an option-rich environment may involve some costs to well-being, but these are relatively minor. And the benefits may greatly exceed the costs, as seems to be the effect of the market's invisible hand. Indeed, the salutary effects of the market are obviously profound, so much so that they might sustain liberal optimism, say by generating products that keep us alive longer, even if people tend to bungle their lives. We can say what we will about the rat race; the drugs are great.[23]

But confidence is hard to come by in such matters given the vast scales and immense complexities involved. For one thing, the most important sort of freedom for the functioning of the market is economic non-interference. It is less clear that the general population needs high levels of option freedom to gain most of the collective benefits of market forces (e.g., perhaps, Singapore). Thus pharmaceutical companies might keep us well supplied with antibiotics and sleeping pills even if most citizens face relatively constrained futures.

Consider also that the problems of collective action may themselves be profound. One obvious consideration is that personal choices frequently generate negative externalities—costs involuntarily borne by others. These effects are not always obvious, and individually may be miniscule. But cumulatively, they can prove quite harmful. Pollution is the classic case, but "positional externalities" are especially interesting here. For instance, whoever is willing to put in the longest hours at the office tends to be more successful, putting pressure on others to do likewise to remain competitive. Some economists have argued that competitive consumption and related phenomena partly explain recent rises in consumer spending, particularly on status goods, to the point of mass overspending, under-saving, and debt.[24] Even the most innocent personal choices can ramify badly for others, but usually the public impact of any one person's actions is so small that there can be little incentive to behave otherwise.

A further difficulty is fundamental to the standard liberal view of freedom, and it concerns the extensive decoupling of the individual in crucial respects from the community and from the environment.[25] The more freedom individuals have to live as they wish, at least beyond a certain minimum, the less strongly tied they will tend to be to their communities and to the ecosystems that sustain them. This is partly the attraction of option freedom: it allows as much as possible for people's lives to be driven internally rather than by the customs of their communities or the whims of nature. The unbounded society frees us to attain self-fulfillment on our own terms by enabling us to decouple ourselves from the land and society, so that—to the extent possible—the only bonds between these things and ourselves are the bonds we willingly accept.

This has obvious advantages, but it has limitations as well: for human well-being is profoundly dependent on the health and vitality of the community and the land. Community arguably just *is* a form of coupling among diverse individuals, requiring that people adapt their attitudes and behavior to each other in countless ways, on a continuous basis. It thrives on familiarity and trust. Whereas the option-rich society makes it so we don't have to adapt ourselves so much to others—that, again, is much of the point—makes it easy not to know our neighbors well, and in fact gives us incentives not to: for one of the great freedoms it allows is that of mobility, to live wherever one chooses, and wherever the pastures are greenest for one's chosen occupation. Another is the freedom to spend our leisure hours however we wish, choosing from a wide array of attractive options, only some of which—typically not the most convenient ones—require the existence of other people. The enhancement of these freedoms tends to benefit the individual at the expense of community.[26] Wide option freedom appears substantially to be antithetical to the goods of community.

The land is prone to suffer for similar reasons: liberated from the constraints of having to pay close attention to the land and the effects of our activities on it, we are bound to be less aware of those effects, hence less prone to rein them in. These worries, again, are familiar from other literatures. And as of yet, no one has proposed a remotely plausible way to get the option-loving members of a highly industrialized society, whose elephantine appetites draw sustenance from a vast array of ecosystems around the globe, to temper their behavior with appropriate concern for the utterly obscure environmental costs of their choices. (It's hard enough to be considerate to our housemates, or for that matter our own cardiovascular systems, let alone a nameless swamp on the far side of the planet.) These worries are not unique to option-rich societies, of course, and tend to be even worse under totalitarian regimes like the former Soviet Union. But they do mark a potentially severe cost of unbounded living.

These are naturally large issues, but it ought to be clear enough that we cannot take Benign Composition for granted. We should remember that the option-rich society is, in the context of human history, an extremely recent innovation; its long-term viability cannot just be assumed. It may be, when all is said and done, that the truth lies somewhere closer to "malign," or worse, "catastrophic" composition: the option-rich society tends to lead us ultimately to ruin, say because it so decouples us from the environment that we destroy its capacity to sustain us; or because it so decouples us from our communities that they eventually cease to be functional. (Or because it generates too many individuals both alienated from their neighbors and empowered to destroy them, say through basement bio-warfare projects.) I make no conjecture here, but claim only that Benign Composition is not *obviously* correct.

2.4. Liberal sobriety

There are good reasons to doubt liberal optimism. Yet we need not abandon liberalism, and there are excellent moral reasons, rooted in respect for persons, not to (see Chapter 1). In the previous chapter I mentioned two liberal alternatives that seem to me improbable: first, *cruel world liberalism* retains most of the commitments of liberal optimism but gives up LO5, conceding that people will tend not to do well even in the best possible society. *Clouseau liberalism* instead surrenders just LO6, holding that option freedom's considerable benefits accrue to us despite our choices, not because of them. But a more plausible alternative would be to drop—instead of or in addition to LO5 and LO6—liberal optimism's more central commitment, expressed in LO1–LO3, to the great benefits of arbitrarily high levels of option freedom. Call a modest form of such a view *liberal sobriety*. Here it is granted that people usually fare better given higher levels of option freedom. As a general rule, people tend to be better off when they have more control over their lives. However, those benefits will often be surprisingly small, and in a significant range of cases may be nil or even negative. While there is a presumption favoring greater option freedom over lesser, we cannot take for granted, at least for a wide range of situations, that a regime of greater option freedom will thereby tend to make individuals better off—or if it does, the benefits may be substantially dissipated by systematic tendencies toward imprudence, as well perhaps as the inherent and collective problems just noted.

Liberal sobriety may strike some as too optimistic. They might prefer, instead, *liberal pessimism*. The pessimist claims that high levels of option freedom tend to be detrimental to human welfare, and increases in option freedom very often leave people worse off. Beyond these views are various non-liberal positions.

3. THE ECOLOGY OF WELL-BEING

3.1. Individualism and contextualism about well-being

Suppose that liberal optimism must give way to liberal sobriety. A question then arises concerning human environmental needs: which circumstances conduce to human flourishing? In particular, to what extent does human well-being depend on living in the right kind of environment, versus simply having the freedom to live in whatever manner one desires? The question invites us to think about human flourishing from an ecological perspective, from which human beings exist as one species among many, with ecological requirements of our own. Liberal optimists naturally favor an emphasis on individual freedom, holding that humans tend to fare best when the shape of a life is, to the extent possible, determined by the individual who leads it. People should, ideally, face conditions of maximally unbounded and unburdened choice. Call this thesis—designated earlier as LO1, the first component of liberal optimism—*individualism* about the pursuit of well-being.

Contextualists, by contrast, think well-being is better served when individuals' lives are substantially, and non-minimally, shaped by an obliging context. People do best, that is, when the context constrains or guides their choices in certain ways, beyond the minimums imposed by the unalterable facts of human existence. I mean "constraint" to include both limits and burdens on our choices. (Making an option very expensive adds to the constraints you must deal with, though it may not strictly limit your options.) "Obliging contexts" might include certain sorts of communities, cultures, and/or physical environments.[27] Contextualists need not deny the value of free choice, or even of having lots of options. But their regard for such values will be tempered by the belief that, given the character of human needs and our limited capacity for prudence, we tend to fare best when living in circumstances that either constrain our choices somewhat or steer us toward certain options rather than others. Of course, the favored options will need to be *good* ones for human beings: the point is not to restrict choice for its own sake, but to meet human needs. Individualists think this is best done by letting individuals determine for themselves what they need and giving them as much freedom to shape their lives as possible, while contextualists will prefer, given the problematical connection between option freedom and well-being, to focus more directly on people's substantive needs for community, meaningful work, relaxation, whatever. (Those needs need not be universal in a way that should offend any relativist. They could largely be for whatever goods your culture favors. The focus on faring "best" may seem Utopian, since the best usually isn't an option. But knowing what's best for an organism can tell us a lot about what's better and worse for it in the suboptimal conditions we normally face. In practice, individualists will almost always favor expanding the scope and extent of autonomous choice, whereas contextualists will tend to be more cautious about such measures.)

The divide between individualists and contextualists can also be framed as a disagreement about the pursuit of happiness. Individualists see this, naturally, as properly a matter of the individual: happiness is best secured through the individual's prudent exercise of choice, ideally in conditions of unbounded and unburdened choice. If people endowed with wide-open futures wish to be happier, the solution will lie within themselves: in cultivating better judgment and habits of thought and behavior. Contextualists will of course grant a role to such efforts—no one doubts the importance of individual prudence for living well—but they will regard them as only a part of the story. To some extent, the pursuit of happiness will depend, not on personal wisdom, but on being situated in the right social and physical context: living in the right place, with the right people, where this is not simply a matter of personal choice. The pursuit of happiness, in other words, will not be solely, or perhaps even mainly, an individual affair: it will be substantially a societal matter. (Though whether the relevant social variables, like cultural norms, can realistically be *pursued* is another question. The good society could be largely a matter of happy accident rather than conscious decision.)

To see how context might govern or steer choice without necessarily limiting people's options, imagine two societies that make available the same range of occupations, where in one society the cultural norms favor becoming a doctor or a lawyer over most other occupations. The other society, however, has "laissez-faire" attitudes encouraging people to do whatever they want to do. A subtler example can be seen in the contrast between East Asian and Caribbean Latin cultures, which appear to have very different norms regarding emotional expression and other matters relating to happiness. Such norms can "burden" choice by discouraging individuals from choosing paths they might otherwise have taken, and to that extent will be distasteful to the individualist.

This is not to say that individualists are "anti-culture." Rather, their ideal is a "liberating" culture that leaves people's choices unencumbered as much as possible, maximizing the extent to which their lives reflect priorities of their own. (Think of the tolerant ethos endorsed by many American undergraduates.) And while people always internalize many of their cultures' norms, so that "their own" priorities cannot help but reflect such norms, such internalization need not be complete. Probably most people disagree with some aspect of the party line in their cultures. Thus some Latino cultures may disadvantage those sharing the North American penchant for relentless toil in pursuit of ambitious goals. And even those who endorse the party line may not be constitutionally suited to it. Better, from the individualist's perspective, to provide an atmosphere that encourages each person to develop as best suits her nature. The individualistic utopia will be as welcoming to those with the heart of a Russian poet as to those with the bubbly enthusiasm of a cheerleader. And, most importantly, will try as little as possible to steer individuals toward any particular way of living or ideal of the good life. (Individualists will not deny that any situation must favor some options over others; but they will see this as a regrettable fact of life, to be minimized.) Contextualists, by contrast, will reject this sort of neutrality. Through cultural norms or otherwise, their utopia will favor certain ways of living over others.

Recent contextualists notably include the communitarians,[28] but the philosophical pedigree goes back at least to Plato, who charted one of contextualism's most appalling extremes. Aristotle too was probably a contextualist who stressed the importance of living in the right kind of city, where proper human functioning is encouraged. Probably most people historically have lived within, and more often than not endorsed, social forms exhibiting the limited personal control, if not the obliging circumstances, characteristic of contextualism. Notice that rejecting liberal optimism does not compel us to accept contextualism. For instance, liberal sobriety can take the weak form of rejecting merely LO3, the idea that option freedom's benefits are great. You could think that people living in societies with greater option freedom are better off for it, but not by much given their tendencies toward systematic imprudence. Alternatively, it would be possible to accept individualism but not LO2, the idea that more freedom is virtually always better: perhaps people do *best* given maximally unbounded and unburdened self-determination, but still sometimes do better given fewer options rather than more. But many of those motivated to reject liberal optimism by the sorts of worries discussed in this book will likely take the stronger view and favor some form of contextualism over individualism.

Accepting contextualism does not require us to follow communitarians in rejecting liberalism. Contextualists might insist that governments promote substantive goods only when doing so enjoys sufficient popular support, and that they not infringe on individual rights in doing so. Even a libertarian could embrace contextualism, believing for instance that people tend to fare best in certain small-scale societies where people's choices are limited, not by other people's dictates, but by the dictates of living close to the land in a small community. (Notably, the island fishermen I have written about had a strong libertarian streak, and I very much doubt that all of them envied their more option-blessed counterparts on the mainland.) Contextualism is a doctrine about the sources of well-being, not political morality.

The contextualist/individualist divide comes to the fore in thinking about the choice societies have to make between the somewhat incompatible goods of community and individual mobility. The freer people are to pursue the occupation and lifestyle of their choosing, in the place of their choosing, the harder it is to maintain strong community ties and the kinds of personal relationships that come with them. Individualists need not deny the worry, since virtually everyone wants the goods of relationships and community. But they will tend to favor high levels of mobility, believing that the gains from pursuing our dreams outweigh the negatives of weaker communal bonds. Many contextualists will be less sanguine. This sort of dispute may be most familiar from the ongoing debates over the U.S. and European economic models. The contrast is sharper in the disagreement between Feinberg and the Amish (see Chapter 11). Whether Feinberg is correct about the benefits of giving Amish children more schooling and more open futures, the Amish are not crazy to fear that such a policy would threaten one of their most cherished values, that of community.[29] Similarly, the well-known Amish aversion to luxuries and many technologies is not an inane superstition: it is rooted in the less-than-crazy belief that such things weaken community by making people less dependent on each other and promoting vanity and social competition. Indeed, if they can adopt a new technology to make their lives better without compromising their values, they will gladly do so—sometimes before the general population.[30] The Amish way of life appears to embody a strong form of contextualism, holding that human beings tend best to flourish under conditions of constraint, where options are fewer but common tendencies toward imprudence are blunted—and where, perhaps, some of the more important human needs are more easily met. The Amish might be wrong in this, but they are not out of their minds. Their view illustrates the extent to which seemingly reasonable people can depart from the individualistic paradigm.[31]

I suspect that the balance of evidence favors both liberal sobriety and contextualism, but I do not know how one can *show* this given the broad character of these issues. (Though further support may come from a closely related debate in moral psychology.[32]) So I claim only that they should be considered live options: we have good reason to think they may be true, and should take that possibility seriously. We should take neither liberal optimism nor individualism for granted.

Indeed, perhaps the pursuit of happiness will prove to be mainly a societal matter: our prospects for flourishing may depend less on personal wisdom than on living in the right kind of setting, with the right sorts of people.

3.2. The anthropology of well-being

It is doubtful that any serious inquiry into these questions can proceed without taking a step back and examining what human life is like in different sorts of societies, and not just in the societies where philosophers tend to live, governed as they are on individualistic principles. How do people actually fare in the "collectivist" cultures of Asia and other parts of the world? In the working-class neighborhoods of liberal societies where options are fewer, or less accessible, than in more affluent areas? In traditional agrarian, fishing, or pastoral communities? Or, for that matter, in hunter-gatherer societies in which human beings have usually lived? What are the prudential tradeoffs, the pluses and minuses, of life in such societies compared to our own? The interesting question, note, is not "Which society is best," which obscures too much and raises no end of "apples and oranges" problems, but how societies compare in specific respects.[33] So we break the inquiry down into narrower questions, for instance asking what degree and kind of well-being the typical member of a given society enjoys on a typical day. How fulfilling or gratifying are the most common activities people engage in? What proportion of the time can a person expect to suffer from extreme physical or emotional discomfort? And so forth. A reliable food supply and great life-support machines are major points in favor of a society, and most of us would rather live in an environment where "play date" and "quality time" are operative notions than deal with leprosy. But the discussion should not end there.

There are several reasons we shall want to investigate questions of well-being across a wide range of cultures. For starters, it will be hard not to beg important questions about the relative merits of social forms for human flourishing if our reflections are not informed by a decent appreciation of other ways of living, such as those favored by contextualists, and the goods attainable in them.[34] The untutored intuitions of philosophers, who are usually among the chief beneficiaries of the most individualized social forms in human history, must be considered at least a little suspect. (Cf. Feinberg, an indisputably humane thinker, whose discussion of the Amish counsels educational policies that could very well obliterate Amish society and others like it, seemingly with little appreciation of what might be lost in the process.)

Perhaps we should not be surprised if philosophical accounts of well-being frequently employ concepts that may be utterly alien, and perhaps inappropriate, to many cultures: to define the good life for a human being in terms of a plan of life, or the good of accomplishment, or critical reflection on one's deepest values, for instance, might seem pretty innocuous even to those of us who ultimately disagree.[35] But such goods, at least as understood in some of the literature, may have formed little or no part of human life for more than 90 percent of our history, or even in some cultures today. (It is not clear, for example, how far people in some hunter-gatherer societies form meaningful ideas of a future at all, at least beyond the next day or so.[36]) We could of course conclude, so much the worse for those other cultures. But could we offer any non-question-begging reasons for such a conclusion? Just why, for instance, is it necessary to seek accomplishment in one's life, to "make something" of one's life or build toward something at all? Perhaps some people can flourish by simply *being there*. The point is not to deny the value of accomplishment, or to push a relativistic approach to value. It is to note how radically different ideals of human life can be, and how parochial untutored intuition can be. If we understood the gratifications people find in other ways of living, perhaps we would come to a different understanding of human well-being. It is hard to believe that our reflections on the good life would remain untouched by a worldly acquaintance with the ways human beings actually live.

The philosophy of well-being, I am suggesting, needs an anthropology of well-being.

4. OBJECTIONS AND REPLIES

4.1. "Why don't you move there?"

A standard objection to doubts about the value of more options is that if people without so many options can be so well off, why don't *you* join them? Of course I have not claimed that people living in bounded societies are better off on the whole than affluent Westerners. At any rate, this sort of objection is remarkably weak, and one aim of this book is to help us put such wizened tropes behind us. The general point I want to make is that what our choices are is a poor guide to what we take to be good for us. The preceding chapters of this book laid out numerous reasons why we might make *bad* choices. But even reasonable choices can fail to maximize our prospects for well-being.[37] Most obviously, most of us care about things other than our own well-being. Less obviously, even self-interested choices can reasonably fail to maximize expected utility, say when we choose more modest prospects to minimize the risk of catastrophe.[38]

Crucially, most of us have some attachment to the lives we lead, the people we know, and the places we live, however imperfect. (Indeed, the objection assumes a rootless, itinerant mentality that in many cultures through the ages would have seemed repulsive.) In general, people tend to like who they are and to affirm the lives they have made for themselves, and this gives them sound reasons to remain where they are. In all likelihood, I don't want to trade places with you, and you don't want to trade places with me. You may be better off than me, and have a better life than me, but I don't care: your life isn't *my* life. And I'm attached to my life. Whatever you think of Amish well-being, the fact is that most of them have no more interest in trading places with you than you do with them. Perhaps you and I are much better off than they, but the fact that we would not trade places with them, or go and live with them, does not tell us very much.

4.2. Contextualism and freedom

Contextualism does not amount to skepticism about the value of freedom. It does evince doubts about the benefits, beyond certain limits, of one *kind* of freedom, option freedom. But there are other kinds of freedom, not all of which clearly do better in the regimes favored by liberal optimists. The fisherman depicted at the start of this chapter enjoyed, so far as I can tell, relatively little option freedom in life. Yet people like him on the island seemed extraordinarily free, as I noted before. I would suggest that the islanders' remarkable individuality obtained not in spite of the constraints in which they lived, but *because* of those constraints. In part, it reflected life in a tight-knit community of equals, with nothing to hide and no ladders to climb, and hence no point in being anything other than utterly themselves. The relative absence of wage labor or a service economy meant that few people, let alone strangers, were in a position to dictate their doings. And importantly, the islanders' individuality evinced the pride borne of not having your whims catered to, having instead to exercise the considerable skill needed to live in an unforgiving environment, with no help from the outside world. There is a popular image of individuality as simply doing or having whatever you want, like an idle monarch. Perhaps that is one road to individuality. But individuality can also emerge through responding well, and in your own manner, to circumstances of constraint. (As any musician can attest. It is no coincidence that blues and gospel, both highly structured musical forms, are also among the most expressive and liberating.) You need a good deal of latitude for this, but you certainly do not need unbounded and unburdened choice. What chiefly stifles individuality is not constraint, I would suggest, but subjection to an alien will. (An underappreciated corollary of this point is that the introduction of a wage economy, as recently happened on the island, typically involves deep tradeoffs between two kinds of freedom: the greater options of life in a modern economy, on the one hand, and the often greater autonomy of being more fully one's own master, on the other.[39])

Jane Watson, the young woman mentioned at the start of this book who feeds a wolverine appetite for luxury items by carrying a hefty car payment and $8,000 of high-interest debt on a $40,000 income, probably has a lot more options in life than the fisherman had. It is not obviously natural to think of people like her as more *free*.

4.3. A needy species?

A third objection invites us to rethink the arguments against Aptitude: perhaps human needs are such that people don't require much aptitude to profit from high levels of option freedom. According to this objection, individuals have highly diverse natures, so that what they need to flourish is correspondingly diverse. And however error-prone people may be, they are knowledgeable enough about their own natures that their particular needs will more likely be met if they have the power to arrange their lives as they see fit than if they do not. If Jones has a passion for philosophy, and Smith a love affair with ceramic miniatures, they can be pretty foolish and still have a better chance of fulfilling their interests if given the opportunity to engage in those pursuits than if confined in a highly traditional society where those options don't exist. And if this sort of view is right, then it looks like we will need many options indeed if we are going to accommodate the boundless diversity of human tastes, temperaments, talents, and inclinations. This thought is implicit in Feinberg and Mill (see Chapter 11).

The objection takes human beings to be, in an important way, extremely *needy*: whereas most organisms have pretty much the same needs for flourishing as the other members of their species, our natures are strongly idiosyncratic, imposing quite specific and arbitrarily diverse requirements that must be met if we are to find happiness. It is no surprise, then, that we should need a *lot* of options if very many of us are to have our best shot at flourishing. *Homo sapiens*, on this picture, is a high-maintenance animal. Its members have such specific, unique, and inflexible needs that they require a sprawling technological civilization offering each an effectively limitless range of options for living. They can get by with less, but then their prospects for self-fulfillment will be compromised, as Feinberg thought they are for the Amish. Some, including I suspect Amish farmers like David Kline,[40] might call it the "Princess and the Pea" model of human nature. I will call it, less pejoratively, the "special needs" assumption.

Are human beings a needy species in this way? We can all grant that human natures are extremely diverse, with no two people benefiting from exactly the same things. The question is whether our idiosyncrasies are *rigid*, concern matters that are *central* to our well-being, and are well-enough *known* to us—sufficiently, that is, to remove pressure from the Aptitude assumption generated by the psychological findings discussed in earlier chapters. Some people are certainly like this: notably, those described by Mill as having "strong natures," especially forceful personalities like Picasso and Mill himself. Such individuals can benefit from the life of unbounded choice, since they tend to be driven by strong internal compasses that point in atypical directions. Best, probably, to give them the leeway they need to seek their destinations. Conversely, such persons often languish in confining circumstances—this being the stuff of many fictions set in Victorian England—for they cannot be made happy by what satisfies most. They are rather needy individuals in the sense just mentioned.

Having a strong nature may lower the bar for Aptitude. But it is a very strong and surely implausible claim to suggest that *most* people are like this. (Mill didn't think so; he argued that we all benefit from allowing the strong few to develop their talents.) Indeed, the situationist literature suggests the reverse: most of us are pretty adaptable, and tend to conform to those around us. It is not that we are docile sheep; a more charitable and plausible reading of the situationist moral is that we tend to go with the flow, to get along, and make the best of the circumstances we face. When you have to sleep in a hut with your mother-in-law, that probably makes sense.

Perhaps we tend also to be made happy by pretty much the same things, at least in the essentials. Empirical research points to substantial commonalities in the sources of human happiness, with strong and supportive social relations being the most important determinant, probably across all cultures, and engagement in interesting and meaningful activity (particularly if it induces states of "flow"), among other things, also being crucial.[41] But the literature does not tell us whether individuals' needs might still be idiosyncratic enough to require an option-rich regime.[42] Idiosyncrasies are inherently difficult to study.

A more promising route might be to consider the well-being of people living without so many options. On the supposition that people's natures are strongly idiosyncratic, we ought to find substantially lower levels of well-being in strongly bounded societies. There are two difficulties here: first, we don't yet have very robust measures of well-being across cultures, since the usual self-report-based methods are subject to cultural biases; and second, option-rich societies may tend to exhibit higher levels of well-being for reasons having nothing to do with their ability to accommodate personal eccentricities. But suppose we had evidence that the members of some highly bounded societies actually find their way of life pretty satisfying, limits to their well-being owing mainly to extrinsic factors like periodic hunger and disease. Indeed, that their way of life, considered as such, truly *is* fulfilling for most of them, despite the limited menu of options. That would at least weaken the case for a view of human nature as strongly idiosyncratic, particularly since Mill/Feinberg-type arguments for such views tend to emphasize that it is in *what we find fulfilling* that we are most importantly idiosyncratic.

I know of no definitive proof that such societies exist, as we know amazingly little about the quality of life in small-scale societies. Intelligent people continue to argue, for instance, over preposterous caricatures of hunter-gatherers as, alternately, noble or pathetic savages. This state of affairs is a little surreal, given that hunter-gatherer societies comprise the historical norm for human living, providing as well the conditions in which most human evolution occurred, with civilizations only starting to arise in the last 1 to 10 percent of our tenure here on Earth.[43] Whatever their shortcomings, they are not exactly a fringe case. Regarding quality of life, there is no shortage of anecdotes purporting to describe small-scale societies in which many people managed to lead fulfilling lives. Here is one. A colleague who works with a quasi-hunter-gatherer society[44] tells me that the people he studies "love their lives." While their lives are not idyllic, I am told they envy nothing about our civilization except the health care, and have no interest in being "developed." They still live basically as their tribe has done for centuries, and it is not uncommon for members who leave for civilization eventually to return to the traditional life. One member did so even after receiving a college degree and pursuing further studies in the United States, with bright prospects. He found American life "exciting" for the first few months, but it quickly grew too confining and harried—"miserable" was the word—for his tastes. "I don't see how you can take it," he told my colleague. He returned to the tribe. (A neighboring tribe, by contrast, quite likes the offerings of Western civilization, and would probably welcome further economic development—a nice illustration of the diversity of indigenous peoples.)

This is just one anecdote, and we should not infer too much from it. But there is a sizable literature filled with *many* such accounts, from numerous New World reports of "white Indians" abandoning Western civilization to live among indigenous peoples to prominent claims—indeed, according to one critic, the dominant view—in the contemporary anthropological literature about hunter-gatherer bands constituting the "Original Affluent Society."[45] Such portrayals can notoriously be overstated—consider just the question of life expectancy—but they are not spun whole cloth.[46] It is noteworthy that skeptics tend rightly to focus, not on the way of life—which is probably what drives the romanticism—but on the (for our purposes) irrelevant extrinsics such as longevity. It bears remarking as well that life in many "folk" societies appears to exhibit features known to be highly correlated with subjective well-being: in particular, strong social networks and—particularly given the lack of specialization in such societies—challenging, meaningful activities.[47] (Traditional Aborigines doubtless have much to gripe about, but Camus's plaints about the pointlessness of everyday life probably aren't among them.)

Hard empirical data on such questions remain difficult to come by, a state of affairs that is itself worth pondering. But an important recent study of subjective well-being among three small-scale societies—the Maasai, Inughuit, and Amish—found very high levels of reported life (and domain[48]) satisfaction and happiness across the board, and strongly positive overall effect on affect balance and (among the Inughuit) experience sampling measures. Reported life satisfaction among all three groups (5.4 out of 7 for the Maasai and 5.1 for the other two) was higher than that found in American college students (4.9) and Illinois nurses (4.8).[49] This study hardly proves that people in those societies are better off than affluent Westerners, nor even that they are happy. But it certainly is not *obvious* that the typical Amish or Maasai child faces a probable future of frustrated self-fulfillment. To be sure, a hunter-gatherer who does not like hunting will be stuck (I have never heard of such a thing, but I suppose it happens). But so might an affluent Westerner make choices that yield an unrewarding working life. Reading David Kline's account of life in one Amish community, for instance, one would be hard-pressed to regard him or his children, or most of the neighbors he discusses, as *trapped*.[50] By and large, human needs probably aren't that eccentric.

The common tendency to think that human needs are strongly idiosyncratic, requiring a diverse menu of options to give us a decent shot at well-being, may result partly from a confusion about the fact that most people historically, and even today, would have been better off with more control over the way they live. Exploited peasants turning boulders to gravel, browbeaten sweatshop workers, and isolated suburban homemakers have typically confronted, not just a short menu of options in life, but a short menu of *bad* options. Even the privileged, such as Mill's peers, have often been straightjacketed by a thoroughly regimented and oppressive way of life. So in a great many societies, most people have been confined to living in ways that do not suit their natures. However, the fundamental problem may not be the amount of freedom they have to shape their lives the way they want, but the kinds of options they have. Conversely, the advantages of life in affluent Western societies may result more from how good people's options are than from their extensiveness. What I have been suggesting is that some social forms might serve most people's needs even while offering a relatively narrow range of options for living.

Earlier in this section I allowed that individuals with strong natures may tend to require an option-rich environment to flourish. This is not obviously true. One question is how far option-rich environments *make* people needy, proliferating idiosyncratic desires in what is essentially a reverse "sour grapes" phenomenon. Second, if the conditions required for unbounded living weaken community bonds sufficiently, then some community functions may be supplanted by bureaucratic procedures. The bureaucratization of community, with the standardization it requires, may not be favorable to unusual personalities or the development of individuality. Public schools in the United States today, for instance, do not obviously seem like friendly environments for children with strong natures given their tendency toward highly depersonalized and standardized treatment. A third point is that more anonymous social forms, where individuals are more often judged on the basis of superficial information, may foster pressures for individuals to conform to one of some number of standardized personality types, or at least "appearance" types. Of course, tight-knit communities are capable of imposing strict social norms that can hinder individuality and disadvantage atypical personalities in obvious ways. But such communities vary tremendously in this regard, some being more tolerant of difference than others, and can also provide individuals with a level of comfort and personalized attention that affords broad scope for their eccentricities. The psychologist in Malaysia mentioned in Chapter 11, for instance, was visiting another village where he noticed someone darting about from one hiding place to another. When asked about this strange man, the villagers replied, "Oh, that is our thief." He compulsively stole from others, but things always ended up back where they belonged and no one seemed particularly to mind. Obviously not quite sane, this person's oddities were tolerated in a way that would be unlikely in a large-scale bureaucratic society, where he would probably be institutionalized.[51]

5. WHAT MIGHT A POLITICS OF LIBERAL SOBRIETY LOOK LIKE?

5.1. Development policy

The white people, the government comes out here . . . "Look at this poor old woman living in a hogan. Look, it's got a dirt floor, and there's no electricity or running water. We got to *help* this *poor* old woman!" [But] she got her sheep, she got her family, and she's self-sufficient. She's happy and she don't feel poor. This is the way she lived all her life . . . But the government says, look, this is terrible, you're *poor*. We're going to relocate you where there's electricity and water, and build you a nice house. So they relocate her . . . Nobody to help her because her family's somewhere else. And nothing to eat because her sheep are gone . . . So the government has to support her! . . . The government's taken a totally self-sufficient, happy old lady and *made* her poor. *Made* her dependent.

Norman Tulley, a Navajo[52]

As I said at the outset, we will not delve extensively into political questions here. But readers may wonder if the anthropological questions just mentioned will hold any more than academic interest. We have bitten the apple and there is no going back. Yet even if there were no lessons to be gleaned for those of us living in the developed world, there remain very many people in lesser developed regions, millions of them still leading more or less traditional lifestyles, and many of those targeted for development and incorporation into the global economy.[53] We would do well to understand something of the quality of life in those societies before embarking on plans to remake them according to the ideals of liberal optimism. Particularly given that the individuals affected will typically have no say in the matter. And particularly given the record of prior attempts to improve the lives of traditional peoples. (Theirs is not the only well-being at stake: the ongoing mass extinction of the world's cultures[54] represents for us a catastrophic loss of information about human nature and the possibilities for human existence. If trends continue we may soon have no way of living to observe but our own, and precious little perspective on our own species.)

Now clearly, a large portion of the world desperately needs economic and other development. Billions of people would benefit immensely from greater educational opportunities, better jobs, and other kinds of wisely planned development. Many countries are too poor and life in them is too hard. The struggling Indian women that Martha Nussbaum so compellingly depicts could plainly use more money and, in many other ways, a lot more option freedom.[55] One need not be a liberal optimist to see that. It does not follow, however, that expanding people's option freedom should be the sole aim of development policy, or that all policies that enhance people's option freedom will be a good idea. All policies have costs, and the points raised in this book should at the very least make it clear that the costs associated with option freedom can be surprisingly high. This will sometimes tilt the balance of reasons against option-enhancing policies. Environmental costs present a fairly obvious case here: plausibly, we will not want to bring everyone on earth to the living standard of an affluent American.

A stronger point also seems plausible: policies that increase people's options in life may sometimes leave them worse off, even looking simply at the impact of the options themselves. Consider the fictional example of San Marco, a mostly working-class island state whose residents enjoy, on average, an exceptionally high level of happiness, due largely to strong community bonds and a culture that emphasizes the enjoyment of life. (They have a *lot* of holidays and festivals.) Educational attainments there are modest, with most stopping at a high school degree before going on to work in various blue-collar occupations, usually with a 40-hour week: manufacturing, auto mechanic, hairdresser, fisher, etc. People mostly find their jobs at least to be tolerable, if not enjoyable, and not terribly stressful. Employment levels are high and serious poverty is low. The government has before it a proposal to raise the island's level of development substantially, by encouraging more high-tech and other white-collar businesses to locate there and by embarking on an ambitious program to make it easy for most young adults to attend college, allowing them to get at least a four-year degree and to work in a much wider range of mostly higher-paying jobs. Let's assume the costs would be manageable. Should they go ahead with the proposal? It depends, naturally; some of the likely benefits are plain, for instance that those with exceptional talents or strong natures may be better able to develop their potential or pursue their dreams. But some questions about the potential downsides need to be asked: how many of them, for instance, would become the victims of inaccurate forecasting, positive illusions, lay rationalism, and other idiosyncrasies of their less-than-modern brains? How many would choose occupations that would be more stressful or time-consuming, or otherwise leave them less happy than the jobs they would have had otherwise? (Many would now have a *career* to look after, rather than simply having a job or a trade.) In short, would the choices made available to them make them more likely to enjoy happiness or well-being? I do not think the answer to the question is obviously "yes." Consider this as well: what will happen to community and personal ties on the island once this policy transpires? It is unlikely they will remain as strong, and as supportive and fulfilling, as before. Chances are that many youths will use their newfound freedom to leave the island to pursue their careers, and in general the greater mobility—including an influx of outsiders to work in the new businesses—will erode the sense of community, perhaps until there is no more of it than one finds in a typical American suburb. And what will happen to the island's culture of relishing the present? Perhaps this will be supplanted, with so many people now having careers to mind, by a culture of accomplishment, with the attendant drive always to be working, building toward something. (The festivals being replaced, perhaps, by the occasional cocktail party where associates and allies trade boasts about how little they sleep.)

Places like San Marco may be the exception, rather than the rule. But they probably are not the stuff of mere fiction. It seems at least possible that an ostensibly enlightened development policy that plainly gives people more options and more control over their lives could nonetheless leave them worse off. We probably should not just assume that this sort of development will invariably promote human flourishing.

The island described at the start of this chapter is no longer so rustic, and in economic terms it is quite a success story: the material standard of living is much higher than it once was, and children growing up there enjoy much more freedom to shape their lives than their grandparents or great-grandparents did. I cannot say with confidence whether the *quality* of life is better than it was, but it may well be: the island could be an exceedingly harsh place to live, particularly in the old days of truly traditional living when, as one old-timer put it, they were often "cold and hungry." Things like modern health care, boat motors, and refrigeration were a substantial boon to the quality of life there, and it is doubtful that many of the present islanders would wish to do without them. (While developers were never very popular there, neither were strict preservationists, typically outsiders, who wished to freeze the place in time.)

It is less clear, however, whether the expansion of their horizons has made them better off. Inequalities among the islanders have grown, the community has frayed as locals and newcomers vie for the biggest slices of the pie, and the distinctive lifestyle and attitudes of the islanders, which were finely attuned to the local environment, are substantially being replaced by mainland ways that do not conduce to appreciating or enjoying the place as it is. Now busy and overcrowded for much of the year, the island has less room for the relaxed mindset fondly described as a variety of coma. The island's visual centerpiece, the harbor, has been obscured by unsightly buildings, and waters that once teemed with creatures for a boy's aquarium now seem to hold more slime than animal life. With most residents no longer fishing—the trade survives largely through charity—the chief vocation is tourism, and the old independence is largely a memory. They have become utterly dependent on the global economy, and the unique dialect and culture of the island are heading for extinction. Once self-described as "poor and proud," the islanders are not so poor any more, but neither are they quite so proud, their merits now tending to be measured by the cash value of their holdings rather than their skills on the water. The island remains a special place, but it is less special now, and more like everyplace else. Life there is more comfortable, certainly, but whether it is more fulfilling is less certain. The same individuals who told my parents of cold and hunger sometimes intimated that islanders were happier then, and some regard life as harder for young islanders than it was for previous generations. Naturally, some islanders see things differently. But such sentiments were not rare, and I suspect that few are without regrets.[56]

5.2. Politics in the industrialized world

Domesticated biotechnology, once it gets into the hands of housewives and children, will give us an explosion of diversity of new living creatures, rather than the monoculture crops that the big corporations prefer. New lineages will proliferate to replace those that monoculture farming and deforestation have destroyed. Designing genomes will be a personal thing, a new art form as creative as painting or sculpture.

Freeman Dyson, "Our Biotech Future"

Suppose we conclude that the social forms characteristic of the United States, Europe, and other affluent industrial democracies are not well-suited to human nature, or that the option freedoms sought in those nations otherwise tend to exact far heavier costs in human well-being than liberal optimists have assumed. It may seem natural at such a juncture to call for radical policy changes in those countries. Yet we are some way from any such conclusion. For even if we can confidently identify social arrangements that promote human welfare better than our own, some of those forms may not be available to us, or the costs of getting there, moral or otherwise, may be prohibitive.

But offhand it is plausible that policy instruments could accomplish *something* in such nations.[57] After all, many sorts of errors are predictable, and some problems are not easily addressed at the individual level (e.g., Sections 2.2–2.3). Thus, for instance, narrowly focused measures might help compensate for common errors, say by setting default options on retirement plans that counteract status quo biases. On a broader scale, there is a movement to promote well-being by rebuilding or preserving local communities. It is possible that future policy will tilt more heavily toward fostering community, even if that means somewhat less mobility or less option freedom otherwise. Governments are already deeply involved in such matters, so the only question is how far questions of well-being will enter directly into their deliberations, and whether those will sometimes favor less option freedom over greater. Policies in the United States, for instance, promoted the exodus of middle class citizens to far flung suburbs, arguably to the detriment of social connectedness and happiness. Similarly, there are questions about how to maintain a healthy economy in the face of global competition without undermining the very community you are trying to benefit. Perhaps Ireland can sustain its presently vibrant economy, and Italy boost its lagging economy, without ending up like Florida. Further policies might be devised to help reduce time pressures on individuals, yielding a slower and less stressful—if also less prosperous—existence. And then there is our "biotech future," which promises a vast expansion of option freedom for those who can afford to partake in it. Should its progress be permitted to continue unchecked we shall witness, I suspect, a manifold *reductio* of liberal optimism. Perhaps governments could do something to preserve a more humane, or at least human, future.

I do not mean to advocate these or any other policy measures, since many difficult questions, economic concerns included, remain to be addressed. One worry, for instance, is how far a given intervention would worsen unemployment, which is well known to have seriously adverse effects on happiness.[58] The point is simply to illustrate some of the possibilities. Note that probably all of the sorts of policies just mentioned involve paternalistic restrictions on people's option freedom. The utility of such measures will be limited, naturally, by the less than stellar capacity of governments to devise wise policies and implement them in an honest and competent manner. (A problem, note, that traditional economic approaches are not entirely immune to, as some of those who have been on the receiving end of the International Monetary Fund's none-too-light-handed wisdom, for instance, might observe.[59]) But it would take a fairly radical—and empirically extremely bold—skepticism about government efficacy to justify a blanket dismissal of all such measures as hopelessly ineffective.

A more realistic concern is that *too many* paternalistic interventions aimed at promoting happiness will prove effective. Perhaps an example can be found in the Buddhist kingdom of Bhutan, which has sharply limited certain kinds of options, for instance banning television until recently, in response to reasonable worries about their impact on people's happiness. There is good evidence that the introduction of television in Bhutan and elsewhere brought declines in quality of life.[60] Yet it is questionable whether such measures can be justified, at least in developed nations, even if they would promote well-being. The science of happiness may, in short, create significant opportunities for the erosion of personal freedom in the name of personal welfare. This would not commit us to accepting such policies. For we could, and should, continue to endorse traditional liberal constraints on paternalistic meddling with personal liberty, presumably on the grounds that our rationality—however bounded—entitles us to broad claims to non-interference, even if that ultimately leaves us worse off. Only a regime that thus respected personal dignity and autonomy could, on such a view, be consistent with our rights.

Perhaps it would help to clarify the state's moral purposes were we to emphasize, among our basic entitlements, our right to the pursuit of *un*happiness.

"But I don't want comfort. I want God, I want poetry, I want real danger, I want freedom, I want goodness. I want sin."

"In fact," said Mustapha Mond, "you're claiming the right to be unhappy."

"All right then," said the Savage defiantly, "I'm claiming the right to be unhappy."

"Not to mention the right to grow old and ugly and impotent; the right to have syphilis and cancer; the right to have too little to eat; the right to be lousy; the right to live in constant apprehension of what may happen to-morrow; the right to catch typhoid; the right to be tortured by unspeakable pains of every kind." There was a long silence.

"I claim them all," said the Savage at last.

Mustapha Mond shrugged his shoulders. "You're welcome," he said.

Aldous Huxley, *Brave New World*

Afterword

In a series of experiments starting in 1957, psychologist Harry Harlow placed some unfortunate baby rhesus monkeys in a variety of circumstances to see how they would develop. Some were raised in more or less the usual fashion—albeit in a lab—by real monkey mothers. The others were placed with wire surrogate mothers, some covered in addition with terrycloth. Harlow discovered that baby rhesus monkeys prefer terrycloth mothers to chicken-wire mothers, even when the latter dispense the milk, and that in neither case do the monkeys do well. All of them, basically, went crazy, those with the terrycloth mothers less so than those blessed only with chicken-wire mothers. As one textbook put it, "the actions of monkeys raised by surrogates and without their peers became bizarre later in life. They had stereotyped patterns of behavior such as moving in circles or clutching themselves and rocking constantly back and forth while staring vacantly. They exhibited excessive and misdirected aggression, sometimes attacking infants or injuring themselves."[1] These results were, somewhat disconcertingly, taken to be informative.

It would be possible to perform a similar experiment on human beings. We might, for instance, create a civilization in which important human psychological needs, say for attachment and affection, were not well fulfilled—in a manner of speaking, a land of chicken-wire mothers. (This would require a very large grant.) Such a civilization might resemble the less-than-happy society B described at the start of this book. What would psychologists studying well-being in this world find? It is not inconceivable—by now it should seem all too conceivable—that most people would report, sincerely, being happy, and generally being satisfied with their lives. Perhaps their unhappiness manifests itself in ways that do not command their attention, or their ideas of happiness and well-being are skewed by the fact that the way they feel is how people, in their experience, normally feel. In essence, they don't know any mothers other than the chicken-wire variety. And if this is, in addition, a technologically sophisticated civilization, its residents might be impressed by the advanced features that could be fitted to their surrogate moms—speakers emitting pleasant music, cocktail and medicine dispensers, heated mesh, etc. Individuals might choose from a huge array of possible "mothers." And no lice, fleas, or ticks.

It might also seem as though the possibilities for improving people's happiness are very limited. While the lucky ones who get terrycloth mothers do better than the ones with bare wire, the respondents will nonetheless share the fact of lame surrogates for mothers, and the happiness of individuals with real mothers will be unknown. Heritability estimates may be exaggerated in such circumstances, since variations in happiness among surrogate-raised individuals will owe more to genes than variations between surrogate-raised and "real-mother" individuals. This could produce a false impression that happiness lies mainly in the genes, depending largely on an innate "set point."

These psychologists might, finally, scratch their heads over a puzzling finding: despite the splendid accoutrements of their surrogate mothers, and despite the high levels of reported happiness, the denizens of this world exhibit a remarkably pronounced incidence of mental illness. This sort of datum could mark one end of a bell curve of more or less pervasive distress—those individuals pushed over the edge and made crazy by a way of life that suits few people very well. But in light of the tangible positives of this civilization, its psychologists might conclude, instead, that there is just a minority of people who, inexplicably, have lost out: the regrettable casualties of progress.

Notes

NOTES TO PREFACE

1. Wilson 2002, p. xvii.
2. Preston 1995, p. 116. The author fictionalized the name, as the individual was, fittingly, nonplussed about having his real name revealed to a stranger.
3. Carlson 2005, p. 5.
4. Ibid., p. xv.

NOTES TO CHAPTER 1

1. August 27, 2001, p. 34. I have changed the name. I owe the Parker quote to Annas 2003.
2. Nozick 1974.
3. On happiness versus well-being, see the end of this section, and Chapter 2.
4. Freedman 1978.
5. See, e.g., Williams 1985. In this book I will use 'ethical theory' as a broad term for value theory, including not just moral theory but the study of non-moral values as well.
6. Anscombe 1958/1997.
7. Annas 2004.
8. Nussbaum 2004.
9. Perhaps the best evidence for this can be found in the work of Annas and Nussbaum themselves. See, e.g., their excellent volumes, Annas 1993 and Nussbaum 1994.
10. Plato, *Crito*, trans. Benjamin Jowett.
11. Fellow travelers in this endeavor arguably include, among others, Gilbert 2006 and Schwartz 2004, whose books develop similar themes to those explored here. See also Lane 2000 and Offer 2006. I do not know if these authors would like this way of classifying them.
12. The respective subject keywords were happiness, well-being, flourishing, and welfare; and moral, morality, ethics, ethical, virtue, and virtues. Title word searches revealed almost identical proportions.
13. But see Griffin 1986. Also, Sidgwick 1907/1966 and, though not strictly Utilitarian, Sumner 1996.
14. If anyone can lay claim to the title of "godfather" of the science of happiness it is Diener, who has conducted many of the most important studies and trained a sizable proportion of the leading figures in the contemporary literature. Major figures from this era also include, among others, Ruut Veenhoven 1984, Mihaly Csikszentmihalyi 1990, Richard Easterlin 1974, and Alex Michalos 1985. For a good history, showing that research on subjective well-being actually dates at least to the 1920s, see Angner 2005. But the field did not really begin to gel until around the time of Diener 1984, with the first extensive survey of the literature appearing

in Myers 1992. More recent reviews include Argyle 2002, Diener, Suh et al. 1999, and Diener and Oishi 2005. The definitive anthologies for the subjective well-being literature are Kahneman, Diener et al. 1999, and Eid and Larsen 2008; see also Huppert, Baylis et al. 2006. Surveys by economists include Frey and Stutzer 2002 and Layard 2005. Ruut Veenhoven maintains a large online database of subjective well-being research, the World Database of Happiness. For overviews of positive psychology, see Seligman 2002, Peterson 2006, Linley, Joseph et al. 2006, Snyder and Lopez 2002, Gable and Haidt 2005, and the January 2000 issue of *American Psychologist.*

15. The new wave of philosophical work on (psychological) happiness, which is just now starting to gather steam, began with the publication of L. W. Sumner's excellent monograph, *Welfare, Happiness and Ethics* (1996). An earlier review of philosophical work is Den Uyl and Machan 1983; for an anthology, see Cahn and Vitrano 2008. Though not mainly focused on happiness, Valerie Tiberius's important book, *The Reflective Life*, also engages with empirical research on happiness and otherwise shares affinities with the present volume (Tiberius forthcoming). See also Flanagan 2007 and Kenny and Kenny 2006; Fred Feldman and Neera Badhwar also have major projects under way. Several fine books on "happiness" have come out in the last fifteen years, including Almeder 2000, Annas 1993, White 2006, and McMahon 2005. Annas's book has particularly influenced my thinking. But in the terminology of this volume, these books focus more broadly on well-being, not happiness (see Chapter 2).

16. Though not unheard of, as Gorgias and Callicles demonstrate in Plato's *Gorgias.* Some economists maintain such a view of "utility" while not claiming this to be identical with well-being.

17. I will codify the view more precisely in Chapter 12.

18. Chapter 9 will employ a narrower conception of subjectivism.

19. Bentham effectively founded Utilitarianism (1780/1969). He espoused a simple form of hedonism that equates well-being with feelings of pleasure, differentiated only by intensity.

20. Haidt 2006.

21. Nietzsche 1887/1996, p. 24. The Burroughs line is from his poem, "Thanksgiving Day, Nov. 28, 1986."

22. Cf. Hursthouse 1999, Foot 2001. Thanks to Neera Badhwar for pointing out the commonality.

23. "The Happiness Gap," *The New York Times*, October 30, 2007.

24. Sumner 1996.

25. For a typical example, see, e.g., the *New American Dream Survey Report 2004*, by the Center for a New American Dream. In a nationally representative poll of 1,269 adults, 93 percent agreed, among other things, that "Americans are too focused on working and making money and not enough on family and community." See also Myers 2000a.

26. See, e.g., Seligman 1990, Diener and Seligman 2004, and Peterson, Maier et al. 1995, which argue persuasively that the rise in depression is not just an artifact. On trends in happiness, see e.g., Easterlin 1974, 2005.

27. Wilson 2002.

28. Miller Jr. 2002, p. 333; the measures are actually in kilocalories. For the footprint figures, see the *Living Planet Report 2006*, by the WWF.
29. Thermally reconstituted: Moore 2005. Weeds: Quammen 1998. Dust: Bissell 2002.
30. I am not entirely comfortable relating my experiences on the island in this book, for several reasons. Most importantly, personal anecdotes tendered by a philosopher with an axe to grind don't make very strong evidence for anything. Despite these reservations I discuss the island, mainly because I don't know how else to direct the reader's attention to certain kinds of points.
31. Cf. Scitovsky 1976.
32. I learned of this story from Slouka 1996.
33. This take on junk food, and the quote, I owe to Michael Pollan, "Unhappy Meals," *The New York Times*, January 28, 2007.
34. For an interesting variation on the experience machine theme, see Banks 1963, which depicts a future in which people wear hearing-aid-like virtual reality devices, "ear friends," that provide pleasant illusions while they go about their business. Only about ten percent of the time are they fully connected with their surroundings. I am grateful to Bill Rehg for referring me to this story.
35. I am of course trading in crude generalizations, with plenty of exceptions.
36. Though they are hardly eccentric. See, e.g., Carlson 2005, Raphael 1976. Carlson's book gives a taste of a community much like the island I've referred to, but at a far more advanced stage of development.

NOTES TO CHAPTER 2

1. On the senses of 'happiness', see Haybron 2000, 2003, as well as Thomas 1968, Goldstein 1973, and Davis 1981b.
2. In this book I will use these terms interchangeably. Some would object to this practice, for instance believing 'welfare' too closely aligned with Utilitarian doctrines. But theories of "welfare" and "flourishing" seem clearly to concern a common subject matter—what benefits a person, is in her interest, makes her life go better for her. Reserving different terms for different theories simply obscures the issues.
3. In earlier work I called this "prudential," as distinct from "psychological" or "perfectionist" happiness (2000). But these usages suggest that these are different species of a common genus, so I will refer to the "well-being" and "psychological" *senses* of 'happiness.' The "perfectionist" usage, which corresponds to the notion of a good life discussed later, is sufficiently marginal that I will not discuss it. I suspect it results from the sort of confusion discussed at the end of Chapter 8. (As well, the use of 'perfectionist' for it now seems to me very misleading.)
4. Recent philosophers who appear to accept hedonism about happiness include Brandt 1959, 1979, 1989, 1992; Campbell 1973, Carson 1978a, 1978b, 1979, 1981; Davis 1981b, 1981a; Ebenstein 1991, Griffin 1979, 1986; Mayerfeld 1996, 1999; Sen 1987a; Sprigge 1987, 1991; and Wilson 1968. Fred Feldman is developing a hedonistic account of happiness to complement his theory of well-being (2004). Casual references to happiness in the philosophical literature frequently assume it

to be hedonistic. Hedonism has adherents in psychology as well, such as Allen Parducci 1995 and Daniel Kahneman 1999.

5. Philosophical proponents of views making life satisfaction central to or exhaustive of happiness appear to include Barrow 1980, 1991; Benditt 1974, 1978; Brülde 2007, Buss 2004, Campbell 1973, Montague 1967, Nozick 1989, Rescher 1972, 1980; Sumner 1996, 2000; Telfer 1980, and Von Wright 1963. Those making life satisfaction central or identical to well-being (often using the word 'happiness' for it) appear to include Almeder 2000; Kekes 1982, 1988, 1992; McFall 1989; Meynell 1969; Scruton 1975; Tatarkiewicz 1976; Thomas 1968; and Tiberius and Plakias forthcoming, among others. Empirical researchers often identify life satisfaction and happiness—notably, Ruut Veenhoven 1984, 1997.

6. The view has not, to my knowledge, been explicitly defended in the literature prior to Haybron 2001b, 2005 (though see Wilson 1968, and many informal references elsewhere). But affect-based empirical research on "happiness," which has typically been viewed as hedonistic, may be better characterized in terms of an emotional state theory (e.g., in the focus on moods and emotions versus physical pleasures and pains). See, e.g., Kahneman 1999, 2000b, Michalos 1980. Thanks to Anna Alexandrova for pointing out the connection with Kahneman's work.

7. Schimmack 2008, Diener, Scollon et al. 2003. See also the references to this literature in Chapter 1. Among philosophers, Sumner 1996 and Brülde 2007 defend hybrid views (Sumner calls his a "life satisfaction" account).

8. An exception is Seligman 2002. His 'authentic happiness' view of well-being seems unrelated to Sumner's and mine, though Seligman's view and mine accord emotional states, notably flow, a central role in well-being. His "meaning" component may resemble the (conjectured) "narrative role fulfillment" aspect of my view (Chapter 9).

9. This is just a variant of Nozick's experience machine case. The description of the case was: "George is generally very cheerful, highly satisfied with his life, and feels deeply fulfilled. He enjoys his life greatly and has a very pleasant experience on the whole. But he does not realize that his wife, children and friends can't stand him, ridiculing him behind his back. They pretend to love him only because he is wealthy. If he knew these things, he would be devastated. But he remains ignorant of the facts even into old age, and feels completely satisfied through the end of his life. He never learns the truth." Earlier variants of this survey, with 18 respondents, yielded similar results.

10. Likely examples include Austin 1968, Hare 1963, Nozick 1989, and Smart 1973.

11. There are exceptions. Chekola 2007 and Murphy 2001, for instance, appear to use 'happiness' as a descriptive term for a life that is successful from the agent's point of view.

12. On the aforementioned claims, see Sumner 1996 and Diener and Diener 1996. For a possible example of subjectivism, see Diener, Sapyta et al. 1998. The authors do not claim that subjective well-being suffices for well-being. For an acknowledgement that there are other values besides subjective well-being, see Diener and Scollon 2003.

13. For a helpful example, see Kraut 1979, 2002, 2007. We might wish to make an exception for accounts that focus on *ideal* states of well-being: well-being conceived

as a goal in life. 'Happiness' seems apt for this notion. But note that this sort of project risks confusion with inquiry into the good life more broadly (see Chapter 8, §2.5).

14. Parfit 1984. Excellent surveys of the philosophical literature appear in Sumner 1996 and Crisp 2005.

15. Hedonists about well-being include, among many others, Epicureans and classical Utilitarians. Recent defenses include Crisp 2006a, 2006b; Feldman 2004, Heathwood 2006, Mendola 2006, Sprigge 1987, and Tännsjö 2007.

16. Such theories include, to name a few, those of Brandt 1979, Hare 1981, Harsanyi 1982, Rawls 1971, and Sidgwick 1907/1966. For related views, see Carson 2000, Darwall 1983, Griffin 1986, 2000; Keller 2004, and Railton 1986a, 1986b. (Griffin is probably better classified as a list theorist, below.)

17. Sumner 1996, 2000; see also Brülde 2007.

18. "Happy slave" worries, directed against hedonistic and desire theories, concern adaptation: desires adapt to the possibilities people face. So, e.g., oppressed individuals may content themselves with impoverished lives. See, e.g., Elster 1983, Nussbaum 2000b, Sen 1987b.

19. For broadly Aristotelian views see, e.g., Foot 2001, Hurka 1993, Hursthouse 1999, Kraut 2002, 2007; MacIntyre 1999, Nussbaum 1988, 1992, 1993, 2000b, 2000a; and Toner 2006. The Aristotelian literature has yet to integrate fully with the contemporary literature on well-being, so it is often difficult to tell where an author stands on well-being. (Hurka, e.g., rejects a "well-being" interpretation of his view, yet there is considerable overlap in concerns.) For related views, see Darwall 2002, Finnis 1980, LeBar 2004, Murphy 2001, Raz 2006, and Sher 1997. Other accounts sharing much in common with Aristotelian views include Stoic and Platonic theories. On Stoic views, see Annas 1993, 1998, 2003, and Becker 1999. Broadly Platonic views include Adams 2002 and Gentzler 2004.

20. See, e.g., Annas 1993.

21. For general discussion, see Gewirth 1998 and Feinberg 1992a. See also Brink 2003. For a review of eudaimonic psychology, see Ryan and Deci 2001.

22. For a related view, see Warner 1987.

23. Likely examples include Arneson 1999, Brink 1989, Gert 1998, Griffin 1986, 2000, 2007; Hooker 2000, Scanlon 1993, 1999; and Slote 2001. Scanlon's view might be considered broadly Aristotelian (Raz 2006). Finnis 1980 and Murphy 2001 offer lists grounded in a broadly Aristotelian Natural Law framework. For discussion of list items, see Becker 1992.

24. There is some question whether the concept of well-being really denotes a single category, or whether any single concept can do all the work expected of the concept of well-being (Griffin 2007, Raz 1986, 2004; Scanlon 1999). We may want to distinguish multiple concepts of well-being, for instance a concept of how the *person* is doing, versus how the person's *life* is going for her (Kagan 1992, 1994; Griffin 2000). Or even conclude that we don't need a distinct concept of well-being at all (Hurka 1993). While I am sympathetic to some of these concerns, I will not try to sort them out in this book. If anything, I expect they will resolve in favor of the views defended here.

25. Among those who have taken the distinction seriously, see Kekes 1988, 2002; Simpson 1975, and Swanton 2003, pp. 57, 59. Valerie Tiberius discusses something

similar in a wonderful new book, offering a theory of the good life from the individual's point of view (forthcoming). This is not strictly an account of either well-being or the good life. This seems to me an important innovation, and it represents a version of the "methodological eudaimonism" that informs this book (see Chapter 3).

26. See Rawls and Korsgaard on the "concept/conception" distinction (Rawls 1971, Korsgaard 1996, pp. 113–14). In philosophical parlance, 'normative' is basically synonymous with 'evaluative'. The major moral theories, like Utilitarianism, also involve substantive normative claims, so much of this discussion applies to that literature as well.

27. Darwall 2002.

28. Mackie 1977.

29. E.g., Gibbard 1990.

NOTES TO CHAPTER 3

1. For the reader not fluent in American rural vernacular, there is an expression for futility, "That dog won't hunt."

2. I have paraphrased the original statement. Thanks to Jerry Fodor for this. His comments on a related paper largely stimulated me to write this chapter.

3. For a review of most of the literature of this sort, see Den Uyl and Machan 1983. With a few exceptions, philosophers pretty much gave up on the theory of happiness after this.

4. For convenience, I shall often write as if there is a single long-term psychological folk concept of happiness. Perhaps there isn't; there does not, at any rate, seem to be a single *well-defined* concept.

5. Block 1995.

6. See Sumner 1996 on normative adequacy.

7. This proposal is analogous to the approach Paul Griffiths takes towards the emotions (1997).

8. A nice brief summary of the approach appears in Nichols 2006.

9. I use terms like 'kind' and 'category' very loosely here, with no particular metaphysical commitments in mind.

10. I borrow the term 'philosophically primary' from L. W. Sumner 1996.

11. For discussion, see Nichols 2006. The terminology of paraphrasing hails from Quine.

12. Justin Fisher has been developing a related approach, "pragmatic conceptual analysis," in much greater detail. For further discussion and references, see Fisher 2006a, 2006b.

13. A forceful challenge to this claim relates to the phenomenon of adaptation, which has led some to suggest that happiness functions to track *changes* in well-being, not well-being itself. This important argument deserves a more extensive response than I will offer in this book, but I discuss some reasons for skepticism in Chapter 6, as well as Chapters 5 and 10. I do not claim happiness can serve as a proxy for well-being in *all* contexts.

14. Haybron 2003.

15. Sumner 1996.

16. I am grateful to Matthew Cashen for pressing me on these questions. See, e.g., Cashen ms.
17. James 1890/1981, p. 462.
18. For a sampling of the growing literature on this, see Doris and Stich 2005, Knobe and Doris forthcoming, Machery, Mallon et al. 2004, Nahmias, Morris et al. forthcoming, Weinberg, Nichols et al. 2001, and Woolfolk, Doris et al. 2006.
19. Annas 1993. For a similar—but more subjectivist—approach, see Tiberius forthcoming.

NOTES TO CHAPTER 4

1. See Chapter 2 for references.
2. By "pleasant states of mind" I mean mental states that contain pleasantness, not states that are pleasant in the extrinsic way that a sunny day is pleasant. See Feldman 2004 for a careful discussion of the difficulties of stating hedonistic theses accurately. Because 'pleasure' has unhelpful connotations, I prefer to focus on 'pleasantness,' but generally use the terms interchangeably.
3. Stuart Rachels defends the use of 'unpleasure' in Rachels 2004.
4. Sumner 1996, chapter 4.
5. Feldman 1997a, 1997b, 2002, 2004.
6. Haybron 2001b.
7. I will discuss some reasons for favoring internalism in Chapter 9. For more extensive philosophical commentary on theories of pleasure, see Alston 1967, Cowan 1968, Crisp forthcoming, Edwards 1979, Feldman 1997a, 2004; Goldstein 1985, Gosling 1969, 1992; McCloskey 1992, Marshall 1998, Perry 1967, Rachels 2000, 2004; Sobel 1999, 2002, and Sumner 1996. The most thorough treatment is Katz 2006. An excellent overview of current scientific work on pleasure and related matters appears in Kahneman, Diener et al. 1999.
8. For a similar point, see Braybrooke 1989.
9. The title of a Stoic manual by Epictetus.
10. I will suggest in Chapter 7, however, that happiness requires more than a mere predominance of positive affect.
11. In the article on which most of the material for this chapter is based, I discuss this aspect of happiness at greater length under the heading of "mood base" (Haybron 2001b).
12. Affective states such as mood figure prominently in most psychological accounts, and indeed my own view is inspired by that literature. (However, I take a narrower view of the relevant affective states than psychologists generally do.) A helpful discussion appears in Diener and Larsen 1993.
13. On the dispositionality of moods, see Lormand 1985, 1996, and Griffiths 1997. For overviews of scientific work on moods, see Ekman and Davidson 1994, Frijda 1993, and Morris 1999.
14. Thanks to Fred Feldman, as well as Anna Alexandrova and Matthew Cashen, for pressing me on this issue.
15. Internalist accounts might also entail certain dispositions, such as the disposition to *seem* unpleasant under certain introspective conditions. A more exact account will address such possibilities, but here I will remark only that such dispositions

seem largely to be causally inert, quite unlike (say) the dispositions constitutive of irritability.

16. Hedonists may object that happiness ascriptions are bound to be backward-looking on any credible view of happiness. I discuss this objection, and note that answering it reveals an important further problem for hedonism, as well as life satisfaction theories, in my discussion of "present-anchoring" in Haybron 2001b.

17. The meaning of "depth" should become somewhat clearer in Chapter 7. Two points of clarification. First, nonreductive forms of hedonism (see §5), can construe "pleasure" in thicker terms that, e.g., incorporate emotional states in their entirety. Second, I have not claimed that happiness can be purely dispositional, so that zombies or the comatose might be happy. (I will allow in §5.2 that happiness-constitutive *states* can be purely dispositional, but this is a weaker claim; see Chapter 7.) Thanks to Fred Feldman for bringing these issues to my attention.

18. This is the standard use of 'positive' and 'negative' in the psychological literature. For want of a better alternative, I will use these terms differently, so that they do not entail anything about actual pleasantness. I explain later.

19. "Melancholy is the pleasure of being sad." Thanks to John Bennett for advice on the translation.

20. Thanks to Valerie Tiberius for noting this possibility.

21. Hence, in part, my incorporation of mood propensity into the emotional state theory of happiness. For simplicity I focus mainly on prediction, but similar points should apply, *mutatis mutandis*, for explanation.

22. I am grateful to Anna Alexandrova for pointing out that Dan Hausman has made essentially the same point regarding economic theory (Hausman 1992/2008).

NOTES TO CHAPTER 5

1. Gilbert 2006, p. 151. Bickham was imprisoned for defending himself against Klansmen who had shot him. The first quote is reported to be the tormented philosopher's last words (Monk 1990, p. 579).

2. See Nozick 1989, Sumner 1996, and Almeder 2000. See Chapter 2 for further references.

3. e.g., Sumner 1996, p. 161.

4. Diener and Diener 1996, Biswas-Diener, Vittersø et al. 2005, Inglehart and Klingemann 2000, Argyle 2002, Myers 1992, 2000; Biswas-Diener and Diener 2001, Diener and Seligman 2004.

5. Biswas-Diener and Diener 2001.

6. Sumner 1996, p. 145. Some of Sumner's remarks suggest that he might allow for life satisfaction in the absence of a strictly global judgment, but his views seem open to different readings, and in any event his account seems strongest with the global judgment requirement. (The reasons for this should become apparent in what follows.)

7. Andrews and Withey 1976. For the preceding instrument, see Veenhoven 1997. The most popular instrument is the five-item Satisfaction With Life Scale, or SWLS (Diener, Emmons et al. 1985). It is probably a bit less susceptible to the concerns raised about norms and perspectives, mainly because it is partly a measure of perceived well-being, not life satisfaction. See Haybron 2007b. The "ladder of

life" scale, which asks people to rate their lives on a scale from worst possible life to best possible, is still more like this (Cantril 1965). This is probably why it tends to yield less positive results than other instruments.

8. I will often use 'life satisfaction attitudes' as generic, covering attitudes of dissatisfaction as well.

9. Sumner 1996, p. 145.

10. See, e.g., Slote 1982 and Velleman 1991.

11. This point has also been made by Carson 1981 and Davis 1981b.

12. Sandvik, Diener et al. 1993.

13. Suh, Diener et al. 1998.

14. Glatzer 1991. E.g., the two studies found 37 and 46 percent reporting "frequent spells of complete exhaustion or fatigue."

15. Benditt 1974, 1978.

16. Schwarz and Strack 1991, 1999. These articles provide excellent overviews of the literature on this subject. For brevity I refer mostly to them.

17. Strack, Martin et al. 1988.

18. Handicapped: Strack, Schwarz et al. 1990. Hardships: Dermer, Cohen et al. 1979. See Schwarz and Strack 1991.

19. Schwarz and Strack 1999, p. 79.

20. Ibid., p. 77.

21. Schwarz and Strack 1991, 1999.

22. Schwarz and Strack 1999, p. 80.

23. Kahneman 1999.

24. See, e.g., Schimmack and Oishi 2005, Eid and Diener 2004, Pavot 2008.

25. Schimmack and Oishi 2005.

26. The proviso about cultures concerns the influence of norms, discussed below.

27. E.g., Morris 1999.

28. Written September 4, 2003, and printed in the *New York Times*, "The Things They Wrote," March 24, 2004.

29. Depending on his priorities, it is also possible that his life was going well for him, as he might have been doing what he most valued, caring little about the sacrifices. But the case need not be like that.

30. Again, I focus on well-being because happiness is supposed to be a proxy for it.

31. Thanks to Bengt Brülde, who originally suggested this term for an earlier paper from which this material is drawn. Only belatedly did I see the need for it.

32. I am using 'ethical' broadly, incorporating virtues that we don't necessarily think of as moral.

33. It occurs to me that the claims about norms in this section resemble a point raised against certain metaethical theories by D'Arms and Jacobson (2000), namely that what counts as an appropriate response to a value can depend on factors other than the presence of that value. E.g., it may be inappropriate to envy a friend's success, even if that state of affairs is in fact enviable.

34. This sort of case shows clearly the compatibility of my arguments with even strong forms of subjectivism.

35. For interesting discussions of the way brief reflections on gratitude can have lasting impacts, probably in this unreflective way, see Emmons and McCullough 2003, Emmons 2008, and Lyubomirsky, Sheldon et al. 2005.

36. Haybron 2007b.
37. Note that we need not imagine her emotional state as highly volatile. People in her position sometimes oscillate in their attitudes toward their lives while remaining somewhat depressed throughout. Emma-like variations in life satisfaction can occur even as *both* the agent's life conditions and internal state remain largely unchanged.
38. Annas 1993, p. 29.
39. My arguments here do not mean we should expect people's self-reports to be all over the map (and indeed they are not). It is likely that certain norms and perspectives tend to predominate, at least in a given culture. I discuss empirical research supporting variation in perspectives and norms in Haybron 2007b.
40. There is some question whether perspectives and norms can really be distinguished in this way. I have left the notion of a perspective undefined, preferring to rely on the intuitive idea of a "way of looking at things." But on even the most expansive understanding of a perspective we can still distinguish the question of which facts command the majority of your attention from the question of which norms govern your evaluations. That distinction is all my discussion requires. For a good discussion of perspective, see Tiberius 2002.
41. On the various standards applied in life satisfaction judgments, see Michalos 1985.
42. Assuming we have the relevant attitudes in the first place, which we saw is not a trivial assumption.
43. See, e.g., Gilbert 2006, p. 167.
44. Adams 1997.
45. "For Richer or for Poorer, to Our Visa Card Limit," *New York Times*, July 13, 2003. Emphasis added. I have changed last names.
46. This does not mean that we should expect life satisfaction reports to be all over the map. There will almost certainly be regularities in the norms and perspectives that people rely on.
47. The problem thus cannot be avoided by restricting the class of life satisfaction judgments to those made given adequate reflection, taking the "right" perspective, etc., as e.g. Tiberius and Plakias forthcoming do.
48. I discuss aggregative views further in Haybron 2007b.
49. I develop the points in this paragraph at greater length in Haybron 2007b.
50. This generalization gets much weaker across cultures and subcultures (including income groups), where norms will often differ systematically. See Chapter 10.
51. As I noted above and discuss further in Haybron 2007b, the SWLS and ladder of life scales may fare a bit better in relation to these issues than others. On the limits of purely affective measures, see e.g., Alexandrova 2005.
52. Ubel and Loewenstein forthcoming, discussing the findings of Torrance 1976; they note similar but less pronounced results for colostomy patients. The study involving life satisfaction is Riis, Loewenstein et al. 2005. Experience sampling measures of affect also showed no significant difference; while I suspect the instrument missed some genuine hedonic differences (see Chapter 10), the results do suggest that happiness fails to fully track well-being, or other important values, in this sort of case. (This is by no means to say that we should take the patients' extreme preferences as final regarding their well-being; I suspect they would not hold up under reflective scrutiny. My point is that life satisfaction reports can fail to give us the sort of information they are supposed to provide.)

53. This sort of instrument, which would hopefully be less susceptible to attitudinal norms and perspectival variation, might in effect amount to a "D-index" (as in dissatisfaction), similarly to the U-index employed to assess hedonic negatives (Kahneman and Krueger 2006).

54. A related possibility would be "subjective preference satisfaction," which more closely mirrors the traditional concerns of economists. See Chapter 9, §5, to see how such measures might connect with my account of well-being.

NOTES TO CHAPTER 6

1. From Chapter 52 of Edward Gibbon's *Decline and Fall of the Roman Empire*.
2. Davis 1981b.
3. Ibid., p. 113.
4. When I write "happiness consists in X," I usually mean "the (un)happiness-constituting states are X." And while I will usually write 'happiness', the points will generally apply, *mutatis mutandis*, to unhappiness.
5. For a persuasive argument that 'emotion' ranges over multiple psychological kinds, see Griffiths 1997.
6. Hemingway 1952, p. 10.
7. Ibid., p. 105.
8. Ibid., p. 127. Thanks to Ron Haybron for noting that Santiago's dream was unaffected by his recent adventures.
9. I noted in the last chapter that life satisfaction plausibly has an important emotional component. But the intellectual component has to be quite central on standard versions of the view.
10. This term is usefully evocative, but potentially misleading: 'flourishing' is normally used as an evaluative term, whereas ascriptions of happiness entail no value claims. Moreover, happiness could in principle be disordered, in which case we would not think of it as "psychic flourishing."
11. Interestingly, Belliotti 2004 takes a working definition of happiness as "relatively enduring joy, peace, or exuberance," which mirrors the three dimensions distinguished here.
12. Mill 1979.
13. From Preston 1995, p. 21.
14. It is awkward to speak of endorsement as but one species of "affirmation," but I can find no better terms.
15. Diener and Emmons 1984, Schimmack 2008.
16. It may be misleading to use depression here, since it usually involves more than a lack of vitality. But I am not claiming these axes to be orthogonal, and it can be useful to highlight the difference between depression and sadness.
17. Reginster 2004, Solomon 1998.
18. Csikszentmihalyi 1990, 1999; Nakamura and Csikszentmihalyi 2002. Seligman's view of well-being as "authentic happiness" includes engagement in this sense as a central element (Seligman 2002).
19. Csikszentmihalyi 1990.
20. See Woolfolk and Wasserman 2005.
21. E.g., Nesse 2000.

22. An unpublished manuscript. Excerpts were published in Haybron 1991.
23. My views here owe much to a wonderful discussion of tranquility by Charles Griswold (1996).
24. Cf. Barrow 1991 on "enmeshment," and Ebenstein 1991 on harmony with the external world.
25. Mill 1991. Also suggestive is this bit from a letter Jung wrote to Freud: "What we now find in the individual psyche—in compressed, or one-sidedly differentiated form—may be seen spread out in all its fulness in times past" (McGuire 1974, cited by Staude 1976, pp. 313–14).
26. Thanks to Scott Berman for help on the term.
27. As I noted in Chapter 1 (e.g., the Burroughs quote), the individual's own intellect can have an analogous impact.
28. From Allen Ginsburg, "America."
29. Do not all affective states involve appraisals, and so fall within the endorsement dimension? No: exuberance and calm, to name just two.
30. Given the special difficulties of this subject matter, researchers may want to enlist the aid of novelists and others in the arts who specialize in depicting the nuances of human experience.
31. See, e.g., Headey and Wearing 1989, 1992; Cummins 2003, Lykken and Tellegen 1996 and Lykken 1999, Suh, Diener et al. 1996, and Diener and Oishi 2005.
32. Millgram 2000, Railton ms.
33. See, e.g., Diener, Lucas et al. 2006, Lucas, Clark et al. 2004a, 2004b; Lucas 2008, Diener 2008, Lyubomirsky, Sheldon et al. 2005, Easterlin 2003, 2005a; Inglehart and Klingemann 2000, and Headey 2007, 2008.
34. See, e.g., Elster 1983, Nussbaum 2000b, Sen 1987b.
35. Nussbaum 2000b. These cases are meant to illustrate (*inter alia*) the force of adaptation worries.
36. See Chapter 5, Haybron 2007b. For more on "affect type" and related biases, see Chapter 10.
37. This should become clearer in the next chapter. I argue more fully for the claim in Haybron 2001a, and hope to develop that discussion further in future work. For related suggestions, see Lazarus 1994, Morris 1999, Prinz 2004.
38. See, for instance, Argyle 1999, 2002; Layard 2005, Myers 1992, 2000b; Myers and Diener 1995, Seligman 2002, Helliwell and Putnam 2004. For a useful caution about simple lists of sources of happiness, see Diener 2008.
39. For some evidence on this count, see Seligman 2002, Seligman, Steen et al. 2005, Lyubomirsky, Sheldon et al. 2005, and various articles in Eid and Larsen 2008. An excellent popular treatment is Lyubomirsky 2007. On the ancients, see Nussbaum 1994.
40. For worries along these lines, see Woolfolk 2002, Woolfolk and Wasserman 2005.
41. This is not a criticism of positive psychology, of which this book is basically a part. First, societal and institutional questions form a large part of the field (Diener and Seligman 2004). Even at the individual level, there are plenty of people who could benefit greatly from positive psychology interventions. Note that some of the recommendations *are* to change how one lives—e.g., exercise. My point is that some of the most important variables will be very difficult to change without corresponding changes in the social context. See especially Chapter 12.

NOTES TO CHAPTER 7

1. From a letter to Emerson's sister-in-law, Lucy Brown, March 2, 1842.
2. Bob Marley, "Satisfy My Soul."
3. I note some further evidence to this effect in Chapter 9.
4. I will note some further evidence for the central peripheral/distinction and its connection with the self, and thereby to the theory of well-being, in Chapter 9.
5. It is possible that these too are essential properties, or that centrality just requires having enough of these properties, including dispositionality. But I see no need to make either claim.
6. Cf. DeLancey 2006.
7. For brevity, I sometimes use 'moods' to refer to central affective states generally. See Haugeland 1981, p. 271 for a description of moods that parallels my characterization of centrality.
8. Recent philosophical accounts of mood include, among others, Armon-Jones 1991, DeLancey 2006, Griffiths 1997, Lormand 1985, 1996; Prinz 2004, and Sizer 2000. I differ from some authors in holding that moods typically have non-dispositional, phenomenal aspects. See also Ekman and Davidson 1994, Frijda 1993, Morris 1999, and Parkinson, Totterdell et al. 1996.
9. See Kubovy 1999. This seems to me to non-trivially resemble Plato's tripartite psychology (Plato 1992), but I will not pursue this vexed question here.
10. Frankfurt 1987.
11. Or, possibly, that his emotional condition was otherwise positive in a deeper manner than merely his mood, and that this state disposed him to respond favorably. I will return to this possibility at the end of this section.
12. See the discussion of present-anchoring in Haybron 2001b.
13. This case differs from having one's mood constantly pushed in one direction. Mood propensities take at least two forms: as *thresholds* for the triggering of moods, and as ongoing *tendencies* toward certain moods.
14. See, e.g., Parkinson, Totterdell et al. 1996.
15. Cf. research on the connection between serotonin levels in vervet monkeys and social dominance—e.g., Raleigh, McGuire et al. 1991. See also evolutionary theories of depression, e.g., Nesse 2000. I discuss the functions of various types of affect in Haybron 2001a, and expect to return to this question in future work.
16. Parkinson, Totterdell et al. 1996.
17. "At some basic level": the qualifier reflects the relative immutability and near-innateness of temperament. Other factors also contribute to our characteristic emotional dispositions, such as our values and habits of thought.
18. However, consider someone grieving the loss of her spouse. She may be fine so long as nothing reminds her of the loss. The problem is that *lots* of things serve as reminders, thus triggering her grief. This person is strongly disposed toward negative moods, and appears to be less happy thereby. Yet the disposition is not wholly generalized. It is a good question what exactly distinguishes this sort of case from a disposition to cheer up when writing poetry.
19. This is partly why I once incorporated the categorical basis—"mood base"—into the account rather than mood propensity (2001b). Mood propensity now strikes me as more plausible, though not much hangs on the choice.

20. Thanks to Anna Alexandrova and Matthew Cashen for pressing me on these matters. I address some objections to the inclusion of mood propensities (Hill forthcoming), and elaborate further on the reasons for incorporating them in an account of happiness, in Haybron ms. An additional argument for mood propensities concerns the phenomenon of "present-anchoring" in ascriptions of happiness, which I discuss in Haybron 2001b.

21. Previously I suggested the term 'thymic state', from the Greek *thumos* or *thymos*, and following the use of the root in expressions like "dysthymia" (Haybron 2001b). This may be preferable, but I will not press it here.

22. Ito and Cacioppo 1999.

23. Significantly, no students chose the "no opinion" option, suggesting that all respondents were reasonably comfortable making determinations of happiness based purely on emotional information.

24. Results were consistent from one section to the next, and respondents evinced remarkable candor in responses to other questions. The other questions touched on happiness only in asking them how happy they believed themselves and those they know to be.

25. Fredrickson and Losada 2005, p. 685. See also Fredrickson 2008, Larsen and Prizmic 2008. The criteria for flourishing and languishing are drawn from Keyes 2002, which mirrors DSM criteria for assessing mental illness.

26. See e.g., Krueger, Kahneman et al. 2007.

27. See also the discussion of "present-anchoring" in Haybron 2001b.

28. Cf. Griswold 1996.

29. As I noted in an earlier discussion of present-anchoring (Haybron 2001b), in such cases we often qualify the ascription by saying that the person is "basically" happy, emphasizing the discrepancy between the deeper and shallower aspects of the person's emotional condition.

30. Darwall 2002.

31. Cf. Railton's "delta meter" metaphor (Railton ms); see also Millgram 2000. The debate here might be framed as between "delta meter" vs. "welfarometer" models of happiness.

32. I am influenced here by Fredrickson's "broaden and build" model of positive emotion, and will follow her terminology (Fredrickson 2001, 2008). This model may be too narrow, however, for states in the attunement dimension, which may be more about acceptance of one's circumstances than improving one's position. Perhaps it should be "sustain, broaden, and build."

33. This because it matters little whether the changes sought come about through one's own behavior or through the behavior of others. One way to seek change is to signal concerned others that one needs a change.

34. E.g., Diener and Seligman 2002.

35. Kahneman 1999, p. 7, emphasis added. Mill 1979.

36. E.g., Solomon 2003.

37. Stone and Shiffman 1999, Csikszentmihalyi and Larson 1987, Csikszentmihalyi and Hunter 2003, Kahneman, Krueger et al. 2004. For reviews of measurement techniques, see Larsen and Fredrickson 1999, Larsen and Prizmic 2005, Kahneman and Krueger 2006, and Pavot 2008. As I noted in Chapter 5, there are reasons for continuing with life satisfaction-type measures in research on well-being.

38. Kahneman and Krueger 2006. On the need for measures of positive affect, see Huppert and Whittington 2003.

39. Fordyce 1988. Simply having an item asking about *feelings* of being stressed is likely to omit much, since stressful living can compromise our experience well beyond clear-cut episodes of feeling stressed.

40. For a stress measure, see the General Health Questionnaire (e.g., Gardner and Oswald 2001).

41. E.g., Davidson 2004, Urry, Nitschke et al. 2004, Blanchflower and Oswald 2008.

42. See Chapter 10.

NOTES TO CHAPTER 8

1. Rodzinski 1979, pp. 164–5, cited in Carson 2000, p. 273. Thanks to Thomas Carson for bringing this translation to my attention.

2. For the crucial distinction between happiness and well-being, see Chapter 2.

3. For references, see Chapter 2.

4. See, e.g., Dorsey forthcoming, Sumner 1992, 1996, and Hooker 1996.

5. This usage of 'perfectionism' may not be ideal, but I know of no better term for the family of views in question (which is a genuine family; see §2.4). My arguments *do not equate perfection with moral virtue*, and most of them (including the "Angela" case) apply even to wholly non-moralistic views of perfection. Some perfectionists, like Hurka 1993, do not claim to offer accounts of well-being, in which case my arguments will not strictly apply. But they will make it very hard to deny, as Hurka does, that something like an account of well-being is needed.

6. For a good recent discussion, with references, see Brown 2005.

7. I originally employed 'individualism' for this view, and 'non-individualism' for externalism, but that terminology might sow confusion given the very different sort of individualism discussed in Chapter 12.

8. Some externalists, Aristotle included, might agree with this, though whether they truly satisfy it is another question.

9. See, e.g., Nussbaum 2000b.

10. For more discussion, see Chapter 2.

11. While my arguments will often focus on the sorts of goods that hedonists and desire theorists privilege, I will not assume any such view. I focus on those goods simply because they are relatively uncontroversial.

12. Williams 1985, p. 46.

13. Callicles is the immoralist depicted in Plato's *Gorgias*.

14. Though notice that we might find it intuitive both that a moral monster's life is to some extent impoverished *and* that she nonetheless manages to flourish. Hannibal Lecter might be like that.

15. It may help to apply Hooker's sympathy test (1996): would sympathy be an appropriate response to the slaveholder? This test is not obviously decisive, but (as Hooker notes) sympathy need not be inappropriate even in cases like this. Imagine you are an abolitionist relation of the slaveholder, whom you love despite his conduct.

16. Recall that I use 'happy life' for the well-being sense of 'happiness', and sometimes the abstract noun 'happiness' as well, but only when the context makes the meaning clear enough. See Chapter 2 for discussion.

17. See, e.g., Hursthouse 1999, p. 175, Kraut 1979, and Swanton 2003, p. 86.

18. Sumner 1992, pp. 4–5, Sumner 1996, p. 24. I have modified the case slightly for convenience.

19. It might be argued that Angela herself wouldn't see things this way: from her perspective, her life goes better for her than it would have if she'd taken the retirement. I rebut this objection, and note a special difficulty for the related claim that virtue will never seem a sacrifice to the virtuous agent, in Haybron 2007c.

20. Cases like Angela's suggest that even the strongest emphasis on actualization cannot yield plausible claims about well-being. But some readers might dispute my handling of her case while granting my description of Frank.

21. See, e.g., Crisp forthcoming.

22. *Nichomachean Ethics*, Bk. VII 13.

23. Likewise for unpleasant experiences. Aristotle does not seem explicitly to connect his discussion of pleasure with unpleasure, but any disvalue the latter has will presumably need somehow to connect, negatively, with virtuous activity. As I note later, the problems may be even more acute here than for pleasure.

24. *Nichomachean Ethics* 1174b24.

25. See, e.g., Annas 1993, p. 380.

26. As Mark Murphy points out, pain is a difficulty here since it appears to be a "positive reality" rather than a privation (2001, p. 97). Suffering seems analogous on this point.

27. Presumably we must distinguish this from *mal*functioning, since suffering usually involves no malfunction, and indeed can be crucial to proper functioning.

28. *Nichomachean Ethics* 1174b33.

29. I have been influenced here by Eric Brown's reading of Aristotle (Brown 2005).

30. Some of Aristotle's claims about pleasure may seem to suggest that no such conflict is possible, since pleasures that conflict with virtue wouldn't really be pleasures. This seems to me dubious however one reads him, but in any event I am talking about what we ordinarily refer to by 'pleasure', not necessarily what Aristotle calls pleasure.

31. Note that cases like the immoral slaveholder or Genghis Khan suggest that moral virtue probably forms no fundamental part of well-being at all. And cases like Sumner's philosopher, and perhaps Angela, put pressure even on the modest idea that non-moral excellences could form any fundamental part of well-being. (*Contra* the reading of my arguments in Dorsey forthcoming, responding to Haybron 2007c. I have revised the text here to reduce confusion.)

32. Sumner 1992, 1996, 1998.

33. My claim here is neutral between two possibilities: the relevant differences could reside in the concepts themselves, or simply in the roles these concepts play in evaluative thought.

34. Simon Keller is developing a view of well-being as success, construed more narrowly than here (Keller 2004).

35. Darwall 2002.

36. While Aristotelians will deny this is complete perfection, I have argued that they cannot withhold the ascription of perfection entirely without retreating to an intolerable conception of perfection.

37. In describing values as normative for certain attitudes I am not taking a stand on Darwall's claim that welfare is to be *understood* in terms of care rather than the reverse (Darwall 2002). I am saying only that the correctness or appropriateness of such attitudes depends on the (perceived or actual) presence of the relevant values.

38. See, e.g., Haidt 2007, Haidt and Graham 2007, Prinz 2007.

39. I am grateful to Hurka for pressing me on this point (which is not to say he would endorse my claims here).

40. Annas 1993, p. 27.

41. My take on Aristotle in this section is reasonable, I think, but not uncontroversial. But my concern is mainly to explain why perfectionist views seem compelling to so many, whatever Aristotle himself believed.

42. Or perhaps more accurately: we take up a perspective in which we think about how deliberation from the goal-setting perspective should go. I will set aside the qualification for convenience.

43. See, e.g., Annas 1993, especially ch. 1, where she argues that for the ancients the idea that eudaimonia is the ultimate goal that should structure all our activities was considered a virtually empty, platitudinous claim.

44. Annas 2006, p. 520–1.

45. Annas 1993, p. 46.

46. Here I am talking about ethical eudaimonism, not just welfare eudaimonism—see Chapter 2.

47. e.g., Foot 2001.

NOTES TO CHAPTER 9

1. *Nicomachean Ethics* 1178a2–7, trans. H. Rackham.

2. Sumner 1996. See also Scanlon 1993, Arneson 1999. Sumner's characterization of subjectivism is not without difficulties; see Sobel 1997. But those concerns do not impact the broad distinction discussed here.

3. Rosati 1996a, pp. 298–9, Railton 1986a. The italics are mine. The term "internalist intuition" hails from Loeb 1995. For a compelling argument against this putative desideratum, see Darwall 2002. Rosati observes that the autonomy argument may itself be used to defend the internalist intuition.

4. See also Almeder 2000, Kekes 1982, 1988, 1992; McFall 1989, Meynell 1969, Tatarkiewicz 1976, and Thomas 1968, among others. A nice statement of the contemporary subjectivist outlook appears in Kraut 1979. He also offers some of the sharpest critiques (Kraut 1994/1996, 2002, 2007).

5. I shall understand "values" to encompass an agent's general sense of what matters. This might be understood, e.g., along the lines of higher-order desires (Frankfurt 1971). I focus on agents' values because, even though subjectivist accounts of well-being typically give weight to "mere" preferences or desires, subjectivists will surely want to keep these subordinate in importance to agent's values. For instance, "alien" desires for what an agent considers undesirable, such as a smoker's cravings, should not be allowed to trump the agents' best judgment.

6. I borrow this idea from Sumner 1996, though he employs a life satisfaction (or hybrid) view of happiness.
7. This example resembles one used by L. W. Sumner 1992.
8. Informed-desire theories may be qualified in various ways that do not materially affect the arguments here.
9. While I am prepared to insist for the sake of argument that no amount of reflection could alter Henry's or Claudia's preferences, I think such a case unlikely. The point of stipulating that they would not change their minds is simply to make clear that their welfare doesn't wholly *depend* on what they do, or would, think. Subjectivists and objectivists alike believe that optimal reflection will typically lead people to the right values.
10. Thanks to Roger Crisp, Matthew Cashen, and Anna Alexandrova for bringing the latter objection to my attention.
11. For further discussion, see Chapter 7.
12. The linguistic data are not unequivocal, since we can naturally say things like "I am a bit annoyed by that fly." Perhaps they only apply to physical pleasures, as Roger Crisp has suggested to me.
13. E.g., Parfit 1984.
14. On social identity, see, e.g., Appiah 1993, and Sandel 1998. Ideal identity concerns an agent's ideals and values. See Flanagan and Rorty 1990, Frankfurt 1971, 1987; Taylor 1985, 1989; and Watson 1975. See also Williams 1973, 1981. A good critical discussion of Taylor appears in Flanagan 1990. On practical identity, see, e.g., Korsgaard 1996. On self-esteem identity, see Copp 2002. (He defines the self in terms of the potential grounds of an individual's self-esteem.) Finally, on narrative identity, see MacIntyre 1981, Dennett 1991, and Velleman 2006.
15. "Characteristically" because happiness itself alters our emotional dispositions while it lasts.
16. For this reason the term 'emotional self' might be clearer, but it is more awkward and alien to ordinary usage.
17. At least non-derivatively. Exceptions would involve people whose self-conception is tied to these things—a "health nut," for instance. In such cases matters like health are important to who we are, but only derivatively.
18. Note that, while identity is not the only part of the self, it is plausible that major changes in the self should often have implications for one's identity: if *who* one is changes, one's *sense* of who one is liable to change as well.
19. Although some of my claims presuppose that our emotional natures do not always track our desires or values. Thanks to Martha Nussbaum for bringing this worry to my attention.
20. Another sort of case involves changing the way one thinks about things, say by adopting a more optimistic explanatory style (see, e.g., Seligman 2002). It may seem odd to think of this as a way of changing one's emotional nature or emotional self. But when such efforts succeed we do often describe them as altering the self—not just changing what I think or do, say, but changing *myself*. Admittedly the change in one's emotional propensities is cognitively grounded, but it is not at all clear that who we are, emotionally speaking, must be definable independently of how we think. Again, we are not simply talking about temperament.

21. Sumner 1996, 2000.
22. The authenticity constraint does not seem limited to the happiness-related aspect of self-fulfillment. Insofar as self-fulfillment has other dimensions, it is plausible that they too will need to meet an authenticity requirement.
23. Rawls 1971.
24. While richness seems quite plausible as a constraint on self-fulfillment, I am not certain that it is best incorporated under the heading of authenticity.
25. Sumner goes further into the details in his book (1996).
26. Korsgaard 1996, p. 100.
27. This is not to deny that he might be living in accordance with some aspects of who he is. But in this case the conflict outweighs the agreement.
28. See Pigou 1932. Sumner has a good discussion of this move in his (1996).
29. To be fair, no view of pleasure is especially attractive. Pleasure is an elephantine problem for virtually any non-hedonistic axiology: neither desire nor anything else seems capable of explaining its value. Its value just seems *brute*. Perhaps pleasure can be understood as a kind of subjective fulfillment: an aspect of nature-fulfillment that is essentially tied to the subjective point of view. (A further type of "subjectivism" centers not on agent sovereignty but on the subjective point of view more broadly—the agent's experience. In this sense pleasure is a subjective good. But this sort of subjectivism has very different allures from the type that concerns this chapter.) On the objective value of pleasure, see Goldstein 1973, 1983, 1985, 1989; Carson 2000, and Scanlon 1993. For an excellent discussion of pleasure's value, see Crisp 2006a, 2006b.
30. For a related but independent discussion of Sumner's views see an excellent paper by Mark LeBar (2004, p. 200).
31. See also LeBar 2004, p. 199.
32. At least, it does on a plausible reading of "own best judgment."
33. Cf., for instance, Berlin 1969.
34. Loeb 1995, Rosati 1995. Such worries seem significantly worse here than for Sumner.
35. For references, see the discussion of positive illusions in Chapter 11.
36. See, e.g., Annas 1993.
37. Gewirth 1998. Cf. Rosati's discussion of the intuition underlying the autonomy-based argument for internalism about a person's good (which underwrites much of subjectivism's appeal): the intuition is that "the good of a creature must suit *its own nature*" (Rosati 1996, p. 323). See also Rawls 1971, esp. secs. 40, 65, 79, 85–6.
38. See, e.g., Annas 1993.
39. Aristotle hardly considered affect unimportant—he thought it an essential part, and "completion," of virtuous activity—but he regarded it as properly integrated with, and subordinate to, reason.
40. Or, similarly, one's children. Having children does seem generally to be a benefit, at least long term, but I am not sure it makes you happier (aside from various moments of joy or fulfillment that are hard to achieve otherwise).
41. See, e.g., Frankfurt on wholeheartedness (1987), and Copp on self-esteem identity (2002). In fact I suspect that emotions play an essential role in *any* part of the self, the "rational" self thus being part of a thoroughly emotional self. I will set this possibility aside here, however.

42. I am grateful to Talia Bettcher for helping me to see the importance of this point.
43. See Aristotle, *Nicomachean Ethics*, 1098a1−3.
44. "Internalist eudaimonism" might be a convenient alternative.
45. For a similar claim, see Scanlon 1993, pp. 187−8.
46. A similar point appears in Hooker 1996.

NOTES TO CHAPTER 10

1. The reference is to Thomas Nagel's famed discussion of whether we can know what it's like to be a bat (1974).
2. See Haybron 2007a.
3. Some excellent discussions that come close, however, are Schwitzgebel forthcoming, Lambie and Marcel 2002, and Gilbert 2006. For other helpful discussions of matters closely related to this chapter, see Berridge 1999, Berridge and Winkielman 2003, Winkielman and Berridge 2004, and Schooler, Ariely et al. 2003. See also Bargh and Chartrand 1999, Kahneman 1999, Nisbett and Wilson 1978, Simons and Chabris 1999, and Zajonc 1980, 1994. For those unfamiliar with the "basketball" video used by Simons and Chabris, I highly recommend viewing it *before* someone gives away the surprise. It can be downloaded, with instructions, at <http://viscog.beckman.uiuc.edu/media/ig.html>. Most viewers find the result astonishing.
4. Wilson 2002.
5. Gilbert, Pinel et al. 2002, p. 308. The line originally appeared in Gilbert, Pinel et al. 1998. Gilbert seems more open to the possibility of substantial error in a more recent work (2006).
6. See, e.g., Berridge 1999, Berridge and Winkielman 2003, Winkielman and Berridge 2004, and Prinz 2004. A noteworthy exception is Lambie and Marcel 2002.
7. My discussion will apply only indirectly to life satisfaction views of happiness (Chapter 5). AI is nonetheless significant for determining how seriously we should take attitudes of life satisfaction. For if we don't know how pleasant our experience is, we can hardly expect to make informed judgments about the satisfactoriness of our lives.
8. Eric Schwitzgebel has recently made some interesting observations along these lines (forthcoming); see also the discussion of alexithymia in Lambie and Marcel 2002, p. 251. By misidentification I have in mind issues akin to linguistic failures, though the differences between this and some of the problems of AI that I discuss below can be difficult to make out. Thanks to Joseph Neisser for bringing this worry to my attention.
9. "Focused" is vague, and it is tempting to put the point in terms of intentionality. But the intentionality of sensory affects like pains is controversial. And those who think pains purely sensory states without intentional content can still grant that our perception of pain is typically of something with a fairly definite location. Hence "focused."
10. For references to the literature on moods, see Chapter 7.
11. See Schooler, Ariely et al. 2003.
12. See Csikszentmihalyi 1990, 1999.
13. To borrow an expression from Mill's essay on individuality (1991).

14. See, e.g., Lazarus 1994, Morris 1999, Prinz 2004, and Haybron 2001a.

15. See the discussion of dual process psychology in Chapter 11.

16. See, e.g., Wilson and Gilbert 2003.

17. See, e.g., Ekman 1994. However, there is some evidence that even these emotions can be elusive. E.g., one study had sufferers of a spider phobia engage in a series of increasingly difficult interactions with spiders, from walking toward a spider in a jar to letting it walk on their hands (Arntz 1993). Those who received naltrexone, an opioid antagonist, refused to proceed with the tasks at a significantly earlier stage than those who received a placebo, indicating an enhanced fear response. Yet self-reports of fear in both groups were essentially the same at all stages. It is not implausible that naltrexone recipients experienced heightened fear but failed to notice it.

18. Interestingly, Ned Block has been using essentially the same example in his work (Block 1995); his use is independent and predates mine. Evidently the experience is not idiosyncratic.

19. See, e.g., Rosenthal 2002, Chalmers 1997, Church 1995, Prinz 2004, and Searle 1990. The fact that we can come to know about an affect under certain conditions, like after a sudden change, does not affect the point—namely, that *as things are*, we are unable to discern it.

20. Evans and Johnson 2000. Consider also the experience of a dull persistent pain; for related findings with anxiety, see Lambie and Marcel 2002. Frederick and Loewenstein report that noise is actually one of the things to which people do *not* seem to adapt (1999). This is surely correct for some types of noise. But it is equally clear that adaptation, at least to steady noise, can occur (see, e.g., Glass and Singer 1972, Glass, Singer et al. 1977). (There are also multiple forms of adaptation—physiological, hedonic, etc.) Frederick and Loewenstein also express skepticism about adapting to depression and pain *qua* unpleasant experience, but they do not address the questions raised here.

21. It is possible that subjects' experience was degraded in ways that did not escape their notice, but weren't captured by the self-report instrument. For instance, we need to distinguish between the unpleasantness of the *noise* and the unpleasantness of the *affect* (e.g., the stress response) it causes. And given the subtlety of the feelings involved, it is also possible that differences were obscured by the use of a coarse-grained, four-point scale to elicit self-reports.

22. Kahneman has made a related suggestion regarding a "satisfaction treadmill" (1999, 2000b). However, the mechanism he suggests for this involves not fading awareness but escalating aspirations: we need more pleasure to be satisfied or to consider ourselves happy.

23. See the discussion of alexithymics in Lambie and Marcel 2002, and Schwitzgebel 2004 on introspective training.

24. For a good collection of scientific papers on cultural issues and happiness, see Diener and Suh 2000.

25. Suh, Diener et al. 1998.

26. Levenson, Ekman et al. 1992.

27. See Frederick and Loewenstein 1999. The phenomenon is not of course limited to numerical scales.

28. This differs from simple elusiveness in that it concerns not failing to be aware of certain affects but failing to take them into account when making judgments.

29. One study, for example, found that anxiety and tension correlated with life satisfaction at only -0.17, whereas feelings of depression and dejection correlated much more strongly, at -0.46 (Pilcher 1998). This might simply reflect differences in how much subjects cared about these affects, though the differences are rather large. In fact the study instruments *themselves* sometimes incorporate affect-type biases. E.g., the popular Fordyce emotions questionnaire only assesses joy–sadness-type affects (Fordyce 1988).

30. Recall the earlier suggestion that claims about the need for affects to fade with time to free up cognitive resources may not apply to states of the latter sorts. References to the adaptation literature appear in Chapter 6.

31. For references, see Wilson and Gilbert 2003.

32. The term 'expectation effect' may be a bit misleading given that researchers use it to characterize the way people's expectations of a future event can affect their experience of it. But talk of 'theories' of affect, a more common way of describing these issues, fails to encompass normative beliefs about what *should* occur, and it seems to me that these can affect our judgments similarly. It also seems a bit too intellectualized.

33. Schooler, Ariely et al. argue that self-appraisals of affect draw heavily on inferences like this (2003). Cases like the one just described may sometimes involve a sort of irritability that doesn't feel like anything at all, since an irritable mood could be little or no more than a disposition to overreact to things (Chapter 4). But I am imagining a case where one really does feel irritable, but doesn't recognize it until led to do so by inference from one's behavior.

34. I.e., he is what I will call a "Pollyanna." I discuss this notion in §3.3.

35. Schwitzgebel discusses a case of a woman who consistently claims to find gardening unpleasant, evidently sincerely, yet manifests all the signs of joy while doing it (Schwitzgebel forthcoming).

36. This is an example given by Frederick and Loewenstein 1999, who suggest that scale norming can affect the reported valence of a person's experience.

37. For references, see Wilson and Gilbert 2003.

38. Kahneman, Fredrickson et al. 1993, Kahneman 1999, 2000b, 2000a.

39. Redelmeier, Katz et al. 2003, cited in Kahneman and Frederick 2002.

40. Redelmeier and Kahneman 1996, cited in Kahneman 2000a.

41. Schwarz and Strack 1999.

42. Insofar as one's current experience is complex, with positive and negative affects, this bias might generate a form of present-AI as well.

43. Wex 2005, p. 114.

44. For discussion and references, see Headey and Wearing 1992, Cummins 1995, Diener and Diener 1996, p. 183, Biswas-Diener, Vitterso et al. 2005, Argyle 1996, pp. 23–4, and Taylor and Brown 1988.

45. Lykken and Tellegen 1996. This is from their Minnesota twin studies, with a sample of 2,310 subjects.

46. Seidlitz 1993, cited in Diener and Diener 1996.

47. I will return to the universality of positivity biases in the next chapter, but it is possible that even kvetches have positivity biases in important realms, and even tend to view their lives favorably given the right context.

48. King and Napa 1998.

49. But not meaningless—multinational surveys yield interesting regularities that are unlikely to be due simply to cultural norms. See the papers collected in Diener and Suh 2000. On differences in norms, see Eid and Diener 2001.

50. For a trenchant discussion of the importance of cultural norms, see Wierzbicka 2004. Naturally such biases can affect actual well-being as well as reports—optimists probably tend to feel better than pessimists. The question here is how far they can influence judgments independently of actual well-being.

51. Oishi 2002. A different result, however, was obtained by Scollon, Diener et al. 2004.

52. Kim 2004.

53. Krueger, Kahneman et al. 2007. I am grateful to Alan Krueger for sharing this study with me.

54. Kahneman and Riis 2005.

55. Similarly, Martha Nussbaum discusses a survey of widows and widowers in India a year after the Great Bengal Famine of 1943. 45.6 percent of widowers rated their health as "ill" or "indifferent," while only 2.5 percent of widows did (in fact none reported "indifferent"). Yet the widows' health was actually *worse* (Nussbaum 2000b, p. 139).

56. Oddly, life satisfaction scores in this study were not unequivocally lower among the French, with Americans being more likely to use the extremes of the scale, perhaps due to differences in norms.

57. The U-Index assesses the percentage of time people spend in predominantly unpleasant states (see Chapter 7).

58. Lyubomirsky, King et al. 2005.

59. For reviews, see Diener and Biswas-Diener 2002 and Biswas-Diener 2008.

60. For discussion and references, see Morris 1999, Schwarz and Strack 1999.

61. Evidently, at least Schooler, Ariely et al. have (2003, p. 45).

62. Ubel and Loewenstein forthcoming report having conversations with kidney transplantation patients who say "only after being relieved of kidney failure did they realize how unhappy they used to be when they had to receive dialysis three times a week." Given that measures of affect fail to find any difference between such patients and controls (Chapter 5), this could be evidence that those measures are missing something, perhaps due to AI.

63. Diener and Diener 1996, Biswas-Diener, Vittersø et al. 2005.

64. Ito and Cacioppo 1999.

65. Some of the higher "negative" response rates come from studies using a three-point scale where there is no negative option, the least favorable possibility being "not too happy" (vs. "very" or "pretty" happy). See, e.g., Gurin, Veroff et al. 1960, cited in Diener and Diener 1996, where 11 percent chose this option, and a recent Pew survey, in which 15 percent chose it ("Are We Happy Yet?" February 13, 2006, from the Pew Research Center). Moreover, some of these studies, including the Pew study, use a very confused instrument, popularized by the General Social

Survey, that appears to be measuring life satisfaction more than happiness; the question starts out asking "how would you say things are these days in your life" (to which, incidentally, "pretty happy" does not seem an obviously intelligible answer). As I noted above, life satisfaction measures tend to yield less positive results than self-reports of happiness.

66. Andrews and Withey 1976. While this study nominally assesses life satisfaction (which at any rate tends to yield similar, if somewhat less rosy, results), the response scale appears to measure happiness instead (Argyle 2002), and the results are more typical of happiness than life satisfaction studies.

67. Based on a national sample of 1,027 adults. Report titled, "Most Americans 'Very Satisfied' with their Personal Lives," December 31, 2007, from Gallup, Inc.

68. The WVS data appear in Inglehart and Klingemann 2000.

69. Stone and Shiffman 1999, Csikszentmihalyi and Hunter 2003, Pavot 2008.

70. Brandstatter 1991. See also Kahneman, Krueger et al. 2006, where subjects reported being in a "bad" or "a little low or irritable" mood for an average of 20 percent or more of the time depending on demographic. Since the measure likely missed important negatives, this suggests that many people were well over 20 percent in negative affect.

71. Krueger, Kahneman et al. 2007. The latter figures suggest both that very low levels of negative affect are possible on these measures and that even these measures probably skew positive.

72. See, e.g., Ryan and Deci 2001, Ryff 1989, Ryff and Singer 1998, and Keyes 2002.

73. Keyes 2002; see also Keyes 2005, 2007. My adjustment is based on Keyes' report of an 8.5 percent "pure depression" (not languishing) rate *for the last 12-month period*. Since depressive episodes last six months on average (below), this should probably be cut in half to yield a current prevalence.

74. Seligman 1990.

75. Ohayon 2007.

76. Kessler, DuPont et al. 1999.

77. 1993. Clinical evaluations were based on subjects' descriptions of various personal recollections. The stress tests are essentially an example of using mood inductions to measure happiness (see Chapter 7).

78. The BDI correlated with self-reported happiness at -0.54 in the Fordyce study (1988).

79. For a discussion of "repressors" who seem clueless about high levels of anxiety, see Lambie and Marcel 2002.

80. For instance, someone with a traumatic childhood may be happy but susceptible to extreme distress when made to reflect on the past (though some might question how happy such individuals really are).

81. National Institute for Occupational Safety and Health (1999), citing a large study by Northwestern National Life.

82. "Stress and Mind/Body Health," February 23, 2006, posted at: <http://www.greenbergresearch.com/articles/1670/1889_APAStressReport.pdf>.

83. "Tired of Having Too Much to Do?" *The Boston Globe*, February 20, 2003. From research by ACNielsen.

84. Research by the Families and Work Institute, cited by Veninga 2000.

85. Kessler, DuPont et al. 1999, Kessler, Chiu et al. 2005. The diagnosis requires at least six months of anxiety, and GAD tends to be longer-lasting than MD.

86. Kessler, Chiu et al. 2005.

87. Lepine 2002.

88. Twenge 2000.

89. Kessler, Chiu et al. 2005.

90. Kessler, Berglund et al. 2005.

91. Figures from Medco, reported in "F.D.A. Expands Suicide Warning on Drugs," *The New York Times*, May 3, 2007.

92. During the period 1999–2002. From "Health, United States, 2007," from the National Center for Health Statistics, Centers for Disease Control.

93. This figure, and the other prescription numbers cited in the remainder of this paragraph, come from IMS Health, Inc. I am grateful for IMS Health's permission to use these data.

94. My calculation assumes a population of 299 million (U.S. Census Bureau), and an average of one prescription per individual treated. The calculation is very conservative, since adults comprise only three-fourths of the U.S. population (U.S. Census Bureau), and a single prescription may be used for more than one month. (Accordingly, the IMS figures yield substantially lower rates of antidepressant use than the CDC study, with 10,647,168 prescriptions for SSRI's in that month. Using the same assumptions, this yields a rate of only 3.6 percent, less than half the CDC's 8 percent. Yet usage rates are generally believed to have *risen* substantially since the CDC study.)

95. Pearson, Johnson et al. 2006.

96. Quan 2006.

97. Lauderdale, Knutson et al. 2006.

98. "Loneliness Can Be the Death of Us," *The Boston Globe*, April 22, 1996.

99. McPherson, Brashears et al. 2006.

100. Self-abuse: Whitlock, Eckenrode et al. 2006. Suicide: National College Health Assessment: Reference Group Report. Baltimore: American College Health Association, Fall 2006.

101. Csikszentmihalyi and Hunter 2003, Csikszentmihalyi 1999, Csikszentmihalyi and Schneider 2000, Luthar and Becker 2002, Luthar 2003.

102. Csikszentmihalyi 1999, p. 823.

103. For a good collection of papers on the use of introspective evidence in cognitive science, see Jack and Roepstorff 2003, 2004. See also Jack and Shallice 2001, and Jack and Roepstorff 2002. See also Schwitzgebel and Hurlburt 2007.

104. See also Chapter 5, Haybron 2007b. A lucid discussion of the issue appears in Gilbert 2006.

105. See, e.g., Diener 1994, Argyle 1996, Diener, Suh et al. 1997, Diener, Suh et al. 1999, Larsen and Fredrickson 1999, Larsen and Prizmic forthcoming.

106. Lyubomirsky, King et al. 2005, Oishi and Koo 2008, Kahneman and Krueger 2006.

107. See Chapter 5, Haybron 2007b.

108. See, e.g., Diener and Seligman 2004, Lucas, Clark et al. 2004b, Argyle 2002, Frey and Stutzer 2002, and Layard 2005.

109. Some details have been changed to protect the innocent.

NOTES TO CHAPTER 11

1. Navin Johnson's words, from the Carl Reiner film, were spoken by Steve Martin.
2. Sterelny 2003.
3. Feinberg 1992b, p. 84; emphasis added. Harvard economist Edward Glaeser recently offered a particularly explicit statement of this sentiment in the popular media (Glaeser 2007; see Chapter 12).
4. For good reviews, see Gilbert 2006, Hsee and Hastie 2006, Trout 2005, Shafir and LeBoeuf 2002. See also Botti and Iyengar 2006, Camerer, Issacharoff et al. 2003, Camerer, Loewenstein et al. 2005, Diener and Seligman 2004, Frank 1999a, Kahneman 1994, 2003; Kahneman and Thaler 2006, Offer 2006, Rabin 1998, Schooler, Ariely et al. 2003, Schwartz 2000, Schwartz 2004, Stich 1999, Sunstein and Thaler 2003, Thaler 2000. I will not review the economic literature detailing the role of liberal optimism in classical economic thought, as economists' views in this regard are so well-known, but references can be found in many of the articles just cited (see, e.g., Botti and Iyengar 2006).
5. For a helpful discussion, see Pettit 2003.
6. Cf. Pettit on option freedom as "non-limitation" (2003).
7. "Roughly" and similar provisos are meant to allow for a fringe of special cases like trivial options.
8. Again, many of the points to follow can be adapted to a wide range of prudential goods, and thus could be maintained even by those who consider happiness badly overrated.
9. For helpful discussion and review of the rationality question, see Samuels, Stich et al. 2002a, 2002b.
10. See, e.g., Loewenstein 1996, Frederick, Loewenstein et al. 2003, Offer 2006, Oswald and Powdthavee 2007.
11. For reviews, see Wilson and Gilbert 2003, Gilbert 2006, Wilson and Gilbert 2005, as well as Wilson, Gilbert et al. 2002 and Gilbert, Pinel et al. 1998.
12. Brickman and Campbell 1971, Suh, Diener et al. 1996.
13. Gilbert, Pinel et al. 1998.
14. Gilbert, Driver-Linn et al. 2002. The authors previously called it a "durability bias" (Gilbert, Pinel et al. 2002).
15. Kahneman and Tversky 1979. A better known effect is *focalism*, or the focusing illusion, where a narrow focus on the matter of interest causes us to overlook other factors that impact our happiness (Wilson, Wheatley et al. 2000, Schkade and Kahneman 1998, and Kahneman 1999). A further possible source is worth mentioning: some things may loom too large in prospect because we fail to anticipate changes in comparison classes; e.g., we may want a higher-status job because we correctly envision that being higher status *when around our current peers* would make us happier, forgetting that we will later be comparing ourselves to a different group of higher-status peers. This would be an instance of "projection bias" (see, e.g., Loewenstein and Angner 2003).
16. Dunn, Wilson et al. 2003.
17. The *locus classicus* in this literature is Taylor and Brown 1988; see also Taylor and Brown 1994. An excellent recent discussion appears in Gilbert 2006. My discussion draws largely on their articles, and further references can be found there. There

has been considerable debate about various particulars, notably whether positive illusions really promote well-being (see, e.g., Colvin and Block 1994, Colvin, Block et al. 1995, Badhwar forthcoming). But there seems little question that positive illusions are prevalent, at least in the West. As well, my purposes do not require positive illusions across the board: significant tendencies toward excessive optimism and to overrate one's life, both of which seem to be well established, will suffice. Other philosophical discussions include Tiberius forthcoming, Flanagan 1991, 2007 and Elga 2005.

18. A seminal source on "unrealistic optimism" is Weinstein 1980.

19. "Not Insured, and Not Worried," *The New York Times*, October 6, 1999.

20. E.g., Heine, Lehman et al. 1999.

21. See, e.g., Endo, Heine et al. 2000, Sedikides, Gaertner et al. 2003, Mezulis, Abramson et al. 2004, Sedikides, Gaertner et al. 2005. For doubts, see Heine 2005, Heine and Hamamura 2007.

22. The difficulty of speaking generically of "positive illusions," as if they constituted a natural kind, is fairly plain. One complication is the body of literature on "negativity bias" and the idea that generally "bad is stronger than good" in human psychology (see, e.g., Baumeister, Bratslavsky et al. 2001, Rozin and Royzman 2001). It appears that, while we do tend to put a positive spin on ourselves and our lives, we also tend to react much more strongly to negative than positive information. The latter may in part be why we do the former: if the bad is hard on us, we may be motivated to view ourselves as favorably as we can. Negativity bias can raise problems of its own.

23. Markus and Kitayama 1991.

24. Kline 1990, pp. xviii–xix.

25. The term, and the characterization of the issue, hails from Hsee, Hastie et al. 2003. (Although I simplify in some respects.) For related issues, see Frey and Stutzer 2004, Amir and Ariely 2007.

26. Tversky and Griffin 1991.

27. Hsee, Zhang et al. 2003. See also Hsee and Hastie 2006.

28. This fact presents a problem for scientific research on well-being: how do you apply scientific methods to what is often impossible to articulate, much less quantify? A recent review of the hunter-gatherer literature, for example, expresses bafflement at the widespread acceptance of the "original affluent society" view among anthropologists, despite serious flaws in the best-known quantitative studies used to support the idea that many hunters enjoy a very high quality of life (Kaplan 2000; for the origins of this view, see Sahlins 1968). Perhaps the idea persists, not because of neo-Rousseauian romanticism, but because the researchers who have actually dwelt among hunters have often observed a way of life whose gratifications are substantial but not readily quantified (see, e.g., Bird-David 1992, p. 25, who notes that "most specialists . . . recognized, if only intuitively, that Sahlins 'had a point' ").

29. See, e.g., a 2004 poll by Widmeyer Research for the Center for a New American Dream at <http://www.newdream.org/about/PollResults.pdf>.

30. See, e.g., Carlson 2005.

31. Wolff 1994, pp. 176–83.

32. One could readily imagine well-meaning development agencies "gifting" villages with this sort of contrivance—perhaps resulting mainly in more time spent watching television. See also "Seven Amish Farms," in Berry 1981.

33. The literature on this is massive. See, e.g., various papers in Kahneman and Tversky 2000.
34. Kahneman, Knetsch et al. 1990.
35. Kermer, Driver-Linn et al. 2006.
36. See, e.g., Kahneman 1999.
37. See, e.g., Gilbert, Pinel et al. 1998, Gilbert 2006, Ross and Wilson 2003.
38. Yiddish for "no evil eye," or "knock on wood."
39. See Haybron 2007b.
40. See, e.g., Larrick 2004, Shafir and LeBoeuf 2002, Trout 2005.
41. See Gollwitzer and Kinney 1989, Taylor and Gollwitzer 1995. A further problem is that conscious deliberation in some domains, including complex decisions, may tend to yield worse results (Wilson and Schooler 1991, Wilson, Lisle et al. 1993, Dijksterhuis, Bos et al. 2006).
42. Gilbert 2006, p. 214.
43. On credit card debt and the savings rate, see Schor 1998, 1999; on bankruptcies, see Frank 1999b. The U.S. Department of Commerce reported that the personal savings rate in 2005 was −0.5 percent (see "As Personal Savings Fall, a Comeuppance Is Due," *The New York Times*, February 4, 2006).
44. Schor 1992.
45. For the reader raised by two parents: would you prefer that one of them left the family, or that your family was poor? Perhaps many of these children would be better off in some third world countries, with intact families. The preceding figures on family breakdown are cited in Layard 2005.
46. Census figures reported in the New York Times, "Who Americans Are and What They Do, in Census Data," December 15, 2006. The cited figure was 1,548 hours of television per year.
47. *Ibid.* By contrast, in 1970 79 percent placed developing "a meaningful philosophy of life" at the top—itself not necessarily a great idea, but probably better than rank greed.
48. David Brooks, "A Nation of Grinders," *The New York Times*, June 29, 2003.
49. David Brooks, "The Triumph of Hope Over Self-Interest," *The New York Times*, January 12, 2003.
50. Cutler, Glaeser et al. 2003, Vasan, Pencina et al. 2005. A recent article in a U.S. Department of Agriculture magazine suggests, incredibly, that Americans' rapid weight gain in recent decades may be a "rational response" to changing technology and prices (Kuchler, Golan et al. 2005). This is reportedly a common view among economists (Oswald and Powdthavee 2007); if so, it is surely a *reductio* of their position.
51. Cited in Andrews 2004.
52. Thanks to Gerardo Camilo for discussion, and for suggesting examples along these lines.
53. For useful discussion and reviews of the relevant literature, see Barkow 1997, Nesse and Berridge 1997, Buss 2000, Grinde 2002, Nesse 2004, Nesse 2005, and Hill and Buss 2008. A major aspect of this work is "mismatch theory," according to which much contemporary ill-being arises from a mismatch between the EEA and the current environment.

54. See, e.g., Everett 2005.
55. This theme is prominent in Gerd Gigerenzer's work (see, e.g., Gigerenzer 2002). His and other work in ecological rationality and evolutionary psychology is often positioned in sharp opposition to the heuristics and biases literature we have been discussing, notably by the authors themselves. But the conflict is largely artificial—there is no incompatibility between evolutionary psychology and the idea that people systematically make errors in certain domains (on this, see Samuels, Stich et al. 2002a). Quite the contrary.
56. See Wegner and Bargh 1998, Bargh and Chartrand 1999, Haidt 2001, Shafir and LeBoeuf 2002, Kahneman 2003, Stanovich 2004, Hassin, Uleman et al. 2005, Bargh and Williams 2006, 2006, Bargh and Morsella 2008, Wegner 2003.
57. The old classic here is Nisbett and Wilson 1978.
58. Gazzaniga 1970.
59. Bargh, Chen et al. 1996.
60. Haidt 2006. See also Haidt 2001, as well as Knobe and Leiter 2007 and Leiter 2007. John Doris has been working on a variant of such a model as well.
61. For reviews, see Ross and Nisbett 1991 and Doris 2002.
62. And perhaps as well on other situational factors, though it seems likely that social factors will have the strongest systematic effect. Note that there is little controversy over the core situationist thesis, that human behavior is remarkably sensitive to situational influence. The debate centers on the much stronger claim that personality variables aren't that important. Apparently most researchers now grant a large role to both types of variables.
63. This sort of view appears to be gathering steam. See especially Haidt 2001, 2007, 2008. John Doris and Shaun Nichols have been developing a similar view in talks and unpublished work. Other sentimentalists working in a similar vein include, to name a few, Greene 2008, Knobe and Leiter 2007, Nichols 2004, Prinz 2007.
64. Interestingly, Kant seems not to be among those holding this view, as the pessimistic quote above suggests. But his liberalism does not depend on liberal optimism, as Mill's does. Humean sentimentalism about motivation, on which reason alone cannot motivate people to act, is compatible with rationalism in the sense intended here. For Humeans can still accord a special place to reflective deliberation.

NOTES TO CHAPTER 12

1. Glaeser 2007, and Wolff 1994, p. 113. The Sng'oi, or Senoi, are a mountain-dwelling indigenous people in Malaysia. The closest thing to a systematic anthropological treatment, to my knowledge, is Denton 1968, which Wolff tells me discusses a related but different tribe (personal communication).
2. For another illustration of this point, see Crawford 2006.
3. On exceptions, see, e.g., Dworkin 1982. The notions of option freedom and bounded choice employed here were explained in Chapter 11.
4. *Ceteris paribus*, that is. This claim is not entailed by the first, since some increases in freedom may have serious drawbacks while not offering *enough* freedom to gain certain important benefits. The focus on average well-being may need refinement, since I am setting aside issues about distribution. We might think a society better

promotes well-being if, e.g., it insures people better against catastrophes, even if average welfare is diminished.

5. Such theories of justice tend to focus on meeting certain minimums rather than increasing people's capabilities or resources without limit. But the general sentiment seems to be that almost all increases in capabilities or resources are, in themselves, at least desirable (even if they go beyond the requirements of justice). See, e.g., Sen 2000.

6. See, e.g., Mill 1991b, Feinberg 1992b, and Glaeser 2007.

7. "Call Me Local," *The New York Times*, August 30, 2006.

8. Though those lacking these freedoms may not resent it; Amish, Inughuit, and Maasai subjects in one series of studies all tended to report being satisfied with their privacy (Biswas-Diener, Vitterso et al. 2005).

9. E.g., Peterson 1999, Ryan and Deci 2001.

10. I hinted at the start of this chapter that the specialization that comes with affluence may tend to yield *helplessness* more than control, a point echoed by Wolff 1994. Twenge, Zhang et al. 2004 reports that, on average, college students in 2002 felt less control over their lives than 80 percent of college students did in the early 1960s.

11. For fascinating discussions of the psychological literature, see Barry Schwartz 2000, 2004 and Botti and Iyengar 2006. I draw heavily on Schwartz's work in what follows. A prescient philosophical discussion appears in Dworkin 1982. See also Gilbert 2006, chapter 9.

12. Offer 2006. This has the opposite effect of loss aversion, which can involve sticking too firmly to our commitments.

13. Schwartz 2000.

14. Iyengar, Wells et al. 2006.

15. Iyengar and Lepper 2000.

16. For discussion, see Botti and Iyengar 2006.

17. Schwartz, Markus et al. 2006.

18. Peterson, Maier et al. 1995, Schwartz 2000, 2004.

19. From Iris Murdoch: " 'Happiness,' said Willy, 'is a matter of one's most ordinary everyday mode of consciousness being busy and lively and unconcerned with self. To be damned is for one's ordinary everyday mode of consciousness to be unremitting agonising preoccupation with self' " Murdoch 1968, p. 187.

20. See, e.g., Nisbett 2003, as well as Seligman 1990 on individualism and the rise of the "California self." See also Twenge 2002, which finds changes in personality over recent decades. It is possible that cultures focused on the promotion of option freedom also tend to foster materialistic values, which are believed to undercut well-being (Kasser 2002). But we should not assume that greater affluence in a society always yields greater materialism. Poorer people are often quite materialistic.

21. Thoreau: "This curious world we inhabit is more wonderful than convenient; more beautiful than it is useful; it is more to be admired and enjoyed than used" (speech to graduating class at Harvard, 1837, quoted in Berry 1990, p. 138). See also Plato's acid take on the "democratic man," *The Republic* 561c–d.

22. "The Yucatec Maya: A Case Study in Marriage and the Family," from the *Faces of Culture* series.

23. One limitation of market forces that I will only mention in passing is that they respond only to people's choices, or rather suppliers' expectations about choices, and this may not very well reflect what people *want*, or care about. We've seen numerous sources of divergence due to irrationality and the like, but it is also important to note that people very often lack well-defined preferences, thus being very sensitive to framing effects and contextual influences. The fact that people choose one good over another may thus have nothing to do with their priorities. On preference instability, see the papers collected in Lichtenstein and Slovic 2006, as well as Kahneman and Tversky 2000.

24. See, e.g., Frank 1999a, Layard 2005.

25. I am keeping this informal and imprecise, intending to gesture at certain forms of decoupling that should be easy to discern. But there are some respects in which the same social arrangements may yield tighter forms of coupling, for instance the way the global economy links distant people who previously did not interact at all.

26. E.g., Putnam 2000, Lane 2000.

27. I will often omit the reference to "obliging," since it should be clear that not just any context will do. Other empirically-oriented work on well-being that may be sympathetic to a contextualist outlook includes, e.g., Schwartz 2000, 2004; Eckersley 2006, Helliwell and Putnam 2004, Putnam 2000, Diener and Seligman 2004, Lane 2000, Offer 2006, and Layard 2005. I do not know how many of these authors would endorse contextualism.

28. E.g., MacIntyre 1981 and Sandel 1998.

29. See the discussion of Feinberg at the start of Chapter 10.

30. McKibben 2003. As McKibben points out, the noteworthy fact about the Amish is not their refusal of many technologies but the simple fact that they think *at all* about whether a new technology is worth adopting.

31. Obviously, you might agree with the Amish on these points while objecting to major features of their culture.

32. In the moral case, the question is how far the moral life, at least ideally, depends on context: does the morally good life typically depend overwhelmingly on the individual's character and wisdom? Or does it substantially depend on the salutary influences of an obliging context? Individualism in moral psychology has recently come under fire from situationists and others, notably Jonathan Haidt, whose "social intuitionist" account of moral judgment takes moral deliberation and reflection to be primarily a social or collective affair and not, for the most part, something that individuals effectively undertake on their own. See Chapter 11 for references. John Doris and Shaun Nichols have also been exploring what I would call moral contextualism.

33. A similar point is made by Diener 2008.

34. Recall my remarks to this effect at the end of Chapter 6.

35. For some possible examples, see Arneson 1999, Brink 1989, Griffin 1986, Hurka 1993, Rawls 1971.

36. For a stark example, see Everett 2005 on the Pirahã, whose conceptual scheme is said to be restricted to "concrete, immediate experience," where this extends as far as the memories of those with direct experience. It is questionable whether the notion of a life plan could meaningfully be applied to such people, still more so

whether they could appreciate the practice of critically reflecting on one's values. And it is very dubious indeed that some philosophers' notions about the merits of certain activities would find much sympathy among them (e.g., Raz on hunting 1986, p. 161). Against the idea that they are primitive, Everett writes that the Pirahã "are some of the brightest, pleasantest, most fun-loving people that I know" (p. 621n).

37. I will set aside special issues relating to children, though they raise further difficulties for the trope in question.

38. This sort of strategy is familiar from the "maximin" principle employed by Rawls 1971.

39. Hints of the tradeoffs can be seen in the back-and-forth work lives of some Hatteras fishermen in Carlson 2005.

40. Kline was quoted in Chapter 11.

41. For references, see Chapter 6.

42. Cross-national studies sometimes find fairly strong correlations between indicators of wealth like GDP per capita and self-reported life satisfaction and happiness, e.g., Inglehart and Klingemann 2000, though individual nations vary and there is some question about the effect above poverty level. But it is not clear how far these results reflect dividends in happiness from increasing levels of option freedom, versus the benefits of other items that tend to accompany greater GDP, or simply artifacts of cultural differences in judgment and reporting. (Recall the possibility, noted in Chapter 10, that positivity biases may correlate with wealth.) As well, low-GDP nations tend to follow a Western economic model on which they are, by the standards they've accepted, doing poorly. But of course there are other models of society, on which GDP may be less important.

43. The fact that non-hunters are so numerous at present is irrelevant to questions of historical norms. If all wolves were put in captivity and bred to vast numbers in just a few years, outnumbering the wolves ever to see the wild, the historical norm for wolves would not be to live in cages.

44. "Quasi" because they grow some of their food.

45. Sahlins 1968. For the critic's take, see Kaplan 2000. Recall as well the quote from Bird-David in Chapter 11. On "white Indians," see Axtell 1986.

46. For a good discussion of romanticizing tendencies, see Edgerton 1992. As his discussion makes clear, some indigenous peoples lead patently unenviable lives (e.g., the Siriono). For a more optimistic take on the history of quality of life, see Veenhoven 2005, 2008.

47. Among them perhaps being the hunt: for a bracing illustration of the experience of a reluctant hunter, see Michael Pollan, "The Modern Hunter-Gatherer," *The New York Times*, March 26, 2006. See also Lee 2002, as well as the literature on Wilson's "biophilia" hypothesis, which holds that we evolved with a natural affinity for natural environments (e.g., Kellert and Wilson 1993).

48. Except that the Amish reported low levels of satisfaction with *self*, probably due to religious norms.

49. For the study, see Biswas-Diener, Vitterso et al. 2005. Biswas-Diener 2008 also discusses related research, including similar work done in Peru. The comparative data appear in Diener and Scollon 2003 and Flanagan 2007. A further avenue

worth exploring is cross-cultural research on physiolological indicators of stress such as cortisol levels; e.g., McDade, Stallings et al. 2000, Harrison 2001.

50. Kline 1990.

51. Wolff 1994, p. 187. The *Washington Post* reported on a major study by the World Health Organization that tracked outcomes of 3,300 schizophrenia patients in twelve countries, starting in 1967 with follow-ups thirty years later. The consistent result, found initially and in later follow-ups, was that patients in poor countries like India, Nigeria, and Columbia had much higher rates of recovery, with half to two-thirds becoming symptom-free, than those in wealthy countries like Denmark, England, and the United States, where only a third recovered to this extent (Hopper, Harrison et al. 2007, cited in "Social Network's Healing Power Is Borne Out in Poorer Nations," *The Washington Post*, June 27, 2005). When a reporter asked Darrel Regier, the director of research for the American Psychiatric Association, whether schizophrenia patients might be better off in Nigeria than in New York, he replied, "God, no!" It was not explained why he said this.

52. Preston 1995, pp. 213–14.

53. At the time of this writing, millions of small farmers worldwide are being forced, if they wish to survive, to quit their ancestral lands to seek other work in the global economy. One factor driving this state of affairs may be a belief among policymakers in distant cities that most of these farmers will ultimately be better off, with more opportunities and higher incomes than they would otherwise have expected. For a differing view, see "On India's Despairing Farms, a Plague of Suicide," *The New York Times*, September 19, 2006.

54. Sutherland 2003.

55. Nussbaum 2000.

56. In part it seems the island suffered a Tragedy of the Commons, in which each local could benefit by selling to developers, since the monetary gain is large and the incremental effect of one sale on the island is minimal. But taken together, the impact of many such sales may be intolerable.

57. The literature here is growing rapidly. For starters, see Camerer, Issacharoff et al. 2003, Diener 2000, 2006; Diener and Seligman 2004, Dolan and White 2007, Frank 1999a, Kahneman, Krueger et al. 2004a, Helliwell 2006, Kenny and Kenny 2006, Layard 2005, 2006; Sunstein and Thaler 2003, Trout 2005. For doubts about happiness-based policy, some defending more optimistic views of well-being in Western societies, see (to mention a few) Glaeser 2006, 2007, Badhwar 2006, Wilkinson 2007, Lebergott 1993. For excellent discussions of some complexities, see Adler and Posner forthcoming and Frey and Stutzer 2007.

58. Lucas, Clark et al. 2004b. In fact, focusing on unemployment—versus, say, economic growth—could be an example of happiness-based policy (e.g., Oswald 1997).

59. On overconfidence among economists, see Angner 2006.

60. Layard 2005, pp. 77–90.

NOTES TO AFTERWORD

1. Kimble, Garmezy et al. 1984, p. 299.

Bibliography

Adams, R. M. (2002). *Finite and Infinite Goods*. New York: Oxford University Press.

Adams, V. H. I. (1997). "A paradox in African American quality of life." *Social Indicators Research* 42: 205–19.

Adler, M. and E. Posner (forthcoming). "Happiness Research and Cost-Benefit Analysis." *Journal of Legal Studies*.

Alexandrova, A. (2005). "Subjective Well-Being and Kahneman's 'Objective Happiness'." *Journal of Happiness Studies* 6: 301–24.

Almeder, R. (2000). *Human Happiness and Morality*. Buffalo, NY: Prometheus Press.

Alston, W. P. (1967). "Pleasure." In *The Encyclopedia of Philosophy*, ed. P. Edwards. New York: Macmillan, 341–7.

Amir, O. and D. Ariely (2007). "Decisions by rules: The case of unwillingness to pay for beneficial delays." *Journal of Marketing Research* XLIV, 142–52.

Andrews, F. M. and S. B. Withey (1976). *Social Indicators of Well-Being*. New York: Plenum Press.

Andrews, L. B. (2004). "The Many Faces of Human Cloning." (Bibliotheca Alexandrina).

Angner, E. (2005). "The Evolution of Eupathics: The Historical Roots of Subjective Measures of Well-Being." Available at SSRN: <http://ssrn.com/abstract=799166>.

_____ (2006). "Economists as Experts: Overconfidence in theory and practice." *Journal of Economic Methodology* 13(1): 1–24.

Annas, J. (1993). *The Morality of Happiness*. New York: Oxford University Press.

_____ (1998). "Virtue and Eudaimonism." In *Virtue and Vice*, eds. E. F. Paul, F. D. Miller Jr., and J. Paul. New York: Cambridge University Press, 37–55.

_____ (2003). "Should Virtue Make You Happy?" In *Eudaimonia and Well-Being: Ancient and Modern Conceptions*, eds. L. J. Jost and R. A. Shiner. Kelowna, British Columbia: Academic Printing and Publishing, 1–19.

_____ (2004). "Happiness as Achievement." *Daedalus* 133(2): 44–51.

_____ (2006). "Virtue Ethics." In *The Oxford Handbook of Ethical Theory*, ed. D. Copp. New York: Oxford University Press, 515–36.

Anscombe, G. E. M. (1958/1997). "Modern Moral Philosophy." In *Virtue Ethics*, eds. R. Crisp and M. Slote. New York: Oxford University Press, 26–44.

Appiah, K. A. (1993). "Identity, Authenticity, Survival: Multicultural Societies and Social Reproduction." In *Multiculturalism: Examining the Politics of Recognition*, ed. C. Taylor, et al. Princeton, NJ: Princeton University Press.

Argyle, M. (1996). "Subjective Well-Being." In *In Pursuit of the Quality of Life*, ed. A. Offer. New York: Oxford University Press, 18–45.

_____ (1999). "Causes and Correlates of Happiness." In *Well-Being: The Foundations of Hedonic Psychology*, eds. D. Kahneman, E. Diener, and N. Schwarz. New York: Russell Sage Foundation, 3–25.

_____ (2002). *The Psychology of Happiness*. New York: Routledge.

Armon-Jones, C. (1991). *Varieties of Affect*. Toronto: University of Toronto Press.

Arneson, R. J. (1999). "Human Flourishing versus Desire Satisfaction." In *Human Flourishing*, eds. E. F. Paul, F. D. Miller Jr., and J. Paul. New York: Cambridge University Press, 113–42.

Arntz, A. (1993). "Endorphins stimulate approach behavior, but do not reduce subjective fear. A pilot study." *Behavioural Research and Therapy* 31(4): 403–5.

Austin, J. (1968). "Pleasure and Happiness." *Philosophy* 43: 51–62.

Axtell, J. (1986). *The Invasion Within: The Contest of Cultures in Colonial North America*. New York: Oxford University Press.

Badhwar, N. (2006). "Experiments in Living." *The Philosophers' Magazine* (35): 58–61.

_____ (forthcoming). "Is Realism Really Bad for You? A Realistic Response." *Journal of Philosophy*.

Banks, R. E. (1963). "The Ear-Friend." In *6 and the Silent Scream*, ed. I. Howard. New York: Belmont Books.

Bargh, J. A. and T. L. Chartrand (1999). "The unbearable automaticity of being." *American Psychologist* 54(7): 462–79.

Bargh, J. A., M. Chen, et al. (1996). "Automaticity of social behavior: Direct effects of trait construct and stereotype activation on action." *Journal of Personality and Social Psychology* 71(2): 230–44.

Bargh, J. A. and E. Morsella (2008). "The Unconscious Mind." *Perspectives on Psychological Science* 3(1): 73–9.

Bargh, J. A. and E. L. Williams (2006). "The Automaticity of Social Life." *Current Directions in Psychological Science* 15(1): 1–4.

Barkow, J. H. (1997). "Happiness in evolutionary perspective." In *Uniting Psychology and Biology: Integrative Perspectives on Human Development*, eds. N. L. Segal, G. E. Weisfeld, and C. C. Weisfeld. Washington, DC: American Psychological Association, 397–418.

Barrow, R. (1980). *Happiness and Schooling*. New York: St. Martin's Press.

_____ (1991). *Utilitarianism: A Contemporary Statement*. Brookfield, VT: Edward Elgar.

Baumeister, R. F., E. Bratslavsky, et al. (2001). "Bad is stronger than good." *Review of General Psychology* 5: 323–70.

Becker, L. C. (1999). *A New Stoicism*. Princeton, NJ: Princeton University Press.

_____ (1992). "Good Lives: Prolegomena." In *The Good Life and the Human Good*, eds. E. F. Paul, F. D. Miller Jr., and J. Paul. New York: Cambridge University Press, 15–37.

Belliotti, R. A. (2004). *Happiness Is Overrated*. New York: Rowman & Littlefield.

Benditt, T. M. (1974). "Happiness." *Philosophical Studies* 25: 1–20.

_____ (1978). "Happiness and Satisfaction—A Rejoinder to Carson." *The Personalist* 59: 108–9.

Bentham, J. (1780/1969). "An Introduction to the Principles of Morals and Legislation." In *A Bentham Reader*, ed. M. P. Mack. New York: Pegasus, 73–144.

Berlin, I. (1969). "Two Concepts of Liberty." In *Four Essays on Liberty*, ed. I. Berlin. New York: Oxford University Press.

Berridge, K. C. (1999). "Pleasure, pain, desire, and dread: Hidden core processes of emotion." In *Well-Being: The Foundations of Hedonic Psychology*, eds. D. Kahneman, E. Diener, and N. Schwarz. New York: Russell Sage Foundation Press, 525–57.

Berridge, K. C. and P. Winkielman (2003). "What Is an Unconscious Emotion?" *Cognition & Emotion* 17: 181–211.

Berry, W. (1981). *The Gift of Good Land.* San Francisco: North Point Press.

_____ (1990). *What Are People For?* New York: North Point Press.

Bird-David, N. (1992). "Beyond 'the original affluent society': A culturalist reformulation." *Current Anthropology* 33(1): 25–47.

Bissell, T. (2002). "Eternal Winter: Lessons of the Aral Sea Disaster." *Harper's* (April), 41–56.

Biswas-Diener, R. (2008). "Material Wealth and Subjective Well-Being." In *The Science of Subjective Well-Being*, eds. M. Eid and R. J. Larsen. New York: Guilford Press, 307–23.

Biswas-Diener, R. and E. Diener (2001). "Making the Best of a Bad Situation: Satisfaction in the Slums of Calcutta." *Social Indicators Research* 55(3): 329–52.

Biswas-Diener, R., J. Vitterso, et al. (2005). "Most People are Pretty Happy, but There is Cultural Variation: The Inughuit, The Amish, and The Maasai." *The Journal of Happiness Studies* 6(3): 205–26.

Blanchflower, D. G. and A. J. Oswald (2008). "Hypertension and Happiness Across Nations." *Journal of Health Economics* 27(2): 218–33.

Block, N. (1995). "On a Confusion About A Function of Consciousness." *Behavioral and Brain Sciences* 18: 227–47.

Botti, S. and S. S. Iyengar (2006). "The Dark Side of Choice: When Choice Impairs Social Welfare." *Journal of Public Policy and Marketing* 25(1): 24–38.

Brandstatter, H. (1991). "Emotions in everyday life situations: Time sampling of subjective experience." In *Subjective Well-Being: An Interdisciplinary Perspective*, eds. F. Strack, M. Argyle, and N. Schwarz. New York: Pergamon Press, 173–92.

Brandt, R. B. (1959). *Ethical Theory.* Englewood Cliffs, NJ: Prentice-Hall.

_____ (1979). *A Theory of the Good and the Right.* New York: Oxford University Press.

_____ (1989). "Fairness to Happiness." *Social Theory & Practice* 15: 33–58.

_____ (1992). *Morality, Utilitarianism, and Rights.* New York: Cambridge University Press.

Braybrooke, D. (1989). "Thoughtful Happiness." *Ethics* 99: 625–36.

Brickman, P. and D. T. Campbell (1971). "Hedonic relativism and planning the good society." In *Adaptation-Level Theory: A Symposium*, ed. M. H. Apley. New York: Academic Press, 287–301.

Brink, D. O. (1989). *Moral Realism and the Foundations of Ethics.* New York: Cambridge University Press.

_____ (2003). *Perfectionism and the Common Good: Themes in the Philosophy of T. H. Green.* New York: Oxford University Press.

Brown, E. (2005). "Wishing for Fortune, Choosing Activity: Aristotle on External Goods and Happiness." *Proceedings of the Boston Area Colloquium in Ancient Philosophy* 21: 57–81.

Brülde, B. (2007). "Happiness theories of the good life." *Journal of Happiness Studies* 8(1): 15–49.

Buss, D. M. (2000). "The Evolution of Happiness." *American Psychologist* 55(1): 15–23.

Buss, S. (2004). "The Irrationality of Unhappiness and the Paradox of Despair." *Journal of Philosophy* CI(4): 171–200.

Cahn, S. M. and C. Vitrano, eds. (2008). *Happiness: Classical and Contemporary Readings in Philosophy.* New York: Oxford University Press.

Camerer, C., S. Issacharoff, et al. (2003). "Regulation for Conservatives: Behavioral Economics and the Case for 'Asymmetric Paternalism'." *University of Pennsylvania Law Review* 151: 1211–54.

Camerer, C., G. Loewenstein, et al. (2005). "Neuroeconomics: How neuroscience can inform economics." *Journal of Economic Literature* 34(1): 9–64.

Campbell, R. (1973). "The Pursuit Of Happiness." *Personalist* 54: 325–37.

Cantril, H. (1965). *The Pattern of Human Concerns*. New Brunswick, NJ: Rutgers University Press.

Carlson, T. (2005). *Hatteras Blues*. Chapel Hill, NC: University of North Carolina Press.

Carson, T. L. (1978a). "Happiness and Contentment: A Reply to Benditt." *The Personalist* 59: 101–7.

——— (1978b). "Happiness and the Good Life." *Southwestern Journal of Philosophy* 9: 73–88.

——— (1979). "Happiness and the Good Life: a Rejoinder to Mele." *Southwestern Journal of Philosophy* 10: 189–92.

——— (1981). "Happiness, Contentment, and the Good Life." *Pacific Philosophical Quarterly* 62: 378–92.

——— (2000). *Value and the Good Life*. Notre Dame, IN: University of Notre Dame Press.

Cashen, M. (ms). "Happiness, Eudaimonia, and Descriptive Adequacy." Washington University in St. Louis.

Chalmers, D. (1997). "Availability: The Cognitive Basis of Experience?" In *The Nature of Consciousness*, eds. N. Block, O. Flanagan, and G. Guzeldere. Cambridge, MA: MIT Press, 421–4.

Chekola, M. (2007). "Happiness, Rationality, Autonomy and the Good Life." *Journal of Happiness Studies* 8(1): 51–78.

Church, J. (1995). "Fallacies or Analyses?" *Behavioral and Brain Sciences* 18: 227–47.

Colvin, C. R. and J. Block (1994). "Do positive illusions foster mental health? An examination of the Taylor and Brown formulation." *Psychological Bulletin* 116: 3–20.

Colvin, C. R., J. Block, et al. (1995). "Overly positive self-evaluations and personality: Negative implications for mental health." *Journal of Personality and Social Psychology* 68: 1152–62.

Copp, D. (2002). "Social Unity and the Identity of Persons." *Journal of Political Philosophy* 10(4): 365–91.

Cowan, J. L. (1968). *Pleasure and Pain: A Study in Philosophical Psychology*. New York: Macmillan.

Crawford, M. B. (2006). "Shop Class as Soulcraft." *The New Atlantis* (Summer), 7–24.

Crisp, R. (2005). "Well-Being." In *The Stanford Encyclopedia of Philosophy*, ed. E. N. Zalta. URL = <http://plato.stanford.edu/entries/well-being/>.

——— (2006a). "Hedonism Reconsidered." *Philosophy and Phenomenological Research* 73(3): 619–45.

——— (2006b). *Reasons and the Good*. New York: Oxford University Press.

——— (forthcoming). "Hedonism Reconsidered." *Philosophy and Phenomenological Research*.

Csikszentmihalyi, M. (1990). *Flow: The Psychology of Optimum Experience*. New York: Harper & Row.

——— (1999). "If we are so rich, why aren't we happy?" *American Psychologist* 54(10): 821–7.

Csikszentmihalyi, M. and J. Hunter (2003). "Happiness in everyday life: The uses of experience sampling." *Journal of Happiness Studies* 4(2): 185–99.

Csikszentmihalyi, M. and R. Larson (1987). "Validity and reliability of the experience-sampling method." *Journal of Nervous and Mental Disease* 175(9): 526–36.

Csikszentmihalyi, M. and B. Schneider (2000). *Becoming Adult: How Teenagers Prepare for the World of Work*. New York: Basic Books.

Cummins, R. A. (1995). "On the trail of the gold standard for subjective well-being." *Social Indicators Research* 35: 179–200.

_____ (2003). "Normative Life Satisfaction: Measurement Issues and a Homeostatic Model." *Social Indicators Research* 64(2): 225–56.

Cutler, D. M., E. L. Glaeser, et al. (2003). "Why have Americans become more obese?" *Journal of Economic Perspectives* 17(3): 93–118.

D'Arms, J. and D. Jacobson (2000). "Sentiment and Value." *Ethics* 110(July): 722–48.

Darwall, S. (1983). *Impartial Reason*. Ithaca, NY: Cornell University Press.

_____ (2002). *Welfare and Rational Care*. Princeton, NJ: Princeton University Press.

Davidson, R. J. (2004). "Well-being and affective style: neural substrates and bio-behavioural correlates." *Philosophical Transactions of the Royal Society B: Biological Sciences* 359(1449): 1395–411.

Davis, W. (1981a). "Pleasure and Happiness." *Philosophical Studies* 39: 305–18.

_____ (1981b). "A Theory of Happiness." *American Philosophical Quarterly* 18: 111–20.

DeLancey, C. (2006). "Basic Moods." *Philosophical Psychology* 19(4): 527–38.

Den Uyl, D. and T. R. Machan (1983). "Recent Work on the Concept of Happiness." *American Philosophical Quarterly* 20: 115–33.

Dennett, D. (1991). *Consciousness Explained*. Boston: Little, Brown, & Co.

Denton, R. K. (1968). *The Semai: A Nonviolent People of Malaya*. New York: Holt, Reinhart and Winston.

Dermer, M., S. J. Cohen, et al. (1979). "Evaluative judgments of aspects of life as a function of vicarious exposure to hedonic extremes." *Journal of Personality and Social Psychology* 37(2): 247–60.

Diener, E. (1984). "Subjective Well-Being." *Psychological Bulletin* 95: 542–75.

_____ (1994). "Assessing Subjective Well-Being: Progress and Opportunities." *Social Indicators Research* 31: 103–57.

_____ (2000). "Subjective well-being: The science of happiness and a proposal for a national index." *American Psychologist* 55(1): 34–43.

_____ (2006). "Guidelines for national indicators of subjective well-being and ill-being." *Journal of Happiness Studies* 7(4): 397–404.

_____ (2008). "Myths in the Science of Happiness, and Directions for Future Research." In *The Science of Subjective Well-Being*, eds. M. Eid and R. J. Larsen. New York: Guilford Press, 493–514.

Diener, E. and R. Biswas-Diener (2002). "Will Money Increase Subjective Well-Being?" *Social Indicators Research* 57: 119–69.

Diener, E. and C. Diener (1996). "Most People Are Happy." *Psychological Science* 7(3): 181–5.

Diener, E. and R. A. Emmons (1984). "The independence of positive and negative affect." *Journal of Personality and Social Psychology* 47(5): 1105–17.

Diener, E., R. A. Emmons, et al. (1985). "The satisfaction with life scale." *Journal of Personality Assessment* 49: 71–5.

Diener, E. and R. J. Larsen (1993). "The Experience of Emotional Well-Being." In *Handbook of Emotions*, eds. M. Lewis and J. M. Haviland. New York: The Guilford Press, 405–15.

Diener, E., R. E. Lucas, et al. (2006). "Beyond the Hedonic Treadmill: Revising the Adaptation Theory of Well-Being." *American Psychologist* 61(4): 305–14.

Diener, E. and S. Oishi (2005). "The Nonobvious Social Psychology of Happiness." *Psychological Inquiry* 16(4): 162–7.

Diener, E., J. J. Sapyta, et al. (1998). "Subjective well-being is essential to well-being." *Psychological Inquiry* 9(1): 33–7.

Diener, E. and C. N. Scollon (2003). "Subjective well-being is desirable, but not the summum bonum." *Minnesota Interdisciplinary Workshop on Well-Being* (Minneapolis).

Diener, E., C. N. Scollon, et al. (2003). "The evolving concept of subjective well-being: The multifaceted nature of happiness." *Advances in Cell Aging and Gerontology* 15: 187–219.

Diener, E. and M. Seligman (2004). "Beyond Money: Toward an economy of well-being." *Psychological Science in the Public Interest* 5(1): 1–31.

Diener, E. and M. E. Seligman (2002). "Very happy people." *Psychological Science* 13(1): 81–4.

Diener, E., E. Suh, et al. (1997). "Recent Studies on Subjective Well-Being." *Indian Journal of Clinical Psychology* 24: 25–41.

Diener, E., E. M. Suh, et al. (1999). "Subjective Well-Being: Three Decades of Progress." *Psychological Bulletin* 125(2): 276–302.

Diener, E. and E. M. Suh, eds. (2000). *Culture and Subjective Well-Being*. Cambridge, MA: MIT Press.

Dijksterhuis, A., M. W. Bos, et al. (2006). "On Making the Right Choice: The Deliberation-Without-Attention Effect." *Science* 311(5763): 1005–7.

Dolan, P. and M. P. White (2007). "How can measures of subjective well-being be used to inform public policy?" *Perspectives on Psychological Science* 2(1): 71–85.

Doris, J. M. (2002). *Lack of Character*. New York: Cambridge University Press.

Doris, J. M. and S. P. Stich (2005). "As a Matter of Fact: Empirical Perspectives on Ethics." In *The Oxford Handbook of Contemporary Philosophy*, eds. F. Jackson and M. Smith. New York: Oxford University Press, 114–52.

Dorsey, D. (forthcoming). "Three Arguments for Perfectionism." *Noûs*.

Dunn, E. W., T. D. Wilson, et al. (2003). "Location, location, location: The misprediction of satisfaction in housing lotteries." *Personality and Social Psychology Bulletin* 29: 1421–32.

Dworkin, G. (1982). "Is More Choice Better Than Less?" In *Midwest Studies in Philosophy, vol. vii: Social and Political Philosophy*, eds. P. A. French, T. E. Uehling, Jr., and H. K. Wettstein. Minneapolis: University of Minnesota Press, 47–61.

Easterlin, R. A. (1974). "Does Economic Growth Improve the Human Lot?" In *Nations and Households in Economic Growth: Essays in Honor of Moses Abramovitz*, eds. P. A. David and M. W. Reder. New York: Academic Press.

——— (2003). "Explaining Happiness." *Proceedings of the National Academy of Sciences of the United States of America* 100(19): 11176–83.

_____ (2005a). "Building a Better Theory of Well-Being." In *Economics and Happiness*, eds. L. Bruni and P. L. Porta. New York: Oxford University Press. 1: 29–65.

_____ (2005b). "Feeding the illusion of growth and happiness: A reply to Hagerty and Veenhoven." *Social Indicators Research* Vol 74(3) Dec 2005: 429–43.

Ebenstein, A. O. (1991). *The Greatest Happiness Principle: An Examination of Utilitarianism*. New York: Garland.

Eckersley, R. (2006). "Is modern Western culture a health hazard?" *International Journal of Epidemiology* 35(2): 252–8.

Edgerton, R. B. (1992). *Sick Societies: Challenging the Myth of Primitive Harmony*. New York: Free Press.

Edwards, R. B. (1979). *Pleasures and Pains: a Theory Of Qualitative Hedonism*. Ithaca, NY: Cornell University Press.

Eid, M. and E. Diener (2001). "Norms for experiencing emotions in different cultures: Inter- and intranational differences." *Journal of Personality and Social Psychology* 81(5): 869–85.

_____ (2004). "Global judgments of subjective well-being: Situational variability and long-term stability." *Social Indicators Research* 65(3): 245–77.

Eid, M. and R. J. Larsen, eds. (2008). *The Science of Subjective Well-Being*. New York: Guilford Press.

Ekman, P. (1994). "All Emotions Are Basic." In *The Nature of Emotion*, eds. P. Ekman and R. J. Davidson. New York: Oxford University Press, 15–19.

Ekman, P. and R. J. Davidson, eds. (1994). *The Nature of Emotion*. New York: Oxford University Press.

Elga, A. (2005). "On overrating oneself . . . and knowing it." *Philosophical Studies* 123: 115–24.

Elster, J. (1983). *Sour Grapes*. New York: Cambridge University Press.

Emmons, R. A. (2008). "Gratitude, Subjective Well-Being, and the Brain." In *The Science of Subjective Well-Being*, eds. M. Eid and R. J. Larsen. New York: Guilford Press, 469–89.

Emmons, R. A. and M. E. McCullough (2003). "Counting blessings versus burdens: an experimental investigation of gratitude and subjective well-being in daily life." *Journal of Personality and Social Psychology* 84(2): 377–89.

Endo, Y., S. J. Heine, et al. (2000). "Culture and positive illusions in close relationships: How my relationships are better than yours." *Personality and Social Psychology Bulletin* 26(12): 1571–86.

Epictetus (1925). *The Discourses as Reported by Arrian, The Manual, and Fragments*. Cambridge, MA: Harvard University Press.

Evans, G. W. and D. Johnson (2000). "Stress and Open-Office Noise." *Journal of Applied Psychology* 85(95): 779–83.

Everett, D. L. (2005). "Cultural Constraints on Grammar and Cognition in Pirahã." *Cultural Anthropology* 46(4): 621–46.

Feinberg, J. (1992a). "Absurd Self-Fulfillment." In *Freedom and Fulfillment*, ed. J. Feinberg. Princeton, NJ: Princeton University Press, 297–330.

_____ (1992b). "The Child's Right to an Open Future." In *Freedom and Fulfillment*, ed. J. Feinberg. Princeton, NJ: Princeton University Press, 76–97.

Feldman, F. (1997a). "On the Intrinsic Value of Pleasures." *Ethics* 107: 448–66.

Feldman, F. (1997b). *Utilitarianism, Hedonism, and Desert*. New York: Cambridge University Press.

___ (2002). "The Good Life: A Defense of Attitudinal Hedonism." *Philosophy and Phenomenological Research* 65: 604–28.

___ (2004). *Pleasure and the Good Life*. New York: Oxford University Press.

Finnis, J. (1980). *Natural Law and Natural Rights*. New York: Oxford University Press.

Fisher, J. C. (2006a). "Pragmatic Conceptual Analysis." University of Arizona, PhD dissertation.

___ (2006b). "Pragmatic Conceptual Analysis." *Online Philosophy Conference*. URL = <http://experimentalphilosophy.typepad.com/online_philosophy_confere/2006/05/justin_fisher.html>.

Flanagan, O. (1990). "Identity and Strong and Weak Evaluation." In *Identity, Character, and Morality*, eds. O. Flanagan and A. O. Rorty. Cambridge, MA: MIT Press, 37–65.

___ (1991). *Varieties of Moral Personality*. Cambridge, MA: Harvard University Press.

___ (2007). *The Really Hard Problem: Meaning in a Material World*. Cambridge, MA: MIT Press.

Flanagan, O. and A. O. Rorty (1990). "Introduction." In *Identity, Character, and Morality*, eds. O. Flanagan and A. O. Rorty. Cambridge, MA: MIT Press, 1–15.

Foot, P. (2001). *Natural Goodness*. New York: Oxford University Press.

Fordyce, M. W. (1988). "A Review of Research on the Happiness Measures: A Sixty Second Index of Happiness and Mental Health." *Social Indicators Research* 20: 355–82.

Forster, E. M. (1909/2001). "The Machine Stops." In *Selected Stories*. New York: Penguin Classics.

Frank, R. (1999a). *Luxury Fever*. New York: Simon and Schuster.

___ (1999b). "Market Failures." *The Boston Review* (Summer).

Frankfurt, H. (1971). "Freedom of the Will and the Concept of a Person." *Journal of Philosophy* 68(1): 5–20.

___ (1987). "Identification and Wholeheartedness." In *Responsibility, Character, and the Emotions*, ed. F. Schoeman. New York: Cambridge University Press, 27–45.

Frederick, S. and G. Loewenstein (1999). "Hedonic Adaptation." In *Well-Being: The Foundations of Hedonic Psychology*, eds. D. Kahneman, E. Diener, and N. Schwarz. New York: Russell Sage Foundation Press, 302–29.

Frederick, S., G. Loewenstein, et al. (2003). "Time discounting and time preference: A critical review." In *Time and Decision: Economic and Psychological Perspectives on Intertemporal Choice*, eds. G. Loewenstein, D. Read, and R. F. Baumeister. New York: Russell Sage Foundation, 13–86.

Fredrickson, B. L. (2001). "The role of positive emotions in positive psychology: The broaden-and-build theory of positive emotions." *American Psychologist* 56(3): 218–26.

___ (2008). "Promoting Positive Affect." In *The Science of Subjective Well-Being*, eds. M. Eid and R. J. Larsen. New York: Guilford Press, 449–68.

Fredrickson, B. L. and M. F. Losada (2005). "Positive Affect and the Complex Dynamics of Human Flourishing." *American Psychologist* 60(7): 678–86.

Freedman, J. (1978). *Happy People: What Happiness Is, Who Has It, and Why*. New York: Harcourt, Brace, Jovanovich.

Frey, B. S. and A. Stutzer (2002). *Happiness and Economics*. Princeton, NJ: Princeton University Press.

—— (2004). "Economic consequences of mispredicting utility." IEW Working Paper No. 218. Available at SSRN: <http://ssrn.com/abstract=639025>.

—— (2007). "Should National Happiness Be Maximized?" Zurich IEER Working Paper No. 306. Available at SSRN: <http://ssrn.com/abstract=936289>.

Frijda, N. H. (1993). "Moods, Emotion Episodes, and Emotions." In *Handbook of Emotions*, eds. M. Lewis and J. M. Haviland. New York: Guilford Press, 381–403.

Gable, S. L. and J. Haidt (2005). "What (and Why) Is Positive Psychology?" *Review of General Psychology* 9(2): 103–10.

Gardner, J. and A. J. Oswald (2001). "What Has Been Happening to the Quality of Workers' Lives in Britain?" Economics Research Paper No. 617, University of Warwick.

Gazzaniga, M. (1970). *The Bisected Brain*. New York: Appleton-Century-Crofts.

Gentzler, J. (2004). "The Attractions and Delights of Goodness." *Philosophical Quarterly* 54(216): 353–67.

Gert, B. (1998). *Morality: Its Nature and Justification*. New York: Oxford University Press.

Gewirth, A. (1998). *Self-Fulfillment*. Princeton, NJ: Princeton University Press.

Gibbard, A. (1990). *Wise Choices, Apt Feelings*. Cambridge, MA: Harvard University Press.

Gigerenzer, G. (2002). *Adaptive Thinking: Rationality in the Real World*. New York: Oxford University Press.

Gilbert, D. (2006). *Stumbling on Happiness*. New York: Knopf.

Gilbert, D. T., E. Driver-Linn, et al. (2002). "The trouble with Vronsky: Impact bias in the forecasting of future affective states." In *The Wisdom in Feeling: Psychological Processes in Emotional Intelligence*, eds. L. F. Barrett and P. Salovey. New York: Guilford Press, 114–43.

Gilbert, D. T., E. C. Pinel, et al. (1998). "Immune neglect: A source of durability bias in affective forecasting." *Journal of Personality and Social Psychology* 75: 617–38.

—— (2002). "Durability Bias in Affective Forecasting." In *Heuristics and Biases: The Psychology of Intuitive Judgment*, eds. T. Gilovitch, D. Griffin, and D. Kahneman. New York: Cambridge University Press, 292–312.

Glaeser, E. L. (2006). "Paternalism and Psychology." *University of Chicago Law Review* 73(1): 133–56.

—— (2007). "Coercive Regulation and the Balance of Freedom." *Cato Unbound* May 11. URL = <http://www.cato-unbound.org/2007/05/11/edward-glaeser/coercive-regulation-and-the-balance-of-freedom/>.

Glass, D. C., J. E. Singer, et al. (1977). "Behavioral and Physiological Effects of Uncontrollable Environmental Events." In *Perspectives on Environment and Behavior*, ed. D. Stokols. New York: Plenum.

Glass, D. C. and J. E. Singer (1972). *Urban Stress: Experiments on Noise and Social Stressors*. New York: Academic Press.

Glatzer, W. (1991). "Quality of life in advanced industrialized countries: The case of West Germany." In *Subjective Well-Being*, eds. F. Strack, M. Argyle, and N. Schwarz. Elmsford, NY: Pergamon Press, 261–79.

Goldstein, I. (1973). "Happiness: The Role of Non-Hedonic Criteria in Its Evaluation." *International Philosophical Quarterly* 13: 523–34.

Goldstein, I. (1983). "Pain and Masochism." *Journal of Value Inquiry* 17: 219–23.

—— (1985). "Hedonic Pluralism." *Philosophical Studies* 48: 49–55.

—— (1989). "Pleasure and Pain: Unconditional, Intrinsic Values." *Philosophy and Phenomenological Research* 50(2): 255–76.

Gollwitzer, P. M. and R. F. Kinney (1989). "Effects of deliberative and implemental mind-sets on illusion of control." *Journal of Personality and Social Psychology* 56: 531–42.

Gosling, J. C. B. (1969). *Pleasure and Desire*. Oxford: Clarendon Press.

—— (1992). "Pleasure." In *Encyclopedia of Ethics*, eds. L. C. Becker and C. B. Becker. New York: Garland, 978–81.

Greene, J. (2008). "The Secret Joke of Kant's Soul." In *Moral Psychology, Volume 3: The Neuroscience of Morality: Emotion, Brain Disorders, and Development*, ed. W. Sinnott-Armstrong. Cambridge, MA: MIT Press.

Griffin, J. (1979). "Is Unhappiness Morally More Important Than Happiness?" *Philosophical Quarterly* 29: 47–55.

—— (1986). *Well-Being: Its Meaning, Measurement, and Moral Importance*. Oxford: Clarendon Press.

—— (2000). "Replies." In *Well-Being and Morality*, eds. R. Crisp and B. Hooker. New York: Oxford University Press, 281–313.

—— (2007). "What Do Happiness Studies Study?" *Journal of Happiness Studies* 8(1): 139–48.

Griffiths, P. E. (1997). *What Emotions Really Are*. Chicago, IL: University of Chicago Press.

Grinde, B. (2002). "Happiness in the Perspective of Evolutionary Psychology." *Journal of Happiness Studies* 3(4): 331–54.

Griswold, C. (1996). "Happiness, Tranquillity, and Philosophy." *Critical Review* 10(1): 1–32.

Gurin, G., J. Veroff, et al. (1960). *Americans View Their Mental Health*. New York: Basic Books.

Haidt, J. (2001). "The emotional dog and its rational tail: A social intuitionist approach to moral judgment." *Psychological Review* 108(4): 814–34.

—— (2006). *The Happiness Hypothesis*. New York: Basic Books.

—— (2007). "The new synthesis in moral psychology." *Science* 316(5827): 998–1002.

—— (2008). "Morality." *Perspectives on Psychological Science* 3(1): 65–72.

Haidt, J. and J. Graham (2007). "When Morality Opposes Justice: Conservatives Have Moral Intuitions that Liberals May Not Recognize." *Social Justice Research* 20: 98–116.

Hare, R. M. (1963). *Freedom and Reason*. Oxford: Oxford University Press.

—— (1981). *Moral Thinking*. Oxford: Oxford University Press.

Harrison, G. A. (2001). "Comparative Stress in Human Societies." *Journal of Physiological Anthropology* 20(2): 49–53.

Harsanyi, J. (1982). "Morality and the Theory of Rational Behaviour." In *Utilitarianism and Beyond*, eds. A. Sen and B. Williams. Cambridge: Cambridge University Press, 39–62.

Hassin, R. R., J. S. Uleman, et al. (2005). *The New Unconscious*. New York: Oxford University Press.

Haugeland, J. (1981). "The Nature and Plausibility of Cognitivism." In *Mind Design: Philosophy, Psychology, and Artificial Intelligence*, ed. J. Haugeland. Montgomery, VT: Bradford Books, 243–81. Orig. published in *Behavioral and Brain Sciences*, 1978.

Hausman, D. M. (1992/2008). "Why Look Under the Hood?" In *The Philosophy of Economics*, ed. D. M. Hausman. New York: Cambridge University Press, 183–7.

Haybron, D. M. (2000). "Two Philosophical Problems in the Study of Happiness." *The Journal of Happiness Studies* 1(2): 207–25.

——— (2001a). "Happiness and Ethical Inquiry: An Essay in the Psychology of Well-Being." Ph.D. Dissertation, Rutgers University.

——— (2001b). "Happiness and Pleasure." *Philosophy and Phenomenological Research* 62(3): 501–28.

——— (2003). "What Do We Want from a Theory of Happiness?" *Metaphilosophy* 34(3): 305–29.

——— (2005). "On Being Happy or Unhappy." *Philosophy and Phenomenological Research* 71(2): 287–317.

——— (2007a). "Do We Know How Happy We Are?" *Noûs* 41(3): 394–428.

——— (2007b). "Life Satisfaction, Ethical Reflection and the Science of Happiness." *The Journal of Happiness Studies* 8: 99–138.

——— (2007c). "Well-Being and Virtue." *Journal of Ethics & Social Philosophy* II(2).

——— (ms). "Mood Propensity as a Constituent of Happiness."

Haybron, R. (1991). "Once Upon an Island." *The Gamut* 33: 5–21.

Headey, B. (2007). "The Set-Point Theory of Well-Being Needs Replacing : On the Brink of a Scientific Revolution?" DIW Berlin: German Institute for Economic Research.

——— (2008). "The Set-Point Theory of Well-Being: Negative Results and Consequent Revisions." *Social Indicators Research* 85(3): 389–403.

Headey, B. and A. Wearing (1989). "Personality, life events, and subjective well-being: Toward a dynamic equilibrium model." *Journal of Personality and Social Psychology* 57: 731–9.

——— (1992). *Understanding Happiness: A Theory of Subjective Well-Being*. Melbourne: Longman Cheshire.

Heathwood, C. (2006). "Desire Satisfactionism and Hedonism." *Philosophical Studies* 128: 539–63.

Heine, S. J. (2005). "Where Is the Evidence for Pancultural Self-Enhancement? A Reply to Sedikides, Gaertner, and Toguchi (2003)." *Journal of Personality and Social Psychology* 89: 531–8.

Heine, S. J. and T. Hamamura (2007). "In search of East Asian self-enhancement." *Personality and Social Psychology Review* 11(1): 4–27.

Heine, S. J., D. R. Lehman, et al. (1999). "Is there a universal need for positive self-regard?" *Psychological Review* 106: 766–94.

Helliwell, J. F. (2006). "Well-Being, Social Capital and Public Policy: What's New?*." *The Economic Journal* 116(510): C34–C45.

Helliwell, J. F. and R. Putnam (2004). "The Social Context of Well-Being." *Philosophical Transactions of the Royal Society* 359(1449): 1435–46.

Hemingway, E. (1952). *The Old Man and the Sea*. New York: Simon and Schuster.

Hill, S. (forthcoming). "Haybron on Mood Propensity and Happiness." *The Journal of Happiness Studies*.

Hill, S. E. and D. M. Buss (2008). "Evolution and Subjective Well-Being." In *The Science of Subjective Well-Being*, eds. M. Eid and R. J. Larsen. New York: Guilford Press, 62–79.

Hooker, B. (1996). "Does Moral Virtue Constitute a Benefit to the Agent?" In *How Should One Live?*, ed. R. Crisp. New York: Oxford University Press, 141–55.

—— (2000). *Ideal Code, Real World*. New York: Oxford University Press.

Hopper, K., G. Harrison, et al. (2007). *Recovery from schizophrenia: An international perspective: A report from the WHO Collaborative Project, the international study of schizophrenia*. New York: Oxford University Press.

Hsee, C. K. and R. Hastie (2006). "Decision and experience: Why don't we choose what makes us happy?" *Trends in Cognitive Sciences* 10(1): 31–7.

Hsee, C. K., J. Zhang, et al. (2003). "Lay rationalism and inconsistency between predicted experience and decision." *Journal of Behavioral Decision Making* 16: 257–72.

Huppert, F. A., N. Baylis, et al., eds. (2006). *The Science of Well-Being*. New York: Oxford University Press.

Huppert, F. A. and J. E. Whittington (2003). "Evidence for the independence of positive and negative well-being: Implications for quality of life assessment." *British Journal of Health Psychology* 8: 107–22.

Hurka, T. (1993). *Perfectionism*. New York: Oxford University Press.

Hursthouse, R. (1999). *On Virtue Ethics*. New York: Oxford University Press.

Inglehart, R. and H.-D. Klingemann (2000). "Genes, Culture, Democracy, and Happiness." In *Culture and Subjective Well-Being*, eds. E. Diener and E. M. Suh. Cambridge, MA: MIT Press, 165–83.

Ito, T. A. and J. T. Cacioppo (1999). "The psychophysiology of utility appraisals." In *Well-Being: The Foundations of Hedonic Psychology*, eds. D. Kahneman, E. Diener, and N. Schwarz. New York: Russell Sage Foundation Press, 470–88.

Iyengar, S. S. and M. R. Lepper (2000). "When choice is demotivating: Can one desire too much of a good thing?" *Journal of Personality and Social Psychology* 79: 995–1006.

Iyengar, S. S., R. E. Wells, et al. (2006). "Doing Better but Feeling Worse: Looking for the 'Best' Job Undermines Satisfaction." *Psychological Science* 17(2): 143–50.

Jack, A. and A. Roepstorff (2002). "Retrospection and cognitive brain mapping: from stimulus-response to script-report." *Trends in Cognitive Science* 6(8): 333–9.

——, eds. (2003). *Trusting the Subject? Vol. 1*. Charlottesville, VA: Imprint Academic.

——, eds. (2004). *Trusting the Subject? Vol. 2*. Charlottesville, VA: Imprint Academic.

Jack, A. and T. Shallice (2001). "Introspective physicalism as an approach to the science of consciousness." *Cognition* 79: 161–96.

James, W. (1890/1981). *The Principles of Psychology*. Cambridge, MA: Harvard University Press.

Kagan, S. (1992). "The Limits of Well-Being." *Social Philosophy and Policy* 9(2): 169–89.

—— (1994). "Me and My Life." *Proceedings of the Aristotelian Society* 94: 309–24.

Kahneman, D. (1994). "New Challenges to the Rationality Assumption." *Journal of Institutional and Theoretical Economics* 150(1): 18–36.

—— (1999). "Objective Happiness." In *Well-Being: The Foundations of Hedonic Psychology*, eds. D. Kahneman, E. Diener, and N. Schwarz. New York: Russell Sage Foundation, 3–25.

—— (2000a). "Evaluation by moments: past and future." In *Choices, Values, and Frames*, eds. D. Kahneman and A. Tversky. New York: Cambridge University Press, 693–708.

_____ (2000b). "Experienced Utility and Objective Happiness: A Moment-Based Approach." In *Choices, Values, and Frames*, eds. D. Kahneman and A. Tversky. New York: Cambridge University Press, 673–92.

_____ (2003). "A perspective on judgment and choice: Mapping bounded rationality." *American Psychologist* 58(9): 697–720.

Kahneman, D., E. Diener, et al., eds. (1999). *Well-Being: The Foundations of Hedonic Psychology*. New York: Russell Sage Foundation Press.

Kahneman, D. and S. Frederick (2002). "Representativeness Revisited: Attribute Substitution in Intuitive Judgment." In *Heuristics and Biases: The Psychology of Intuitive Judgment*, eds. T. Gilovitch, D. Griffin, and D. Kahneman. New York: Cambridge University Press, 49–81.

Kahneman, D., B. L. Fredrickson, et al. (1993). "When More Pain Is Preferred to Less: Adding a Better End." *Psychological Science* 4(6): 401–5.

Kahneman, D., J. L. Knetsch, et al. (1990). "Experimental Tests of the Endowment Effect and the Coase Theorem." *The Journal of Political Economy* 98(6): 1325–48.

Kahneman, D. and A. B. Krueger (2006). "Developments in the Measurement of Subjective Well-Being." *The Journal of Economic Perspectives* 20: 3–24.

Kahneman, D., A. B. Krueger, et al. (2004a). "Toward National Well-Being Accounts." *The American Economic Review* 94: 429–34.

_____ (2004b). "A Survey Method for Characterizing Daily Life Experience: The Day Reconstruction Method." *Science* 306(5702): 1776–80.

_____ (2006). "Would You Be Happier If You Were Richer? A Focusing Illusion." *Science* 312(5782): 1908–10.

Kahneman, D. and J. Riis (2005). "Living, and thinking about it: two perspectives on life." In *The Science of Well-Being*, eds. F. A. Huppert, N. Baylis, and B. Keverne. New York: Oxford University Press, 285–304.

Kahneman, D. and R. H. Thaler (2006). "Anomalies: Utility Maximization and Experienced Utility." *Journal of Economic Perspectives* 20(1): 221–34.

Kahneman, D. and A. Tversky (1979). "Prospect theory: An analysis of decision under risk." *Econometrica* 47: 411–30.

_____, eds. (2000). *Choices, Values, and Frames*. New York: Cambridge University Press.

Kaplan, D. (2000). "The darker side of the 'original affluent society'." *Journal of Anthropological Research* 56: 301–24.

Kasser, T. (2002). *The High Price of Materialismm*. Cambridge, MA: MIT Press.

Katz, L. J. (2006). "Pleasure." In *The Stanford Encyclopedia of Philosophy*, ed. E. N. Zalta. URL = <http://plato.stanford.edu/entries/pleasure/>.

Kekes, J. (1982). "Happiness." *Mind* 91: 358–76.

_____ (1988). *The Examined Life*. Lewisburg: Bucknell University Press.

_____ (1992). "Happiness." In *Encyclopedia of Ethics*, eds. L. C. Becker and C. B. Becker. New York: Garland, 430–5.

_____ (2002). *The Art of Life*. Ithaca, NY: Cornell University Press.

Keller, S. (2004). "Welfare and the Achievement of Goals." *Philosophical Studies* 121(1): 27–41.

Kellert, S. R. and E. O. Wilson (1993). *The Biophilia Hypothesis*. Washington, DC: Island Press.

Kenny, A. and C. Kenny (2006). *Life, Liberty and the Pursuit of Utility*. Charlottesville, VA: Imprint Academic.

Kermer, D. A., E. Driver-Linn, et al. (2006). "Loss Aversion Is an Affective Forecasting Error." *Psychological Science* 17(8): 649–53.

Kessler, R. C., P. Berglund, et al. (2005). "Lifetime Prevalence and Age-of-Onset Distributions of DSM-IV Disorders in the National Comorbidity Survey Replication." *Archives of General Psychiatry* 62(6): 593–602.

Kessler, R. C., W. T. Chiu, et al. (2005). "Prevalence, Severity, and Comorbidity of 12-Month DSM-IV Disorders in the National Comorbidity Survey Replication." *Archives of General Psychiatry* 62(6): 617–27.

Kessler, R. C., R. L. DuPont, et al. (1999). "Impairment in pure and comorbid generalized anxiety disorder and major depression at 12 months in two national surveys." *American Journal of Psychiatry* 156(12): 1915–23.

Keyes, C. L. (2002). "The mental health continuum: From languishing to flourishing in life." *Journal of Health and Social Behavior* 43(2): 207–22.

—— (2005). "Mental Illness and/or Mental Health? Investigating Axioms of the Complete State Model of Health." *Journal of Consulting and Clinical Psychology* 73(3): 539–48.

—— (2007). "Promoting and Protecting Mental Health as Flourishing: A Complementary Strategy for Improving National Mental Health." *American Psychologist* 62(2): 95–108.

Kim, D.-Y. (2004). "The Implicit Life Satisfaction Measure and Its Cross-Cultural Applications." *3rd Annual Hawaii International Conference on Social Sciences*.

Kimble, G. A., N. Garmezy, et al. (1984). *Principles of Psychology*. New York: John Wiley & Sons.

King, L. A. and C. K. Napa (1998). "What makes a life good?" *Journal of Personality and Social Psychology* 75(1): 156–65.

Kline, D. (1990). *Great Possessions: An Amish Farmer's Journal*. San Francisco: North Point Press.

Knobe, J. and J. Doris (forthcoming). "Strawsonian Variations: Folk Morality and the Search for a Unified Theory." In *The Oxford Handbook of Moral Psychology*, eds. J. Doris, G. Harman, et al. New York: Oxford University Press.

Knobe, J. and B. Leiter (2007). "The Case for Nietzschean Moral Psychology." In *Nietzsche and Morality*, eds. B. Leiter and N. Sinhababu. New York: Oxford University Press.

Korsgaard, C. M. (1996). "The Sources of Normativity." In *The Sources of Normativity*, ed. C. M. Korsgaard. New York: Cambridge University Press, 1–166.

Kraut, R. (1979). "Two Conceptions of Happiness." *The Philosophical Review* 138: 167–97.

—— (1994/1996). "Desire and the Human Good." In *Value, Morality and the Good Life*, eds. P. Moser and T. L. Carson. New York: Oxford University Press.

—— (2002). *Aristotle: Political Philosophy*. New York: Oxford University Press.

—— (2007). *What is Good and Why*. Cambridge, MA: Harvard University Press.

Krueger, A. B., D. Kahneman, et al. (2007). "National Time Accounting: The Currency of Life."

Kubovy, M. (1999). "On the Pleasures of the Mind." In *Well-Being: The Foundations of Hedonic Psychology*, eds. D. Kahneman, E. Diener, and N. Schwarz. New York: Russell Sage Foundation Press, 134–54.

Kuchler, F., E. Golan, et al. (2005). "Obesity Policy and the Law of Unintended Consequences." *Amber Waves* 3(3): 26–33.

Lambie, J. A. and A. Marcel (2002). "Consciousness and the varieties of emotion experience: A theoretical framework." *Psychological Review* 109: 219–59.

Lane, R. D. (2000). *The Loss of Happiness in Market Democracies*. New Haven, CT: Yale University Press.

Larrick, R. P. (2004). "Debiasing." In *Blackwell Handbook of Judgment & Decision Making*, eds. D. J. Koehler and N. Harvey. Oxford: Blackwell, 316–37.

Larsen, R. J. and B. L. Fredrickson (1999). "Measurement Issues in Emotion Research." In *Well-Being: The Foundations of Hedonic Psychology*, eds. D. Kahneman, E. Diener, and N. Schwarz. New York: Russell Sage Foundation Press, 40–60.

Larsen, R. J. and Z. Prizmic (2005). "Measuring Emotions: Implications of a Multimethod Perspective." In *Handbook of Multimethod Measurement in Psychology*, eds. E. Diener and M. Eid. Washington, DC: American Psychological Association.

_____ (2008). "Regulation of Emotional Well-Being: Overcoming the Hedonic Treadmill." In *The Science of Subjective Well-Being*, eds. M. Eid and R. J. Larsen. New York: Guilford Press, 258–89.

_____ (forthcoming). "Multimethod Measurement of Emotion." In *Handbook of Psychological Measurement*, eds. M. Eid and E. Diener. Washington, DC: American Psychological Association.

Lauderdale, D. S., K. L. Knutson, et al. (2006). "Objectively measured sleep characteristics among early-middle-aged adults: the CARDIA study." *American Journal of Epidemiology* 164(1): 5–16.

Layard, R. (2005). *Happiness: Lessons From a New Science*. New York: Penguin.

_____ (2006). "Happiness and Public Policy: a Challenge to the Profession." *The Economic Journal* 116(510): C24–C33.

Lazarus, R. (1994). "The Stable and the Unstable in Emotions." In *The Nature of Emotion*, eds. P. Ekman and R. J. Davidson. New York: Oxford University Press, 79–85.

LeBar, M. (2004). "Good for You." *Pacific Philosophical Quarterly* 85: 195–217.

Lebergott, S. (1993). *Pursuing Happiness: American Consumers in the Twentieth Century*. Princeton, NJ: Princeton University Press.

Lee, R. B. (2002). *The Dobe Jul'Hoansi*. Belmont, CA: Wadsworth.

Leiter, B. (2007). "Nietzsche's Theory of the Will." *Philosophers' Imprint* 7(7).

Lepine, J.-P. (2002). "The epidemiology of anxiety disorders: Prevalence and societal costs." *Journal of Clinical Psychiatry* 63(suppl 14): 4–8.

Levenson, R. W., P. Ekman, et al. (1992). "Emotion and autonomic nervous system activity in the Minangkabau of West Sumatra." *Journal of Personality and Social Psychology* 62: 972–88.

Lichtenstein, S. and P. Slovic (2006). *The Construction of Preference*. New York: Cambridge University Press.

Linley, P., S. Joseph, et al. (2006). "Positive psychology: Past, present, and (possible) future." *The Journal of Positive Psychology* 1(1): 3–16.

Loeb, D. (1995). "Full-Information Theories of Individual Good." *Social Theory and Practice* 21(1).

Loewenstein, G. (1996). "Out of control: Visceral influences on behavior." *Organizational Behavior and Human Decision Processes* 65(3): 272–92.

Loewenstein, G. and E. Angner (2003). "Predicting and indulging changing preferences." In *Time and Decision: Economic and Psychological Perspectives on Intertemporal Choice*, eds. G. Loewenstein, D. Read, and R. Baumeister. New York: Russell Sage Foundation, 351–91.

Lormand, E. (1985). "Toward a Theory of Moods." *Philosophical Studies* 47: 385–407.

—— (1996). "Nonphenomenal Consciousness." *Noûs* 30(2): 242–61.

Lucas, R. E. (2008). "Personality and Subjective Well-Being." In *The Science of Subjective Well-Being*, eds. M. Eid and R. J. Larsen. New York: Guilford Press, 171–94.

Lucas, R. E., A. E. Clark, et al. (2004a). "Re-Examining Adaptation and the Setpoint Model of Happiness: Reactions to Changes in Marital Status." *Journal of Personality and Social Psychology* 84: 527–39.

—— (2004b). "Unemployment alters the set point for life satisfaction." *Psychological Science* 15(1): 8–13.

Luthar, S. S. (2003). "The culture of affluence: Psychological costs of material wealth." *Child Development* 74(6): 1581–93.

Luthar, S. S. and B. E. Becker (2002). "Privileged but pressured? A study of affluent youth." *Child Development* 73(5): 1593–1610.

Lykken, D. (1999). *Happiness*. New York: Golden Books.

Lykken, D. and A. Tellegen (1996). "Happiness is a stochastic phenomenon." *Psychological Science* 7(3): 186–9.

Lyubomirsky, S. (2007). *The How of Happiness*. New York: Penguin.

Lyubomirsky, S., L. King, et al. (2005). "The Benefits of Frequent Positive Affect: Does Happiness Lead to Success?" *Psychological Bulletin* 131(6): 803–55.

Lyubomirsky, S., K. M. Sheldon, et al. (2005). "Pursuing Happiness: The Architecture of Sustainable Change." *Review of General Psychology* 9(2): 111–31.

McCloskey, H. J. (1992). "Pain and Suffering." In *Encyclopedia of Ethics*, eds. L. C. Becker and C. B. Becker. New York: Garland, 927–9.

McDade, T. W., J. F. Stallings, et al. (2000). "Culture change and stress in Western Samoan youth: Methodological issues in the cross-cultural study of stress and immune function." *American Journal of Human Biology* 12(6): 792–802.

McFall, L. (1989). *Happiness*. New York: Peter Lang.

McGuire, W. (1974). *The Freud/Jung Letters*. Princeton, NJ: Princeton University Press.

MacIntyre, A. (1981). *After Virtue*. Notre Dame, IN: University of Notre Dame Press.

—— (1999). *Dependent Rational Animals*. Chicago: Open Court.

McKibben, B. (2003). *Enough*. New York: Owl Books.

McMahon, D. M. (2005). *Happiness: A History*. New York: Atlantic Monthly Press.

McPherson, M., M. E. Brashears, et al. (2006). "Social Isolation in America: Changes in Core Discussion Networks over Two Decades." *American Sociological Review* 71(3): 353–75.

Machery, E., R. Mallon, et al. (2004). "Semantics, Cross-Cultural Style." *Cognition* 92: B1–B12.

Mackie, J. L. (1977). *Ethics: Inventing Right and Wrong*. New York: Penguin.

Markus, H. R. and S. Kitayama (1991). "Culture and the self: Implications for cognition, emotion, and motivation." *Psychological Review* 98(2): 224–53.

Marshall, G. (1998). "Pleasure." In *Routledge Encyclopedia of Philosophy*, ed. E. Craig. New York: Routledge.

Mayerfeld, J. (1996). "The Moral Asymmetry of Happiness and Suffering." *Southern Journal of Philosophy* 34: 317–38.

——— (1999). *Suffering and Moral Responsibility*. New York: Oxford University Press.

Mendola, J. (2006). "Intuitive Hedonism." *Philosophical Studies* 128(2): 441–77.

Meynell, H. (1969). "Human Flourishing." *Religious Studies* 5: 147–54.

Mezulis, A. H., L. Y. Abramson, et al. (2004). "Is There a Universal Positivity Bias in Attributions? A Meta-Analytic Review of Individual, Developmental, and Cultural Differences in the Self-Serving Attributional Bias." *Psychological Bulletin* 130: 711–47.

Michalos, A. (1980). "Satisfaction and Happiness." *Social Indicators Research* 8: 385–422.

——— (1985). "Multiple Discrepancies Theory." *Social Indicators Research* 16: 347–413.

Mill, J. S. (1979). *Utilitarianism*. Indianapolis: Hackett.

——— (1991). "On Liberty." In *On Liberty and Other Essays*, ed. J. Gray. New York: Oxford University Press.

Miller Jr., G. T. (2002). *Living in the Environment*. Belmont, CA: Wadsworth.

Millgram, E. (2000). "What's the Use of Utility." *Philosophy and Public Affairs* 29(2): 113–36.

Monk, R. (1990). *Ludwig Wittgenstein: The Duty of Genius*. New York: Penguin.

Montague, R. (1967). "Happiness." *Proceedings of the Aristotelian Society* 67: 87–102.

Moore, A. (2005). "Fast-Cooking the Biosphere." *EMBO reports* 6(12): 1110–13.

Morris, W. N. (1999). "The Mood System." In *Well-Being: The Foundations of Hedonic Psychology*, eds. D. Kahneman, E. Diener, and N. Schwarz. New York: Russell Sage Foundation Press, 169–89.

Murdoch, I. (1968). *The Nice and the Good*. New York: Penguin.

Murphy, M. C. (2001). *Natural Law and Practical Rationality*. New York: Cambridge University Press.

Myers, D. G. (1992). *The Pursuit of Happiness: Who is Happy, and Why*. New York: William Morrow and Co.

——— (2000a). *The American Paradox*. New Haven: Yale University Press.

——— (2000b). "The Funds, Friends, and Faith of Happy People." *American Psychologist* 55(1): 56–67.

Myers, D. G. and E. Diener (1995). "Who Is Happy?" *Psychological Science* 6(1): 10–19.

Nagel, T. (1974). "What Is It Like to Be a Bat?" *Philosophical Review* LXXXIII(4): 435–50.

Nahmias, E. A., S. G. Morris, et al. (forthcoming). "Is Incompatibilism Intuitive?" *Philosophy and Phenomenological Research*.

Nakamura, J. and M. Csikszentmihalyi (2002). "The concept of flow." In *Handbook of Positive Psychology*, eds. C. R. Snyder and S. J. Lopez. New York: Oxford University Press, 89–92.

Nesse, R. M. (2000). "Is Depression an Adaptation?" *Archives of General Psychiatry* 57: 14–20.

——— (2004). "Natural selection and the elusiveness of happiness." *Philosophical Transactions of the Royal Society* 359: 1333–47.

——— (2005). "Evolutionary Psychology and Mental Health." In *The Handbook of Evolutionary Psychology*, ed. D. M. Buss. New York: John Wiley & Sons, 903–27.

Nesse, R. M. and K. C. Berridge (1997). "Psychoactive drug use in evolutionary perspective." *Science* 278(3): 63–6.

Nichols, S. (2004). *Sentimental Rules*. New York: Oxford University Press, 242–69.

——(2006). "Folk Intuitions on Free Will." *Journal of Cognition and Culture* 6(1–2): 57–86.

Nietzsche, F. (1887/1996). *On the Genealogy of Morals*. New York: Oxford University Press.

Nisbett, R. E. (2003). *The Geography of Thought*. New York: Free Press.

Nisbett, R. E. and T. D. Wilson (1978). "Telling more than we can know: verbal reports on mental processes." *Psychological Review* 84: 231–59.

Nozick, R. (1974). *Anarchy, State, and Utopia*. New York: Basic Books.

——(1989). *The Examined Life*. New York: Simon and Schuster.

Nussbaum, M. (1988). "Nature, Function, and Capability: Aristotle on Political Distribution." *Oxford Studies in Ancient Philosophy*, suppl. vol. I: 145–84.

——(1992). "Human Functioning and Social Justice: In Defense of Aristotelian Essentialism." *Political Theory* 20: 202–46.

——(1993). "Non-Relative Virtues: An Aristotelian Approach." In *The Quality of Life*, eds. M. Nussbaum and A. Sen. New York: Oxford University Press. 242–69.

——(1994). *The Therapy of Desire*. Princeton, NJ: Princeton University Press.

——(2000a). "Aristotle, Politics, and Human Capabilities: A Response to Antony, Arneson, Charlesworth, and Mulgan." *Ethics* 111(1): 102–40.

——(2000b). *Women and Human Development: The Capabilities Approach*. New York: Cambridge University Press.

——(2004). "Mill between Aristotle and Bentham." *Daedalus* 133(2): 60–8.

Oatley, K. and J. M. Jenkins (1996). *Understanding Emotions*. Cambridge, MA: Blackwell.

Offer, A. (2006). *The Challenge of Affluence: Self-Control and Well-Being in the United States and Britain since 1950*. New York: Oxford University Press.

Ohayon, M. M. (2007). "Epidemiology of depression and its treatment in the general population." *Journal of Psychiatric Research* 41(3–4): 207–13.

Oishi, S. (2002). "The experiencing and remembering of well-being: A cross-cultural analysis." *Personality and Social Psychology Bulletin* 28(10): 1398–1406.

Oishi, S. and M. Koo (2008). "Two New Questions about Happiness: Is Happiness Good? and Is Happier Better?" In *The Science of Subjective Well-Being*, eds. M. Eid and R. J. Larsen. New York: Guilford Press, 290–306.

Oswald, A. J. (1997). "Happiness and Economic Performance." *The Economic Journal* 107(445): 1815–31.

Oswald, A. J. and N. Powdthavee (2007). "Obesity, Unhappiness, and the Challenge of Affluence: Theory and Evidence." *The Economic Journal* 117(521): F441–F454.

Parducci, A. (1995). *Happiness, Pleasure, and Judgement: The Contextual Theory and Its Applications*. Mahwah, NJ: L. Erlbaum Associates.

Parfit, D. (1984). *Reasons and Persons*. Oxford: Oxford University Press.

Parkinson, B., P. Totterdell, et al. (1996). *Changing Moods: The Psychology of Mood and Mood Regulation*. New York: Addison Wesley.

Pavot, W. (2008). "The Assessment of Subjective Well-Being: Successes and Shortfalls." In *The Science of Subjective Well-Being*, eds. M. Eid and R. J. Larsen. New York: Guilford Press, 124–40.

Pearson, N. J., L. L. Johnson, et al. (2006). "Insomnia, Trouble Sleeping, and Complementary and Alternative Medicine: Analysis of the 2002 National Health Interview Survey Data." *Archives of Internal Medicine* 166(September 18): 1775–82.

Perry, D. L. (1967). *The Concept of Pleasure*. The Hague: Mouton & Co.

Peterson, C. (1999). "Personal Control and Well-Being." In *Well-Being: The Foundations of Hedonic Psychology*, eds. D. Kahneman, E. Diener, and N. Schwarz. New York: Russell Sage Foundation Press, 288–301.

—— (2006). *A Primer in Positive Psychology*. New York: Oxford University Press.

Peterson, C., S. Maier, et al. (1995). *Learned Helplessness: A Theory for the Age of Personal Control*. New York: Oxford University Press.

Pettit, P. (2003). "Agency-Freedom and Option-Freedom." *Journal of Theoretical Politics* 15(4): 387–403.

Pigou, A. C. (1932). *The Economics of Welfare*. London: Macmillan.

Pilcher, J. (1998). "Affect and Daily Event Predictors of Life Satisfaction in College Students." *Social Indicators Research* 43: 291–306.

Plato (1992). *Republic*. Indianapolis: Hackett.

Preston, D. (1995). *Talking to the Ground*. Albuquerque, NM: University of New Mexico Press.

Prinz, J. J. (2004). *Gut Reactions*. New York: Oxford University Press.

—— (2007). *The Emotional Construction of Morals*. New York: Oxford University Press.

Putnam, R. (2000). *Bowling Alone*. New York: Simon and Schuster.

Quammen, D. (1998). "Planet of Weeds." *Harper's* (October): 57–69.

Quan, S. F. (2006). "Invited Commentary: How Much Do We Really Sleep?" *American Journal of Epidemiology* 164(1): 17–18.

Rabin, M. (1998). "Psychology and Economics." *Journal of Economic Literature* XXXVI: 11–46.

Rachels, S. (2000). "Is Unpleasantness Intrinsic to Unpleasant Experiences?" *Philosophical Studies* 99(2): 187–210.

—— (2004). "Six Theses About Pleasure." *Philosophical Perspectives* 18(1): 247–67.

Railton, P. (1986a). "Facts and Values." *Philosophical Topics* 14(2): 5–31.

—— (1986b). "Moral Realism." *Philosophical Review* 95(2): 163–207.

—— (ms). "The Problem of Well-Being: Respect, Equality, and the Self."

Raleigh, M. J., M. T. McGuire, et al. (1991). "Serotonergic Mechanisms Promote Dominance Acquisition in Adult Male Vervet Monkeys." *Brain Research* 559: 181–90.

Raphael, R. (1976). *Edges: Human Ecology of the Backcountry*. Lincoln, NB: University of Nebraska Press.

Rawls, J. (1971). *A Theory of Justice*. Cambridge, MA: Harvard University Press.

Raz, J. (1986). *The Morality of Freedom*. New York: Oxford University Press.

—— (2004). "The Role of Well-Being." *Philosophical Perspectives* 18(1): 269–94.

—— (2006). "Darwall on Rational Care." *Utilitas* 18(4): 400–14.

Redelmeier, D. and D. Kahneman (1996). "Patients' memories of painful medical treatments: real-time and retrospective evaluations of two minimally invasive procedures." *Pain* 66: 3–8.

Redelmeier, D., J. Katz, et al. (2003). "Memories of colonoscopy: A randomized trial." *Pain* 104(1–2): 187–94.

Reginster, B. (2004). "Happiness as a Faustian Bargain." *Daedalus* 133(2): 52–9.

Rescher, N. (1972). *Welfare: The Social Issues In Philosophical Perspective*. Pittsburgh: Pittsburgh University Press.

—— (1980). *Unpopular Essays on Technological Progress*. Pittsburgh: University of Pittsburgh Press.

Riis, J., G. Loewenstein, et al. (2005). "Ignorance of Hedonic Adaptation to Hemodialysis: A Study Using Ecological Momentary Assessment." *Journal of Experimental Psychology: General* 134(1): 3–9.

Rodzinski, W. (1979). *A History of China*. Oxford: Pergamon Press.

Rosati, C. (1995). "Persons, Perspectives, and Full Information Accounts of the Good." *Ethics* 105(1): 296–325.

_____ (1996). "Internalism and the Good for a Person." *Ethics* 106(January): 297–326.

Rosenthal, D. M. (2002). "How Many Kinds of Consciousness?" *Consciousness and Cognition* 11: 653–65.

Ross, L. and R. E. Nisbett (1991). *The Person and the Situation: Perspectives of Social Psychology*. Philadelphia: Temple University Press.

Ross, M. and A. E. Wilson (2003). "Autobiographical memory and conceptions of self: Getting better all the time." *Current Directions in Psychological Science* 12(2): 66–9.

Rozin, P. and E. B. Royzman (2001). "Negativity bias, negativity dominance, and contagion." *Personality and Social Psychology Review* 5(4): 296–320.

Ryan, R. M. and E. L. Deci (2001). "On happiness and human potentials: A review of research on hedonic and eudaimonic well-being." *Annual Review of Psychology* 52: 141–66.

Ryff, C. D. (1989). "Happiness is everything, or is it? Explorations on the meaning of psychological well-being." *Journal of Personality and Social Psychology* 57(6): 1069–81.

Ryff, C. D. and B. Singer (1998). "The contours of positive human health." *Psychological Inquiry* 9(1): 1–28.

Sahlins, M. (1968). "Notes on the Original Affluent Society." In *Man the Hunter*, eds. R. B. Lee and I. DeVore. New York: Aldine Publishing, 85–9.

Samuels, R., S. Stich, et al. (2002a). "Ending the rationality wars: How to make disputes about human rationality disappear." In *Common Sense, Reasoning and Rationality*, ed. R. Elio. New York: Oxford University Press.

_____ (2002b). "Reasoning and Rationality." In *Handbook of Epistemology*, eds. I. Niiniluoto, M. Sintonen, and J. Wolenski. Dordrecht: Kluwer, 1–50.

Sandel, M. (1998). *Liberalism and the Limits of Justice*. New York: Cambridge University Press.

Sandvik, E., E. Diener, et al. (1993). "The assessment of well-being: A comparison of self-report and nonself-report strategies." *Journal of Personality* 61: 317–42.

Scanlon, T. M. (1993). "Value, Desire, and Quality of Life." In *The Quality of Life*, eds. A. Sen and M. Nussbaum. New York: Oxford University Press.

_____ (1999). *What We Owe to Each Other*. Cambridge, MA: Harvard University Press.

Schimmack, U. (2008). "The Structure of Subjective Well-Being." In *The Science of Subjective Well-Being*, eds. M. Eid and R. J. Larsen. New York: Guilford Press, 97–123.

Schimmack, U. and S. Oishi (2005). "The influence of chronically and temporarily accessible information on life satisfaction judgments." *Journal of Personality and Social Psychology* 89(3): 395–406.

Schkade, D. A. and D. Kahneman (1998). "Does living in California make people happy? A focusing illusion in judgments of life satisfaction." *Psychological Science* 9(5): 340–6.

Schooler, J. W., D. Ariely, et al. (2003). "The Pursuit and Assessment of Happiness Can Be Self-Defeating." In *The Psychology of Economic Decision*, eds. I. Brocas and J. Carillo. New York: Oxford University Press.

Schor, J. (1992). *The Overworked American*. New York: Basic Books.

—— (1998). *The Overspent American*. New York: Harper Perennial.

—— (1999). "The New Politics of Consumption." *The Boston Review* (Summer).

Schwartz, B. (2000). "Self-Determination: The Tyranny of Freedom." *American Psychologist* 55(1): 79–88.

—— (2004). *The Paradox of Choice*. New York: HarperCollins.

Schwartz, B., H. R. Markus, et al. (2006). "Is Freedom Just Another Word for Many Things to Buy?" *The New York Times*, February 26.

Schwarz, N. and F. Strack (1991). "Evaluating One's Life: A Judgment Model of Subjective Well-Being." In *Subjective Well-Being*, eds. F. Strack, M. Argyle, and N. Schwarz. Elmsford, NY: Pergamon Press, 27–47.

—— (1999). "Reports of Subjective Well-Being: Judgmental Processes and Their Methodological Implications." In *Well-Being: The Foundations of Hedonic Psychology*, eds. D. Kahneman, E. Diener, and N. Schwarz. New York: Russell Sage Foundation Press, 61–84.

Schwitzgebel, E. (2004). "Introspective training apprehensively defended: Reflections on Titchener's lab manual." In *Trusting the Subject?* vol. 2, eds. A. Jack and A. Roepstorff. Charlottesville, VA: Imprint Academic. 2, 58–76.

—— (forthcoming). "The Unreliability of Naive Introspection." *Philosophical Review*.

Schwitzgebel, E. and R. T. Hurlburt (2007). *Describing Inner Experience? Proponent Meets Skeptic*. Cambridge, MA: MIT Press.

Scitovsky, T. (1976). *The Joyless Economy*. New York: Oxford University Press.

Scollon, C. N., E. Diener, et al. (2004). "Emotions Across Cultures and Methods." *Journal of Cross-Cultural Psychology* 35(3): 304–26.

Scruton, R. (1975). "Reason and Happiness." In *Nature and Conduct*, ed. R. S. Peters. New York: Macmillan, 139–61.

Searle, J. (1990). "Who Is Computing with the Brain?" *Behavioral and Brain Sciences* 13(4): 632–42.

Sedikides, C., L. Gaertner, et al. (2003). "Pancultural self-enhancement." *Journal of Personality and Social Psychology* 84: 60–79.

—— (2005). "Pancultural self-enhancement reloaded: A meta-analytic reply to Heine." *Journal of Personality and Social Psychology* 89(4): 539–51.

Seidlitz, L. (1993). "The organization and retrieval of valenced life events by happy and unhappy persons." Urbana-Champaign, IL: University of Illinois.

Seligman, M. E. (1990). "Why is there so much depression today? The waxing of the individual and the waning of the commons." In *Contemporary Psychological Approaches to Depression*, ed. R. E. Ingram. New York: Plenum, 1–9.

—— (2002). *Authentic Happiness*. New York: Free Press.

Seligman, M. E., T. A. Steen, et al. (2005). "Positive psychology progress: Empirical validation of interventions." *American Psychologist* 60(5): 410–21.

Sen, A. (1987a). *Commodities and Capabilities*. New York: Oxford University Press.

—— (1987b). *On Ethics and Economics*. Oxford: Basil Blackwell.

—— (2000). *Development as Freedom*. New York: Anchor Books.

Shafir, E. and R. A. LeBoeuf (2002). "Rationality." *Annual Review of Psychology* 53: 491–517.

Shedler, J., M. Mayman, et al. (1993). "The Illusion of Mental Health." *American Psychologist* 48(11): 1117–31.

Sher, G. (1997). *Beyond Neutrality: Perfectionism and Politics*. New York: Cambridge University Press.

Sidgwick, H. (1907/1966). *The Methods of Ethics*. New York: Dover Publications.

Simons, D. J. and C. F. Chabris (1999). "Gorillas in our midst: sustained inattentional blindness for dynamic events." *Perception* 28: 1059–74.

Simpson, R. (1975). "Happiness." *American Philosophical Quarterly* 12: 169–76.

Sizer, L. (2000). "Towards a Computational Theory of Mood." *British Journal of the Philosophy of Science* 51: 743–69.

Slote, M. (1982). "Goods and Lives." *Pacific Philosophical Quarterly* 63: 311–26.

_____ (2001). *Morals from Motives*. New York: Oxford University Press.

Slouka, M. (1996). *War of the Worlds: Cyberspace and the High-Tech Assault on Reality*. New York: Basic Books.

Smart, J. J. C. (1973). "An Outline of a System of Utilitarian Ethics." In *Utilitarianism: For and Against*, eds. J. J. C. Smart and B. Williams. New York: Cambridge University Press, 3–74.

Snyder, C. R. and S. J. Lopez, eds. (2002). *Handbook of Positive Psychology*. New York: Oxford.

Sobel, D. (1997). "On the Subjectivity of Welfare." *Ethics* 107(3): 501–8.

_____ (1999). "Pleasure As a Mental State." *Utilitas* 11(2): 230–4.

_____ (2002). "Varieties of Hedonism." *Journal of Social Philosophy* 33(2): 240–56.

Solomon, R. C. (1998). "The Virtues of a Passionate Life: Erotic Love and the 'Will to Power'." In *Virtue and Vice*, eds. E. F. Paul, F. D. Miller Jr., and J. Paul. New York: Cambridge University Press, 91–118.

_____ (2003). *Not Passion's Slave: Emotions and Choice*. New York: Oxford University Press.

Sprigge, T. L. S. (1987). *The Rational Foundations of Ethics*. New York: Routledge & Kegan Paul.

_____ (1991). "The Greatest Happiness Principle." *Utilitas* 3(1): 37–51.

Stanovich, K. E. (2004). *The Robot's Rebellion*. Chicago, IL: University of Chicago Press.

Staude, J. R. (1976). "From Depth Psychology to Depth Sociology: Freud, Jung, and Levi-Strauss." *Theory and Society* 3(3): 303–38.

Sterelny, K. (2003). *Thought in a Hostile World: The Evolution of Human Cognition*. Oxford: Blackwell.

Stich, S. (1999). "Is Man a Rational Animal?" In *Questioning Matters: An Introduction to Philosophical Inquiry*, ed. D. Kolak. Mountain View, CA: Mayfield Publishing, 221–36.

Stone, A. A. and S. S. Shiffman (1999). "Ecological Momentary Assessment." In *Well-Being: The Foundations of Hedonic Psychology*, eds. D. Kahneman, E. Diener, and N. Schwarz. New York: Russell Sage Foundation Press, 26–39.

Strack, F., L. Martin, et al. (1988). "Priming and communication: Social determinants of information use in judgments of life satisfaction." *European Journal of Social Psychology* 18: 429–42.

Strack, F., N. Schwarz, et al. (1990). "The salience of comparison standards and the activation of social norms: Consequences for judgments of happiness and their communication." *British Journal of Social Psychology* 29: 303–14.

Suh, E., E. Diener, et al. (1996). "Events and subjective well-being: Only recent events matter." *Journal of Personality and Social Psychology* 70: 1091–102.

—— (1998). "The shifting basis of life satisfaction judgments across cultures: Emotions versus norms." *Journal of Personality and Social Psychology* 74(2): 482–93.

Sumner, L. W. (1992). "Two Theories of the Good." In *The Good Life and the Human Good*, eds. E. F. Paul, F. D. Miller Jr., and J. Paul. New York: Cambridge University Press, 1–14.

—— (1996). *Welfare, Happiness, and Ethics*. New York: Oxford University Press.

—— (1998). "Is Virtue Its Own Reward?" In *Virtue and Vice*, eds. E. F. Paul, F. D. Miller Jr., and J. Paul. New York: Cambridge University Press, 18–36.

—— (2000). "Something In Between." In *Well-Being and Morality*, eds. R. Crisp and B. Hooker. New York: Oxford University Press, 1–19.

Sunstein, C. R. and R. H. Thaler (2003). "Libertarian Paternalism Is Not an Oxymoron." *University of Chicago Law Review* 70(4): 1159–1202.

Sutherland, W. J. (2003). "Parallel Extinction Risk and Global Distribution of Languages and Species." *Nature* 423(15 May): 276–9.

Swanton, C. (2003). *Virtue Ethics: A Pluralistic Approach*. New York: Oxford University Press.

Tännsjö, T. (2007). "Narrow Hedonism." *Journal of Happiness Studies* 8(1): 79–98.

Tatarkiewicz, W. (1976). *Analysis of Happiness*. The Hague: Martinus Nijhoff.

Taylor, C. (1985). "What Is Human Agency?" In *Human Agency and Language: Philosophical Papers*, ed. C. Taylor. Cambridge: Cambridge University Press. Orig. published 1977, in T. Mischel, *The Self: Psychological and Philosophical Issues*.

—— (1989). *Sources of the Self: The Making of Modern Identity*. Cambridge, MA: Harvard University Press.

Taylor, S. E. and J. D. Brown (1988). "Illusion and Well-Being: A Social-Psychological Perspective on Mental Health." *Psychological Bulletin* 103: 193–210.

—— (1994). "Positive illusions and well-being revisited: Separating fact from fiction." *Psychological Bulletin* 116: 21–7.

Taylor, S. E. and P. M. Gollwitzer (1995). "Effects of Mindset on Positive Illusions." *Journal of Personality and Social Psychology* 69(2): 213–26.

Telfer, E. (1980). *Happiness*. New York: St. Martin's Press.

Thaler, R. H. (2000). "From Homo Economicus to Homo Sapiens." *Journal of Economic Perspectives* 14(1): 133–141.

Thomas, D. A. L. (1968). "Happiness." *Philosophical Quarterly* 18: 97–113.

Tiberius, V. (2002). "Perspective: A Prudential Virtue." *American Philosophical Quarterly* 39(4): 305–24.

—— (forthcoming). *The Reflective Life*. New York: Oxford University Press.

Tiberius, V. and A. Plakias (forthcoming). "'How's it Going?': Ethics, Positive Psychology, and Conceptions of Well-Being." In *The Oxford Handbook of Moral Psychology*, eds. J. Doris, G. Harman, et al. New York: Oxford University Press.

Toner, C. H. (2006). "Aristotelian Well-Being: A Response to L. W. Sumner's Critique." *Utilitas* 18: 218–31.

Torrance, G. (1976). "Social preferences for health states: An empirical evaluation of three measurement techniques." *Socioeconomic Planning Science* 10: 129–36.

Trout, J. D. (2005). "Paternalism and Cognitive Bias." *Law and Philosophy* 24: 393–434.

Tversky, A. and D. Griffin (1991). "Endowment and Contrast in Judgments of Well-Being." In *Subjective Well-Being*, eds. F. Strack, M. Argyle, and N. Schwarz. Elmsford, NY: Pergamon Press, 101–18.

Twenge, J. M. (2000). "The age of anxiety? The birth cohort change in anxiety and neuroticism, 1952–1993." *Journal of Personality and Social Psychology* 79(6): 1007–21.

_____ (2002). "Birth cohort, social change, and personality: The interplay of dysphoria and individualism in the 20th century." In *Advances in Personality Science*, eds. D. Cervone and W. Mischel. New York: Guilford Press.

Twenge, J. M., L. Zhang, et al. (2004). "It's beyond my control: A cross-temporal meta-analysis of increasing externality in locus of control, 1960–2002." *Personality and Social Psychology Review* 8(3): 308–19.

Ubel, P. A. and G. Loewenstein (forthcoming). "Pain and suffering awards: It shouldn't be (just) about pain and suffering." *Journal of Legal Studies*.

Urry, H. L., J. B. Nitschke, et al. (2004). "Making a life worth living: neural correlates of well-being." *Psychological Science* 15(6): 367–72.

Vasan, R. S., M. J. Pencina, et al. (2005). "Estimated risks for developing obesity in the Framingham heart study." *Annals of Internal Medicine* 143: 473–80.

Veenhoven, R. (1984). *Conditions of Happiness*. Dordrecht: D. Reidel.

_____ (1997). "Advances in Understanding Happiness." *Revue Québécoise de Psychologie* 18: 29–79.

_____ (2005). "Is Life Getting Better? How Long and Happily Do People Live in Modern Society?" *European Psychologist* 10(4): 330–43.

_____ (2008). "Sociological Theories of Subjective Well-Being." In *The Science of Subjective Well-Being*, eds. M. Eid and R. J. Larsen. New York: Guilford Press, 44–61.

Velleman, J. D. (1991). "Well-Being and Time." *Pacific Philosophical Quarterly* 72(1): 48–77.

_____ (2006). *Self to Self*. New York: Cambridge University Press.

Veninga, R. L. (2000). "Building Trust in a Changing Environment." *Health Progress* (November/December).

Von Wright, G. H. (1963). *The Varieties of Goodness*. London: Routledge & Kegan Paul.

Warner, R. (1987). *Freedom, Enjoyment, and Happiness: An Essay on Moral Psychology*. Ithaca, NY: Cornell University Press.

Watson, G. (1975). "Free Agency." *Journal of Philosophy* 72(8): 205–20.

Wegner, D. M. (2003). "The illusion of conscious will." *Journal of Nervous and Mental Disease* 191(2): 69–72.

Wegner, D. M. and J. A. Bargh (1998). "Control and automaticity in social life." In *The Handbook of Social Psychology*, eds. D. Gilbert, S. Fiske, and G. Lindzey. New York: Oxford University Press.

Weinberg, J., S. Nichols, et al. (2001). "Normativity and Epistemic Intuitions." *Philosophical Topics* 29: 429–60.

Weinstein, N. D. (1980). "Unrealistic optimism about future life events." *Journal of Personality and Social Psychology* 39: 806–20.

Wex, M. (2005). *Born to Kvetch*. New York: St. Martin's Press.

White, N. P. (2006). *A Brief History of Happiness*. Oxford: Blackwell.

Whitlock, J., J. Eckenrode, et al. (2006). "Self-Injurious Behaviors in a College Population." *Pediatrics* 117: 1939–48.

Wierzbicka, A. (2004). "'Happiness' in cross-linguistic & cross-cultural perspective." *Daedalus* (Spring): 34–43.

Wilkinson, W. (2007). "In Pursuit of Happiness Research: Is it Reliable? What Does it Imply for Policy?" *Cato Institute Policy Analysis Series* (590).

Williams, B. (1973). "A Critique of Utilitarianism." In *Utilitarianism: For and Against*, eds. J. J. C. Smart and B. Williams. New York: Cambridge University Press.

—— (1981). "Persons, Character, and Morality." In *Moral Luck*, ed. B. Williams. New York: Cambridge University Press, 1–19.

—— (1985). *Ethics and the Limits of Philosophy*. Cambridge: Harvard University Press.

Wilson, E. O. (2002). *The Future of Life*. New York: Knopf.

Wilson, J. (1968). "Happiness." *Analysis* 29: 13–21.

Wilson, T. D. (2002). *Strangers to Ourselves: Discovering the Adaptive Unconscious*. Cambridge, MA: Harvard University Press.

Wilson, T. D. and D. T. Gilbert (2003). "Affective Forecasting." In *Advances in Experimental Social Psychology*, ed. M. Zanna. New York: Elsevier. 35: 345–411.

—— (2005). "Affective Forecasting: Knowing What to Want." *Current Directions in Psychological Science* 14(3): 131–4.

Wilson, T. D., D. T. Gilbert, et al. (2002). "Making sense: The causes of emotional evanescence." In *Economics and Psychology*, eds. J. Carillo and I. Brocas. New York: Oxford University Press, 209–33.

Wilson, T. D., D. J. Lisle, et al. (1993). "Introspecting about reasons can reduce post-choice satisfaction." *Personality and Social Psychology Bulletin* 19(3): 331–9.

Wilson, T. D. and J. W. Schooler (1991). "Thinking too much: Introspection can reduce the quality of preferences and decisions." *Journal of Personality and Social Psychology* 60(2): 181–92.

Wilson, T. D., T. P. Wheatley, et al. (2000). "Focalism: A source of durability bias in affective forecasting." *Journal of Personality and Social Psychology* 78(5): 821–36.

Winkielman, P. and K. C. Berridge (2004). "Unconscious Emotion." *Current Directions in Psychological Science* 13(3): 120–3.

Wolff, R. (1994). *What It Is to Be Human*. Freeland, WA: Periwinkle Press.

Woolfolk, R. L. (2002). "The power of negative thinking: Truth, melancholia, and the tragic sense of life." *Journal of Theoretical and Philosophical Psychology* 22(1): 19–27.

Woolfolk, R. L., J. M. Doris, et al. (2006). "Identification, situational constraint, and social cognition: Studies in the attribution of moral responsibility." *Cognition* 100(2): 283–301.

Woolfolk, R. L. and R. H. Wasserman (2005). "Count No One Happy: Eudaimonia and Positive Psychology." *Journal of Theoretical and Philosophical Psychology* 25(1): 81–90.

Zajonc, R. (1980). "Feeling and thinking: preferences need no inferences." *American Psychologist* 35: 151–75.

—— (1994). "Evidence for Nonconscious Emotions." In *The Nature of Emotion*, eds. P. Ekman and R. J. Davidson. New York: Oxford University Press, pp. 293–7.

Index